This book is dedicated to the memory of our father, Irving Wallace, who was 1 OF A KIND

AMY WALLACE is the co-author of four previous volumes of *The Book of Lists*, as well as several other popular reference books. She also wrote the biography *The Prodigy*, the novel *Desire*, and the best-selling memoir *Sorcerer's Apprentice: My Life with Carlos Castaneda*. Her most recent work is an all-new anniversary edition of her classic, *The Psychic Healing Book*. She currently lives in Los Angeles, California, with her two cats, Hank and Bella.

DAVID WALLECHINSKY is the author of numerous books including *The Peoples' Almanac*, *David Wallechinsky's 20th Century: History With the Boring Parts Left Out* and *The Complete Book of the Olympics*. He is also vice-president of the International Society of Olympic Historians.

The Book of Lists

Contributors

A.E.	Ann Elwood	K.H.J.	Kristine H. Johnson
A.K.	Aaron Kass	K.P.	Karen Pedersen
A.W.	Amy Wallace	L.B.	Linda Bosson
A.T.	Alan Tigay	L.C.	Linda Chase
B.F.	Bruce Felton	L.K.L.	Linda K. Laucella
B.F.G.	Bryan F. Griffin	L.K.S.	Laurie K. Strand
C.D.	Carol Dunlap	L.O.	Laurel Overman
C.F.	Chris Fishel	M.B.T.	Marguerite B. Thompson
C.O.M.	Carol Orsag-Madigan	M.J.H.	Michael J. Hayes
C.Ro.	Christopher Rouse	M.J.T.	Michael J. Toohey
C.R.M.	Claude R. Mowry	M.W.	Mike Ward
C.S.	Carl Sifakis	N.C.S.	Nancy C. Sorel
D.B.	Danny Biederman	N.R.	Nicholas Rennison
D.L.	Don Lessem	P.F.	Pamela Fields
D.P.M.	David P. Monahan	P.S.H.	Paul S. Hagerman
D.W.	David Wallechinsky	R.A.	Randy Alfred
D.W.B.	David W. Barber	R.C.B.	Richard C. Brown
E.H.C.	Ernest H. Corfine	R.H.	Robert Hendrickson
E.F.	Ed Fishbein	R.J.F.	Rodger J. Fadness
E.N	Edward Nizalowski	R.K.R.	R. Kent Rasmussen
F.B.	Fern Bryant	R.S.	Ray Spangenburg
F.H.	Frank Henry	R.T	Richard Trubo
H.A.K.	H. Arthur Klein	R.W. S.	Roy W. Sorrels
I.W.	Irving Wallace	S.B.	Sue Berkman
J.Ba.	James Barnett	S.C.B.	Scott Bradley
J.Be.	Jeremy Beadle	S.R.	Steven Raichlen
J.B.M.	Joseph B. Morris	S.S.	Steven Sherman
J.F.	Josh Fishel	T.C.	Tim Conaway
J.Hu.	Jannika Hurwitt	T.D.	Tom Dodds
J.R.L.	James R. Longacre	W.A.D.	William A. DeGregorio
K.A.	Kayti Adkins	W.D.	Wendy Dreskin
K.A.M.	Kenneth A. Michaelis		
K.A.R.	Karla Rosenbusch		

Lists without initials were written by A.W. and D.W.

The Book of Lists

David Wallechinsky
and Amy Wallace

CANONGATE
Edinburgh · New York · Melbourne

First published in the US in 1977 by William Morrow

UK edition first published in Great Britain in 2004 by
Canongate Books Ltd, 14 High Street,
Edinburgh EH1 1TE

This edition published by Canongate Books in 2005

1

British Library Cataloguing-in-Publication Data
A catalogue record for this book is available on request from the British Library

ISBN 1 84195 661 9

Typeset in Bodoni by Palimpsest Book Production Limited,
Polmont, Stirlingshire

Printed and bound in Great Britain by
Clays Ltd, St Ives plc

Designed by James Hutcheson

www.canongate.net

Contents

Acknowledgements viii

Introduction ix

1. PEOPLE 1
2. MOVIES 32
3. THE ARTS 66
4. FOOD AND HEALTH 94
5. ANIMALS 124
6. WORK AND MONEY 154
7. SEX, LOVE AND MARRIAGE 168
8. CRIME 188
9. WAR, POLITICS AND WORLD AFFAIRS 226
10. TRAVEL 260
11. LITERATURE 278
12. WORDS 316
13. SPORTS 336
14. DEATH 364
15. MISCELLANEOUS 402

INDEX 443

Acknowledgements

The authors warmly thank Flora Wallechinsky for long hours of typing, organising and troubleshooting, Elijah and Aaron Wallechinsky and Macho Boubekour for help with typing, and Jaime Loucky for his creative research. Our love and thanks to our mother for her support and encouragement. To Chris Fishel, for his wonderful work and ingenuity as staff writer; to Danny Biederman for organising the celebrity lists; to Scott Bradley, for his work as researcher and writer of celebrity biographies and as editor with Amy; to Allison Berry, for abstracting texts and research. Warm thanks to Jamie Byng, our publisher at Canongate Books, whose vision and enthusiasm inspired us throughout. And with gratitude to Canongate's wonderful and enthusiastic staff, including our two editors, Helen Bleck and Nick Rennison. Thanks also to our agents, Ed Victor, for his long, long support of *The Book of Lists* series, and Wendy Shmalz, the model of equanimity and humour. And special thanks to Jeremy Beadle for being available for consultations, for providing good advice and for always being a friend in need.

Amy would like to extend special thanks to Allison Berry for helping to keep her life running and to Scott Bradley for having saved his school lunch money at 13 to buy *The Book of Lists*, only to grow up to become part of its creation; and to Richard Jennings for support and keeping the wolves from the door.

This edition would not have been possible without the many people who worked on previous editions of *The Book of Lists*, in particular Vicki Baker, Carol Orsag-Madigan, Anita Taylor, Helen Ginsburg, Elizabethe Kempthorne, Judy Knipe, Fern Bryant, Roger Fadness, Lee Clayton and Torene Svitil.

Most of all, we wish to thank the millions of readers who wondered, and the many who asked 'When is the next *Book of Lists* coming out?' We welcome ideas and contributions from our readers for future editions; and thank you all for helping us create a genre that has lasted for three decades, and is more popular than ever.

The authors can be reached at viciousgnu@aol.com

Introduction

As Oscar Wilde observed, the only sin is to be bored. We believe it is an equal sin to be boring, and if the great wit was correct, then the authors and millions of *Book of Lists* readers are quite unblemished by sin: for we place a high value on curiosity.

The original 1977 volume of *the Book of Lists*, and its all-new sequels, inspired nearly 200 imitation volumes. These have included books of lists about movies, rock'n'roll, Judaism, the Bible, general sports, and countless other subjects. The books spawned games, toilet paper with lists on it, CD-Roms, calendars and television shows. We had no idea that *The Book of Lists* would become a bestseller, let alone a phenomenon. We thought we were just having fun.

The *Book of Lists* rose to number 1 on the bestseller lists, and was published all over the world. Young readers wrote to tell us they'd bought our book for fun, and were using it to spice up their schoolwork. Older readers locked themselves in bathrooms, curled up in bed, took the book to parties and demanded more editions. We invited their contributions, which came pouring in, and we featured many of them in the editions that followed.

Although we are pleased to have popularised a genre that so many people enjoy, we do not pretend to have been its founders. That honour goes to the Reverend Nathaniel Wanley, author of *Wonders of the Little World*, a book of lists first published in 1678. We didn't know about the Reverend Wanley when we wrote our own *Book of Lists*, but a glance through his table of contents shows striking similarities: 'Of such People and Nations as have been scourged and afflicted by small and contemptible things', 'Of such as having been extremely Wild, and Prodigal, or Debauched in their Youth, have afterwards proved excellent Persons', 'Of such as have been seized with an extraordinary joy, at what hath followed there-upon'.

The trend never died down, and in recent years has had a dazzling renaissance. We appear to live in an age in which the volume of information available to us is far too overwhelming for our minds to process. The everyday lists we all make are a balm to a cluttered mind; list-making puts things in order, it clarifies, it helps coax truth from the cracks of the universe, and it invites our favourite question: 'What if . . . ?'

In the present volume, we have updated our readers' favourite lists, prepared an array of new material, and included lists from a wide variety of notables and celebrities, such as Ian Rankin, Philip Pullman, Johnny Cash, Brian Eno, Elmore Leonard and Ben Schott, to name only a few.

We owe much of the inspiration for this volume to our father, Irving Wallace, who always hoped we'd continue to compile new editions. Whenever possible, we have concentrated on lists that cause readers to laugh out loud, gasp, shake their heads in wonder, or call out 'Wait until you hear this!' To quote Mark Twain's introduction to *The Adventures of Huckleberry Finn*: 'Persons attempting to find a motive in this narrative will be prosecuted; persons attempting to find a moral in it will be banished; persons attempting to find a plot in it will be shot.'

Chapter 1

AGES OF 25 PEOPLE HAD THEY LIVED TO 2005

10 MEN WHO CRIED IN PUBLIC

IF 27 FAMOUS MEN WERE KNOWN BY THEIR MOTHERS' MAIDEN NAMES

9 PEOPLE WITH EXTRA LIMBS AND DIGITS

10 FAMOUS NOSES

10 MEETINGS BETWEEN FAMOUS PEOPLE AND PEOPLE NOT YET FAMOUS

17 FAMOUS PEOPLE WHO WERE EXPELLED FROM SCHOOL

9 TATTOOED CELEBRITIES

10 PEOPLE WITH THE MOST SQUARE MILES OF THE EARTH'S SURFACE NAMED AFTER THEM

8 UNNAMED WOMEN OF THE BIBLE

6 PEOPLE WHOSE NAMES WERE CHANGED BY ACCIDENT

8 ALMOST INDESTRUCTIBLE PEOPLE

13 MOTHERS OF INFAMOUS MEN

People

FRANCESCO LENTINI, THE THREE-LEGGED MAN – WITH ONE OF HIS FIVE CHILDREN
– see p.6

Ages of 25 People Had They Lived to 2005

1.	Dylan Thomas, (1914–53), poet	91
2.	John F. Kennedy (1917–63), president	88
3.	Rocky Marciano (1923–69), boxer	82
4.	Malcolm X (1925–65), civil rights activist	80
5.	Marilyn Monroe (1926–62), actress	79
6.	Ernesto 'Che' Guevara (1928–67), revolutionary leader	77
7.	Anne Frank (1929–45), diarist	76
8.	Martin Luther King, Jr (1929–68), clergyman and civil rights leader	76
9.	James Dean (1931–55), actor	74
10.	Sylvia Plath (1932–63), poet	72
11.	Elvis Presley (1935–77), singer	70
12.	John Lennon (1940–80), musician	65
13.	Bruce Lee (1940–73), martial artist and actor	65
14.	Otis Redding (1941–67), musician	64
15.	Ritchie Valens (1941–59), singer	64
16.	Jimi Hendrix (1942–70), musician	63
17.	Janis Joplin (1943–70), singer	62
18.	Jim Morrison (1943–71), musician	62
19.	Bob Marley (1945–81), singer	60
20.	Marc Bolan (1947–77), musician	58
21.	John Belushi (1949–82), comedian	56
22.	Douglas Adams (1952–2001), science fiction writer	53
23.	Princess Diana (1961–97), royalty	44
24.	Kurt Cobain (1967–94), musician	38
25.	River Phoenix (1970–93), actor	35

10 Men Who Cried In Public

1. JESUS CHRIST, RELIGIOUS LEADER
After Lazarus died, Jesus led his disciples to visit Lazarus's sisters, Mary and Martha. When the friends of Lazarus agreed to show Jesus the cave where Lazarus's body was laid, Jesus wept.

2. BILL CLINTON, AMERICAN PRESIDENT
On the morning of his inauguration, President Clinton and his family attended services at Washington's Metropolitan African Methodist Episcopal church. As the choir sang hymns, tears rolled down Clinton's cheeks. Clinton teared up frequently as his years in office continued. Once, when caught on camera laughing

and joking at a funeral, Clinton suddenly realised he was being filmed. Having learned 'the Nixon lesson', he instantly grew serious and tears came to his eyes. Right-wing TV host Rush Limbaugh played the tape in slow motion repeatedly, sending his studio audience into fits of mirth. Tom Lutz, the author of *Crying: The Natural & Cultural History of Tears*, observed that crying for male politicians was 'a 1990s version of kissing babies'.

3. DAVID, WARRIOR KING
When David and his troops returned to the city of Ziklag, after being sent home by the princes of the Philistines, they discovered that the Amalekites had invaded the city and taken captive all of the women and children, including David's two wives. David and his followers immediately 'lifted up their voices and wept until they had no more power to weep'.

4. PAUL GASCOIGNE, ENGLISH FOOTBALLER
Paul Gascoigne arrived at the Italia 90 World Cup as an up-and-coming young footballer with a gift for the unexpected on the field and a reputation for being, in his manager's words, 'as daft as a brush' off it. He left it a national folk hero. And all because millions of English football fans, glued to their TV sets back home, saw him weep. In the semi-final England were playing old rivals Germany – then still just West Germany. Gazza, whose performances in earlier rounds had helped his team to overcome a poor start to the competition, was again playing like a man inspired. Then tragedy struck. Gascoigne was booked for a reckless tackle. Even if England made it to the final, he would not play in the match. As the realisation hit home, Gazza's face crumpled and the tears began to flow. England went on to lose the match on penalties but Gazza had been taken to the nation's hearts and all the sorry antics of his later career have been unable quite to destroy that earlier image of him as a little boy lost on the world football stage.

5. JOHN LEE HOOKER, AMERICAN BLUES MUSICIAN
Hooker, the revered American blues musician, told an interviewer in 1998, 'You can't get no deeper than me and my guitar. I open my mouth, and it's there. I get so deep the teardrops come to my eyes. That's why I wear my dark glasses, so you won't see the teardrops.'

6. MICHAEL JORDAN, AMERICAN BASKETBALL PLAYER
Michael Jordan cried openly when, while playing with the Chicago Bulls, he won his first NBA title in 1991 and this drew no comment from the press. Then, when he won his fourth title in

1996, he wept once more, falling onto the floor in a foetal position and sobbing when the game ended. This time TV announcers explained that Jordan's father had been murdered a year and a half before; the game was played on Father's Day, and Jordan had made an incredible comeback after retiring for two years.

7. RICHARD NIXON, AMERICAN PRESIDENT
During a 1977 television interview, Nixon told David Frost, 'I never cry – except in public.' Nixon's most famous public weep occurred in 1952 after he made his notorious 'Checkers speech' and Dwight Eisenhower decided to allow him to remain on the Republican ticket as the vice-presidential candidate. Watching this performance, Nixon's college drama coach, Albert Upton, who had taught the future politician how to cry, remarked, 'Here goes my actor.'

8. ELVIS PRESLEY, AMERICAN SINGER
Presley cried so frequently in public that his nicknames included 'The Cry Guy', 'The Prince of Wails', 'The Golden Tearjerker', 'The Cheerful Tearful', 'Squirt-Gun Eyes' and 'America's Number One Public Weeper'.

9. NIKOLAI RYZHKOV, RUSSIAN PRIME MINISTER
Ryzhkov was Prime Minister during Mikhail Gorbachev's reign. He received his nickname, 'The Weeping Bolshevik', for crying in front of the press when visiting Armenia after the brutal earthquake of 1988. Opposition critics treated him as an object of ridicule, a pathetic clown. Running for Parliament in 1995, he countered accusations that tears proved him too weak to hold a position of power, implying others would have wept had they seen the same horrors. By changing public opinion to that of viewing tears not as a weakness but as a sign of humanity, Ryzhkov won the election.

10. NORMAN SCHWARZKOPF, AMERICAN MILITARY LEADER
Towards the end of the 1991 Persian Gulf War, General Schwarzkopf was interviewed on television by Barbara Walters. His eyes welled up with tears as he answered personal questions. Walters said, 'Generals don't cry'. Schwarzkopf replied, 'Grant, after Shiloh, went back and cried. Sherman went back and cried . . . and these are tough old guys . . . Lincoln cried.' He added that he held back his tears in front of his troops during the war for the purpose of morale; although he could cry in front of them during a Christmas Eve service, where he was embodying the role of father figure, rather than commanding officer.

If 27 Famous Men Were Known by Their Mothers' Maiden Names

In our society a married woman loses part of her identity through taking her husband's family name. Should her children happen to become famous, her husband's family is immortalised while her own family is consigned to oblivion. (Picasso is one of the few famous men who chose to use his mother's name, partly because it was less common than Ruiz, his father's name.) It seems fitting to turn the spotlight, for once, upon the maternal branch responsible for contributing half the genetic endowment of the world's immortals and mortals.

1. William Arden (*Shakespeare*)
2. Isaac Ayscough (*Newton*)
3. Johann Sebastian Lämmerhirt (*Bach*)
4. George Ball (*Washington*)
5. Thomas Randolph (*Jefferson*)
6. Johann Wolfgang Textor (*von Goethe*)
7. Wolfgang Amadeus Pertl (*Mozart*)
8. Napoleon Ramolino (*Bonaparte*)
9. Ludwig Keverich (*van Beethoven*)
10. Abraham Hanks (*Lincoln*)
11. Charles Wedgwood (*Darwin*)
12. Charles Barrow (*Dickens*)
13. Karl Pressburg (*Marx*)
14. Sigmund Nathanson (*Freud*)
15. George Bernard Gurly (*Shaw*)
16. Winston Jerome (*Churchill*)
17. Albert Koch (*Einstein*)
18. Charlie Hill (*Chaplin*)
19. Ernest Hall (*Hemingway*)
20. Frank Garaventi (*Sinatra*)
21. Mick Scutts (*Jagger*)
22. Sylvester Labofish (*Stallone*)
23. Stephen Pillsbury (*King*)
24. Arnold Jedrny (*Schwarzenegger*)
25. Michael Scruse (*Jackson*)
26. Osama Ghanem (*bin Laden*)
27. Tiger Punsawad (*Woods*)

– M.B.T.

9 People with Extra Limbs and Digits

1. MYRTLE CORBIN (1868–19??)
'The woman from Texas with four legs' was the only freak who could challenge the 'King of Freaks' Frank Lentini as a box-office attraction. ('Freak' expresses dramatic physical deviation from the norm and was not offensive to those in the sideshows.) The body of a twin grew from between Myrtle's legs, well developed from the waist down and completely functional. Myrtle was married and, according to her billing, had five children – three from her own body and two from her twin's.

2. JEAN BAPTISTA DOS SANTOS (1843–?)
Born in Cuba, Jean (or Juan) was a good-looking, well-proportioned boy who happened to have two fully-functioning penises and an extra pair of legs behind and between his own, united along their length. His mental and physical capacities were considered above normal and so, according to one report, was his 'animal passion' and sexual functioning. He was exhibited in Havana in 1865 and later in Paris, where he is alleged to have had an affair with the three-legged courtesan, Blanche Dumas, who had two vaginas.

3. FOLDI FAMILY
Written up in the book called *Anomalies and Curiosities of Medicine* in 1896, the Foldi family was described as living in the tribe of the Hyabites in 'Arabia' for many generations. Each member of the large family had 24 digits. They confined their marriages to other members of the tribe, so the trait was usually inherited. In fact, if a baby was born with only 10 fingers and 10 toes, it was sacrificed as the product of adultery.

4. LALOO (1874–1905)
Laloo was a Muslim born in Oovonin, Oudh, India. He had an extra set of arms, legs and sex organs from a headless twin attached to his body at the neck. He, too, travelled with carnivals and circuses in the US and Europe and was written up in many medical textbooks. He married in Philadelphia in 1894 and his wife travelled with him. His 'parasitic twin' was male, but the circuses liked to advertise it as female to add to Laloo's strangeness.

5. FRANCESCO LENTINI (1889–1966)
For years acknowledged as the 'King of Freaks', Frank Lentini had three legs, two sets of genital organs, four feet and sixteen

toes. In order to counter his depression at being deformed, Lentini's parents took him to an institution for handicapped children, where he saw boys and girls who were far worse off than he was. 'From that time to this,' he would later recall, 'I've never complained. I think life is beautiful and I enjoy living it.' He could use the third leg, which grew out of the base of his spine, as a stool. In his circus act he used it to kick a football the length of the sideshow tent. Born in Rosolini, Sicily, he moved to the US at the age of nine. He married and raised four children.

6. JEAN LIBBERA (1884–1934)
'The Man with Two Bodies' was born in Rome. He travelled with several circuses displaying his miniature 'twin', named Jacques. Jacques had hips, thighs, arms and legs. A German doctor using
X-rays found a rudimentary structure resembling a head inside Jean's body. Jean covered Jacques with a cape when he went out. Walking with his wife and four children he looked just like any other family man.

7. LOUISE L. (1869–?)
Known as 'La Dame á Quatre Jambes' ('the lady with four legs'), Louise was born in France. Attached to her pelvis was a second, rudimentary pelvis from which grew two atrophied legs. There were two rudimentary breasts where the legs joined her body. In spite of this handicap, Louise not only married but gave birth to two healthy daughters.

8. SHIVSHANKARI YAMANAPPA MOOTAGERI (1978–)
A young woman from Karnataka, India, Shivshankari has a third leg with nine toes growing out of the middle of her body. She views her anomaly as a divine blessing and supports her family by exhibiting herself locally.

9. BETTY LOU WILLIAMS (1932–1955)
Betty Lou Williams was the daughter of poor black share-croppers. She looked pretty and shapely in her two-piece bathing suit on the sideshow stage – but growing out of her left side was the bottom half of a body, with two legs and one misplaced arm. Betty, who died at the age of 23, made a good living during the Depression. Her friends say she died of a broken heart, jilted by a man she loved. However, the more probable cause of her death was complications from an asthma attack, aggravated by the second head inside her body.

10 Famous Noses

1. RUDOLF I OF HAPSBURG (German king and Holy Roman Emperor, 1218–91)
According to one historian of anatomy, Rudolf 'had so large a nose that no artist would ever paint its full dimension'.

2. MICHELANGELO (Italian artist, 1475–1564)
Michelangelo's nose was so squashed against his face that, in the words of one historian, 'his forehead almost overhangs the nose'. As a boy, Michelangelo had mercilessly teased the painter Pietro Torrigiano while Torrigiano was trying to study some art inside a church. Angered, Torrigiano turned on young Michelangelo and, in his own words, 'dealt him such a blow on the nose that I felt the bone and the cartilage yield under my fist as if they had been made of crisp wafer. And so he'll go with my mark on him to his dying day'.

3. MATTHEW PARKER (English clergyman, 1504–75)
Matthew Parker's name entered the English language as 'Nosey' Parker – meaning someone who pokes his nose into other people's business. Parker was Archbishop of Canterbury under Queen Elizabeth I. Though shy and modest, he was over-inquisitive about Church matters, and his enemies began to call him 'Nosey' Parker.

4. TYCHO BRAHE (Danish astronomer, 1546–1601)
Brahe lost the bridge of his nose in a swordfight when he was 20 and replaced it with a silver one.

5. CYRANO DE BERGERAC (French dramatist, 1619–55)
He really was a living person. He is said to have fought 1,000 duels over insults concerning his enormous nose.

6. THOMAS WEDDERS (English circus freak, 1700s)
Wedders had the longest-known nose of any human being in history. It measured 7½ inches in length. He was exhibited throughout England and was said to be mentally retarded.

7. JOSEF MYSLIVEČEK (Czech composer, 1737–81)
Nicknamed 'The Bohemian', Mysliveček was known for his operas *Armida* and *Il Bellerofonte*, and for the fact that he had no nose. In 1777, suffering from a venereal disease, he went to a third-rate doctor who told him that the only way to cure the disease was to remove his nose. So off it came. This led to the collapse of his career and he died in poverty.

8. DUKE OF WELLINGTON (British soldier and statesman, 1769–1852)
In addition to the more familiar (and more respectful) nickname of 'The Iron Duke', Wellington was also called 'Old Nosey' by many of his soldiers because of his prominent nose. During the Peninsular War, Wellington was riding near the frontlines when he was challenged by a sentry. Unfortunately, he had forgotten the day's password. Fortunately, the sentry recognised his nose. 'God bless your crooked nose, sir,' the soldier is said to have remarked. 'I would rather see it than 10,000 men.'

9. KATE ELDER, *alias* FISHER (American brothel owner, 1870s)
Elder was famous in the Wild West as 'Big Nose' Kate. Her nose was of the bulbous variety. She ran a house of ill repute in Dodge City, Kansas, and was the mistress of bad man Doc Holliday. Once when Holliday, in an argument over a poker hand, slit his opponent's throat and was about to be arrested, 'Big Nose' Kate set the livery stable afire, creating a distraction that allowed her lover to escape.

10. MEHMET OZYUREK (Long Nose Contest Winner)
Ozyurek is the only two-time winner of the Longest Nose competition in Rise, Turkey. Proudly displaying his 3½-inch nose, he won the inaugural contest in 1997 and then regained the title in 2000.

– I.W. & J.Be.

10 Meetings Between Famous People and People Not Yet Famous

1. NEW YORK, CITY, 1789. GEORGE WASHINGTON IS INTRODUCED TO WASHINGTON IRVING
As the President browsed in a Broadway shop, a servant of the Irving family spotted him from the street and hustled inside with six-year-old Washington Irving in tow. Informed that the lad had been named after him, the Chief Executive stroked the head that later would conjure up Rip Van Winkle and wished the boy well. *Note*: This pat on the head has been passed on through generations of Americans to the present-day recipient. An older Washington Irving bestowed it upon his publisher, George Putnam, who in turn gave it to young Allan Nevins, the future Pulitzer Prize-winning historian. Years later, at an informal

gathering at the Irving Wallace home, Nevins conferred the historic pat on 10-year-old Amy Wallace saying, 'Amy, I pat you on behalf of General George Washington.' Amy refused to wash her hair for a week afterwards. As *The Book of Lists* was going to print, she bestowed the historic pat upon baby Daniel, son of the owners of Clementines, one of Los Angeles' most popular restaurants.

2. **LONDON, 1836. ELIZABETH BARRETT BROWNING ATTENDS A DINNER FOR WILLIAM WORDSWORTH**
Elizabeth Barrett, not yet either married to Robert Browning or very well-known, was a great admirer of Wordsworth. John Kenyon, a friend of the Barrett family, arranged for Elizabeth to attend a dinner in the poet's honour. Although she was nervous (she said that she trembled 'in my soul and my body') about being seated next to Wordsworth, he was kind and even recited one of Dante's sonnets for her entertainment. Eight years later, Barrett paid tribute to Wordsworth by mentioning him in 'Lady Geraldine's Courtship'.

3. **ÉTRETAT, FRANCE, 1868. ALGERNON CHARLES SWINBURNE MEETS GUY DE MAUPASSANT**
The 18-year-old Maupassant, later one of France's greatest writers, witnessed the near-drowning of a swimmer who turned out to be the eccentric English poet Swinburne. (According to some versions of the incident, including Maupassant's own, he was actually in on the rescue, but this is disputed by more objective accounts.) When Maupassant introduced himself, the poet invited him to dinner at his villa. Swinburne's guest was shocked by the main dish – roast monkey – and the presence of a large ape, which pushed the young Frenchman's head aside whenever he tried to drink.

4. **LEGHORN, ITALY, 1897. ENRICO CARUSO SINGS FOR GIACOMO PUCCINI**
Near the beginning of his career, Caruso was hired by Arturo Lisciarelli to star as Rudolfo in a production of Puccini's *La Boheme*. Lisciarelli took advantage of Caruso's eagerness to sing the part by booking him for a mere 15 lire per performance, but added, rather vaguely, that the fee would be increased to 1,000 lire if Puccini liked him. When Caruso found out that Puccini lived nearby, he made a 25-mile trip to see the composer at his villa. After Caruso sang several measures, Puccini exclaimed, 'Who sent you? God?' Despite the composer's praises, Lisciarelli held Caruso to the original terms of his contract.

5. **NEW YORK, NEW YORK, 1910. SARAH BERNHARDT MEETS LILLIAN GISH IN THE WINGS**
Before going west to become a star in D.W. Griffith's epic films, Miss Gish landed a dancing role in Sarah Bernhardt's show. As they waited together in the wings for the opening curtain, the Divine Sarah stroked the young girl's delicate curls admiringly and uttered something to her in French, a language Miss Gish had never before heard.

6. **NEW YORK CITY, c.1945. NANCY REAGAN DATES CLARK GABLE**
Gable dated the future first lady – then known as Nancy Davis and an aspiring actress – on three occasions during a visit to New York. Although gossip columnists speculated about a possible marriage, the relationship never was particularly romantic. Gable simply enjoyed seeing the town with Nancy and making her laugh, while she hero-worshipped Gable and wondered how long it would last. Once when they attended a party, she was convinced that Gable would leave her the moment a more glamorous woman appeared. When he stayed, it gave her self-confidence a great boost.

7. **NEW HAVEN, CONNECTICUT, 1948. GEORGE BUSH MEETS BABE RUTH**
Ruth was in New Haven to donate a signed manuscript of *The Babe Ruth Story* to the Yale library. Ruth presented the book to the captain of the Yale baseball team, first baseman George Bush. Later that day, with the Sultan of Swat watching from the stands, the future US president went two-for-four and led Yale to a 14–2 blowout over Princeton.

8. **GAINESVILLE, FLORIDA, 1962. TOM PETTY MEETS ELVIS PRESLEY**
When future rock star Petty was 11 years old, Elvis arrived in his hometown to shoot scenes for the movie *Follow That Dream*. Since his uncle was involved with making the film, Petty was able to visit the set and meet the king of rock and roll. Petty remembered, 'He didn't have much to say to us, but for a kid at an impressionable age, he was an incredible sight.' Straightaway, Petty traded his slingshot for a friend's collection of Elvis records.

9. **WASHINGTON, DC, 1963. BILL CLINTON SHAKES HANDS WITH JOHN F. KENNEDY**
In the summer of 1963, Clinton was named one of the delegates to Boys Nation, an American Legion program in which a select

group of high school juniors travelled to Washington to watch national politics in action. The highlight of the trip was the delegates' visit to the White House, where a gangly, crew-cut Clinton briefly shook hands with President Kennedy. The moment was recorded for posterity (and future Clinton campaigns) in a photo and on film. When Clinton returned home to Arkansas, he was set on a political career. His mother, Virginia Kelley, remembered, 'I'd never seen him so excited about something. When he came back from Washington, holding this picture of himself with Jack Kennedy, and the expression on his face – I just knew that politics was the answer for him.'

10. CHELTENHAM, ENGLAND, LITERARY FESTIVAL, 1963. JOHN FOWLES MEETS IRIS MURDOCH
When bestselling author John Fowles was on the verge of success, but not yet famous, he was a panellist at the Cheltenham Festival. He was prepared to attack the famous authoress Iris Murdoch, but instead found her 'a gentle creature with a good mind'. Mrs Fowles felt Murdoch ignored them. Years later, when Fowles' fame was enormous, Murdoch invited the Fowleses to lunch. He recorded the following exchange in his diary:
I.M.: Are you religious?
J.F.: Not at all . . .
I.M.: Nor am I.
J.F.: in the normal sense of the word.
I.M.: Ah. (long Pinter-like silence, contemplation of the lawn outside.) I expect you have a nice intellectual circle at Lyme Regis? [The extremely remote country area where Fowles lived.]
J.F.: Are you mad?

– W.A.D. & C.F.

17 Famous People Who Were Expelled from School

1. TORI AMOS (1963–), SINGER AND SONGWRITER
At the age of five, Amos was the youngest person accepted to the Peabody Conservatory in Baltimore, Maryland. Six years later, she was expelled for refusing to read sheet music. The experience inspired the title of her first album, *Y Kant Tori Read?*

2. **JOHN BARRYMORE (1882–1942), ACTOR**
American actor John Barrymore was 16 when he was expelled from Georgetown Academy in Washington, DC. A faculty member recognised him, in the company of several other young men, entering a bordello where they had gone to celebrate Washington's Birthday. The next day, when asked to name the other men, Barrymore refused and was expelled.

3. **HUMPHREY BOGART (1899–1957), ACTOR**
The son of a successful physician with inherited wealth, young Bogart was sent to Phillips Academy of Andover, Massachusetts, and after a year was thrown out for 'irreverence' and 'uncontrollable high spirits'. Since attending Yale was suddenly out of the question, Bogie joined the US Navy.

4. **TINA BROWN (1953–), MAGAZINE EDITOR**
Former editor-in-chief of *Vanity Fair* and currently editor-in-chief of the *New Yorker*, Brown was expelled from three boarding schools by the time she was 16. 'I got other girls to run away,' she recalled, 'and I organised protests because we weren't allowed to change our underpants.' At one school the headmistress found her diary, 'and opened it where I had described her bosom as an unidentified flying object'.

5. **JACKIE COLLINS (1941–), NOVELIST**
At 16, Collins was expelled from Francis Holland School in England for (among other crimes) truancy, smoking behind a tree during lacrosse, selling readings from her diary of naughty limericks and waving at the neighbourhood flasher. Says Collins, 'I was a *bad* girl.' She later sent her own daughters to the same school.

6. **SALVADOR DALI (1904–89), ARTIST**
In 1926 Spanish ultra-modernist painter Salvador Dali was expelled from the Escuela Nacional de Bellas Artes de San Fernando in Madrid when he refused to allow his professors to critique his paintings.

7. **ROGER DALTREY (1944–), MUSICIAN**
Daltrey was expelled from Acton County Grammar School in England. 'I was an evil little so-and-so,' he remembers, 'I didn't fit in.' The headmaster who expelled him commented, 'When you have 500 boys in uniform, and one in a teddy boy outfit, no wonder he didn't fit in.'

8. GUSTAVE FLAUBERT (1821–80), AUTHOR
The 18-year-old Flaubert was first in his philosophy class at the College Royal. Nevertheless, he led a revolt against a substitute teacher, and when the noisy students were ordered to copy 1,000 lines of poetry as punishment, Flaubert organised a petition in protest. The headmaster was unmoved, and Flaubert and two other boys were expelled.

9. WILLIAM RANDOLPH HEARST (1863–1951), PLUTOCRAT
In 1885, American newspaper publisher William Randolph Hearst was expelled from Harvard, halfway through his junior year. He had given each of his professors a chamber pot adorned with the professor's name and picture.

10. JEAN-CLAUDE KILLY (1943–), SKI CHAMPION
Killy began skiing at the age of three, and by the time he was a teenager he often cut school to attend ski competitions. 'Once you start racing in France,' he said, 'your schooling is finished.' He was expelled at 15 because of chronic truancy.

11. BENITO MUSSOLINI (1883–1945), DICTATOR
At the age of nine, Mussolini was sent 20 miles from home to a boarding school in Faenza, Italy, run by Salesian priests. The recalcitrant youth was nearly expelled for throwing an inkpot at a teacher who had struck him with a ruler. Finally he went too far – he stabbed a fellow student in the buttocks with a knife. The future dictator was permanently dismissed.

12. EDGAR ALLAN POE (1809–49), AUTHOR
In 1831 American author and poet Edgar Allan Poe was expelled from West Point when he refused to attend drills and classes for several weeks.

13. RICHARD PRYOR (1940–), COMEDIAN
Pryor was expelled from a Catholic grammar school in Peoria, Illinois, when the nuns discovered that his grandmother ran a string of brothels. At 16, he was expelled from Central High School for punching a science teacher named Mr Think.

14. PERCY BYSSHE SHELLEY (1792–1822), POET
In 1811, while a student at Oxford, the poet Shelley and his close friend Thomas Jefferson Hogg sent a pamphlet entitled 'The Necessity of Atheism', a summary of the arguments of John Locke and David Hume, to the heads of the colleges. When both students refused to answer questions about the pamphlet, they were summarily expelled.

15. LEON TROTSKY (1879–1940), POLITICAL LEADER
At approximately the age of 10, Russian Communist leader Leon Trotsky was expelled from secondary school in Odessa, Russia, after he incited his classmates to howl at their teacher. Trotsky, however, was the school's best pupil and was readmitted the following year.

16. OWEN WILSON (1968–), ACTOR AND SCREENWRITER
Wilson was expelled from prep school after he and two friends stole the answers to a maths exam. 'I got called into the headmaster's office and he handed me a geometry problem and told me to do it. When I couldn't, he pointed out I had just completed a similar one on the exam.' The next year, Wilson was enrolled in the New Mexico Military Institute, where, he noted, 'I learned to follow rules, even the ones I thought were stupid.'

17. ORVILLE WRIGHT (1871–1948), INVENTOR
In 1883, during the sixth grade, American inventor and aviator Orville Wright was expelled from his elementary school in Richmond, Indiana, for mischievous behaviour.

– R.J.F. & The Eds

9 Tattooed Celebrities

1. DAVID BECKHAM
Beckham has a large crucified figure in the centre of his back. Above and below are the names of his sons, Romeo and Brooklyn. Among his other tattoos are his wife's name misspelled in Hindi and the Roman numeral VII, representing his number when he played for Manchester United.

2. NICOLAS CAGE
On his back is a monitor lizard wearing a top hat.

3. WINSTON CHURCHILL
Had an anchor on his arm. His mother, Jenny, had a snake on her right wrist.

4. EMINEM
The singer has several tattoos including one on his wrist that says 'Slit Here', three in honour of his daughter and an open grave with the words 'Rot in Pieces' dedicated to his ex-wife.

5. JANET JACKSON
Just below her bikini line she has what appears to be Mickey Mouse and Minnie Mouse having sex.

6. **PETER JACKSON**
When the actors in *The Lord of the Rings* were tattooed with an Elfish design for 'The 9' to represent the Fellowship of the Ring, director Jackson was tattooed with an Elfish '10'.

7. **JOHN MELLENCAMP**
The singer has Jesus on his right arm and Woody Woodpecker on his left.

8. **CHARLIE SHEEN**
Among his dozen tattoos are an open zipper with an eyeball peering out and, on his chest, a note that says 'Back in 15 minutes'.

9. **MIKE TYSON**
Besides the obvious Maori-style tattoo on his face, Tyson has pictures of Mao Tse Tung on his right arm, tennis player Arthur Ashe on his left arm, Che Guevara on his stomach and his second wife, Dr Monica Turner, on his left forearm.

10 People With the Most Square Miles of the Earth's Surface Named After Them

	Square miles
1. AMERIGO VESPUCCI, Italian explorer	
Total area:	16,243,000
North America	9,360,000
South America	6,883,000
2. VICTORIA, British queen	
Total area:	1,188,100
Queensland (Australia)	666,790
Victoria (Australia)	227,620
Great Victoria Desert (Australia)	127,000
Victoria Island (Canada)	83,000
Victoria Island (Antarctica)	60,000
Lake Victoria (Africa)	26,000
Victoria Strait (Canada)	6,000
3. MAUD, Norwegian queen	
Total area:	1,102,000
Queen Maud Land (Antarctica)	1,081,000

Queen Maud Mountains (Antarctica)	15,000
Queen Maud Gulf (Canada)	6,000

4. JAMES WEDDELL, British seal hunter and explorer

Weddell Sea (Antarctica)	1,080,000

5. ABEL JANZOON TASMAN, Dutch explorer

Total area:	925,100
Tasman Sea (Pacific Ocean)	900,000
Tasmania (Australia)	24,900
Tasman Peninsula (Australia)	200

6. CHRISTOPHER COLUMBUS, Italian explorer

Total area:	920,200
Colombia	440,830
British Columbia (Canada)	365,950
Columbia Plateau (US)	100,000
Colon department (Honduras)	3,430
Colon department (Panama)	3,150
District of Columbia and 10 US counties named for Columbus (combined area)	6,790

7. VITUS BERING, Russian explorer

Bering Sea (Arctic Ocean)	879,000

8. IBN-SAUD, Saudi king

Saudi Arabia	865,000

9. CHARLES WILKES, US naval officer

Wilkes Land (Antarctica)	660,000

10. WILLEM BARENTS, Dutch explorer

Barents Sea (Arctic Ocean)	592,000

8 Unnamed Women of the Bible

1. NOAH'S WIFE
   She is mentioned five times in the book of Genesis, but only in the context of being one of a group who is present. This is surprising considering how talented and efficient she must have been to have been suddenly uprooted from her home and asked to set up housekeeping in a gopherwood ark filled with birds, snakes, insects and full-grown animals of every species. This

woman, who kept everything in order in the ark for 12 months, is known to us today, not by her own name, but only as 'Noah's wife', (Gen. 6:18; 7:7 and 13; 8:16 and 18).

2. THE PHARAOH'S DAUGHTER

Her father, probably Ramses II, decreed that it was necessary to kill all male children born to the Hebrews because the Hebrew population in Egypt was growing too quickly. One day the pharaoh's daughter was bathing in the Nile with her attendants when she noticed a basket containing a three-month-old baby boy. She realised that he was a Hebrew child and decided to raise him rather than allow him to be killed by her father. The baby's sister, Miriam, was standing nearby and offered to find a Hebrew woman to suckle the child. The baby's mother, Jochebed, conveniently close at hand, was summoned and hired as a nurse to care for the child. The pharaoh's daughter later named the baby Moshe, or Moses, and he grew up to become the greatest leader and teacher in the history of the Jews. The woman who saved his life and raised and educated him was known in various history books as Thermuthis, Myrrina or Mercis. However, the authors of the Bible referred to her only as 'the pharaoh's daughter'. (Exod. 2:5–10)

3. THE WOMAN PATRIOT OF THEBEZ

Abimelech was a tyrant who ruled over Shechem for three years during the twelfth century BC. Having taken power by slaughtering 69 of his 79 brothers, he continued his bloody ways by killing the entire population of the town of Shechem when they revolted against him. Moving on to the neighbouring town of Thebez, he was about to set it ablaze when 'a certain woman' appeared on the roof of the town tower and dropped a piece of a millstone on Abimelech's head, crushing his skull. Humiliated by the prospect of being killed by a woman, Abimelech ordered one of his followers to run him through with a sword. With Abimelech dead, his supporters dispersed and Thebez was saved. (Judg. 9:50–55)

4. THE WISE WOMAN OF ABEL

When Sheba, the son of Bichri, led a revolt against King David, David sent his commander-in-chief, Joab, to track down the rebel and kill him. Joab finally found the culprit hiding in the walled city of Abel. Joab and his soldiers began the destruction of the city, but stopped when a wise woman called out to them to discuss the situation. Joab explained that if the people of Abel turned the rebel Sheba over to him, he and his soldiers would leave them alone. The wise woman easily convinced her people that this was a good deal. Sheba was quickly decapitated, his head thrown over the wall to Joab, and the city of Abel was saved. (II Sam. 20:15–22)

5. BARZILLAI'S DAUGHTER
When this Gileadite woman married, she retained her own name rather than take her husband's. In fact, her husband, a priest, took *her* family's name. Despite this early display of feminism, or perhaps because of it, the Bible authors do not tell us her name, but refer to her merely as 'one of the daughters of Barzillai'. (Neh.7:63)

6. THE SHULAMITE SWEETHEART
According to some scholars, the Song of Songs tells the story of a young Shulamite maiden who attracted the attention of King Solomon. He forced her to come to Jerusalem and tried to convince her to marry him, but she resisted him and insisted on remaining faithful to her shepherd lover. Eventually Solomon gave up and allowed her to return home, while he was forced to continue living with the 700 women he had already married. (Song of Solomon)

7. HERODIAS' DAUGHTER
Known to the historian Josephus as Salome, this most famous of all dancers is not given a name in the New Testament. King Herod was so impressed by the dancing of Herodias' daughter that he offered her any gift, including half his kingdom. After consulting her mother, who was angry with John the Baptist for publicly denouncing her as an incestuous adulterer, she asked for the head of John the Baptist on a platter. She got it and promptly turned over the grisly prize to her mum. (Matt. 14:6; Mark 6:22)

8. THE ADULTEROUS WOMAN
Caught in the act of adultery, this woman was brought before Jesus by the scribes and Pharisees, who pointed out that the law required that such an offence be punished by stoning. Jesus ignored them at first and then said, 'He that is without sin among you, let him first cast a stone at her.' One by one her accusers slithered away, and she was not punished. (John 8:3–ll)

6 People Whose Names Were Changed by Accident

1. IRVING BERLIN (1888–1989), songwriter
He was born Israel Baline, but the sheet music for his first composition, 'Marie from Sunny Italy', credited the song to 'I. Berlin'. Baline preferred the mistake over his actual name.

2. WILLIAM FAULKNER (1897–1962), novelist
After William Falkner's first book, *The Marble Faun* (1924), was published, he discovered that a 'u' had been inserted into his last name. He decided to live with the new spelling rather than go through the hassle of correcting the error.

3. ULYSSES S. GRANT (1822–85), general and US president
The future Civil War general was born Hiram Ulysses Grant. The prospect of entering the US Military Academy with the initials 'H.U.G.' embarrassed him, so the new cadet reversed the order of his names and started signing himself U.H. Grant. He soon learned that Rep. Thomas L. Hamer, who had sponsored his appointment to West Point, had mistakenly enrolled him as Ulysses Simpson Grant, 'Simpson' being the maiden name of Grant's mother. Grant, finding nothing objectionable in the initials 'USG', adopted the new name.

4. BUDDY HOLLY (1936–59), singer and songwriter
When Charles 'Buddy' Holley signed his first contract with Decca Records, his last name was misspelled as 'Holly'. Reasoning that others in the recording industry would make the same error, Buddy kept the new spelling.

5. DIONNE WARWICK (1940–), singer
When her first record, 'Don't Make Me Over' was released in 1962, a printing error made Dionne Warrick over into Dionne Warwick.

6. OPRAH WINFREY (1954–), television personality
Her parents intended to name her 'Orpah' after Ruth's sister-in-law in the Old Testament. However, the name was misspelled 'Oprah' on her birth certificate. Winfrey has used it ever since.

– C.F.

8 Almost Indestructible People

1. GRIGORI RASPUTIN
   The Russian mystic and orgiast held enormous political power at the court of the Romanovs from 1905 until his murder in 1916. That this decadent, vulgar peasant should hold such sway over the Empress Alexandra infuriated a group of five power-hungry aristocrats, who set out to destroy him. They arranged for Rasputin to take midnight tea at the home of Prince Felix Yussupov. Some accounts say that Rasputin drank voluminous amounts of poisoned or opiated wine and remained unaffected, to Yussupov's great consternation. The frightened Prince contrived an excuse to go upstairs, where the waiting gang furnished him with a gun, then followed him downstairs. According to Rasputin's daughter, Maria, the men assaulted her father and 'used him sexually'. Then Yussupov shot him. Again, according to Maria, they viciously beat Rasputin and castrated him, flinging the famed penis across the room. One of the conspirators – a doctor – pronounced the victim dead; but Yussupov, feeling uneasy, began to shake the body violently. The corpse's eyelids twitched – and opened. Suddenly, Rasputin jumped to his feet and gripped Yussupov by the shoulders. Terrorised, Prince Felix pulled himself free; Rasputin fell to the floor, and the other men dashed upstairs. In the midst of the brouhaha, they heard noises in the hallway: Rasputin had crawled up the stairs after them. Two more shots were fired into him, and again he was beaten with harrowing violence. The men (still doubting his death) bound Rasputin's wrists. Carrying him to a frozen river, they thrust his body through a hole in the ice. Rasputin was still alive. The icy water revived him, and he struggled against his bonds. When his body was found two days later, his scarred wrists and water-filled lungs gave this proof, as did his freed right hand, which was frozen in the sign of the cross.

2. SAMUEL DOMBEY
   Dombey was a black gravedigger in post-Civil War Orleans. Because he worked for such low rates, his fellow gravediggers decided to put an end to their competition. They called upon a certain Dr Beauregard, reputed to have magical powers, to use his $50 'supreme curse' involving an owl's head. The next morning, as Dombey began to dig a new grave, he heard a loud explosion. Someone, apparently injured, staggered from a

nearby clump of bushes. There Dombey found a gun which, overloaded with buckshot, had blown up. Later, a much-bandaged Dr Beauregard threatened to curse anyone who questioned him. The gravediggers took matters into their own hands. They placed a keg of explosive powder under the cot in the tool shed where Dombey took his daily nap and lit it while he slept. The explosion blasted Dombey out the doorway and plopped him 20 feet away. The tool shed was completely destroyed, but Dombey was unhurt. The local police nicknamed him Indestructible Sam. But the best (or worst) was yet to come: Indestructible Sam was soon captured by masked men and taken in a boat to Lake Pontchartrain. Sam's hands and feet were tied, and he was dumped into the depths of the lake. These particular depths, however, turned out to be only 2 feet; Sam wriggled free of his bonds and walked ashore. Next, Dombey's foes tried arson – and as Dombey ran from his burning home, he received a full load of buckshot in his chest. Firemen saved the house and rushed Sam to the hospital, where he lived up to his nickname. Sam had the last laugh. He continued to dig graves, and died at 98, having outlived every one of his jealous competitors.

3. MICHAEL MALLOY
In 1933, a down-and-out drunken Irishman became the victim of an extraordinary series of murder attempts. Malloy was a bum who frequented the speakeasy of one Anthony Marino in the Bronx. Marino and four of his friends, themselves hard up, had recently pulled off an insurance scam, murdering Marino's girlfriend and collecting on her policy; pitiful Michael Malloy seemed a good next bet. The gang took out three policies on him. Figuring Malloy would simply drink himself to death, Marino gave him unlimited credit at the bar. This scheme failed – Malloy's liver knew no bounds. The bartender, Joseph Murphy, was in on the plot and substituted antifreeze for Malloy's whisky. Malloy asked for a refill and happily put away six shots before passing out on the floor; after a few hours, he perked up and requested another drink. For a week Malloy guzzled antifreeze nonstop. Straight turpentine worked no better, and neither did horse liniment laced with rat poison. A meal of rotten oysters marinated in wood alcohol brought Malloy back for seconds. In an ultimate moment of culinary inspiration, Murphy devised a sandwich for his victim: spoiled sardines mixed with carpet tacks. Malloy came back for more.

The gang's next tactic was to dump the drunk into a bank of wet snow and pour water over him on a night when the temperature had sunk to -14°F. No luck. So Marino hired a professional killer, who drove a taxi straight at Malloy at 45 mph, throwing him into the air – and then ran over him again for good measure. After a disappearance of three weeks, Malloy walked into the bar, told the boys he'd been hospitalised because of a nasty car accident, and was 'sure ready for drink'. Finally, the desperate murderers succeeded – they stuffed a rubber hose into Malloy's mouth and attached it to a gas jet until his face turned purple. The scheme was discovered, and four members of the five-man 'Murder Trust' (as the tabloids dubbed Marino & Co.) died in the electric chair. One New York reporter speculated that if Mike Malloy had sat in the electric chair, he would have shorted out every circuit in Sing Sing.

4. DR ARTHUR WARREN WAITE'S FATHER-IN-LAW AND MOTHER-IN-LAW

Dr Waite was a New York dentist whose wife was the only daughter of a rich drug manufacturer in Grand Rapids, Michigan. Waite decided to remove the only two obstacles in his path to riches: his parents-in-law. The doctor's efforts are neatly chronicled in Carl Sifakis's book *A Catalogue of Crime*. Setting to work on his mother-in-law, Waite took her for a drive in a heavy rain with the windshield open. He put ground glass in her marmalade. He introduced into her food all sorts of bacteria and viruses – those that cause pneumonia, influenza, anthrax and diphtheria. The lady did catch a cold, but that was all. In disgust, Waite shifted his attention to his father-in-law, trying the same disease producers – with absolutely no effect. He filled the old man's rubber boots with water, dampened his sheets, opened a container of chlorine gas in his bedroom while he slept. Nothing. Then he tried giving the old man calomel, a purgative, to weaken him, and then a throat spray loaded with typhoid bacteria. People started commenting on how well the old man looked. Waite got off the disease kick and switched to arsenic. Amazingly, the poison failed. Finally, Waite polished off the old man by smothering him with a pillow. By now, however, other relatives were suspicious, and an autopsy on the father-in-law's body was ordered. Heavy traces of arsenic were found; although this was not the cause of death, the arsenic was traced to Waite and he finally confessed to his crime.

5. **HERBERT 'THE CAT' NOBLE**

This Dallas racketeer earned his nickname after the first nine attempts on his life. He was shot at so often that he was also called 'The Clay Pigeon'. His third moniker was 'The Sieve' because he had been riddled by so many bullets. The murder attempts were made by another Dallas gangster, the crude, illiterate 'Benny the Cowboy' Binion. A retired police captain revealed the details of their rivalry to Ed Reid and Ovid Demaris, authors of the *Green Felt Jungle*, an exposé of Las Vegas crime. Binion was taking a 25% cut of Noble's crap games and wanted to up it to 40%. Noble refused, and the fireworks began. In a dramatic car chase, Binion's thugs splattered Noble's car with bullets, and one slug lodged in Noble's spine. Binion moved to Las Vegas, but the feud continued long-distance – Benny wanted to save face by employing hired killers to nail Noble. Hollis 'Lois' Green, a depraved murderer, succeeded in wounding Noble on his third attempt. The following year, in 1949, explosives were found attached to Noble's car, and he was soon shot again. Real tragedy struck when Noble's beloved wife, Mildred, was literally blown to bits by an explosion of nitrogelatin planted in his car. This loss unhinged Noble's mind – his prematurely grey hair (he was 41) turned snow-white, he lost 50 lbs, and he began to drink heavily. Another shooting put him in the hospital, where he was fired upon from across the street. Noble's attempts at retaliation included equipping a plane with bombs to drop on Binion's home, but Noble was shot again before he could carry out his plan. Next, Noble miraculously survived the bombing of his business and a nitroglycerin explosion in one of his planes. Binion finally killed Herbert the same gruesome way he killed Mildred – with nitrogelatin hidden near Noble's mailbox. On August 7, 1951, the top part of Noble's body was blown right over a tree – there was nothing left of the bottom. The retired police captain who revealed all this commented, 'I think Noble had more downright cold-blooded nerve than anyone I've ever known. He was ice in water in a tight place.'

6. **DAVID HARGIS**

The 23-year-old Marine drill instructor was murdered in San Diego on July 21, 1977 – but it wasn't easy. His wife, 36-year-old Carol, took out an insurance policy on her husband to the tune of $20,000. Her accomplice was 26-year-old Natha Mary Depew. First, the ladies went to the woods to find a rattlesnake; instead

they found a tarantula, which they made into a pie. David didn't really like the taste of the tarantula pie, so he only ate a few pieces. The women then tried to (1) electrocute him in the shower, (2) poison him with lye, (3) run him over with a car and (4) make him hallucinate while driving by putting amphetamines in his beer. Their plan to inject a bubble into his veins with a hypodermic needle – thereby causing a heart attack – failed when the needle broke. They considered putting bullets into the carburettor of David's truck, but Depew objected because she wanted to keep the truck after his death. Frustrated, they resorted to a more old-fashioned method – they beat him over the head with a 6½-lb metal weight while he slept. This worked. The murderesses were apprehended while trying to dump the body into a river. Depew told the jury, 'If it had not been for Carol I would never have touched him . . . He looked so beautiful lying there sleeping.'

7. BERNADETTE SCOTT
Between 1979 and 1981, Peter Scott, a British computer programmer, made seven attempts to kill his 23-year-old wife after taking out a $530,000 insurance policy on her. First he put mercury into a strawberry flan, but he put in so much mercury that it slithered out. Next, Peter served Bernadette a poisoned mackerel, but she survived her meal. Once in Yugoslavia and again in England, Peter tried to get her to sit on the edge of a cliff, but she refused. When Bernadette was in bed with chicken pox, her husband set the house on fire, but the blaze was discovered in time. His next arson attempt met with the same result. Bernadette had her first suspicion of foul play when Peter convinced her to stand in the middle of the street while he drove their car toward her, saying he wanted to 'test the suspension'. He accelerated, but he swerved away moments before impact. 'I was going to run her over but I didn't have the courage', he later confessed to the police. Pleading guilty to several charges, he was jailed for life. The Scotts had been married for two years.

8. ALAN URWIN
According to the *Daily Mirror*, after his wife left him, Urwin, a 46-year-old former miner from Sunderland, England, made seven suicide attempts in a three-month period in 1995. Having survived three drug overdoses, he wound an electrical wire about his body, got into a tub of water, and plugged the wires into an outlet. The fuse blew out and he suffered a minor electric shock. He then tried to hang himself with the same piece of

wire, but it snapped and he fell to the floor, very much alive. For his sixth attempt, he broke a gas pipe in his bedroom and lay next to it. When this didn't kill him, he lit a match. The explosion blew away the gable end of his semi-detached house, along with the windows and part of the roof. He was pulled out of the wreckage suffering nothing worse than some flash burns. He was convicted of arson and placed on two years' probation. A few months later, he was on speaking terms with his ex-wife and was considerably more cheerful.

13 Mothers of Infamous Men

1. AGRIPPINA, THE YOUNGER (mother of NERO, monstrous Roman emperor)
   Raised by her grandmother, Agrippina was accused of having had incestuous relations with her brother Caligula. Lucius Domitius Ahenobarbus (later called Nero) was the product of her first marriage. She was believed to have poisoned her second husband before embarking upon a third marriage, which was to her uncle, Emperor Claudius I. She held such sway over Claudius that she convinced him to set aside his own son and make her son Nero heir to the throne. When Nero was 16, she poisoned Claudius, thus setting the stage for Nero to be proclaimed emperor. Resentful of his mother's continuing interference, Nero later arranged to have her assassinated.

2. HANNAH WATERMAN ARNOLD (mother of BENEDICT ARNOLD, American traitor in the Revolutionary War)
   Hannah belonged to a prominent family and when, as a young widow, she married Benedict Arnold III, she brought with her considerable wealth inherited from her first husband. Unfortunately, her new husband squandered this fortune, and as his ineptitude increased, Hannah assumed a dominant position in the household. She achieved a reputation as a long-suffering, pious woman, and she was pitied by her neighbours. When her young son, Benedict Arnold IV, was sent away to school, she wrote him long letters advising him as to proper Christian behaviour. Hannah lost five of her seven children in a yellow-fever epidemic, and thereafter she was obsessed by fears of death. She continually exhorted young Benedict and his sister to submit to God's will and urged them to be prepared do die at any moment. Hannah herself died when her son Benedict was 18.

3. MARY ANN HOLMES BOOTH (mother of JOHN WILKES BOOTH, assassin of Abraham Lincoln)
Eighteen-year-old Mary Ann was a London flower girl when she first met Junius Brutus Booth, a talented but dissolute tragedian. Already legally married, Junius fell madly in love with the gentle, warmhearted Mary Ann. In 1821, he accompanied her to the US. Eventually she bore Junius 10 children, and John Wilkes was her ninth and favourite child. Although she was acknowledged as his wife in America, Mary Ann's existence was kept secret from Junius's legal wife in England. However, in 1846, his double life was exposed, and in 1851 he obtained a divorce and at last wed Mary Ann. John Wilkes was devoted to his mother, and it is reputed that his dying words after he had assassinated Abraham Lincoln were 'Tell Mother . . . tell Mother . . . I died for my country.'

4. BARBARA BUSH (mother of GEORGE BUSH, JR., president of the United States)
Born on June 8, 1925, Barbara Pierce grew up in Rye, New York, a wealthy suburb of New York City. Her father was an executive in the publishing industry. When Barbara was 16 years old, she met George Bush at a country club dance. Three years later she dropped out of Smith College so that the two could marry. While her husband pursued a career in the oil industry and eventually entered politics, Barbara gave birth to six children, of whom George Jr was the oldest. (A daughter, Robin, died of leukaemia at the age of four.) George Jr was not a perfect son. Saddled with a serious alcohol problem until the age of 40, he was arrested at least three times, once for stealing a wreath, once for public rowdiness at a Yale–Princeton football game and once, when he was 30 years old, for driving under the influence of alcohol. As First Lady of the United States, Barbara Bush worked hard to promote literacy programmes.

5. TERESA CAPONE (mother of AL CAPONE, US gangster)
Born in Italy, Teresa emigrated with her husband to New York City, in 1893, where she worked as a seamstress to help support her family in Brooklyn's Italian colony. Alfonso, Teresa's fourth son, was forced to take over as head of the household when his father died in 1920. By that time, Al had already begun to establish his underworld connections. Later, during the periods when he was imprisoned, Teresa visited him regularly and she always maintained, 'Al's a good boy.'

6. MARIE ÉLÉNORE MAILLÉ DE CARMAN (mother of the MARQUIS DE SADE, noted debauchee and author)
Marie Élénore, lady-in-waiting in a royal family related to the de Sades, married the Count de Sade in 1733 and gave birth to a son, the future Marquis de Sade, in 1740. By 1750, the count had become increasingly difficult to live with, and as a result Marie Élénore removed herself to a Carmelite convent in Paris, where she remained until her death in 1777. Despite her pleas to the king, her son was imprisoned numerous times for his debauchery. Upon hearing of his mother's impending death, he escaped from prison and hurried to Paris. Unfortunately, he arrived too late and was rearrested through the efforts of his mother-in-law. During his subsequent 13 years in prison the marquis wrote the books which made him infamous.

7. VANNOZZA DEI CATTANEI (mother of CESARE BORGIA, ruthless Renaissance politician)
Vannozza was the mistress of Cardinal Rodgrigo Borgia (who later became Pope Alexander VI), and bore him at least four children, of whom Cesare was reputedly the first. During the course of her life Vannozza also had four husbands, the last one hand-picked by the pope. Always known for her piety, by the time of her death in 1518 she had left so much money to the Church where she was buried that Augustine monks were still saying masses for her soul 200 years later.

8. EKATERINA GHELADZE DZHUGASHVILI (mother of JOSEPH STALIN, dictator of the USSR)
Born in 1856 in a Georgian village, Ekaterina was the daughter of serfs. After her marriage to Beso Dzhugashvili she supported her new family by working as a washerwoman and seamstress. When her son Joseph was born, she hoped he would become a priest, and throughout her life she was disappointed at his choice of a different career. Ekaterina never learned to speak Russian, and even after her son's rise to power, she had no desire to leave her home in the Caucasus.

9. KLARA PÖLZL HITLER (mother of ADOLF HITLER, Nazi dictator)
A simple, uneducated Bavarian girl, 18-year-old Klara joined the household of her second cousin, 'Uncle' Alois Hitler, whose mistress she became and whom she eventually married. Three of her children died in infancy prior to the birth of Adolf, and Klara was always fearful of his death as well. Disappointed in

her marriage, she pinned all hopes on her surviving son. When she died of breast cancer in 1908, Hitler was overcome with grief.

10. ZERELDA COLE JAMES (mother of JESSE JAMES, US bandit)
Married at the age of 17, Zerelda went west with her husband Robert to homestead in Missouri in the early 1840s. Jesse was their second son. The elder James died while Jesse was still a boy, and Zerelda then married a man named Simms. The marriage failed, but she embarked upon a third marriage, this one to Dr Reuben Samuels. Throughout the bank-robbing careers of Jesse and his younger brother Frank, Zerelda remained loyal to her sons. A very pious woman, Zerelda would often attend church in Jesse's company. Zerelda was described by a newspaper reporter who interviewed her in later years as 'graceful in carriage and gesture, calm and quiet in demeanor, with a ripple of fire now and then breaking through the placid surface'. Perhaps it was this fire which she had imparted to her sons.

11. ROSA MALTONI MUSSOLINI (mother of BENITO MUSSOLINI, Italian dictator)
Born in a small Italian village in 1858, Rosa Maltoni was known for her retiring and gentle disposition. While employed as a schoolteacher in the village of Dovia, she met and married the village blacksmith, Alessandro Mussolini. Benito, their first child, was constantly in trouble and the source of much anxiety to Rosa. She was worn out and disheartened when she died of meningitis in 1905.

12. ALIA GHANEM (mother of OSAMA BIN LADEN, terrorist leader of al-Qaeda)
The daughter of a Syrian merchant, Alia Ghanem married Mohammed bin Laden, a prominent Saudi citizen of Yemeni origin, when she was 22 years old. Having experienced a more worldly society, she did not fit into the bin Laden family and was known sarcastically as 'The Slave'. Osama, who was mockingly called 'The Son of the Slave', was her only child by bin Laden. Pushed to the outskirts of the bin Laden clan, Alia had to watch as her son was raised by others. Mohammed died when Osama was 10 years old, and it was only then that he was sent to live with his mother. They lived together for only a few months, after which Osama went back to live with an uncle. Alia Ghanem later married another Saudi businessman, but she did remain in contact with her son.

13. SUBHA TULFAH AL-MUSSALLAT (mother of SADDAM HUSSEIN, dictator of Iraq)
Subha's husband, Hussein al-Majid, either died or abandoned the family before Saddam's birth. Subha considered having an abortion, but was talked out of it by a midwife. She gave birth to Saddam in a mud-brick house outside Tikrit belonging to her brother, Khairaillah al-Talfa. Subha, in a deep depression, could not take care of her newborn son, so she left him with Khairaillah. Saddam did not live with his mother until he was three years old, when Khairaillah was imprisoned for taking part in an anti-British,
pro-Nazi uprising. By this time, Subha had married her first cousin, Hasan al-Ibrahim, known as 'Hasan the Liar'. Hasan refused to send his stepson to school and forced him to steal chickens and sheep. At the age of 10 Saddam, wanting to go to school and fed up with his stepfather's abuse, ran away from home to live with his uncle Khairaillah. Despite her indifferent parenting, when Subha died in 1982 her son ordered a huge shrine built at government expense in Tikrit to honour the 'Mother of Militants'.

– F.B.

Chapter 2

14 MOVIE STARS WHO FELL IN LOVE ON THE SET

23 ACTORS AND ACTRESSES WHO TURNED DOWN GREAT ROLES

15 FILM SCENES LEFT ON THE CUTTING ROOM FLOOR

37 FAMOUS WRITERS WHO WORKED FOR THE MOVIES

8 MEMORABLE LINES ERRONEOUSLY ATTRIBUTED TO FILM STARS

17 MOVIE STARS AND HOW THEY WERE DISCOVERED

PATRICK ROBERTSON'S 10 TALES OF THE MOVIES

ANTHONY BOURDAIN'S 10 GRITTIEST, MOST UNCOMPROMISING CRIME FILMS

STEPHEN KING'S 6 SCARIEST SCENES EVER CAPTURED ON FILM

10 MOVIES THAT WERE PART OF HISTORY

WILLIAM FRIEDKIN'S 10 FAVOURITE MOVIES

KEVIN MACDONALD'S 10 FAVOURITE DOCUMENTARIES OF ALL TIME

WALTER MATTHAU'S 10 FAVOURITE COMEDIES OF ALL TIME

Movies

SEABISCUIT INFLATABLE EXTRAS – see p.56

14 Movie Stars Who Fell in Love on the Set

1.-2. VIVIEN LEIGH and LAURENCE OLIVIER

Cast as lovers in *Fire over England* (1937), Leigh and Olivier had little difficulty playing the parts convincingly. They were both married when they became powerfully infatuated with each other. Leigh was the opposite of Olivier's cool, calm wife, and he was a contrast to her intelligent but rather dry and unromantic husband. The affair was ill-timed: Olivier's wife was about to give birth and she guessed what was going on. At the christening party for his newborn son, Olivier stepped outside with Leigh and returned with lipstick on his cheek. On the set they were known as 'the lovers'. This was all too true for Olivier, who complained to another actor that he was exhausted. 'It's not the stunts,' he groaned. 'It's Vivien. It's every day, two, three times. She's bloody wearing me out.' He also felt guilty, 'a really wormlike adulterer, slipping in between another man's sheets'. Eventually the two passionate actors divorced their respective spouses and married in 1940. Twenty years later they divorced, and Olivier married his third wife, actress Joan Plowright.

3.-4. RONALD REAGAN and JANE WYMAN

Jane Wyman had a hard time getting going with Ronnie, as he was known on the set of *Brother Rat* (1938). Even before they were cast as lovers she had noticed him around the studio and suggested, 'Let's have cocktails at my place.' He innocently replied, 'What for?' Wyman didn't realise how straightlaced Ronnie was – although she was divorcing her husband, she was still officially married. When they finally began dating, they discovered they had little in common. She liked night-clubbing; he jabbered away about sports. Wyman loathed athletics, but she took up golf, tennis and ice-skating to be near Ronnie. 'She's a good scout,' Reagan told his mother after one date.

Reagan lived near his parents and visited them every day. Jane found his devotedness and general goodness intimidating. It wasn't until the sequel to *Brother Rat* – *Brother Rat and a Baby* (1940) – that they began to date seriously. While their courtship was romantic, the proposal, Wyman recalled, 'was about as unromantic as anything that ever happened. We were about to be called for a take. Ronnie simply turned to me as if the idea were brand-new and had just hit him and said, "Jane, why don't we get married?"' They were wed in 1940 and divorced in 1948.

5.-6. KATHARINE HEPBURN and SPENCER TRACY
Having seen Tracy's work, Hepburn got him to act opposite her in MGM's *Woman of the Year* (1942), in which they would play feuding columnists who fall in love. The first time they met she said, 'I'm afraid I'm a little tall for you, Mr Tracy.' Their producer, Joseph Mankiewicz, turned to Hepburn and said, 'Don't worry, Kate, he'll soon cut you down to size.'

After a few days of sparring on the set – at first Tracy referred to his co-star as 'Shorty' or 'that woman' – an attraction began to develop between them. Tracy was married and, although he lived apart from his wife, was a Catholic who wouldn't consider divorce. As the pair fell in love, their relationship was treated with unusual respect by the gossip columnists and was rarely referred to in print. One of the great Hollywood love affairs, their romance lasted 25 years, until Tracy's death in 1967 from a heart attack.

Explaining the phenomenal success of their screen chemistry, Hepburn said, 'Certainly the ideal American man is Spencer. Sport-loving, a man's man . . . And I think I represent a woman. I needle him, I irritate him, and I try to get around him, yet if he put a big paw out, he could squash me. I think this is the sort of romantic ideal picture of the male and female in the United States.'

7.-8. LIZ TAYLOR and RICHARD BURTON
The furor that attended the Burton–Taylor affair during the making of *Cleopatra* (1962) in Rome was as bombastic as the film they were starring in. Newspapers all over the world carried photos of the courting couple. Taylor was married at the time to Eddie Fisher, her fourth husband; Burton was also married.

In her memoirs, Taylor recalled their first conversation on the set. After the usual small talk, 'he sort of sidled over to me and said, "Has anybody ever told you that you're a very pretty girl?" And I said to myself, *Oy gevaldt*, here's the great lover, the great wit, the great intellectual of Wales, and he comes out with a line like that.' Chemistry prevailed, however, and soon there was electricity on-screen and off between the two stars. There were breakups and reconciliations, stormy fights and passionate clinches, public denials and private declarations, Liz's drug overdose and Richard's brief affair with a model. 'Le Scandale', as Burton called it, grew so public that Liz was denounced by the Vatican and accused of 'erotic vagrancy'. Liz wondered, 'Could I sue the Vatican?' During one love scene, director Joseph Mankiewicz yelled, 'Cut! I feel as though I'm intruding.'

Burton and Taylor married for the first time in 1964, divorced, remarried, and finally redivorced in 1976. Taylor said of *Cleopatra*, 'It was like a disease. An illness one had a very difficult time recuperating from.'

9.-10. HUMPHREY BOGART and LAUREN 'BETTY' BACALL
When Bacall was cast opposite Bogart in *To Have and Have Not* (1944), she was disappointed. She was 19, and it was her first movie role. She said, 'I had visions of playing opposite Charles Boyer and Tyrone Power . . . But when Hawks said it was to be Bogart, I thought, "How awful to be in a picture with that mug, that illiterate . . . He won't be able to think or talk about anything."' Bacall soon learned that she was confusing Bogey with the characters he played. She was so nervous the first day of shooting that her hands were shaking; Bogart was kind and amusing and teased her through it. Soon they were falling in love. He was 25 years her senior, and unhappily married. Though the affair became serious, Bogart was reluctant to leave his wife. His friend Peter Lorre told him, 'It's better to have five good years than none at all.' Meanwhile, the courtship grew intensely romantic. In honour of Bacall's famous line in the movie, 'If you want me, just whistle', Bogart gave Betty a small gold whistle. 'Bogey,' she said, 'is the kind of fellow who sends you flowers.' They were married in 1945 – he cried profusely at the wedding – and had 12 happy years until Bogart's death from cancer in 1957.

11-12. HELENA BONHAM CARTER and KENNETH BRANAGH
The elegant Bonham Carter, famous for, among others, her feminine period roles in E.M. Forster adaptations, met director/actor Kenneth Branagh when he directed her in *Frankenstein*, a film in which they also played lovers. At the time, Branagh was married to the actress Emma Thompson – their marriage ended shortly after *Frankenstein* was released. Said Bonham Carter, 'A third party doesn't break up a relationship. It just means you weren't meant to be.' The British tabloid press made things '. . . very difficult for Ken and I at first'. When the pair went on to co-star in *The Theory of Flight*, the press let up. As for that film's love scenes, Bonham Carter remarked, '. . . it doesn't help to be emotionally involved with the person. It's all acting. Your emotions are never present

really.' Said Branagh, 'Nothing could be more embarrassing than somehow doing anything other than your job . . . for this to be an excuse to play out your relationship . . . That's all bollocks!'

13-14. ANGELINA JOLIE and BILLY BOB THORNTON
One of the twentieth century's most talked about bad-boy cinema stars, director/writer/actor Billy Bob Thornton struggled from poverty to world-wide acclaim with *Slingblade* and a fast-and-furious series of roles and scripts. Equally fast-and-furious is Mr Thornton's propensity for falling in and out of love. He was engaged to Laura Dern, and professed happiness with his calm-at-last domestic life – he was finally spending time with his children by earlier marriages. Then, according to Dern, 'I left our home to work on a movie, and while I was away, my boyfriend got married, and I've never heard from him again.' Thornton and his bright, sexy co-star Angelina Jolie were playing marrieds in 1999's *Pushing Tin* – in May 2000 they tied the knot in a quickie Las Vegas ceremony. The marriage was Thornton's fifth, and was much-publicised: the pair got complementary tattoos, exchanged vials of blood, and were notorious for their ribald public displays of affection. They adopted a Cambodian-born baby in June, 2002, but 11 days after their son was brought to Los Angeles, Thornton abandoned his wife and child. Said Jolie, 'It's clear to me that our priorities shifted overnight.' Jolie had her tattoo removed, Thornton kept his. Laura Dern remarked in an interview that being dumped by Billy Bob was the best thing that could have happened to her.

23 Actors and Actresses Who Turned Down Great Roles

1. MARLON BRANDO
Turned down the role of Frankie, the musician-junkie, in *The Man with the Golden Arm* (1955). Frank Sinatra got the part and re-established his career with an electrifying performance.

2. JAMES CAGNEY
Turned down the role of Alfred P. Doolittle in *My Fair Lady* (1964). The role went to Stanley Holloway. Cagney was offered $1 million but did not want to come out of retirement.

3. **MONTGOMERY CLIFT**
Expressed enthusiasm for the role of the young writer in *Sunset Boulevard* (1950), but later turned it down, claiming that his audience would not accept his playing love scenes with a woman who was 35 years older. William Holden starred with Gloria Swanson in the widely acclaimed film.

4. **SEAN CONNERY**
Long a fan-favourite to play Gandalf, the venerable wizard from J.R.R. Tolkien's *Lord of the Rings* trilogy, the star turned the role down because he did not want to spend 18 months filming in New Zealand. Sir Ian McKellan eventually played the role to wide acclaim in the film trilogy. After the massive success of the first film, *The Fellowship of the Ring*, Connery said, 'I had never read Tolkien, and the script when they sent it to me, I didn't understand . . . bobbits, hobbits . . . I will see it.'

5. **BETTE DAVIS**
Turned down the role of Scarlett O'Hara in *Gone with the Wind* (1939). The role went to Vivien Leigh. Davis thought that her co-star was going to be Errol Flynn, with whom she refused to work.

6. **KIRK DOUGLAS**
Turned down the role of Kid Shelleen in *Cat Ballou* (1965). The role won an Academy Award for Lee Marvin. Douglas's agent convinced him not to accept the comedic role of the drunken gunfighter.

7. **W.C. FIELDS**
Could have played the title role in *The Wizard of Oz* (1939). The part was written for Fields, who would have played the wizard as a cynical con man. But he turned down the part, purportedly because he wanted $100,000 and MGM only offered him $75,000. However, a letter signed by Fields's agent asserts that Fields rejected the offer in order to devote all his time to writing *You Can't Cheat an Honest Man*. Frank Morgan ended up playing the wizard.

8. **JANE FONDA**
Turned down *Bonnie and Clyde* (1967). The role of Bonnie Parker went to Faye Dunaway. Fonda, living in France at the time, did not want to move to the United States for the role.

9. **CARY GRANT**
Producers Albert Broccoli and Harry Saltzman, who had bought the film rights to Ian Fleming's James Bond novels, originally approached Cary Grant about playing 007. Grant declined because he did not want to become involved in a film series. Instead, Sean Connery was cast as Bond, starting with *Dr No* (1962). Fleming's comment on this casting choice: 'He's not exactly what I had in mind'.

10.-11. **GENE HACKMAN and MICHELLE PFEIFFER**
Orion Pictures acquired the film rights to *Silence of the Lambs* in 1988 because Gene Hackman had expressed an interest in directing and writing the screenplay for it. He would also star as serial killer Hannibal Lecter. By mid-1989, Hackman had dropped out of the project. Jonathan Demme took over as director and offered the female lead of FBI agent-in-training Clarice Starling to Michelle Pfeiffer, with whom he had worked in *Married to the Mob* (1988). Pfeiffer felt the film was too dark and decided not to be in it. When *Silence of the Lambs* was made in 1990, the lead roles were played by Anthony Hopkins and Jodie Foster. Both won Academy Awards for their performances.

12. **ALAN LADD**
Turned down the role of Jett Rink in *Giant* (1956). The role went to James Dean. Ladd felt he was too old for the part.

13. **HEDY LAMARR**
Turned down the role of Ilsa in *Casablanca* (1942). Ingrid Bergman took over and, with Bogart, made film history. Lamarr had not wanted to work with an unfinished script.

14. **BURT LANCASTER**
Turned down the lead in *Ben-Hur* (1959). The role of Judah Ben-Hur went to Charlton Heston, who won an Academy Award and added another hit to his career of spectacular blockbusters.

15. **MYRNA LOY**
Turned down the lead (Ellie Andrews) opposite Clark Gable (Peter Warne) in *It Happened One Night* (1934). The role led to an Academy Award for Claudette Colbert. A previous film set on a bus had just failed, and Loy thought the film would not have a chance.

16. MICHAEL MADSEN

After his terrifyingly menacing performance in *Reservoir Dogs* (1992), Michael Madsen was offered the role of Vincent Vega in Quentin Tarantino's next film as director, *Pulp Fiction* (1994). He turned it down because he was involved in the making of *Wyatt Earp* (1994) in which he plays Virgil Earp. *Pulp Fiction* was an enormous success with audiences and critics. *Wyatt Earp* wasn't. John Travolta, who played Vincent Vega, found his career on the up and up while Madsen found himself playing parts in a series of B pictures. 'I wanted to take a walk down to the OK Corral,' Madsen has been quoted as saying. 'If I'd known how long a walk it was gonna be, I'd have taken a cab.'

17.-18. EWAN MCGREGOR and WILL SMITH

Both of these stars turned down the role of Neo in the blockbuster science fiction epic *The Matrix*, which eventually went to Keanu Reeves. McGregor starred as the young Obi-Wan Kenobi in *Star Wars: The Phantom Menace* instead, while Smith – who went on to star in the film version of Isaac Asimov's *I, Robot* – admitted, 'I watched Keanu's performance – and very rarely do I say this – but I would have messed it up. I would have absolutely messed up *The Matrix*. At that point I wasn't smart enough as an actor to let the movie be.'

19. STEVE MCQUEEN

When Paul Newman asked McQueen to star opposite him in *Butch Cassidy and the Sundance Kid* (1969), McQueen insisted on top billing. When his demand was turned down, McQueen refused to appear in the film. Robert Redford played Sundance and became the most sought-after star of the 1970's. McQueen turned down the lead role of Popeye Doyle in *The French Connection* (1971) because he felt the part was too similar to the tough cop he had played in *Bullitt* (1969). Gene Hackman got the part and won an Oscar for it. Finally, when director Francis Ford Coppola offered McQueen the starring role of Captain Willard in *Apocalypse Now* (1979), McQueen declined because he did not want to spend 16 weeks – Coppolla's original shooting schedule – on location in the Philippine jungles, away from his new bride, Ali MacGraw. Martin Sheen, who accepted the role, ended up spending a year and a half on location and almost died from a massive heart attack during the filming. Nonetheless, he turned in an electrifying performance.

20. **GREGORY PECK**
The producer of *High Noon* (1952), Stanley Kramer, originally offered the role of Will Kane, the retiring marshal who stays in town to confront the gunmen out to kill him, to Gregory Peck. Peck turned it down because he thought it was too similar to the part of Jimmy Ringo, an aging gunslinger haunted by his own reputation, which he had played in *The Gunfighter* (1950). Several other actors, including Montgomery Clift, Charlton Heston and Marlon Brando were approached before Gary Cooper was signed to play Kane. He went on to win an Oscar for Best Actor for his performance.

21. **GEORGE RAFT**
Turned down the main roles in *High Sierra* (1941), *The Maltese Falcon* (1941), and *Casablanca* (1942), which became three of Humphrey Bogart's most famous roles. Raft rejected the Sam Spade role in *The Maltese Falcon* because he did not want to work with director John Huston, an unknown at that time.

22. **ROBERT REDFORD**
Turned down the role of Ben Braddock in *The Graduate* (1967). The role made an instant star of Dustin Hoffman. Redford thought he could not project the right amount of naiveté.

23. **EVA MARIE SAINT**
Known for her selectivity in choosing roles, she erred when she turned down the central role in *The Three Faces of Eve* (1957) after reading an early version of the script. Joanne Woodward won an Oscar for her performance in the film.

– R.S. & C.F.

15 Film Scenes Left on the Cutting Room Floor

1. *FRANKENSTEIN* (1931)
In one scene, the monster (Boris Karloff) walks through a forest and comes upon a little girl, Maria, who is throwing flowers into a pond. The monster joins her in the activity but soon runs out of flowers. At a loss for something to throw into the water, he looks at Maria and moves towards her. In all American prints of

the movie, the scene ends here. But as originally filmed, the action continues to show the monster grabbing Maria, hurling her into the lake, and then departing in confusion when Maria fails to float as the flowers did. This bit was deleted because Karloff, objecting to the director's interpretation of the scene, felt that the monster should have gently put Maria into the lake. Though Karloff's intentions were good, the scene's omission suggests a crueller death for Maria, since a subsequent scene shows her bloodied corpse being carried through the village by her father.

2. *KING KONG* (1933)
   The original *King Kong* was released four times between 1933 and 1952, and each release saw the cutting of additional scenes. Though many of the outtakes – including the censored sequence in which Kong peels off Fay Wray's clothes – were restored in 1971, one cut scene has never been found. It is the clip in which Kong shakes four sailors off a log bridge, causing them to fall into a ravine where they are eaten alive by giant spiders. When the movie – with spider sequence intact – was previewed in San Bernardino, California, in late January, 1933, members of the audience screamed and either left the theatre or talked about the grisly sequence throughout the remainder of the film. Said the film's producer, Merian C. Cooper, 'It stopped the picture cold, so the next day back at the studio, I took it out myself.'

3. *TARZAN AND HIS MATE* (1934)
   Considered by many to be the best of the Tarzan films, *Tarzan and His Mate* included a scene in which Tarzan (Johnny Weissmuller), standing on a tree limb with Jane (Maureen O'Sullivan), pulls at Jane's scanty outfit and persuades her to dive into a lake with him. The two swim for a while and eventually surface. When Jane rises out of the water, one of her breasts is fully exposed. Because various groups, including official censors of the Hays Office, criticised the scene for being too erotic, it was cut by MGM.

4. *THE WIZARD OF OZ* (1939)
   The Wizard of Oz originally contained an elaborate production number called 'The Jitter Bug', which cost $80,000 and took five weeks to shoot. In the scene, Dorothy, the Scarecrow, the Cowardly Lion and the Tin Woodsman are on their way to the witch's castle when they are attacked by 'jitter bugs' – furry pink and blue mosquito-like 'rascals' that give one 'the jitters'

as they buzz about in the air. When, after its first preview, the movie was judged too long, MGM officials decided to sacrifice the 'Jitter Bug' scene. They reasoned that it added little to the plot and, because a dance by the same name had just become popular, they feared it might date the picture. (Another number was also cut for previews because some felt it slowed the pacing, but it was eventually restored. It's title was . . . 'Over the Rainbow'.)

5. *THE BIG SLEEP* (1946)
   This movie is famed as a classic despite its notoriously difficult-to-follow plot. As originally filmed, it included an aid for the viewer: Philip Marlowe (Humphrey Bogart) and a DA meet and have a conversation that summarises the plot. The film was finished in 1945, but held back from release until the studio finished rolling out its backlog of World War II films. During the delay, the decision was made to re-shoot several scenes to play up the chemistry between Bogart and Lauren Bacall. Also, a scene was added in which Bogart and Bacall meet in a nightclub and flirt while ostensibly talking about horse racing. In order to keep the running-time of the film the same, the scene of Marlowe and the DA was cut.

6. *SUNSET BOULEVARD* (1950)
   Billy Wilder's film classic about an aging Hollywood film queen and a down-on-his-luck screenwriter originally incorporated a framing sequence which opened and closed the story at the Los Angeles County Morgue. In a scene described by Wilder as one of the best he'd ever shot, the body of Joe Gillis (William Holden) is rolled into the morgue to join three dozen other corpses, some of whom – in voice-over – tell Gillis how they died. Eventually Gillis tells his story, which takes us to a flashback of his affair with Norma Desmond (Gloria Swanson). The movie was previewed with this opening in Illinois and Long Island. Because both audiences inappropriately found the morgue scene hilarious, the film's release was delayed six months so that a new beginning could be shot in which police find Gillis's corpse floating in Norma's pool while Gillis's voice narrates the events leading to his death.

7. *LIMELIGHT* (1952)
   Charlie Chaplin's film about a vaudeville comic on the decline features a scene in which Chaplin, as the elderly Calvero, makes his comeback in a music hall sketch. The routine, which originally

ran to 10 minutes, has Calvero performing onstage with an old colleague, played by Buster Keaton. It has been said that while Chaplin was good, Keaton was sensational. Consequently, Chaplin allowed only a small portion of the scene to remain in release prints.

8. *THE SEVEN YEAR ITCH* (1955)
Originally, the movie included a scene of Marilyn Monroe in the bathtub, getting her toe stuck in the faucet. Although Monroe remained covered by bubbles, the scene ran afoul of the Hollywood censors, so director Billy Wilder cut it.

9. *SPARTACUS* (1960)
Of the 167 days it took Stanley Kubrick to shoot *Spartacus*, six weeks were spent directing an elaborate battle sequence in which 8,500 extras dramatised the clash between Roman troops and Spartacus's slave army. Several scenes in the battle drew the ire of the Legion of Decency and were therefore cut. These included shots of men being dismembered. (Dwarfs with false torsos and an armless man with a phony 'break-away' limb were used to give authenticity.) Seven years later, when the Oscar-winning film was reissued, an additional 22 minutes were chopped out, including a scene in which Varinia (Jean Simmons) watches Spartacus (Kirk Douglas) writhe in agony on a cross. Her line 'Oh, please die, my darling' was excised, and the scene was cut to make it appear that Spartacus was already dead. These cuts were restored to the film in the early '90s.

10. *SPLENDOR IN THE GRASS* (1961)
As filmed, *Splendor in the Grass* included a sequence in which Wilma Dean Loomis (Natalie Wood) takes a bath while arguing with her mother (Audrey Christie). The bickering finally becomes so intense that Wilma jumps out of the tub and runs nude down a hallway to her bedroom, where the camera cuts to a close-up of her bare legs kicking hysterically on the mattress. Both the Hollywood censors and the Catholic Legion of Decency objected to the hallway display. Consequently, director Elia Kazan dropped the piece, leaving an abrupt jump from tub to bed.

11. *DR NO* (1962)
The first of the James Bond films ended with Honey Ryder (Ursula Andress) being attacked by crabs when Bond (Sean Connery) rescues her. The crabs moved too slowly to look truly menacing, so the ending was re-shot without them.

12. *EVERYTHING YOU ALWAYS WANTED TO KNOW ABOUT SEX BUT WERE AFRAID TO ASK* (1972)
'What Makes a Man a Homosexual?' was one of the many vignettes filmed for the Woody Allen movie using the title of Dr David Reuben's bestselling book. The sequence stars Allen as a common spider anxious to court a black widow (Louise Lasser). After doing a mating dance on Lasser's web, Allen makes love to the widow, only to be devoured by her afterwards. The scene was finally cut out of the film because Allen couldn't come up with a suitable way to end the piece.

13. *BIG* (1988)
In this film, Tom Hanks plays Josh, a 12-year-old who becomes an adult literally overnight when he makes a wish on a machine at a carnival. While an adult, Josh falls in love with a woman named Susan (Elizabeth Perkins), but he has to leave her behind when he makes another wish to become 12 again. In the original version, there was an additional scene at the end, in which Josh is back at school and a new girl named Susan arrives. The implication is that Susan went back to the carnival machine to make herself Josh's age. Due to negative audience feedback, the scene was cut from the movie.

14. *JERRY MAGUIRE* (1996)
Jerry Maguire originally included a fictional Reebok advertisement starring Rod Tidwell (Cuba Gooding, Jr.), which was cut from the film by director Cameron Crowe. However, when the movie was broadcast on the Showtime cable network, the commercial was restored, playing under the closing credits. Reportedly, the scene was put back in because of a lawsuit filed by Reebok against Columbia Pictures over the terms of product placement in the film.

15. *TITANIC* (1997)
The film ends with Rose (Gloria Stuart) going to the deck of the research ship investigating the *Titanic* wreck, leaning over the railing, and dropping a necklace with the valuable 'Heart of the Ocean' diamond into the ocean. As originally filmed, the crew members of the research ship see Rose, mistakenly believe that she is planning to jump overboard, and try to talk her out of committing suicide. When they realise what she is actually doing, they try to persuade her to preserve the necklace. Director James Cameron decided that he wanted the scene to focus on Rose, so he re-shot it with her alone.

– D.B. & C.F.

37 Famous Writers Who Worked for the Movies

1. JAMES AGEE (novelist; 1909–1955)
   Films worked on include: *The Quiet One* (1948); *The African Queen* (1951); *The Night of the Hunter* (1955)

2. MAYA ANGELOU (poet; 1928–)
   Georgia, Georgia (1972); *Poetic Justice* (1993)

3. RAY BRADBURY (science-fiction writer; 1920–)
   Moby Dick (1956); *Something Wicked This Way Comes* (1983)

4. BERTOLT BRECHT (playwright; 1898–1956)
   Hangmen Also Die (1943)

5. CHARLES BUKOWSKI (poet and novelist; 1920–1994)
   The Killers (1984); *Barfly* (1987); *Lonely at the Top* (1993)

6. TRUMAN CAPOTE (novelist; 1924–1984)
   Beat the Devil (1954); *The Innocents* (1961)

7. RAYMOND CHANDLER (detective story writer; 1888–1959)
   And Now Tomorrow (1944); *Double Indemnity* (1944); *The Unseen* (1945); *The Blue Dahlia* (1946); *Strangers on a Train* (1951)

8. MICHAEL CRICHTON (novelist; 1942–)
   Westworld (1973); *Coma* (1978); *The Great Train Robbery* (1979); *Jurassic Park* (1993); *Rising Sun* (1993)

9. ROALD DAHL (author; 1916–1990)
   You Only Live Twice (1967); *Chitty Chitty Bang Bang* (1968); *Willy Wonka and the Chocolate Factory* (1971)

10. WILLIAM FAULKNER (novelist; 1897–1962)
    Today We Live (1933); *Road to Glory* (1936); *To Have and Have Not* (1945); *The Big Sleep* (1946); *Land of the Pharaohs* (1955)

11. F. SCOTT FITZGERALD (novelist; 1896–1940)
    A Yank at Oxford (1938); *Three Comrades* (1938); *Gone with the Wind* (1939); *The Women* (1939); *Madame Curie* (1943)

12. CARLOS FUENTES (novelist; 1928–)
    Pedro Paramo (1967); *Muneca Riera* (1971)

13. GRAHAM GREENE (novelist; 1904–91)
    The Green Cockatoo (1937); *The Fallen Idol* (1948); *The Third*

Man (1950); *Saint Joan* (1957); *Our Man in Havana* (1960); *The Comedians* (1967)

14. DASHIELL HAMMETT (detective story writer; 1894–1961)
City Streets (1931); *Mister Dynamite* (1935); *After the Thin Man* (1937); *Another Thin Man* (1939); *Watch on the Rhine* (1943)

15. ERNEST HEMINGWAY (novelist; 1899–1961)
The Spanish Earth (1937); *The Old Man and the Sea* (1956)

16. ALDOUS HUXLEY (novelist and essayist; 1894–1956)
Pride and Prejudice (1940); *Jane Eyre* (1944); *A Woman's Vengeance* (1948)

17. CHRISTOPHER ISHERWOOD (writer; 1904–1986)
Rage in Heaven (1941); *Forever and a Day* (1944); *The Loved One* (1965); *Frankenstein, the True Story* (1973)

18. WILLIAM KENNEDY (novelist; 1928–)
The Cotton Club (1984); *Ironweed* (1987)

19. NORMAN MAILER (novelist; 1923–)
Tough Guys Don't Dance (1987); *King Lear* (1987)

20. LARRY McMURTRY (novelist; 1936–)
The Last Picture Show (1971); *Falling from Grace* (1992)

21. ARTHUR MILLER (playwright; 1915–)
Death of a Salesman (1951); *Let's Make Love* (1960); *The Misfits* (1961); *An Enemy of the People* (1977); *Everybody Wins* (1990)

22. JOHN OSBORNE (playwright; 1929–94)
The Entertainer (1960); *Tom Jones* (1963); *England, My England* (1995)

23. DOROTHY PARKER (short-story writer; 1893–1967)
Suzy (1936); *A Star Is Born* (1937); *Weekend for Three* (1941); *Saboteur* (1942); *The Fan* (1949)

24. S.J. PERELMAN (humorist; 1904–79)
Horse Feathers (1932); *Sitting Pretty* (1933); *Florida Special* (1936); *Boy Trouble* (1939); *Around the World in 80 Days* (1956)

25. HAROLD PINTER (playwright; 1930–)
The Birthday Party (1968); *The Go-Between* (1971); *The Last Tycoon* (1976); *The French Lieutenant's Woman* (1981); *The Trial* (1993)

26. **GEORGE BERNARD SHAW** (playwright; 1856–1950)
Pygmalion (1938); *Major Barbara* (1941); *Caesar and Cleopatra* (1946)

27. **SAM SHEPARD** (playwright; 1943–)
Zabriske Point (1970); *Paris, Texas* (1984); *Silent Tongue* (1993)

28. **NEIL SIMON** (playwright; 1927–)
Barefoot in the Park (1967); *The Sunshine Boys* (1975); *The Goodbye Girl* (1977); *The Lonely Guy* (1984); *Brighton Beach Memoirs* (1986); *Lost in Yonkers* (1993)

29. **JOHN STEINBECK** (novelist; 1902–1968)
The Forgotten Village (1941); *The Pearl* (1948); *The Red Pony* (1949); *Viva Zapata* (1952)

30. **TOM STOPPARD** (playwright; 1937–)
Brazil (1985); *Empire of the Sun* (1987); *The Russia House* (1990); *Shakespeare in Love* (1998)

31. **JIM THOMPSON** (crime novelist; 1906–77)
The Killing (1956); *Paths of Glory* (1957)

32. **GORE VIDAL** (novelist; 1925–)
I Accuse (1958); *Suddenly Last Summer* (1959); *Ben Hur* (1959); *The Best Man* (1961); *Caligula* (1980)

33. **EDGAR WALLACE** (novelist; 1875–1932)
King Kong (1933)

34. **NATHANAEL WEST** (novelist; (1903–40)
Ticket to Paradise (1936); *It Could Happen to You* (1937); *Five Came Back* (1939); *I Stole a Million* (1939); *Let's Make Music* (1940)

35. **THORNTON WILDER** (novelist and playwright; (1897–1975)
The Dark Angel (1935); *Our Town* (1940); *Shadow of a Doubt* (1943).

36. **TENNESSEE WILLIAMS** (playwright; 1911–83)
A Streetcar Named Desire (1951); *Baby Doll* (1956); *Sweet Bird of Youth* (1962)

37. **TOM WOLFE** (journalist and novelist; 1937–)
Three Ways to Love (1969)

– C.F. & F.B.

8 Memorable Lines Erroneously Attributed to Film Stars

1 'Smile when you say that, pardner.'
What Gary Cooper actually said to Walter Huston in *The Virginian* (1929) was, 'If you want to call me that, smile.'

2. 'Me Tarzan, you Jane.'
Johnny Weismuller's first Tarzan role was in *Tarzan, the Ape Man* (1932). He introduced himself to co-star Maureen O'Sullivan by thumping his chest and announcing, 'Tarzan'. He then gingerly tapped *her* chest and said, 'Jane'.

3. 'You dirty rat.'
In fact, James Cagney never uttered this line in any of his roles as a hard-boiled gangster. It has often been used by impersonators, however, to typify Cagney's tough-guy image.

4. 'Come with me to the Casbah.'
Charles Boyer cast seductive glances at Hedy Lamarr throughout *Algiers* (1938), but he never did make this suggestion. Delivered with a French accent, the line appeals to many Boyer imitators who enjoy saying, 'Come weez mee . . .'

5. 'Why don't you come up and see me sometime?'
Cary Grant found himself the recipient of Mae West's lusty invitation, 'Why don't you come up sometime and see me?' in *She Done Him Wrong* (1933).

6. 'Play it again, Sam.'
In *Casablanca* (1942) Ingrid Bergman dropped in unexpectedly at old lover Humphrey Bogart's nightclub, where she asked the piano player to 'Play it, Sam', referring to the song 'As Time Goes By'. Although Bogart's character was shocked at hearing the song that reminded him so painfully of his lost love, he also made Sam play it again – but the words he used were, 'You played it for her, you can play it for me . . . play it.'

7. 'Judy, Judy, Judy.'
Cary Grant has never exclaimed this line in any film, but imitators often use it to display their Cary Grant-like accents.

8. 'I want to be alone.'
In 1955, retired film star Greta Garbo – despairing of ever being free of publicity – said, 'I want to be let alone.' The

melodramatic misinterpretation, however, is the way most people have heard and quoted it.

– K.P.

17 Movie Stars and How They Were Discovered

1. FATTY ARBUCKLE
The hefty comedian got his first break due to a blocked drain. Working as a plumber's assistant, he was summoned to unclog Mack Sennett's pipes in 1913 and the producer immediately offered Arbuckle a job in his Keystone Kops comedies.

2. RICHARD ARLEN
He was working as a film lab runner at Paramount Studios in 1922 when he was struck by a company car and hospitalised with a broken leg. Studio executives took notice and offered him a chance to act.

3. WALTER BRENNAN
He got his start in Hollywood in 1932 when he did a voice-over for a donkey. The actor volunteered to help a film director who was having difficulty getting the animal to bray on cue.

4. ELLEN BURSTYN
She was cast in her first major role in *Tropic of Cancer* (1969) on the basis of a political speech that director Joseph Strick heard her delivering.

5. GARY COOPER
Working as a stunt man, he was noticed by director Henry King on the set of *The Winning of Barbara Worth* at Samuel Goldwyn Studios in 1926.

6. ERROL FLYNN
He was discovered by Cinesound Studios casting director John Warwick in Sydney, Australia, in 1932. Warwick found some amateur footage of Flynn taken in 1930 by Dr Herman F. Erben, a filmmaker and tropical-disease specialist who had chartered navigator Flynn's schooner for a tour of New Guinea headhunter territory.

7. ROCK HUDSON
Hudson, whose original name was Roy Fitzgerald, was working as a truck driver for the Budget Pack Company in 1954 when

another driver offered to arrange a meeting between Fitzgerald and agent Henry Willson. In spite of Fitzgerald's professed lack of faith in his acting abilities, Willson took the aspiring actor under his wing, changed his name to Rock Hudson, and launched his career.

8. JANET LEIGH
She was a psychology student when MGM star Norma Shearer happened to see a photo of her at a ski lodge in northern California where her parents were employed. Shearer took it to the studio with the result that Leigh was given a role in *The Romance of Rosy Ridge* (1947).

9. GINA LOLLOBRIGIDA
An art student in Rome, she was stopped on the street by director Mario Costa. She let loose a torrent of abuse about men who accost defenceless girls and only when she paused for breath was he able to explain that he wanted to screen-test her for *Elisir d'Amore* (1946). She won the part.

10. CAROLE LOMBARD
She met director Allan Dwan in Los Angeles in the spring of 1921. Dwan watched 12-year-old Carole – then tomboy Jane Alice Peters – playing baseball outside the home of his friends Al and Rita Kaufman.

11. IDA LUPINO
She was introduced to director Allan Dwan in England in 1933, while Dwan was casting a film, *Her First Affair*. Forty-one-year-old Connie Emerald was trying out for a part, but Dwan found Connie's 15-year-old daughter Ida better suited for the role.

12. MAE MARSH
One of the first actresses to achieve screen stardom without previous stage experience, Marsh was a 17-year-old salesgirl when she stopped by the Biograph Studios to see her sister, Marguerite Loveridge. She was spotted by director D.W. Griffith, who was having problems because none of his contract players was willing to play the lead in *Man's Genesis* (1912) with bared legs. Marsh had no such inhibitions when Griffith offered her the part.

13. RYAN O'NEAL
He was befriended by actor Richard Egan in 1962 at the gymnasium where both Egan and O'Neal worked out. 'It was just a matter of Ryan himself being so impressive,' said Egan.

14. TELLY SAVALAS
He was teaching adult-education classes in Garden City, New Jersey, when an agent asked him if he knew an actor who could speak with a European accent. He tried out himself and landed a part in *Armstrong Circle Theater* on television.

15. CHARLIZE THERON
The South African-born actress studied dance and modelled in Milan and New York before heading to Los Angeles to pursue her dream of acting. After several difficult months in LA, Theron's discovery came in a Hollywood Boulevard bank. When a teller refused to cash an out-of-town check for her, she threw an enormous tantrum which caught the attention of veteran talent manager John Crosby, who happened to be standing nearby. Crosby handed her his business card as she was being thrown out of the bank. After signing with Crosby, Theron landed a star-making role as a sexy assassin in 1996's *2 Days in the Valley*. She ended her association with Crosby in 1997, and has starred in such films as *The Cider House Rules*, *The Italian Job* and *Monster*, which won Theron the Best Actress in a Leading Role Oscar in 2004 for her portrayal of serial killer Aileen Wuornos.

16. LANA TURNER
She was observed in Currie's Ice Cream Parlor across the street from Hollywood High School in January 1936. Billy Wilkerson, editor of the *Hollywood Reporter*, approached her while she was drinking a Coke.

17. JOHN WAYNE
He was spotted by director Raoul Walsh at Hollywood's Fox lot in 1928. Walsh was on his way to the administration building when he noticed Wayne – then Marion Morrison, a studio prop man – loading furniture from a warehouse onto a truck.

– D.B. & C.F.

Patrick Robertson's 10 Tales of the Movies

Patrick Robertson's earlier selections of movie lore appeared in *The Book of Lists #3* and *The Book of Lists '90s Edition.* He is the author of *The Book of Firsts* and the continuously updated *Guinness Movie*

Facts and Feats, both of which have appeared in many languages, and is currently engaged on *The Book of American Firsts*.

1. DISNEY'S HOLY GRAIL
The rarest and most sought-after cartoon film of all time was rediscovered in 1998 when a 16mm print, bought in London for £2 from the disposal of the Wallace Heaton Film Library in the late 1970s, was identified as the only known copy of Walt Disney's first-ever production, the seven-minute-long *Little Red Riding Hood*. It was made in 1922 at Disney's Laugh-O-Gram Films, a small animation studio he established in Kansas City and which went bankrupt within a year. *Little Red Riding Hood* is particularly notable to Disney buffs because, unlike the later Hollywood cartoons such as Mickey Mouse, it was drawn by the 21-year-old fledgling film-maker himself. The reason that the unique print remained unidentified for so long was that the pirated copy bought by silent-movie collector David Wyatt had been retitled *Grandma Steps Out*. Only when he took it to the Disney company 20 years later was it finally revealed that the holy grail of animated films had been found at last.

2. FATHER OF THE FEATURE
Every movie buff knows that in the early days of cinema all films were one-reelers until D.W. Griffith came along and invented the full-length feature film with epics like *Birth of a Nation* (1915) and *Intolerance* (1916). Right? Wrong. The first full-length feature film was called *The Story of the Kelly Gang*, about desperado Ned Kelly, and it was made in Australia in 1906. And nor was this just a one-off. Other Australian features followed, with no fewer than 16 in 1911, the first year in which other countries began to make full-length movies, with France, Denmark, Germany, Italy, Poland, Russia, Serbia and Spain in the vanguard. In 1912 Hungary made more features than any other country and in 1913 it was Germany. With imports flooding in from France, Germany, Italy and Denmark, American producers were finally forced to accept what they had steadfastly refused to believe: that the kind of unsophisticated people who frequented movie houses were able to concentrate on a story lasting as much as an hour and a half. There was an explosion of production in 1914 with the US releasing no fewer than 212 features, of which one, *Judith of Bethulia*, was indeed by D.W. Griffith. But it is the long-forgotten name of Melbourne theatrical impresario Charles Tait, producer and director of

The Story of the Kelly Gang, which should be honoured as that of the true father of the feature-length movie.

3. THE CRYING GAME

Not all actresses can cry to order and some directors have been known to resort to less than gentle measures to coax tears from the dry-eyed. Maureen O'Sullivan's tear ducts failed to respond in her deathbed scene as Dora in *David Copperfield* (1935) until director George Cukor positioned himself out of camera range of the bed and twisted her feet sharply and painfully. Victor Fleming achieved the same effect with Lana Turner, never noted as one of Hollywood's most accomplished thespians, by jerking her arm behind her back and giving it a vicious twist.

Kim Novak, unable to produce tears on demand in the waterfall scene with William Holden in *Picnic* (1955), asked director Joshua Logan to pinch her arms hard enough to make her cry. The scene took seven takes and after each one a make-up artist swabbed Novak's arms to cover up the marks. Logan was so distressed by the need to inflict physical hurt on his star that he threw up afterwards. Later Ms Novak was to accuse him of unprompted physical abuse when she recalled the episode.

Gregory La Cava was able to obtain convincing tears from Ginger Rogers in response to Katharine Hepburn's calla lilies speech in *Stage Door* (1937) only when he announced to her that a message had just come through to say that her home had been burned to the ground. Norman Tourog directed his own nephew, Jackie Cooper, in *Skippy* (1931). When he was unable to get the 10-year-old to cry on cue, he told him that he would have his dog shot. The ensuing waterworks helped young Cooper on his way to what would be the youngest Oscar nomination for the next 40 years.

Otto Preminger stooped even lower when he needed spontaneous tears from a dozen small Israeli children in a scene in *Exodus* (US 1960) to show fear at an imminent Arab attack. He told them that their mothers no longer wanted them and had gone away never to return.

Whatever the vicissitudes of Hollywood, things were worse for child stars in Hong Kong. Veteran actress Josephine Siao Fong-fond recalled her days as the colony's most famous juvenile of the 1950s: 'If you were shooting a scene where you had to cry, and they were afraid you wouldn't be able to deliver, they simply beat you with a rattan cane till you did.'

4. IRISH EYES WERE SMILING
Ireland had always been notorious for the vigilance of its censors. Surprisingly, though, Roman Polanski's 1962 debut feature, *Knife in the Water*, a film with strong homosexual overtones, passed unscathed. It was argued that homosexuality was quite unknown to the Irish and what they did not understand could not harm them. An earlier generation of censors had been less tolerant. In 1932 the Marx Brothers' slapstick comedy *Monkey Business* was banned lest it provoke the Irish to anarchy.

5. MARRIED TO THE MOB
One of the most notorious examples of oppressive censorship occurred not at the hands of a censorship board but what might be loosely described as a 'pressure group'. The picture was *The Godfather*; those who were affronted were the Mafia, and the pressure group was the Italian-American Civil Rights League, headed by Joseph Colombo. When the League attempted to halt production of the film, producer Albert S. Ruddy decided it would be in the interests of his personal wellbeing and prospects of longevity to meet Mr Colombo and others of its representatives for a full and frank exchange of views. After protracted negotiations, during which the League asserted that the Mafia did not exist and was a figment of collective hysteria, they made him an offer he couldn't refuse. The film could go ahead with no fear of retribution from a non-existent underworld brotherhood provided the word 'Mafia' was wholly excised from the script. Ruddy declared that he had no wish to cast a slur on the blameless lives led by New York's Italian-American community and agreed to the League's suggestion. As it happened, Joseph Colombo was slain before the picture started, by persons alleged to belong to an organised crime syndicate comprised of citizens of the same national origin as himself.

The Godfather (US 1972) was a sensation and became the top-grossing film of 1972 even without mention of the Mafia. But those who decried what they believed was a craven compromise with the mob were mistaken in their criticism. Mario Puzo, author of the original novel and scriptwriter of the film, wryly observed: 'I must say that Ruddy proved himself a hard bargainer, because the word "Mafia" was never in the script in the first place.'

6. PAY RISE
Maybe you can't measure talent in dollars, but the moolah does say something about box office appeal. While the second half of the 1990s saw a stable of male leads (Jim Carrey, Tom Cruise, Tom Hanks, Bruce Willis, Harrison Ford, Mel Gibson, Sylvester Stallone) crashing the $20 million barrier, on the distaff side the upfront fees for A-list leading ladies seemed pegged at a miserly $10 million. (What other profession is allowed to pay women half the rate of men in this day and age?) Then Demi 'Gimme' Moore pushed the envelope with a $12.5 million pay-check for *Striptease*, but the picture bombed. Hard on her heels was Julia Roberts, who then established herself as the undisputed Number 1 female star with her hugely popular successes *Notting Hill* and *The Runaway Bride*. For her next picture, the even bigger *Erin Brockovich*, the flame-haired beauty with the letter-box mouth became the first actress to join the $20 million-up front club. It had taken her 14 years since her debut in a long forgotten 1986 flick called *Blood Red* and she now commanded a fee precisely 20,000 times the $1,000 she was paid on that one.

7. *SEABISCUIT* PICKED A WINNER
The 7,000 extras needed for the racetrack scenes in Universal's *Seabiscuit* (2003) would have put the movie into a severe budget bust at the standard fee of $50-$60 per day. Saviour of the movie was one Joe Biggins, the assistant to the unit production manager – not a role that normally wins plaudits from anyone other than the incumbent's mom. Biggins' inspiration was lifesize inflatable dolls. Cheap to make and transport, they could be inflated three at a time with a portable pump in 12 seconds. Mixed in with a few live performers, the dolls could be computer activated in post-production to simulate crowd movement. With *Seabiscuit* in the can and on budget, a triumphant Biggins set up the Inflatable Crowd Co., offering 15,500 roll-up plastic 'people' at $15 per week compared with a $300 per week tab for humans.

8. SERGEANT VOSS'S PRIVATE ARMY
Between 1923 and 1940 ex-Sergeant Carl Voss commanded a private army. With a strength of 2,112 former World War I servicemen, when it first appeared in the field of opposing American and German troops in *The Big Parade* (1925), the Voss Brigade took up arms again as Riff warriors, Hessians,

Senegalese, Revolutionary Americans, Chinese, Romans, Maoris and Crusaders in the years that followed. They would not only fight on both sides, but were equally adept as foot soldiers and cavalry, and as artillerymen it was said that there was no piece of ordnance they could not handle from the Roman catapult to Big Bertha. Following a stint as Fascist troops in Chaplin's *The Great Dictator* (1940), their last battle was fought in *Four Sons* (1940), some ending as they had begun as German soldiery, others as Czechs. On the eve of America's entry into World War II, the band of veterans was finally routed by the forces of bureaucracy. The Screen Actors Guild decreed that no agent could accept commission from an extra and their commander Sergeant Voss was decreed to be acting as such. After 232 engagements without a serious casualty, the old soldiers faded away.

9. THE LAST STAR OF THE SILENTS

Two actors who had starred in silent movies – and only two – were still performing in the twenty-first century. But with the death of Sir John Gielgud, who made his debut in *Who is the Man* (1924) and his last screen appearance in David Mamet's *Catastrophe* (2000), there is only one surviving. He is Mickey Rooney, who appeared at the age of five in *Not to be Trusted* (1926) as a cigar-smoking midget, giving rise to an ongoing belief that he was a vertically-challenged adult who played child roles. Starring as a teenaged, albeit diminutive, Andy Hardy with Judy Garland as his squeeze helped to lay the myth to rest, but MGM could not resist casting the 5ft 3in. Rooney opposite 6ft 6in. Dorothy Ford in *Love Laughs at Andy Hardy* (1947). These roles and the hundred or so that followed may not have had quite the gravitas of Sir John's, but Mickey outlived him to become not only the silent screen's last active survivor but one of twenty-first-century Hollywood's few actors of such unremitting energy that he puts in as many as four performances a year.

10. MOST MARRIED

The most married of many-times wedded Hollywood stars was B-movie luminary Al 'Lash' La Rue (1917–96), who went to the altar and the divorce court on 10 occasions, finally ending a turbulent life – in which he had been charged with vagrancy, drunkenness, possession of marijuana (while practising as an evangelist) and stealing candy from a baby in Florida, besides scripting porno movies – unmarried.

Anthony Bourdain's 10 Grittiest, Most Uncompromising Crime Films

'Extreme chef' Anthony Bourdain, born in New York in 1956, rose from dishwasher to executive chef at Brasserie Les Halles in New York City via a stint with the CIA (Culinary Institute of America). He is the author of two novels, *Gone Bamboo* (1995) and *Bone in the Throat* (1997), as well as *Kitchen Confidential* (2000), 'part autobiography, part restaurant-goer's survival manual'.

'Is it good? Is it realistic? (That leaves out *The Godfather*). Is it a timeless 'how-to'? Those are the criteria here. No good guys or bad guys – just a moral quagmire of betrayal, lust, greed and crushing, grim inevitability. That's *my* recipe for a good time at the movies!'

1. *THE FRIENDS OF EDDIE COYLE* (1973, dir. Peter Yates)
   You can smell the beer on Robert Mitchum as aging hood/part-time informer Eddie, running out one last scam in a swamp of atmospheric betrayal.
2. *GET CARTER* (1971, dir. Mike Hodges)
   Maybe the most vicious, hardcore – and magnificent – revenge melodrama ever filmed. Accept no substitutes. (The Stallone remake was a sin against God.)
3. *BOB LE FLAMBEUR* (1955, dir. Jean-Pierre Melville)
   Elegant, beautiful, sad and wise caper movie. And the hero gets away!
4. *RIFIFI* (1956, dir. Jules Dassin)
   The *Citizen Kane* of caper flicks.
5. *THE KILLING* (1956, dir. Stanley Kubrick)
   Seedy, delicious – and with Sterling Hayden! Pure crack for film nerds.
6. *THE ASPHALT JUNGLE* (1950, dir. John Huston)
   The jumbo, king-Hell noir to beat all noirs. A crime masterpiece told from the criminals' point of view.
7. *GOODFELLAS* (1990, dir. Martin Scorsese)
   Simply the best American movie ever made. Every word, every move, every inflection thoroughly believable. And funny – as only real mobsters can be.

8. *MEAN STREETS* (1973, dir. Martin Scorsese)
Scorsese's breathtaking low-budget portrait of small-time hoods in Little Italy. It changed everything.

9. *THIEF* (1981, dir. Michael Mann)
An underrated classic. James Caan as a professional safecracker – just out of prison – trying to steal his way to a 'normal' life. Beautiful, grimly realistic, technically groundbreaking.

10. *THE LONG GOOD FRIDAY* (1980, dir. John Mackenzie)
Bob Hoskins owned this part. And yet a shatteringly good Helen Mirren still steals the movie. Brit-crime at its very very best.

Stephen King's 6 Scariest Scenes Ever Captured on Film

The author of such bestselling novels of terror as *Carrie*, *Salem's Lot*, *Night Shift*, *The Stand*, *The Shining*, *The Dead Zone* and *Fire Starter*, Stephen King is the modern master of the macabre. His style is highly visual, revealing an early and strong influence by film. Although he has probably instilled more fear in the hearts of readers than any other contemporary writer, he, too, has experienced chilling moments in the darkness of the cinema.

1. *WAIT UNTIL DARK* (1967, Terence Young)
The moment near the conclusion, when [Alan] Arkin jumps out at Audrey Hepburn, is a real scare.

2. *CARRIE* (1976, Brian De Palma)
The dream sequence at the end, when Sissy Spacek thrusts her hand out of the ground and grabs Amy Irving. I knew it was coming and I still felt as if I'd swallowed a snowcone whole.

3. *I BURY THE LIVING* (1958, Albert Band)
In this almost-forgotten movie, there is a chilling sequence when [Richard] Boone begins to maniacally remove the black pins in the filled graveyard plots and to replace them with white pins.

4. *THE TEXAS CHAINSAW MASSACRE* (1974, Tobe Hooper)
The moment when the corpse seems to leap out of the freezer like a hideous jack-in-the-box.

5. *NIGHT OF THE LIVING DEAD* (1968, George Romero)
The scene where the little girl stabs her mother to death with a garden trowel in the cellar . . . 'Mother, please, I can do it myself.'

6. *PSYCHO* (1960, Alfred Hitchcock)
The shower scene, of course.

Source: Gabe Essoe, *The Book of Movie Lists* (Westport Arlington House, 1981)

10 Movies That Were Part of History

1. *MANHATTAN MELODRAMA*
The film starred William Powell and Clark Gable as two street-wise city kids who grew up in opposite directions – one good, the other headed for the electric chair. The plot was old hat, even in 1934, but the film was enough to draw John Dillinger into the cinema with the 'lady in red'. He had just left the cinema when the tipped-off
G-men sprang their trap and killed him in the ensuing fight.
2. *GRAND ILLUSION*
Directed by pacifist Jean Renoir and starring Erich Von Stroheim, this movie was being shown when the German army marched into Vienna in 1938. Not surprisingly, Nazi stormtroopers invaded the cinema and confiscated the WWI anti-war classic in mid-reel.
3. *THE GREAT DICTATOR*
Produced by, directed by, and starring Charlie Chaplin in 1940, the movie was a brilliant political satire on Nazi Germany. Hitler ordered all prints of the film banned, but when curiosity got the better of him he had one brought in through Portugal and viewed it himself in complete privacy – not once, but twice. History does not record his views on the film.
4. *ROCK AROUND THE CLOCK*
This was a raucous celebration of rock'n'roll starring Bill Haley and his Comets. In London, its young audience took the message to heart in September of 1954. After seeing the film, more than 3,000 Teddy Boys left the cinema to stage one of the biggest riots in Britain up to that time.
5. *FOXFIRE*
Starring Jane Russell and Jeff Chandler, this film – a Universal production dealing with a dedicated mining engineer and his socialite wife – was playing in the tourist-section cinema of the

Andrea Doria on the foggy night in July 1956 when the liner collided with the *Stockholm*. The film was in its last reel when the collision occurred. Fifty people lost their lives in the tragedy.

6. *CAN-CAN*
A 20th Century Fox production starring Frank Sinatra, Shirley MacLaine and Maurice Chevalier, it was just a little too lavish for the taste of Soviet Premier Nikita Khrushchev during his 1959 visit to the studio where it was being filmed. The Cold War heated up briefly when Khrushchev reacted with shocked indignation at the 'perversity' and 'decadence' of dancer MacLaine's flamboyantly raised skirts.

7. *WAR IS HELL*
A double bill featuring two B-style war movies was playing at the Texas Theatre in Dallas, where Lee Harvey Oswald was captured after the assassination of John F. Kennedy in 1963. *War Is Hell*, starring Tony Russell, had just begun when Oswald called attention to himself by ducking into the cinema without paying the 90¢ admission. He was apprehended by the police amid the sound of onscreen gunfire.

8. *I AM CURIOUS YELLOW*
The Swedish film starring Lena Nyman as a sexually active political sociologist was a shocking sensation in 1969. On October 6, 1969, though, Jackie Onassis was the one making headlines after she allegedly gave a professional judo chop to a New York news photographer who took pictures of her leaving the cinema showing the film.

9. *MOHAMMED, MESSENGER OF GOD*
Directed by Moustapha Akkad, this picture, which purported to be an unbiased, authentic study, evoked the wrath of the Hanafi Muslim sect, which assumed that the film would depict the image of the Prophet, an act they consider blasphemous. Demanding that the film be withdrawn from the Washington, DC cinema where it was opening, small bands of Hanafi gunmen invaded the local city hall and two other buildings on March 10, 1977, killing one man and holding more than 100 hostages for two days before surrendering. Their protest turned out to be much ado about nothing. The Prophet was neither seen nor heard in the film; instead, actors addressed the camera as if it were the Prophet standing before them.

10. *THE DEER (GAVAZNHA)*
This Iranian film was being shown in the Cinema Rex cinema in Abadan, Iran, on August 19, 1977, when arsonists set fire to the building, killing at least 377 people (an additional 45 bodies were discovered later in the charred ruins, but these were not included in the official government totals). Police arrested 10 members of a Muslim extremist group that opposed the shah's reforms and had been implicated in other cinema and restaurant fires. However, another version of this incident was sent to the authors by an eyewitness who claims that police chained shut the cinema doors and fended off the crowd outside with clubs and M16s. The fire department, only 10 minutes from the theatre, reportedly did not arrive until the fire had burned itself out. Surprisingly, this witness found most of the people had been burned to death in their seats.

– R.S.

William Friedkin's 10 Favourite Movies

Born August 29, 1935, in Chicago, Illinois, William Friedkin began his career in television and documentaries before moving to features. His early films include such diverse movies as *Good Times* (1967), starring Sonny and Cher, and *The Birthday Party* (1968), adapted from the Harold Pinter play. In 1971, Friedkin directed *The French Connection*, and became the youngest filmmaker in history to win the Best Director Oscar. In 1973, his adaptation of William Peter Blatty's horror novel *The Exorcist* became one of the most successful and controversial films in the history of cinema. His other films include *Sorcerer* (1977), *Cruising* (1980), *To Live and Die in L.A.* (1985), and *The Hunted* (2003). Friedkin is also a passionate classical music and opera fan, and has directed productions of Alban Berg's *Wozzeck* in 1998 and Richard Wagner's *Tannhäuser* in 2004. He lives in Los Angeles, California, with his wife, producer Sherry Lansing.

1. *Citizen Kane* (Orson Welles)
2. *All About Eve* (Joseph C. Mankiewicz)
3. *The Treasure of the Sierra Madre* (John Huston)
4. *Singin' in the Rain* (Stanley Donen and Gene Kelly)
5. *The Band Wagon* (Vincent Minnelli)
6. *Double Indemnity* (Billy Wilder)

7. *2001: A Space Odyssey* (Stanley Kubrick)
8. *The Verdict* (Sidney Lumet)
9. *Fatal Attraction* (Adrian Lyne)
10. *Paths of Glory* (Stanley Kubrick)

Kevin Macdonald's 10 Favourite Documentaries of All Time

Born in Glasgow in 1967, Kevin Macdonald is a documentary film-maker whose films include Channel Four's *Humphrey Jennings: The Man Who Listened To Britain* (2000) and the Oscar-winning *One Day in September* (1999). He also wrote and directed the biography of his grandfather, *Emeric Pressburger: The Life and Death of a Screenwriter* (1994), and his most recent documentary is a short film, *Return to Siula Grande* (2004), about how climbers Joe Simpson and Simon Yates revisited their experience for Macdonald's film *Touching the Void* (2003), inspired by Simpson's book of the same name.

1. *NOW* (Santiago Alvarez, 1965)
   Using pirated stills and archive footage, set to a song by Lena Horne that had been banned in the United States, Cuba's pre-eminent film-maker fashioned a six-minute masterpiece which angrily, yet stylishly, denounces rascism. It inspired me to think that serious subjects need not be handled in an obviously serious way.
2. *THE THIN BLUE LINE* (Errol Morris, 1988)
   A film which contains not only the solution to a real life murder mystery but also a thesis on the nature of knowledge itself.
3. *VIDEO DIARY: 'THE MAN WHO LOVES GARY LINEKER'* (1992)
   The evolution of cheap, high-quality home video cameras has radically altered the documentary over the last decade or so. Suddenly small, personal, domestic stories became easily filmable and the result was a rash of the freshest, most unpretentious films you are ever likely to see. This particular documentary was from the second series of BBC 'Video Diaries' and was made by (and about) an Albanian doctor who lives and works in the most appalling circumstances and who loves to listen to English football on the World Service. He hero-worships the Tottenham Hotspur and England player Gary Lineker. It

makes you cry – and wonder why you complain so much about your life.

4. *THE SORROW AND THE PITY* (Marcel Ophuls, 1969)
It's five hours long, at times confusing and frustrating, but I don't know of any other film with quite the intelligence and humanity of Ophuls' masterwork about a small French town under Nazi occupation. All human life is here.

5. *DIARY FOR TIMOTHY* (Humphrey Jennings 1945)
It could as easily be *Listen to Britain* or *Fires Were Started* – all of them show Jennings' surrealist flair for the striking image that burrows deep into your subconscious. All are full of the epiphanies of everyday life. I understand perfectly why Lindsay Anderson called him the 'only poet of British Cinema'.

6. *THE UNSEEN (*Miroslav Janek, 1996)
A film filled with magic and wonder – it tells the story of a group of blind children at an institution in the Czech Republic who become obsessed with taking photographs.

7. *SHOAH* (Claude Lanzmann, 1985)
The most painful, honest and moving film you are ever likely to see. Lanzmann's sparse epic of the Holocaust is a life changing experience.

8. *GIMME SHELTER (*Albert Maysles, David Maysles and Charlotte Zwerin, 1970)
Not only does it capture the Rolling Stones at their bombastic, glorious best, but its elegant, complex structure means that it has the resonance and thematic depth of a great piece of literature – like some twentieth-century re-telling of *Paradise Lost*.

9. *MARLENE* (Maximilen Schell, 1984)
The most revealing 'portrait film' I know – about one of the most enigmatic public figures of her era: Marlene Dietrich. Overcoming the curmudgeonly exterior of the old battle-axe, Schell reveals the icon's broken heart.

10. *HOOP DREAMS* (Steve James, 1994)
The first documentary I saw in the cinema, it made me realise that documentaries can be more dramatic, more moving, more surprising than any piece of fiction. I'll never forget how the audience stood and cheered when one of the boys scores a decisive point.

Walter Matthau's 10 Favourite Comedies of All Time

Born Walter Matthow on October 1, 1920, to Russian–Jewish immigrants in New York City, Matthau was an amazingly versatile actor who could 'play anything from Scarlett O'Hara to Rhett Butler'. While best known for his comedic performances in such hits as *The Odd Couple*, *The Bad News Bears* and *Grumpy Old Men*, Matthau also played notable dramatic roles in a wide variety of films, including *Fail-Safe*, *Charley Varrick* and *JFK*. He received Best Actor Oscar nominations for his work in *The Sunshine Boys* and *Kotch*, and won an Oscar for Best Supporting Actor in *The Fortune Cookie*. Matthau died of a heart attack on July 1, 2000, just a few months after the release of his final film, *Hanging Up*. He contributed this list to *The Book of Lists* in 1983.

1. *The Odd Couple*
2. *The Producers*
3. *A New Leaf*
4. *Macbeth*
5. *City Lights*
6. *Wuthering Heights*
7. *Death of Salesman*
8. *A Streetcar Named Desire*
9. *Horse Feathers*
10. *Hamlet*

Chapter 3

21 EARLY NAMES OF FAMOUS BANDS

STIRRING OPENING LINES OF 11 NATIONAL ANTHEMS

DR DEMENTO'S 10 WORST SONG TITLES OF ALL TIME

9 ARTISTS WHOSE WORKS WERE PAINTED OVER

8 VALUABLE ART WORKS FOUND UNEXPECTEDLY

DIZZY GILLESPIE'S 10 GREATEST JAZZ MUSICIANS

JOHNNY CASH'S 10 GREATEST COUNTRY SONGS OF ALL TIME

ANDREW MOTION'S TOP 12 DYLAN LYRICS

GEOFF DYER'S '10 SCHOLARLY BOOKS I WOULD LIKE TO WRITE, USING BOB DYLAN LINES AS THEIR TITLES'

ALLEN GINSBERG'S 11 GREATEST BLUES SONGS

RICHARD EYRE'S 9 FAVOURITE THEATRE PRODUCTIONS

IAN RANKIN'S 7 GREAT GIGS

9 DRUMMERS OF NOTE – SELECTED BY BEN SCHOTT

THAT'S ENTERTAINMENT? – 7 PERFECTLY WRETCHED PERFORMERS

10 MOST UNUSUAL VARIETY ACTS OF ALL TIME, BY RICKY JAY

JEREMY BEADLE'S 20 BARMY QUIZ QUESTIONS

The Arts

© Harry Goodwin/Redferns

THE ARTISTS FORMERLY KNOWN AS POLKA TULK – see p.68

21 Early Names of Famous Bands

In the music business, you have to hit not only the right chords but also the right name. Here's a quiz to test your knowledge.

1.	Angel and the Snakes	a.	Bangles
2.	Composition of Sound	b.	Beach Boys
3.	Big Thing	c.	Beatles
4.	Artistics	d.	Bill Haley and His Comets
5.	Carl and the Passions	e.	Black Sabbath
6.	Primettes	f.	Blondie
7.	Tom and Jerry	g.	Byrds
8.	Johnny and the Moondog	h.	Chicago
9.	Caesar and Cleo	i.	Creedence Clearwater Revival
10.	Paramours	j.	Depeche Mode
11.	Polka Tulk	k.	Led Zeppelin
12.	Bangs	l.	Lynyrd Skynyrd
13.	Beefeaters	m.	Mamas and the Papas
14.	Falling Spikes	n.	Righteous Brothers
15.	Sparrow	o.	Simon and Garfunkel
16.	My Backyard	p.	Sonny and Cher
17.	The New Journeymen	q.	Steppenwolf
18.	The Elgins	r.	Supremes
19.	The Four Aces of Western Swing	s.	Talking Heads
20.	The Golliwogs	t.	Temptations
21.	The New Yardbirds	u.	Velvet Underground

Answers: 1 (f), 2 (j), 3 (h), 4 (s), 5 (b), 6 (r), 7 (o), 8 (c), 9 (p), 10 (n), 11 (e), 12 (a), 13 (g), 14 (u), 15 (q), 16 (l), 17 (m), 18 (t), 19 (d), 20 (i), 21 (k)

Stirring Opening Lines of 11 National Anthems

1. ALGERIA
   We swear by the lightning that destroys,
   By the streams of generous blood being shed

By the bright flags that wave
That we are in revolt . . .

2. BOLIVIA
Bolivians, propitious fate has crowned our hopes . . .

3. BURKINA FASO
Against the humiliating bondage of a thousand years
Rapacity came from afar to subjugate them
For a hundred years.
Against the cynical malice in the shape
Of neocolonialism and its petty local servants,
Many gave in and certain others resisted.

4. GUINEA-BISSAU
Sun, sweat, verdure and sea,
Centuries of pain and hope;
This is the land of our ancestors.

5. LUXEMBOURG
Where slow you see the Alzette flow,
The Sura play wild pranks . . .

6. OMAN
O Lord, protect for us Our Majesty the Sultan
And the people in our land,
With honour and peace.
May he live long, strong and supported,
Glorified by his leadership.
For him we shall lay down our lives.

7. PARAGUAY
To the peoples of unhappy America,
Three centuries under a sceptre oppressed.
But one day, with their passion arising,
'Enough,' they said and broke the sceptre.

8. SENEGAL
Everyone strum your koras,
Strike the balafons,
The red lion has roared,
The tamer of the bush with one leap,
Has scattered the gloom.

9. TAIWAN
The three principles of democracy our party does revere.

10. URUGUAY
Eastern landsmen, our country or the tomb!

11. USSR
Unbreakable union of freeborn republics,
Great Russia has welded forever to stand;
Thy might was created by the will of our peoples,
Now flourish in unity, great Soviet land!

Dr Demento's 10 Worst Song Titles of All Time

Radio personality Dr Demento's private collection of more than 200,000 records is said to be one of the world's largest. He puts his library of discs to use on 'The Dr Demento Show', which is heard on 200 radio stations in the US and on the Armed Forces Radio Network.

What's a really bad song title? One that's offensive or inarticulate, I'd say, or one that doesn't readily identify the song it's attached to (Bob Dylan did that for kicks in the Sixties). I think we can leave those alone for now.

Then there are the sort of song titles (often from country music) that are often rather clever, to be truthful, but induce the same sort of groans that often greet a really good pun when heard for the first time.

Some of those are included on this list, along with others that induce groans for altogether different reasons. Qualifiers: 1) This list does not duplicate my two earlier *Book of Lists* contributions. 2) All these songs have been heard at least once on 'The Dr Demento Show'
(I actually like most of these songs).

After each song title the composer credits are shown first (in parentheses) followed by the artist on the recording played on the show.

1. BOOGER ON MY BEER MUG (Dr Peter Rizzo) – Sneaky Pete
2. GROPE ME GENTLY, AIRPORT SECURITY GUARD (Larry Weaver) – Larry Weaver
3. WHO PUT THE BENZEDRINE IN MRS MURPHY'S OVALTINE (Harry Gibson) – Harry the Hipster. (Inspired by the Bing Crosby hit 'Who Put The Overalls In Mrs Murphy's Chowder'.)

4. THE FIVE CONSTIPATED MEN OF THE BIBLE (Scott Hendricks) – Axel the Sot
5. THE DAY TED NUGENT KILLED ALL THE ANIMALS (Wally Pleasant) – Wally Pleasant
6. I'M SELLING MOM'S URINE ON eBAY (Tommy Womack) – Tommy Womack
7. HE WENT TO SLEEP – THE HOGS ATE HIM (Ray Starr, N. Nath, G.C. Redd) – The Stanley Brothers
8. FLUSHED YOU FROM THE TOILETS OF MY HEART (J.D. Blackfoot, Johnny Durzo) – J.D. Blackfoot. (Pronounced 'hort'. Not to be confused with the marginally less groan-inducing 'Flushed From The Bathroom Of Your Heart', a different song, written by Jack Clement and popularised by Johnny Cash.)
9. HE PUT IN A BAR IN THE BACK OF HIS CAR (And He's Driving Himself To Drink) (Sheldon Schwartz, Fred Wolfe, Jules Volk) – Georgie's Tavern Band
10. I STILL WRITE YOUR NAME IN THE SNOW (Chet Atkins, Billy Edd Wheeler) – Chet Atkins. (Wheeler is also known for his eulogy to an outhouse, 'Ode To The Little Brown Shack Out Back'.)

9 Artists Whose Works Were Painted Over

1. UNKNOWN ARTIST (10th century), *Kuan Lin Holding Lotus Blossom*
In 1953, officials of the esteemed Nelson Gallery of Art in Kansas City received a valuable twelfth-century Chinese wall painting that had been damaged during shipping. The horror of the officials was to be short-lived, for as restorer James Roth worked on the mural, he discovered a trace of blue paint underneath a layer of mud and rice husks. After careful, detailed work, a gracious goddess was exposed and identified as an outstanding example of tenth-century painting. It was hailed as one of the greatest Oriental art discoveries in recent years.

2. GIOVANNI BELLINI (1430?–1516); TITIAN (1477–1576), *Feast of the Gods*
It had long been known that the renowned Renaissance painter Titian altered *Feast of the Gods*, a painting by his teacher,

Giovanni Bellini. When the painting was X-rayed in the 1950s, it was discovered that Titian had also painted over several principal figures, altered the composition, and in essence changed the very content of the masterpiece. Art historians now view the two masters' artistry as enhancing the value of the canvas and consider the painting as two original works in one.

3. SANDRO BOTTICELLI (1444?–1510), *Three Miracles St Zenobius*
During the cleaning of this fifteenth-century masterpiece, restorers at the New York Metropolitan Museum of Art noted that a central portion of the painting had been painted over. Technicians using X-rays to examine the area discovered an image of two preserved skeletons lying in a coffin. As the painting had previously been owned by Sir William Abdy of London, it is believed that he had the skeletons painted over in deference to Victorian tastes.

4. LUCAS CRANACH (1472–1553), *Charity*
In this painting of a nude woman nursing her child, puritanical sentiment triumphed over the artist's intentions when a restorer painted a complete set of clothes on the woman. Later the clothing was removed, leaving the painting in its original state.

5. MICHELANGELO (1475–1564), charcoal drawings
The world's only group of mural sketches by the great Renaissance painter, sculptor and architect was found in late 1975 while chapel director Paolo Dal Poggetto was trying to devise an alternative route for moving tourist traffic through Florence's Medici Chapel. Before opening up a storeroom as an exit to the street, restorer Sabino Giovannoni performed tests on the walls. Under several layers of whitewash and grime, he discovered more than 50 large drawings of the human form and one of a horse's head, evidently Michelangelo's record of past works and preliminary sketches of future projects. Art historians believe that Michelangelo, an outspoken Republican, may have rendered the sketches while hiding out from an assassin hired by the Medicis, who were purging Florence of any political opposition.

6. PAUL CÉZANNE (1839–1906), *Portrait of a Peasant*
After recovering a stolen Cézanne, *The Artist's Sister*, in 1962, the St Louis City Art Museum decided to have the painting cleaned and relined. Art conservator James Roth discovered another portrait on the back of the canvas. Painted while

Cézanne was in his early 20s, the new portrait of a peasant raised the value of the original by $75,000. The canvas is mounted so that both portraits may be viewed.

7. **MAURICE UTRILLO (1883–1955), *Execution des Generaux Lecomte & Clement Thomas par les Communards a la Caserne de Chateau Rouge* (a.k.a. *La Caserne*)**
   The painting, an atypical work for Utrillo, provides a dispassionate view of two figures facing a firing squad during the 1871 Paris Commune uprising. The work was bought in Paris in April of 1994 for $87,400 and sold in June at Christie's in London for $109,000. During the two intervening months, the rifles of the firing squad were painted over, apparently to eliminate the reference to an execution. Although Christie's claimed that Utrillo experts Gilbert Petrides and Jean Fabris had authenticated *La Caserne*, both denied having been consulted before the London sale. Fabis added, 'In my opinion, it's a fake, as it was tampered with.'
8. **ARSHILE GORKI (1905–48), aviation murals**
   Two murals of an original 10 painted by Armenian-born artist Arshile Gorki were recovered in 1973 due to the efforts of Mrs Ruth Bowman, a Newark, New Jersey, art historian. Five years after the completion of the 10 murals – commissioned by the Works Progress Administration in 1937 – the Army Air Corps took over Newark Airport, which housed the murals, and put the first of 14 coats of whitewash over them. Every major art text published since 1948 claimed the murals had been lost, but Mrs Bowman decided to investigate the walls further and found two murals intact. The other eight paintings were destroyed when walls were torn down to expedite the installation of new radiators.
9. **DAVID SALLE (1952–), *Jump***
   In September 1980, the artists David Salle and Julian Schnabel traded paintings. The painting that Salle gave Schnabel, *Jump*, consists of two canvases mounted side by side. The right side portrayed a woman and a baby in a bedroom, the left side featured birds. Schnabel decided that the work was incomplete, so he painted Salle's face in orange on the left panel. Salle was not initially pleased with Schnabel's handiwork. When Schnabel first showed him the painting, Salle jumped up and wrestled him to the floor. They later reconciled and sold *Jump* as a joint work to collector Eugene Schwartz.

– E.H.C. & C.F.

8 Valuable Art Works Found Unexpectedly

1. IN A FARMER'S FIELD
In 1820, a Greek peasant named Yorgos was digging in his field on the island of Milos when he unearthed several carved blocks of stone. He burrowed deeper and found four statues – three figures of Hermes and one of Aphrodite, the goddess of love. Three weeks later, the Choiseul archaeological expedition arrived by ship, purchased the Aphrodite, and took it to France. Louis XVIII gave it the name *Venus de Milo* and presented it to the Louvre in Paris, where it became one of the most famous works of art in the world.

2. BENEATH A STREET
On February 21, 1978, electrical workers were putting down lines on a busy street corner in Mexico City when they discovered a 20-ton stone bas-relief of the Aztec night goddess, Coyolxauhqui. It is believed to have been sculpted in the early fifteenth century and buried prior to the destruction of the Aztec civilisation by the Spanish conquistadors in 1521. The stone was moved 200 yards from the site to the Museum of the Great Temple.

3. IN A HOLE IN THE GROUND
In 1978 more than 500 movies dating from 1903 to 1929 were dug out of a hole in the ground in Dawson City, Yukon. Under normal circumstances, the 35-mm nitrate films would have been destroyed, but the permafrost preserved them perfectly.

4. UNDER A BED
Joanne Perez, the widow of vaudeville performer Pepito the Spanish Clown, cleaned out the area underneath her bed and discovered the only existing copy of the pilot for the TV series *I Love Lucy*. Pepito had coached Lucille Ball and had guest-starred in the pilot. Ball and her husband, Desi Arnaz, had given the copy to Pepito as a gift in 1951 and it had remained under the bed for 30 years.

5. ON A WALL
A middle-aged couple in a suburb of Milwaukee, Wisconsin, asked an art prospector to appraise a painting in their home. While he was there he examined another painting that the couple had thought was a reproduction of a work by Vincent

van Gogh. It turned out to be an 1886 original. On March 10, 1991, the painting *Still Life with Flowers* sold at auction for $1,400,000.

6. IN A TRUNK IN AN ATTIC
In 1961 Barbara Testa, a Hollywood librarian, inherited six steamer trunks that had belonged to her grandfather James Fraser Gluck, a Buffalo, New York, lawyer who died in 1895. Over the next three decades she gradually sifted through the contents of the trunks, until one day in the autumn of 1990 she came upon 665 pages that turned out to be the original handwritten manuscript of the first half of Mark Twain's *Huckleberry Finn*. The two halves of the great American novel were finally reunited at the Buffalo and Erie County Public Library.

7. AT A FLEA MARKET
A Philadelphia financial analyst was browsing at a flea market in Adamstown, Pennsylvania, when he was attracted by a wooden picture frame. He paid four dollars for it. Back at his home, he removed the old torn painting in the frame and found a folded document between the canvas and the wood backing. It turned out to be a 1776 copy of the Declaration of Independence – one of 24 known to remain. On June 13, 1991, Sotheby's auction house in New York sold the copy for $2,420,000.

8. MASQUERADING AS A BICYCLE RACK
For years, employees of the God's House Tower Archaeology Museum in Southampton, England, propped their bikes against a 27-inch black rock in the basement. In 2000, two Egyptologists investigating the museum's holdings identified the bike rack as a seventh-century BC Egyptian statue portraying King Taharqa, a Kushite monarch from the region that is modern Sudan. Karen Wordley, the Southampton city council's curator of archaeological collections, said it was a 'mystery' how the sculpture ended up in the museum basement.

Dizzy Gillespie's 10 Greatest Jazz Musicians

Jazz legend John Birks 'Dizzy' Gillespie was born in Cheraw, South Carolina, October 21, 1917. After learning to play piano at the age of four he taught himself to play the trombone, but had switched to the trumpet by the time he was twelve. The leading exponent of 'bebop' jazz, Gillespie was famous for conducting big bands, playing trumpet (many consider him the greatest trumpeter in history), and for his work with Earl 'Fatha' Hines and Charlie Parker, among others. Gillespie's energy was so great that his career never stopped, and at least 10 biographies of the world-famous, beloved revolutionary of jazz have been published. Among his most famous compositions are 'Salt Peanuts', 'Bebop', 'Guachi Guararo (Soul Sauce)', 'Night In Tunisia' and 'Manteca', a pioneering piece in Afro-Cuban style. Gillespie had a stable private life and disdained the addictive drugs favoured by so many jazz heroes. He remained humorous and charming until the end of his life. He died on January 6, 1993, at the age of 75 and the world mourned the loss of a true jazz giant. In 1980, he prepared this list for *The Book of Lists*.

1. Charlie Parker
2. Art Tatum
3. Coleman Hawkins
4. Benny Carter
5. Lester Young
6. Roy Eldridge
7. J.J. Johnson
8. Kenny Clarke
9. Oscar Pettiford
10. Miles Davis

Johnny Cash's 10 Greatest Country Songs of All Time

Johnny Cash, widely considered to be the greatest country music singer and composer in history, died in September of 2003 at the age of 71. Known as 'The Man in Black' (he always wore black), Cash was born the son of a poor sharecropper in Arkansas in 1932, and he sang to himself while picking cotton for 10 hours a day. Cash recorded more than 1,500 songs. He toured worldwide and played for free in prisons throughout America. Among his greatest hits are 'Ring of Fire' and 'I Walk the Line'. His 1975 autobiography, *Man In Black*, has sold well over 1.5 million copies. Cash's death was long and painful, and his last four albums are considered by many to be his greatest work, as they all examine a hard-working man coming to terms with the end of his life. Said Merle Kilgore, one of the co-authors of *Ring of Fire*, 'It's a sad day in Tennessee, but a great day in Heaven. "The Man in Black" is now wearing white as he joins his wife June in the angel band.' June and Johnny were married for 35 years, and her death preceded his by four months. Cash contributed this list to *The Book of Lists* in 1977.

1. 'I Walk the Line', Johnny Cash
2. 'I Can't Stop Loving You', Don Gibson
3. 'Wildwood Flower', Carter Family
4. 'Folsom Prison Blues', Johnny Cash
5. 'Candy Kisses', George Morgan
6. 'I'm Movin' On', Hank Snow
7. 'Walking the Floor over You', Ernest Tubb
8. 'He'll Have to Go', Joe Allison and Audrey Allison
9. 'Great Speckle Bird', Carter Family
10. 'Cold, Cold Heart', Hank Williams

Andrew Motion's Top 12 Dylan Lyrics

Andrew Motion is a poet and biographer. His latest collection of poems, Public Property, *was published in 2003, and he has written lives of Philip Larkin, John Keats and the nineteenth-century artist and criminal Thomas Wainewright. He is Professor of Creative Writing at Royal Holloway College, University of London, and was appointed Poet Laureate in 1999.*

For my money, songs accumulate an even larger baggage of associations than poems. The time I first heard them, the situations – intense or otherwise – in which I have listened to them, the people who introduced them to me, or who I know also like them: all these things become attached to the lyrics as well as the melody, at once broadening the experience of listening and making it more intimate.

Turning over the pages of Bob Dylan's *Lyrics 1962–85* is like opening a Pandora's Box crammed with my life's delights, winces, blushes, broodings, geographies. Which in turn means that reducing his titles to any kind of list is seriously difficult. One song counted in means one (at least one) left out – and the choice is likely to change from day to day.

On the day I'm writing this, 24 May, 2004, my top 12, in album order, is:

1. *Talkin' John Birch Paranoid Blues* – for the comedy in the anger and the wit in the satire

2. *Tomorrow Is a Long Time* – for the tenderness and simplicity

3. *The Times They are A-Changin'* – for saying all the right (but still surprising) things at the right time and every time
4. *All I Really Want to Do* – for the freedom it offers, and for knowing that freedom is difficult to give in fact
5. *Love Minus Zero/No Limit* – for being so damn beautiful
6. *It's All Over Now, Baby Blue* – for 'Leave your stepping stones behind, something calls for you'
7. *Desolation Row* – for getting its arm round so much, with such a strange mixture of ease and effort
8. *All Along the Watchtower* – for the economy of its mystery
9. *Idiot Wind* – for its tender outrage
10. *Hurricane* – for the accuracy of its anger
11. *Man Gave Names to All the Animals* – for its jokes
12. O, and (out of order) *Visions of Johanna* – for all of the above reasons, and more besides

Geoff Dyer's '10 Scholarly Books I Would Like to Write, Using Bob Dylan Lines as Their Titles'

Geoff Dyer is one of the most versatile and least classifiable British writers of his generation. His works include *But Beautiful*, a book about jazz, several novels and *Out of Sheer Rage*, in which Dyer records his journey in search of D.H. Lawrence. *Yoga for People Who Can't Be Bothered to Do It*, an idiosyncratic collection of writings about his travels in places as diverse as Cambodia and New Orleans, was published in 2003.

1. *And Your Mother's Drugs*: Addiction in the Suffragette Movement
2. *Fighting in the Captain's Tower*: Eliot, Pound and the Making of 'The Waste Land'
3. *Alive as You or Me*: A Life of St Augustine
4. *It's Much Cheaper Down in the South American Town*: Globalisation and the Export of Labour
5. *Painting the Passports Brown*: A History of the American Circus

6. *Going Through All These Things Twice*: Nietzsche and the Eternal Recurrence
7. *Hands in Her Back Pockets*: Bette Davis: The Movies and the Myth
8. *Who Really Cares?*: A History of Obscenity
9. *Nearly Any Task*: Masculinity and the New Feminism
10. *I Shall Be Released*: The Bob Dylan Bootleg Industry

Allen Ginsberg's 11 Greatest Blues Songs

Born in New Jersey in 1926, Allen Ginsberg was educated at Columbia University in New York City, where he met fellow writers Jack Kerouac and William S. Burroughs, with whom he formed a creative triad that gave birth to the Beat Movement of the 1950s. Ginsberg's most famous work, *Howl and Other Poems*, was published in 1955, and its graphic, excoriating vision of the failure of the American Dream resulted in both literary acclaim and obscenity charges. Other books by Ginsberg include *Kaddish* (1961), *Reality Sandwiches* (1965), and *First Blues: Songs* (1982). Allen Ginsberg died in 1997. He contributed this list to *The Book of Lists* in 1993.

1. 'James Alley Blues', Richard 'Rabbit' Brown
2. 'Washington DC Hospital Centre Blues', Skip James
3. 'Jelly Bean Blues', Ma Rainey
4. 'See See Rider Blues', Ma Rainey
5. 'Young Woman's Blues', Bessie Smith
6. 'Poor Me', Charles Patton
7. 'Black Girl', Leadbelly
8. 'Levee Camp Moan Blues', Texas Alexander
9. 'Last Fair Deal Gone Down', Robert Johnson
10. 'I'm So Lonesome I Could Cry', Hank Williams, Sr
11. 'Idiot Wind', Bob Dylan

Richard Eyre's 9 Favourite Theatre Productions

One of the world's most respected directors for both stage and screen, Richard Eyre has had a long and distinguished career in the British theatre. For nine years he was artistic director of the

National Theatre, with overall responsibility for a succession of award-winning productions of shows as different as Guys and Dolls *and* The Oedipus Trilogy. *Richard Eyre, who was knighted in 1997, is also a film director whose 2001 movie* Iris, *about the novelist Iris Murdoch, was much acclaimed.*

At the time I saw these productions I thought that they were inspirational and exemplary – perfect syntheses of writing, acting and design. They were truly theatrical, in the sense of exploiting the theatreness of theatre.

1. *WEST SIDE STORY* (1959) by William Shakespeare, Arthur Laurents, Stephen Sondheim and Leonard Bernstein; directed by Jerome Robbins
   Hit me like a thunderbolt – the music, choreography, the energy and the beauty. I had no idea theatre was capable of such things.
2. *THE WARS OF THE ROSES* (1963) by William Shakespeare; directed by Peter Hall
   Made me see that Shakespeare could be contemporary and historical, funny and humane, entertaining and educational.
3. *CORIOLANUS* (1965) by William Shakespeare, adapted by Brecht; directed by Bertolt Brecht and the Berliner Ensemble
   Brilliantly lucid and distilled – everything to the point and the point was political but not polemical.
4. *SAVED* (1965) by Edward Bond; directed by Bill Gaskill
   Like a knife thrust: violent, painful, ascetic, spare – and beautiful.
5. *THE CHANGING ROOM* (1971) by David Storey; directed by Lindsay Anderson
   Ensemble detail and harmony: a celebration of beauty, sport, manual labour which now seems as remote as the pre-Raphaelite movement.
6. *SUMMERFOLK* (1975) by Maxim Gorki; directed by Peter Stein Exquisite, poetic.
7. *THE MAHABHARATA* (1985) by Anon; directed by Peter Brook
   The elements of the production were the elements of life – earth, fire, air and water; it had the brilliance and bravura that could have been attention-seeking were it not obviously the consequence of trying to find the most expressive way of telling the story.

8. *THE DRAGON'S TRILOGY* (1987) written and directed by Robert Lepage
A perfect blend of art and architecture, music, dance, light, dialogue and movement; the writing – and the meaning – was in the whole event.

9. *FUENTE OVEJUNA* (1989) by Lope de Vega; directed by Declan Donellan
A sinuous energy, truth and freshness that defined what every production of every classic should aim for.

Ian Rankin's 7 Great Gigs

Leading exponent of a new sub-genre of crime fiction, dubbed 'tartan noir' by some critics, Ian Rankin is one of Scotland's most successful writers, both critically and commercially. He has published more than a dozen novels set in the parts of Edinburgh the tourists don't see and featuring the maverick and likeable Inspector Rebus. His fiction has won many awards including, most recently, the Edgar Award for Best Novel presented by the Mystery Writers of America. His latest Rebus novel is *Fleshmarket Close* (2004).

1. THE SKIDS
I was just the right age for punk – 17 in 1977. Of course, growing up in a traditional coal-mining community, it didn't do to stand out, so we punks tended to congregate in each other's bedrooms, listening to records and the John Peel show on Radio 1. Then a club opened at the Station Hotel in nearby Kirkcaldy. It happened every Sunday night and was called the Pogo-A-Gogo. Basically, it was the hotel's upstairs ballroom, with a bar serving fizzy lager. But there were also occasional live gigs. By this time, Fife had a punk band of its own – The Skids. The guitarist, Stuart Adamson, had been to the same school as me. There was no stage, band and audience becoming one, writhing on the floor or bouncing to the music. I'd sneak my punk clothes (a boiler-suit spattered with bleach) out of the house and change at a friend's, then his dad would drive us to Kirkcaldy. Great nights, and my first really great gig.

2. BARCLAY JAMES HARVEST
It had taken some persuading, but my parents finally agreed that I could accompany a friend to Edinburgh at the age of 16 to see Barclay James Harvest. I'd then have to stay the night at his house, as there was no way to get home. A huge adventure.

I'd never heard any BJH albums (and, indeed, have never owned any since). It was also my first visit to the Usher Hall, a posh cavern of a place. Were Barclay James Harvest any good? Frankly, no, but that didn't matter. They had dry ice and a light-show and amps turned up to the requisite 11. Tom Robinson was in the support band and I came home with a programme, poster and badge. They say you never forget the first time . . .

3. HAWKWIND . . . SORT OF
Though BJH was my first gig, I'd been lying to pals at school. As far as they were concerned, I'd previously trekked alone to the wilds of Dundee's Caird Hall to see Hawkwind. I made the whole thing up, of course, wanting to impress with my solo efforts. I duly scrawled some signatures on a Hawkwind album sleeve, then crushed and tore it a bit to make it look like there'd been a fracas of sorts. And around this fake artefact I spun the story of my trip. I explained the light show, the nude female dancers, the sonic wondrousness of it all, until I almost began to believe that I really had been there. All in all, a brilliant night, which only exists in my imagination.

4. U2
While a student in Edinburgh, I saw many great gigs (Pere Ubu, Iggy Pop, The Kinks, Ramones, Bauhaus . . .) I also missed a few. A mate tried to get me to go see The Buzzcocks, all because of the support act, a new band called Joy Division. I stayed home and wrote an essay instead, and have regretted it ever since. I also missed out on the Stones at the Playhouse because I had an exam the next day. But one concert that stays with me is U2. They were playing in a disco in Tollcross. I think their first album had just been released. A few hundred sweaty fans, dancing for a solid 90 minutes, and a gang of young men on stage, playing for their professional lives. They were brilliant. And to think, I only went because my mate's girlfriend let him down and he had a ticket going spare.

5. THE PROCLAIMERS
After uni, I moved to London. I'd pretty much stopped going to gigs by that time, apart from jazz nights in Hoxton. But I did make the trip to a pub in Finsbury Park to see a new outfit called The Proclaimers. Until that night, I'd never realised how many Scots had made the move south. The place was

awash with familiar accents and football scarves – everything from Partick to Aberdeen. The twins won me over that night – they were electrifying. It was a pretty rough and drunken crowd, but they had them eating out of their hands. After the gig, I decided to walk home rather than take the tube: that way, I'd have more time to reflect on what I'd just seen and sing a few of the numbers to myself. That's how good a gig it was: it made me want to walk through the rummer parts of night-time London.

6. THE ROLLING STONES
I had to wait a while for my next outstanding London gig. It happened in 2003, in another fairly small venue, the Astoria on Charing Cross Road. I'd managed to miss having dinner with two-thirds of REM (which is another story in itself), and was gutted. Taking pity, my publisher found me a ticket to a secret Rolling Stones gig. This was supposed to be for fan-club members, and took place in the sweltering confines of the Astoria night-club. The audience had come from the four corners of the globe to see the Stones on home ground, playing a set much like the ones they'd have played when they first started. The stage was only about six feet off the ground, with no props or gimmicks. Just a band playing out of their skins. At last I could discern that Keith really is a good guitarist, and that Jagger has the stamina of a man half his age.

7. MOGWAI
Back home in Edinburgh, one of my favourite venues is the Queen's Hall, not so much for the acoustics (iffy) or the views of the stage (even iffier), but for the quality of music it seems to attract. I've seen bands as different as The Residents and the Art Ensemble of Chicago . . . musicians as different as Dick Gaughan and Lloyd Cole, The Durutti Column and Plainsong. But the gig that stands out for me was another recent one – Mogwai. Young men with attitudinal guitars and no need to keep the noise in perspective, as there's no singer to drown out. Their show there in 2003 was colossal, and for the first time I really felt my age. As the volume increased, I found myself at the very back of the hall, plaster falling around me. This was a really, really loud gig. Loud and great. It felt as though the whole hall might elevate, rise from its pinnings into the sky, propelled like a rocket. Which is what the best gigs should do – transport you.

9 Drummers of Note – Selected by Ben Schott

Ben Schott is the bestselling author of Schott's Original Miscellany, *and subsequent miscellanies on* Food & Drink, *and* Sporting, Gaming, & Idling.

His drumming is mediocre at best, and he harbours ambitions to play the Hammond organ to the same standard. Below, in no particular order, are some of Schott's drummers of note.

1. CLYDE STUBBLEFIELD
   Stubblefield was James Brown's 'Funky Drummer', and as such can claim to be the most sampled drummer in the world. Alongside fellow drummers Jabo Starks and Clayton Fillyau, Stubblefield pioneered the tight, crisp and heavily syncopated snare and hi-hat riffs that defined the James Brown sound, and funk itself.

2. JAMES BLADES
   More a percussionist than a drummer, Blades deserves mention as the man who recorded the Morse code 'V for Victory' signal for the BBC during WWII. The 'dot-dot-dot-dash' rhythm was played on an African membrane drum with a timpani mallet and was broadcast up to 150 times a day to encourage the Resistance in Continental Europe. As if this was not enough, James Blades also recorded the famous J. Arthur Rank gong (on small Chinese tam-tam) that was mimed by the boxer Bombardier Billy Wells.

3. CHARLIE WATTS
   Without doubt the most dapper of drummers, Watts merits a place in any drumming line-up for his bespoke suits alone. Like (the much underestimated) Ringo Starr, the essence of Watt's skill lies in playing just enough for the song and no more. When asked what 25 years of rock'n'roll with the Rolling Stones was like, Watts apparently replied: 'It's been one year drumming, and 24 years hanging around.'

4. STEVE GADD
   One of the most recorded drummers in history, Gadd has played with a stellar line-up of musicians from Stanley Clark to Eric Clapton. His work with Paul Simon has justly received high praise: the groove on 'Late In The Evening' and his

fiendishly complex riff on 'Fifty Ways To Leave Your Lover' typify his fluid and effortless style.

5. JOHN 'STUMPY' PEPYS
Tall, geeky and bespectacled, Pepys was the first of six drummers for the band Spinal Tap. His formal technique might seem unsophisticated to modern ears, but he pioneered the simple pop sound of the early 1960s – this is best illustrated in his drumming on the 1965 'Thamesmen' track 'Gimme Some Money'. In 1969 Pepys died in a bizarre gardening accident that to this day remains a mystery.

6. KEITH MOON
Setting aside Moon's antics (both real and apocryphal) his drumming for The Who was as stylish and clever as it was violent and anarchic. Almost any Who track demonstrates the genius of Moon's drumming – from the simple power of 'Substitute' to the flamboyance of 'Won't Get Fooled Again'.

7. RITCHIE HAYWOOD
The drummer for American band Little Feat, Haywood has two apt nicknames: 'the beat behind the Feat' and 'Mr Sophistifunk'. On tracks like 'Dixie Chicken' and 'Sailin' Shoes' Haywood sits just behind the groove, seamlessly melding the styles of rock, zydeco, folk and blues.

8. RONNIE VERRELL
Verrell was a stylish swing drummer who played with some of the great names of jazz, including Ted Heath, Syd Lawrence, David Lund, and Buddie Rich. More important than this, of course, is that he played Animal's drum solo on the theme tune to The Muppet Show.

9. JON BONHAM
Bonham was the typhonic drummer for '70s rock band Led Zeppelin (a band name suggested by Keith Moon, q.v.). Alongside bass-player John Paul Jones, Bonham provided driving, relentless, and (for rock music) astonishingly complex riffs – perhaps best illustrated in 'Fool In The Rain'. The less said about the half-hour drum solo during 'Moby Dick' the better.

That's Entertainment? – 7 Perfectly Wretched Performers

1. HADJI ALI
Billed as 'the Amazing Regurgitator', Hadji Ali enjoyed an improbably widespread popularity at the beginning of the twentieth century as a vaudeville drawing card. His act consisted of swallowing a series of unlikely objects – watermelon seeds, imitation jewels, coins, peach pits – and then regurgitating specific items as requested by his audience. It was impressive, if tasteless, stuff – but his grand finale brought down the house every night. His assistant would set up a tiny metal castle on stage while Ali drank a gallon of water, chased down by a pint of kerosene. To the accompaniment of a protracted drumroll, he would eject the kerosene across the stage in a 6-ft arc and set the castle afire. Then, as flames shot high into the air, he would upchuck the gallon of water and extinguish the blaze.

2. THE CHERRY SISTERS
When impresario Oscar Hammerstein found himself in a financial hole, he decided to try a new approach. 'I've been putting on the best talent and it hasn't gone over,' he told reporters. 'I'm going to try the worst.' On November 16, 1896, he introduced Elizabeth, Effie, Jessie and Addie Cherry to New York audiences at his Olympic Theatre. A sister act that had been treading the vaudeville boards in the Midwest for a few years, the girls strutted out onto the Olympia's stage garbed in flaming red dresses, hats and woollen mittens. Jessie kept time on a bass drum, while her three partners did their opening number:
Cherries ripe Boom-de-ay!
Cherries red Boom-de-ay!
The Cherry Sisters
Have come to stay!
New York audiences sat transfixed, staring goggle-eyed in disbelief, but they proved more merciful than audiences in the Midwest. They refrained from pelting the girls with rubbish and overripe tomatoes at first. Eventually, the Cherry sisters had to put up a wire screen to protect themselves from the inevitable hail of missiles showered on them by their outraged audiences. In later years they denied that anything had ever been thrown at them. Said a writer in the *New York Times*: 'It is sincerely hoped that nothing like them will ever be seen again.' Another critic wrote: 'A locksmith with a strong rasping file could earn

steady wages taking the kinks out of Lizzie's voice.' Despite their reputation as the world's worst act, they played consistently to standing-room-only crowds, wowing their fans with such numbers as 'The Modern Young Man' (a recitation), 'I'm Out Upon the Mash, Boys', 'Curfew Must Not Ring Tonight' and 'Don't You Remember Sweet Alice, Ben Bolt?'

3. RONALD COATES
This nineteenth-century British eccentric may well have been the worst actor in the history of the legitimate theatre. A Shakespearean by inclination, Coates saw no objection to rewriting the Bard's great tragedies to suit his own tastes. In one unforgettable reworking of *Romeo and Juliet*, in which he played the male lead, he tried to jimmy open his bride's casket with a crowbar. Costumed in a feathered hat, spangled cloak and billowing pantaloons – an outfit he wore in public as well – he looked singularly absurd. Coates was frequently hooted and jeered offstage for his inept, overblown performances. Quite often he had to bribe theatre managers to get a role in their productions, and his fellow thespians, fearing violence from the audience, demanded that he provide police protection before they would consent to appear onstage with him. He was slandered and laughed at throughout the British Isles and often threatened with lynching, but he persisted in his efforts to act. During one dramatic performance, several members of the audience were so violently convulsed with laughter that they had to be treated by a physician. Coates was struck and killed by a carriage – but not until 1848, when he was 74.

4. SADAKICHI HARTMANN
It seemed like a good idea at the time. Billing himself as a Japanese–German inventor, Hartmann was, briefly, a fixture in the New York theatre in the early 1900s as he offered soon-to-be-jaded audiences what he called 'perfume concerts'. Using a battery of electric fans, Hartmann blew great billowing clouds of scented smoke towards his audience, meanwhile explaining in thickly-accented English that each aroma represented a different nation. Hartmann, who frequently had trouble with hecklers, rarely made it beyond England (roses) or Germany (violets) before being hooted from the stage.

5. FLORENCE FOSTER JENKINS
A taxi collision in 1943 left would-be diva Florence Foster Jenkins capable of warbling a higher F than she'd ever managed

before. So delighted was she that she waived legal action against the taxi company, presenting the driver with a box of imported cigars instead – an appropriately grand gesture for the woman universally hailed as the world's worst opera singer. The remarkable career of this Pennsylvania heiress was for many years an in-joke among *cognoscenti* and music critics – the latter writing intentionally ambiguous reviews of the performances she gave regularly in salons from Philadelphia to Newport. 'Her singing at its finest suggests the untrammelled swoop of some great bird', Robert Lawrence wrote in the *Saturday Review*. Edward Tatnall Canby spoke of a 'subtle ghastliness that defies description'. But *Newsweek* was the most graphic, noting: 'In high notes, Mrs Jenkins sounds as if she was afflicted with low, nagging backache.' On October 25, 1944, Mrs Jenkins engineered the most daring coup of her career – a recital before a packed Carnegie Hall. That concert, like her others, saw the well-padded matron, then in her 70s, change costume numerous times. She appeared variously as the tinsel-winged 'Angel of Inspiration'; the Queen of the Night from Mozart's *Magic Flute*, and a Spanish coquette, draped in a colourful shawl, with a jewelled comb and a red rose in her hair. Inevitably she seasoned her 'coquette' rendition by tossing rose petals plucked from a wicker basket to the audience. On at least one occasion she inadvertently tossed the basket as well. But she always made certain to retrieve the petals for the next performance.

6. MRS ELVA MILLER

While growing up in Kansas, Elva figured that with practice and training she might have a shot at a career in singing. Her friends and family thought otherwise. However, she made the high school glee club and the church choir and even studied voice at Pomona College in Claremont, California. But with it all, her voice was reminiscent of cockroaches rustling at dawn in a rubbish bin. In the 1960s, still convinced she could sing, Mrs Miller – by now a 50-ish California housewife – recorded on her own a few favourite melodies 'just for the ducks of it'. She persuaded a local disc jockey to give her an airing and finally cut a nightmarish 45" single of the hit song 'Downtown'. It sold 250,000 copies in barely three weeks and made 'The Kansas Rocking Bird', as she was dubbed, the darling of TV variety shows. 'Her tempos, to put it charitably, are freeform', said *Time* magazine. 'She has an uncanny knack for landing squarely between the beat, producing a new ricochet effect that, if nothing else, defies imitation . . . [She] also tosses in a few choruses of whistling for a change of pace.'

7. WILLIAM HUNG
Hung, a 21-year-old engineering student from the University of California at Berkeley, auditioned for the 2004 season of the *American Idol* television show. After Hung sang a tuneless, but enthusiastic, rendition of Ricky Martin's song 'She Bangs', judge Simon Cowell observed, 'You can't sing, you can't dance, so what do you want me to say?' Despite the rejection, repeated showings of the *Idol* clip turned Hung into a cult star. Soon, 'The Real American Idol' was giving off-key performances on talk shows ranging from the *Today Show* to the *Tonight Show*, singing at a nationally televised NBA game, and sharing the stage with the likes of Janet Jackson, Outkast, and Lenny Kravitz at the Wango Tango Music Festival at the Rose Bowl in Pasadena, California. He signed a contract with Koch Entertainment and recorded an album, *Inspiration*, that sold more than 200,000 copies – outselling the debut album by *Idol*'s season one runner-up, Justin Guarini.

– B.F.

10 Most Unusual Variety Acts of All Time, by Ricky Jay

Ricky Jay is an author, actor, sleight-of-hand artist and scholar of the unusual. Most of the performers listed here are included in his histories of remarkable entertainers, *Learned Pigs & Fireproof Women* and *Jay's Journal of Anomalies*.

(*In no particular order*)

1. TOMMY MINNOCK
Shortly before the end of the nineteenth century, this 'human horse', a subject able to withstand excruciating pain, was literally nailed to a cross in a Trenton, New Jersey, music hall. While he was crucified he regaled the audience with his rendition of the popular tune 'After the Ball Is Over'.

2. THEA ALBA
This German schoolgirl wrote with both hands, both feet and her mouth, simultaneously; for a finale she wrote 10 different

numerals at the same time with pieces of chalk extending from pointers on each of her fingers.

3. DANIEL WILDMAN
This eighteenth-century equestrian beekeeper rode around the circus ring on the back of a horse while swarms of bees surrounded his face then moved away to specific locations at his command.

4. MATTHEW BUCHINGER
Born in Germany in 1674, this remarkable man was one of the most well-known performers of his day. He played a dozen musical instruments, danced the hornpipe, and was an expert pistol shot, bowler, calligrapher and magician. His accomplishments seem even more remarkable when one realises he stood only 28 in. high and had no arms or legs.

5. ORVILLE STAMM
Billed as the 'Strongest Boy in the World', he played the violin with an enormous bulldog suspended from the crook of his bowing arm. As an encore he lay on the ground and a piano was placed on his chest; a keyboardist stood on his thighs and pounded out the accompaniment as Orville sang 'Ireland Must Be Heaven 'cause Mother Comes from There'.

6. SIGNORA GIRARDELLI
Entertained audiences in the early nineteenth century by cooking eggs in boiling oil held in her palm, running a red-hot poker over her limbs, and attending to baked goods while inside a blazing oven.

7. ARTHUR LLOYD
Astounded vaudeville fans by producing from his capacious pockets any item printed on paper. Admission tickets to the White House, membership cards to the Communist Party, and ringside tickets to the Dempsey-Carpentier championship fight were among the 15,000 items he could instantly retrieve from his clothing.

8. JEAN ROYER
A seventeenth-century native of Lyons, he swallowed an enormous quantity of water and then spewed it out in continuous graceful arcs for as long as it took to walk 200 paces or recite the 51st Psalm.

9. CLARENCE WILLARD
As 'Willard, the Man Who Grows', he had an act that consisted

of his growing six inches in height while standing next to a volunteer from the audience. A master of manipulating his body, Willard used no trick apparatus of any kind.

10. JOSEPH PUJOL
'Le Petomane', as he was called, was the legendary French musical farter who issued sonorous but odourless notes from his body's most secret orifice.

Jeremy Beadle's 20 Barmy Quiz Questions

Writer and TV presenter Jeremy Beadle first came to major public attention in 1981 when he co-hosted *Game for a Laugh*. Among the other series he has presented are *Beadle's About*, *You've Been Framed* and *Win Beadle's Money*. But before all that, Beadle was the European editor of *The Book of Lists*. He has a personal library of 25,000 volumes. Here Beadle displays his passion for quizzes in typical style.

1. What colour are the breasts of blue tits?
2. To which planet do Abbott & Costello travel in *Abbott & Costello Go To Mars*?
3. How long does morning last on the moon?
4. The Caspian Sea is the world's largest what?
5. Built on the first level of the Eiffel Tower, where would you go to have a meal in Le Restaurant de la Tour Eiffel?
6. In England, what day followed September 2 in 1752?
7. How far down a flagpole should a flag be if it is flying at half-mast?
8. Where does Juliet stand during the famous balcony scene of *Romeo and Juliet*?
9. What religion was Britain's only Jewish prime minister?
10. What type of creature was Buffalo Bill famous for killing?
11. Is the Upper Nile north, south, east or west of the Lower Nile?
12. It was predicted Henry IV would die in Jerusalem and he did. In which town did he die?
13. In the 1948 London Olympics, what stroke was used by the first seven finishers in the 200-m breaststroke final?

14. At the time of writing, the world's population is estimated at 6,222,336,610. Approximately how many of them live on the surface on the earth?

15. Who wrote *The Autobiography of Malcolm X*?

16. In which city were The Plymouth Brethren founded?

17. What was the name of the character played by Clint Eastwood in the 1973 film *The Man With No Name*?

18. On what side of the moon is the Eastern Sea?

19. *The Hitchhiker's Guide to the Galaxy* is a trilogy of how many parts?

20. Including Queen Elizabeth II, how many Queen Elizabeths of England have there been?

ANSWERS

1. Yellow
2. Venus
3. A week
4. Lake
5. New Orleans, Louisiana. The dismantled restaurant was originally on the first level of the Tower from 1937 to 1981.
6. September 14 1752 – it adopted the Gregorian calendar
7. Only the distance equal to its depth, i.e. the top edge is placed where the bottom edge should rest
8. On a floor beside an upper window. There is no mention of a balcony.
9. Christian, Benjamin Disraeli was baptised into the Church of England at the age of 12.
10. Bison – buffalo are found in Africa and India.
11. South (it's higher – more elevated – hence its name)
12. London. He died in the Jerusalem Chapel in Westminster Abbey 1413.
13. Butterfly
14. Exactly none. The actual surface of the earth, as defined by astronomers, is the outer edge of the atmosphere, about 100 miles above our heads.
15. Alex Haley
16. Dublin, about 1827, by the Reverend John Darby
17. Joe
18. West. Owing to a policy decision by the International Astronomical Union reversing lunar east and west, the Eastern Sea is now on the western limb of the moon.

19. Five
20. Five: Edward IV's consort, Henry VII's consort, Queen Elizabeth I, George VI's consort and Queen Elizabeth II

Chapter 4

RATING THE EFFECTS OF 51 PERSONAL CRISES

10 MAMMOTH CHEESES

5 BODY PARTS NAMED AFTER ITALIANS

9 BODY PARTS YOU DIDN'T KNOW HAD NAMES

14 NOTABLE EVENTS THAT HAPPENED UNDER THE INFLUENCE OF ALCOHOL

9 DRINKS NAMED AFTER PEOPLE

RUTH ROGERS' TOP 10 ITALIAN SOUPS

ROSE GRAY'S 10 FAVOURITE ITALIAN WINES

14 HIGHLY UNUSUAL RECIPES

7 GREAT SAUSAGE EVENTS

10 REALLY UNUSUAL MEDICAL CONDITIONS

10 FAMOUS INSOMNIACS

14 HEALTHY INSOMNIA CURES

29 ACTIVITIES AND THE CALORIES THEY CONSUME

Food and Health

© Corbis

MR MARX PREPARES FOR THE LAND OF NOD – see p.120

Rating the Effects of 51 Personal Crises

In the 1920s, Dr Walter Cannon began recording connections between stressful periods in a person's life and the appearance of physical ailments. A decade later, Dr Adolf Meyer compiled a 'life chart', which specifically correlated health problems with a person's particular life circumstances at the time. This process was refined during the 1950s and 1960s and resulted in the creation of the Social Readjustment Rating Scale (SRRS), which ranks 43 life crises on a scale of Life Change Units (LCUs). The ratings were arrived at by researchers who used in-depth interviewing techniques on an international sample of 5,000 people from Europe, the US Central America, Oceania and Japan. Because of the consistency with which marriage was rated as one of the most significant life changes, it was given a value of 50 on the scale, and 42 other life crisis were judged in relation to it. Some cultural differences surfaced (for example, the Japanese ranked minor law violations near the middle of the list and jail terms second from the top), but on the whole there was a remarkable uniformity of results, cutting across all national and socio-economic levels. SRRS supporters contend that there is a direct correlation between annual LCUs and stress-related diseases. One of their studies found that with a 'mild' stress level (150 to 199 LCUs in a single year), health problems increased 37% above the average; with a moderate level (200 to 299 LCUs), the increase was 51%; and with a major crisis level (300 LCUs and above), 79% more health problems occurred. The researchers noted that what counted was the cumulative total, not whether the life changes in themselves were positive or negative. The original chart, produced in 1964 by T.H. Holmes and T.H. Rahe, has since been updated to reflect changing values as well as cross-cultural differences.

Rank	*Life event*	*LCU value*
1.	Death of spouse/mate	87
2	Death of close family member	79
3.	Major injury/illness to self	78
4.	Detention in jail or other institution	76
5.	Major injury/illness to close family member	72
6.	Foreclosure on loan/mortgage	71
7.	Divorce	71
8.	Being a victim of crime	70
9.	Being a victim of police brutality	69

10.	Infidelity	69
11.	Experiencing domestic violence/sexual abuse	69
12.	Separation from or reconciliation with spouse/mate	66
13.	Being fired/laid-off/unemployed	64
14.	Experiencing financial problems/difficulties	62
15.	Death of a close friend	61
16.	Surviving a disaster	59
17.	Becoming a single parent	59
18.	Assuming responsibility for sick or elderly loved one	56
19.	Loss of or major reduction in health insurance/benefits	56
20.	Self/close family member being arrested for violating the law	56
21.	Major disagreement over child support/custody/ visitation	53
22.	Experiencing/involved in auto accident	53
23.	Being disciplined at work/demoted	53
24.	Dealing with unwanted pregnancy	51
25.	Adult child moving in with parent/parent moving in with adult child	50
26.	Child develops behaviour or learning problem	49
27.	Experiencing employment discrimination/sexual harassment	48
28.	Attempting to modify addictive behaviour of self	47
29.	Discovering/attempting to modify addictive behaviour of close family member	46
30.	Employer reorganization/downsizing	45
31.	Dealing with infertility/miscarriage	44
32.	Getting married/remarried	43
33.	Changing employers/careers	43
34.	Failure to obtain/qualify for mortgage	42
35.	Pregnancy of self/spouse/mate	41
36.	Experiencing discrimination/harassment outside the workplace	39
37.	Release from jail	39
38.	Spouse/mate begins/ceases work outside the home	38
39.	Major disagreement with boss/coworker	37
40.	Change in residence	35
41.	Finding appropriate child care/day care	34
42.	Experiencing a large unexpected monetary gain	33
43.	Changing positions (transfer, promotion)	33
44.	Gaining a new family member	33
45.	Changing work responsibilities	32
46.	Child leaving home	30

47. Obtaining a home mortgage 30
48. Obtaining a major loan other than home mortgage 30
49. Retirement 28
50. Beginning/ceasing formal education 26
51. Receiving a ticket for violating the law 22

10 Mammoth Cheeses

1. THE 28½ -TON CHEDDAR
The world's largest block of cheese was 6 ft high, 32 ft long, and 4½ ft wide. It was commissioned in 1995 by Loblaws Supermarket and made by the Agropur dairy cooperative of Quebec, Canada. At 57,508 pounds, the giant cheddar was equivalent to the amount of cheese eaten by 2,500 Canadians in one year.

2. THE 17½ -TON CHEDDAR
Known as the Golden Giant, this enormous chunk of cheese was 14½ ft long, 6½ ft wide and 6 ft high. Produced in 1964 by Steve's Cheese of Denmark, Wisconsin, for the Wisconsin Cheese Foundation, it required 183 tons of milk – the daily production of 16,000 cows. After its manufacture, the cheese was shipped via a special tractor-trailer, called the Cheese-Mobile to the Wisconsin Pavilion at the New York World's Fair. A refrigerated glass enclosure remained its home until 1965. It was then cut up into 2-lb pieces that were put on display until 1968, when they were sold for $3 per package. At the 1978 Wisconsin Cheese Makers' Association convention, the two remaining pieces of the cheese were auctioned off for $200 each.

3. THE 11-TON CHEDDAR
Twelve Canadian cheesemakers collaborated to make a cheese for display at the 1893 Chicago World's Fair. The 'Canadian Mite' was 6 ft tall and 28 ft in circumference. When the Mite was put on display at the Fair's Canadian pavilion, it broke through the floor, and had to be placed on reinforced concrete at the agricultural building. In 1943, a concrete replica of the cheese was unveiled alongside the railroad tracks in Perth, Ontario, to commemorate the fiftieth anniversary of the cheese. For the hundredth anniversary in 1983, Perth organised a week-long celebration.

4. THE 6-TON CHEDDAR
This giant was produced by upstate New York cheesemakers under the direction of W.L. Kilsey for the 1937 New York State Fair at Syracuse. Production began on July 12, 1937. It took

seven weeks to cure and had to be turned frequently to ensure even ripening. It used the milk of 6,000 cows.

5. THE 4-TON CHEDDAR
Made by Canadian cheesemakers, this 7,000-lb-plus giant excited spectators at the 1883 Toronto Fair. Mortician-poet James McIntyre immortalised it in the following cheesy verses:

We have thee, mammoth cheese,
Lying quietly at your ease;
Gently fanned by evening breeze,
Thy fair form no flies dare seize.

6. THE 1,400-LB CHEDDAR
Bestowed upon US President Andrew Jackson by a New York State cheesemaker in 1837, this three-quarter-ton monster ripened in the vestibule of the White House for nearly two years. It was served to the entire city of Washington, DC, when Jackson threw open the doors of the White House to celebrate Washington's Birthday. According to eyewitnesses, the whole atmosphere for a half-mile around was infected with cheese. The birthday cheddar was devoured in less than two hours. Only a tiny morsel was saved for the president.

7. THE 1,200-LB CHESHIRE
In 1801 President Thomas Jefferson received this cheddar-like tribute from the tiny town of Cheshire in the Berkshire Mountains of Massachusetts. Named the Ultra-Democratic, Anti-Federalist Cheese of Cheshire, it was shipped to Washington, DC, by sled, boat and wagon to honour Jefferson's triumph over the Federalists. The originator of the cheese was a preacher named John Leland, who took advantage of all the fuss and publicity to proselytise for his church. Duly impressed, Jefferson donated $200 to Leland's congregation.

8. THE 1,100-LB CHEDDAR
The Great Pennard Cheese, 9 ft in diameter, was a wedding gift to Queen Victoria in 1840. Puzzled and somewhat embarrassed by not knowing what to do with it, the queen was relieved when its makers asked if they could borrow it to exhibit it around England. But when they tried to return the grubby, show-worn cheese, Victoria refused to accept it. After lengthy quarrels over its disposition, the cheddar was finally surrendered to the British Chancery, where it gradually disappeared. In 1989, John Green of West Pennard recreated the Great Pennard Cheese, but added 100 lb.

9. THE 1,000-LB LUNI CHEESE
One of the lesser-known wonders of the ancient world, the 1,000-lb Luni cheese, named after an ancient town in northern Italy, was reported by Pliny in his *Natural History* about AD77. Manufactured in what is now Tuscany, near the famous Carrara marble quarries in central Italy, the Luni cheese was probably made from a mixture of cow's and goat's milk. It is supposed to have tasted like a cross between cheddar and parmesan.

10. THE 1,000-LB CHEDDAR
The largest cheese to travel halfway around the world, this half-ton cheddar was taken to London all the way from New Zealand. It was the star attraction at the Wembley Exposition of 1924.

– S.R. & C.F.

5 Body Parts Named After Italians

1. ORGAN OF CORTI
The organ of hearing in the middle ear. Alfonso Corti (1822–78) was an Italian nobleman who studied medicine and anatomy in Vienna, writing his thesis on the cardiovascular system of reptiles. He published his findings on the inner ear in 1851, the year that he inherited estates and titles from his father and retired from scientific research.

2. EUSTACHIAN TUBE
A tube leading from the middle ear to the throat. Its purpose is to equalise pressure in the ear. It is named after Bartolommeo Eustachio (c.1513–74), considered one of the fathers of anatomy, who lived much of his life in Rome, working as a physician to leading churchmen, including two future saints, Charles Borromeo and Philip Neri.

It has been suggested that Eustachio's discovery of the connection between the middle ear and the pharynx was known to Shakespeare and suggested the means of murder (poison poured in the ear) used by Claudio to kill Hamlet's father.

3. FALLOPIAN TUBES
The pair of tubes that conduct the egg from the ovary to the uterus in the female. They are named after Gabriel Fallopius (1523–62), who spent much of his adult life as a professor of anatomy at Pisa and Padua (early attempts to practise as a surgeon resulted in the deaths of several patients and Fallopius

decided that an academic career was a safer option). He was the first person to coin the word 'vagina' and also invented a kind of contraceptive sheath which he tested out on more than a thousand men in what was, perhaps, the first medical trial of condom efficacy.

4. RUFFINI'S CORPUSCLES
   Sensory nerve-endings that respond to warmth. Named after Angelo Ruffini (1864–1929), who used gold chloride to stain microscope slides of anatomical specimens, thus revealing the tiny and sensitive corpuscles. Ruffini began his career as a country doctor but ended it as a professor at the University of Bologna. His major researches were into the embryology of birds and amphibians.

5. SERTOLI CELLS
   Cells of the testis that serve to nourish sperm cells. Named after histologist Enrico Sertoli (1842–1910) who discovered them in 1865, when he was still a postgraduate student of physiology in Vienna. The year after his discovery Sertoli returned to his native country to fight for Italian forces against an invading army from Austria. His later life was spent as a professor of anatomy and physiology in Milan.

– K.A.M. & N.R.

9 Body Parts You Didn't Know Had Names

1. EPONYCHIUM
   Another term for the cuticle of the fingernail, a narrow band of epidermal tissue that extends down over the margin of the nail wall.

2. FRENUM GLANDIS
   Found in the male reproductive system, this delicate fold of skin attaches the foreskin to the undersurface of the glans.

3. GLABELLA
   A flattened area of the frontal bone (forehead area) between the frontal eminences and the superciliary arches (eyebrows), just above the nose.

4. LUNNULE
   The white crescent-shaped mark at the base of a fingernail.

5. **OTOLITHS**
Particles of calcium carbonate in the utricles and saccules of the inner ears. The otoliths respond to gravity by sliding in the direction of the ground and causing sensitive hairs to bend, thus generating nervous impulses important in maintaining equilibrium.

6. **PHALANX**
One of the bones of the fingers or toes. There are two phalanges in each thumb and big toe, while there are three phalanges in all other fingers and toes, making a total of 14 in each hand or foot.

7. **PHILTRUM**
The vertical groove in the middle portion of the upper lip.

8. **PUDENDUM**
A collective name for the external genitalia of the female; also known as the vulva. It includes the mons pubis, the labia majora, and the labia minora.

9. **CANTHUS**
The corners of the eye where the upper and lower eyelids meet.

– K.A.M. & N.R.

14 Notable Events that Happened Under the Influence of Alcohol

1. **THE VISIT OF KING CHRISTIAN VI OF DENMARK TO THE COURT OF JAMES I (1606)**
In 1606 King Christian IV of Denmark and Norway paid a visit to his royal brother-in-law, James I of England and VI of Scotland. The English courtiers were no strangers to alcohol, but even they were astonished by the prodigious boozing of Christian and his entourage. Several official ceremonies descended into chaos and farce as Danes and English, men and women alike, competed to see who could down the most drink. During a court masque, figures representing Faith, Hope and Charity appeared before the two kings. Faith was so drunk she could not utter a word of her speech and Hope fell over. The Danish king attempted to dance with one of the other actors but tumbled to the floor and had to be carried, comatose, to his room. Indeed most of the performers in the masque, according to a witness, 'went backward or fell down, wine did so occupy their upper chambers'.

2. **THE HANGING OF CAPTAIN KIDD (1701)**
Captain William Kidd was sentenced to death for murder and piracy and led to the gallows at London's Execution Dock on May 23, 1701. The execution itself was a fiasco. As a large group of spectators sang a series of ballads in honour of the pirate, a very drunk public executioner attempted to hang Kidd, who was so smashed that he could hardly stand. Then the rope broke and Kidd fell over into the mud. Though a second attempt at hanging the prisoner succeeded, the sheriff in charge was later harshly criticised in a published editorial for the bungled performance.

3. **BOSTON TEA PARTY (1773)**
In Boston, Massachusetts, 50 colonials and members of the Committee of Correspondence met at the home of a printer named Benjamin Edes at about 4 pm on December 16, 1773. Later that evening, they intended to destroy the tea aboard three ships in Boston harbour as a protest against the British government's taxation of the American colonies. To bolster their resolve, Edes filled a massive punch bowl with a potent rum concoction. Edes's son Peter had the job of keeping the bowl filled, which proved to be an almost impossible task because of the ardour with which the patriots drank. Shortly after 6 pm the men, most of whom were now in a noisy, festive mood, with a few staggering noticeably, departed and marched to Griffin's Wharf, where the tea ships were anchored. For the next three hours they sobered up – a number becoming violently ill – as they dumped heavy tea chests into the harbour – and set off the American Revolution.

4. **THE WEDDING OF THE PRINCE REGENT (1795)**
The Prince Regent, later George IV, was markedly unwilling to make the dynastic marriage expected of the heir to the throne, not least because he was already secretly married to a Roman Catholic commoner, Mrs Fitzherbert. Pressured by his father, George III, the prince agreed to marry Princess Caroline of Brunswick. Meeting his bride three days before the wedding, he was horrified by the prospect of them becoming man and wife and took refuge in drink. At the ceremony he was so drunk he could hardly stand up and had to be supported by his groomsmen. He came to life only to make eyes at his current mistress, Lady Jersey, who was one of the wedding guests. George continued to drink after the vows had been exchanged and spent his wedding night collapsed in a drunken stupor in the fireplace of

his new wife's bedroom. The couple spent only a few nights together – on one of which George's heir Princess Charlotte was conceived – and separated within the year.

5. NAT TURNER REBELLION (1831)
On the night of August 21, 1831, black slave-prophet Nat Turner launched a rebellion in Southampton County, Virginia, that left more than 50 whites and more than 120 blacks dead. Although Turner never touched alcohol, his six followers had feasted on roast pig and apple brandy that night. At the first plantation they attacked, the rebels drank hard cider before massacring the whites living there. Through the night and into the next day, the insurgents raided plantations, killed whites and confiscated horses, weapons and brandy. By noon, Turner's army had expanded to approximately 60 men, but many of them were so intoxicated that they kept falling off their horses. When Turner caught up with one advance party, they were relaxing in the brandy cellar of a plantation. Learning that a group of whites was approaching, Turner rallied his men and put the whites to the fight. But the next day an alarm scattered his new recruits, and he had only 20 men left to fight 3,000 armed white militiamen and volunteers. The rebellion was crushed.

6. LINCOLN'S ASSASSINATION (1865)
On April 14, 1865, actor John Wilkes Booth began drinking at the Kirkwood House bar in Washington, DC, at three in the afternoon. At 4 pm he arrived at Deery's saloon and ordered a bottle of brandy. Two hours later he was drinking whisky at Taltavul's Saloon, next door to Ford's Theater. Having made the final arrangements for his impending crime, Booth returned at 9.30 to Taltavul's, where President Abraham Lincoln's valet, Charles Forbes, his coachman Francis Burns, and his bodyguard John Parker, an alcoholic policeman, were all drinking. At 10.15, while Parker continued to imbibe – thus leaving the president unprotected – Booth left, went next door to Ford's Theater, and shot Lincoln. Meanwhile, George Atzerodt, Booth's fellow conspirator, who was supposed to assassinate Vice President Andrew Johnson, had become so intoxicated and frightened that he abandoned the plan.

7. BATTLE OF THE LITTLE BIGHORN (1876)
A controversy still rages over the extent and level of intoxication of the officers and men of the US 7th Cavalry Regiment at the Battle of the Little Bighorn. It is known that Custer's

second-in-command, Major Marcus Reno, had a half-gallon keg of whisky with him on the expedition. When they reached the Rosebud River four days before the battle, the 7th Cavalry troopers may have replenished their supplies of alcohol off a steamboat carrying cases of whisky. According to Indian veterans of the battle, numerous canteens half full of whisky were found with the bodies of Custer's men. It is a fact that Reno, who was most likely an alcoholic, was intoxicated when besieged by Indians the night after Custer was defeated.

8. THIRD BATTLE OF THE AISNE RIVER (1918)
In May 1918, during WWI, General Erich Ludendorff's German troops reached the Marne River at Château-Thierry, only 37 miles from Paris, during the Third Battle of the Aisne River. On the verge of capturing Paris, but after living without any luxuries for years, the German soldiers invaded France's champagne provinces, where well-stocked wine cellars abounded. Drunkenness quickly spread through the ranks; even the German military police joined the revelries. In the village of Fismes on the morning of May 30, the bodies of soldiers who had passed out littered the streets, making it difficult for trucks to drive through the town on their way to the front lines. The intoxication and subsequent hangovers afflicting the Germans slowed their advance and halted it completely in certain sectors. This enabled the French and Americans to establish new defensive lines, counterattack, and end Ludendorff's offensive, which proved to be the Germans' last chance for victory in WWI.

9. FOUNDING OF ALCOHOLICS ANONYMOUS (1935)
Alcoholics Anonymous came into existence when a New York stockbroker named Bill W. (an AA member uses only his last initial), an alcoholic who had stopped drinking as a result of a spiritual experience, helped a physician named Dr Bob to quit drinking. During a business trip to Akron, Ohio, Bill W. met Dr Bob and shared with him his own experiences as an alcoholic and his method of recovering from alcoholism. Suffering from a severe hangover, the still woozy Dr Bob had his last drink on June 10, 1935. The next day, with Bill W., he found what is now called Alcoholics Anonymous. Neither Bill W., who lived until 1971, nor Dr Bob, who lived until 1950, ever drank again. The fellowship they founded, which is based on the concept of alcoholics helping other alcoholics, now has more than two million members.

10. THE FILMING OF *MY LITTLE CHICKADEE* (1940)
As in almost all of his films, W.C. Fields was intoxicated throughout the production of *My Little Chickadee*. After drinking from two to four martinis with his breakfast each morning, Fields arrived at Universal Studios with a cocktail shaker full of martinis. Apparently at his comic best when drunk, Fields consumed two bottles of gin each day during the filming. Fields's inebriated behaviour often infuriated his co-star, Mae West, especially once, when, in an overly affectionate mood, he prodded and pinched her generous figure and called her 'my little brood mare'. Although he often required an afternoon nap to diminish the effects of his drinking, Fields was never incapacitated by alcohol during his performance in the movie.

11. THE WRITING OF *A CLOCKWORK ORANGE* (1962)
Even though his work sometimes dealt with projected future worlds, English author Anthony Burgess developed his novels from his personal experiences. For example, the brutal rape scene in *A Clockwork Orange* was derived from an incident when his wife was mugged during WWII, which resulted in the death of their expected child. While writing *A Clockwork Orange*, Burgess became so emotionally involved that he frequently had to calm himself by means of alcohol. As he admitted, 'I had to write *A Clockwork Orange* in a state of near drunkenness, in order to deal with material that upset me so much.'

12. THE *EXXON VALDEZ* OIL SPILL (1989)
After striking a reef, the *Exxon Valdez* spilled 250,000 barrels of oil into Alaska's Prince William Sound, forming a slick that covered 2,600 square miles and washed onto 1,000 miles of coastline. At the time of the accident, Captain Joseph Hazelwood was below deck, having left at the helm Third Mate Gregory Cousins, who was not certified, to pilot the tanker in Prince William Sound. After the collision, Hazelwood attempted to pilot the tanker off the reef despite warnings that the ship might break up if he succeeded. Hazelwood also failed to sound a general alarm. In addition, Hazelwood was observed chain-smoking on the bridge until Coast Guard officers arrived and warned him that he could set the whole ship on fire. One of the Coast Guard officers who boarded the ship two and a half hours after the collision reported that Hazelwood's breath smelled of alcohol. When a blood test was administered – a full nine hours after the accident – Hazelwood's blood alcohol level was above the legal level

required to operate a ship. Although Hazelwood admitted that he had drunk alcohol while ashore earlier that day (and witnesses spotted him drinking in two different bars), he denied being impaired at the time of the accident and insisted that the blood alcohol test was inaccurate. Indeed, although a jury convicted Hazelwood on misdemeanour negligence charges (later overturned), he was acquitted of operating a ship while under the influence of alcohol. On the other hand, an investigation by the National Transportation Safety Board concluded that Hazelwood had left the bridge because of 'impairment from alcohol'.

13. THE FAILED SOVIET COUP (1991)
In a last-ditch attempt to undo the reforms of *glasnost*, on August 19, 1991, Communist party hardliners attempted to overthrow Soviet Premier Mikhail Gorbachev. The coup collapsed two days later in the face of resistance led by Boris Yeltsin, President of the Russian Republic. The plotters' failure to act decisively against Yeltsin ensured the failure of the coup. Heavy alcohol consumption contributed to the ineptitude of the plotters. Former Soviet Vice President Gennady Yanayev, the front man for the coup, drank heavily throughout the affair, and was found 'in an alcoholic haze' in his office when the coup collapsed. Another plotter, former Prime Minister Valentin Pavlov, began drinking the first night of the coup, by his own admission. When Pavlov tried unsuccessfully to convince the government to declare a state of emergency, he appeared sick 'or more likely drunk' according to Deputy Prime Minister Shcherbakov. The failed coup ultimately led to the complete disintegration of the Soviet Union.

14. DEATH OF PRINCESS DIANA (1997)
On August 31, 1997, Diana, her boyfriend, Dodi al-Fayed, and their driver Henri Paul, were killed in a car crash in a tunnel in Paris. Paul had been driving at more than 100 mph when he apparently clipped another car and lost control. An investigation found that Paul's blood alcohol level was three times the legal limit. There were also traces of anti-depressants in his blood. Conspiracy theorists – including Dodi's father, Mohammed al-Fayed – have disputed the blood test results. They note that two bodyguards who were with Paul shortly before the crash said that he did not appear drunk and that he acted normally.

– R.J.F. & C.F.

9 Drinks Named After People

1. ALEXANDER
   Made with crème de cacao, gin, or brandy, and cream, this cocktail was named for Alexander the Great, centuries after his death.

2. BLOODY MARY
   Ferdinand L. Petiot, bartender at Harry's New York Bar in Paris, mixed vodka and tomato juice in 1920; American entertainer Roy Barton gave it the name 'bucket of blood' after the club in Chicago. The drink was renamed 'the red snapper' when Petiot spiced it up with salt, pepper, lemon and Worcester sauce. Though it has been said that this 'queen among drinks' was named after Mary, Queen of Scots, it was Queen Mary I of England who was known as 'Bloody Mary'.

3. DOM PÉRIGNON
   Dom Pérignon (1638–1715) entered the religious life at the age of 15. A blind man, his acute senses of taste and smell aided him in making and improving the wines of the Benedictine monastery near Épernay, where he was a cellarmaster. It was Dom Pérignon who perfected the process of fermenting champagne in the bottle – he literally put in the all-important bubbles. Moët et Chandon vineyards later honoured Pérignon's accomplishments by naming its finest vintage after him.

4. PIMM'S
   The typical summer drink of the English upper middle classes was created by James Pimm, nineteenth-century owner of an oyster bar in the City of London. Originally Pimm intended his drink, flavoured with herbs and quinine, to be a digestive tonic, but it was soon being drunk as a cocktail by fashionable Victorian society.

5. HARVEY WALLBANGER
   California surfer Tom Harvey (c. 1970) had a great passion for the 'Italian screwdriver' (orange juice, vodka, Galliano). After a day of surfing, Harvey still couldn't stay off the waves. He would rush to his favourite bar, overindulge himself – and then walk into a wall when it came time to go home.

6. MICKEY FINN
   Mickey Finn was apparently the name of a bartender who worked in Chicago around 1896–1906. He served knockout

drinks (which probably contained chloral hydrate) to his customers so that they could be robbed.

7. ROB ROY
   This concoction of Scotch whisky, sweet vermouth and bitters, topped with a maraschino cherry, bears the nickname of the legendary eighteenth-century Scottish cattle rustler Robert Macgregor.

8. TOM COLLINS
   This drink was named after a nineteenth-century bartender at Limmer's Old House in London who was famous for his gin slings – a tall drink that resembles the Collins mixture of gin, lemon, sugar and soda water.

9. MARGARITA
   There are at least eight different stories relating to the creation of the tequila-based margarita. The most commonly accepted one is that the drink was concocted in 1938 or 1939 by Carlos Herrera, a Mexican bartender who named the drink in honour of a showgirl named Marjorie King, who was allergic to all hard liquor except tequila.

– R.H. & D.B.

Ruth Rogers' Top 10 Italian Soups

With Rose Gray, Ruth Rogers is chef and co-owner of London's lauded River Café Restaurant. The Michelin-starred restaurant was one of the first in Britain to emphasise the flavours of Italian home cooking and employ an all-Italian wine list. She has published several cookery books, including, with Rose Gray, the prize-winning *The River Cafe Cook Book* (1995), *The Italian Kitchen* (1998, accompanying a Channel 4 TV series) and *River Cafe Cook Book Easy* (2003).

1. PAPPA AL POMODORO
   This soup is a traditional, simple soup of Florence made with Tuscan bread, fresh tomatoes and basil. This is my number one favourite.

2. RIBOLLITA
   A November soup with cavalo nero, bread, beans and oil – the new season's oil, newly pressed and cavalo nero just after the first frost.

3. SUMMER MINESTRONE
   Summer vegetables – asparagus, green beans, courgettes and pesto served at room temperature or chilled. Different to winter minestrone.
4. BROAD BEANS, PEA AND POTATO
   A soup for the beginning of summer with new peas and fresh, bright green broad beans.
5. ZUPPA DEI POVERI
   This soup is made of bread, stock, broccoli and melted fontina cheese and comes from the mountain regions of Italy.
6. PORCINI AND POTATO
   I first had this in U Gianco; it is an unusual combination of fresh and raw porcini.
7. ACQUA COTTA
   Porcini, tomato and bread from the Maremma. Acqua Cotta is translated as 'cooked water' and is full of the flavour of tomato and porcini.
8. QUICK FISH
   A really easy soup from our most recent cookbook that can be cooked in 20 minutes.
9. SARDINIAN WILD FENNEL SOUP
   Sliced fennel cooked in a chicken stock. The fennel absorbs the flavours of the chicken stock and the stock is flavoured by the fennel. The ricotta crostini is placed in the bowl with the fennel ladelled over, giving a creamy dimension.
10. CHESTNUT AND CELERIAC SOUP
    An autumn soup which is comforting and warm and so thick that you can eat it with a fork.

Rose Gray's 10 Favourite Italian Wines

With Ruth Rogers, Rose Gray is chef and co-owner of London's famous River Café. She graduated to cooking after a career as teacher of fine art, designer and manufacturer of paper lights and furniture and importer of French cookers. She became chef at Nell's Nightclub, New York in the mid-1980s, and has published several cookery books, including, with Ruth Rogers, the prize-winning *The*

River Cafe Cook Book (1995), *The Italian Kitchen* (1998, accompanying a channel 4 TV series) and *River Cafe Cook Book Easy* (2003). The restaurant has been showered with awards, including a Michelin Star (1998). Rose is also co-founder of the Cooks in Schools charity.

1. PROSECCO SPAGO, N.V.COL VETORAZ
   I love to use this sparkling wine to mix half-and-half with fresh fruit of the season as an aperitivo.
2. RIESLING RENANO LANGHE BIANCO 2001, VAJRA, G D
   An unusual, dry Riesling from a great Barolo producer.
3. PINOT BIANCO 2003, SCHIOPETTO
   This perfect, perfumed Pino Bianco from Friuli complements the fabulous fish dishes of Venice that I love to cook at the River Cafe.
4. VALPOLICELLA CLASSICO 2003, ALLEGRINI
   My favourite summer red. Light, beautifully crafted, young drinking wine. Delicious chilled.
5. AMARONE CLASSICO DELLA VALPOLICELLA 1999, ALLEGRINI
   Amazingly clean. A modern-style of Amerone which I love to use to drink and also to make Amarone Risotto in the winter.
6. CHIANTI CLASSICO 2002, FONTODI
   This year they used all the grapes from their top vineyards in this blend to make a superb concentrated, spicy Chianti. A fantastic buy.
7. CEPPARELLO 1990, ISOLE E OLENA
   My favourite super Tuscan from one of the genius Chianti producers.
8. SYRAH VIGNA DEL BOSCO 2001, MANZANO
   As I love game so much, I love this wine, which is complex with interesting, spicy fruit and savoury flavours.
9. BARBARESCO RABAJA 1997, BRUNO ROCCA
   For Bruno, the wine maker, this is a perfect representation of the elegance of Barbaresco.
10. BAROLO GRANBUSSIA 1989, CONTERNO, ALDO
    When I get my hands on a white truffle from Alba, the pleasure is always completed by a bottle of this brilliant Barolo.

14 Highly Unusual Recipes

Calvin W. Schwabe is a professor of epidemiology and veterinary medicine at Cal State Davis, California, USA. Among his goals is that of helping people overcome existing prejudices about food, and introducing international ways of eating to the Western world. Schwabe serves as an advisor on numerous international committees devoted to nutrition. In 1979, he wrote the groundbreaking work, *Unmentionable Cuisine*, published by The University of Virginia State Press.

1. BRAIN TACOS – Italy (Cevello di agnello alla napoletana)
   Put olive oil in earthenware casserole. Add halved, parboiled lambs' brains, turn over and coat with oil, add salt and pepper, capers, crushed garlic, pitted ripe olives and bread crumbs. Bake in 400° oven for 10–15 minutes. Brain Casserole – Algeria – (Mokh) is an alternative. In Turkey, Brain Salad is commonly eaten.
2. STUFFED KID – Saudi Arabia (Kharuf mahshi)
   This popular dish is not only a temptation for frustrated parents. Rub a skinned, eviscerated kid inside and out with: chopped nuts, parsley or coriander, chopped fresh ginger, salt and pepper. Stuff the kid with cooked rice, mixed nuts (pistachios, almonds, pignolias), sultana raisins or seedless grapes, plus residue of kid rubbing mix. Sew up opening, paint with melted butter, roast on a spit over charcoal (or in a 270–300° oven) until brown and tender. Serve on a mound of the stuffing. Guests sit on the floor and dig in.
3. STIR-FRIED HEART – China (Nan Chow Sin)
   Trim beef or pork heart, cut into one-eighth inches. Julienne. Marinate with sections of scallions in a mix of cornstarch, water, soy sauce, sherry, sugar, salt and minced ginger. Drain vegetables and stir fry medium hot. Pork heart must be thoroughly cooked.
4. UTERUS SAUSAGE – Ancient Rome (Vulvulae botelli)
   'For the cook,' writes Professor Schwabe, 'who has successfully subjugated most of the family's food prejudices . . .'
   Stuff a pig uterus with cumin, leeks, pepper, garum, pounded pork meat and pine nuts. Cook sausage in water and oil with some garum, dill and leeks.
5. STUFFED DORMICE – Ancient Rome
   Prepare a stuffing of dormouse meat or pork, pepper and pine nuts, a tasty broth, asafoetida, and some garum. Stuff the

dormice and sew them up. Bake in oven on a tile. (In 1972, an enterprising chef in Britain revived this recipe, hoping to acquaint modern diners with cuisine of ancient Rome. The results of his mission remain unknown.)

6. FISH SPERM CREPES – France (Pannequets aux laitances)
Spread unsweetened crêpes with a mixture of chopped fish sperm and mushrooms bound with fish-based bechamel sauce. Roll crepes and set in a buttered dish, sprinkle with Parmesan cheese and melted butter; heat dish in a 350° oven until top browns.

7. STUFFED PIG RECTUM SAUSAGE – France (Andouilles de troyes)
Soak a calf's mesentary with the udder of a young beef in cold water, blanch for 30 minutes in boiling water. Dry and cut into small pieces. Sauté a generous amount of chopped mushrooms and some chopped parsley and shallots. Add salt, pepper, nutmeg and a glass of white wine. Remove from heat, and thicken with five egg yolks. Stir in the meat and stuff the mixture into the pig rectum. Tie off both ends, poach sausage for 45 minutes in stock mixed with white wine. Allow to cool in pot.

8. BRAIN FRITTERS – France – (Subrics de cervelle)
Mix small cubes of poached beef brains, chopped buttered spinach (spinach goes well with brain), a crêpe batter and pepper and salt. Fry spoonfuls in hot oil until browned on both sides.

9. RED ANT CHUTNEY – India – (Chindi Chutney)
Collect ants in leaf cups, put directly into the hot ashes of a fire for just a few minutes. Remove ants and make into a paste. Add salt and ground chilli, then bake. This chutney is said to have 'a sharp, clean taste' and is eaten with cocktails and other curries.

10. FERMENTED SHARK – Iceland – (Hakerl)
Schwabe allows that this recipe 'sounds weird', and suggests as an introduction for the family 'shark fillets a la meunière'.

The recipe for fermented shark: Eviscerated sharks are buried in the sand or kept in an open bowl for three years to ferment. The much-prized result resembles in taste a ripe cheese.

11. BEE LARVAE IN COCONUT CREAM – Thailand – (Mang non won)
Marinate larvae, sliced onions and lime leaves in coconut cream with some pepper. Wrap in pieces of linen and steam; serve over rice.

12. KANGAROO RAT RAVIOLI – United States
De-bone kangaroo rats, pass meat through fine blade of grinder. Sauté with bacon fat and garlic. Add chopped cooked spinach or watercress, salt and pepper, and stuff raviolis. (In New Orleans, Louisiana, a variant, alligator and cream cheese ravioli, is served.)

13. CATERPILLAR PRETZELS – Mexico (Gusitanitos di maguey)
Caterpillars of skipper butterflies, which live on the maguey cactus, are toasted or fried and eaten with mescal. Since the maguey is the source of pulque and tequila, 'caterpillar pretzels' are a favourite in Mexico, even available canned.

14. DRAGONFLY NYMPHS – Laos (Mang Por)
Boil dragonfly nymphs. Eat them.

7 Great Sausage Events

1. COMIC SAUSAGE
Epicharmus, a Greek dramatist who lived during the golden age of Sophocles and Aeschylus, wrote a comedy titled *Orya* ('The Sausage') around 500BC. Because the play exists today only as a fragment, we will never know exactly what the Greeks thought was funny about sausage.

2. HEATHEN SAUSAGE
The ancient Romans were so fond of pork sausage spiced with pine nuts and pepper that the dish became a staple of the annual Lupercalian and Floralian festivals. Since these pagan celebrations usually degenerated into orgiastic rites, the early Christians looked upon them with disapproval. When Constantine the Great, a Christian, became emperor in AD324, he outlawed the production and consumption of the sinful sausage. But the Romans refused to cooperate and developed a flourishing black market in sausage. They continued to eat the bootlegged delicacies throughout the reigns of several Christian emperors until the ban was finally lifted.

3. FATAL SAUSAGE
At a simple peasant meal in Wildbad, Germany, in 1793, 13 people shared a single sausage. Within hours they became seriously ill, and six of them died. Their disease became known as botulism – a word coined from the Latin for sausage, *botulus*. The powerfully toxic bacteria *Clostridium botulinum* inside the sausage could have been easily killed by boiling it for two

minutes. Once in the body, botulism toxins attack the nervous system, causing paralysis of all muscles, which brings on death by suffocation.

4. HUMAN SAUSAGE
Adolph Luetgert, a Chicago sausage maker, was so fond of entertaining his mistresses that he had a bed installed in his factory. Louisa Luetgert was aware of her husband's infidelities and, in 1897, their marriage took a dramatic turn for the worse. Louisa subsequently disappeared, and when the police arrived to search Luetgert's factory, they found human teeth and bones – as well as two gold rings engraved 'L.L'. – at the bottom of a sausage vat. During his well-publicised trial, Luetgert maintained his innocence, but he was convicted of murder and spent the rest of his life in prison.

5. MUCKRAKING SAUSAGE
Upton Sinclair's novel *The Jungle*, an exposé of conditions in the Chicago stockyards and meat industry, contained shocking descriptions: 'There was never the least attention paid to what was cut up for sausage . . . there would be meat stored in great piles . . . thousands of rats would race about on it . . . these rats were nuisances, and the packers would put poisoned bread out for them; they would die, and then rats, bread, and meat would go into the hoppers together.' Americans were deeply alarmed by the filth described, and in the same year the book was published, Congress passed the Pure Food and Drug Act of 1906.

6. INSOLENT SAUSAGE
In October 1981, Joseph Guillou, an engineer on the Moroccan tanker *Al Ghassani*, was arrested, fined £50, and sentenced to two years in jail for insulting Morocco's King Hassan. Guillou's offence was hanging a sausage on the hook normally reserved for a portrait of the monarch. A sausage, said Guillou, was 'more useful than a picture of the king'.

7. VICTIM SAUSAGE
During home games at Miller Park, the Milwaukee Brewers baseball team holds 'sausage races' in which people costumed as different types of sausages run around the park between innings. During a game on July 9, 2003, as the runners passed the visiting team's dugout, Randall Simon, the first baseman for the Pittsburgh Pirates, struck the Italian sausage, Mandy Block, with his bat, knocking her to the ground. After the game,

Simon was handcuffed by Milwaukee County sheriff's deputies, taken to a police station, and fined $432 for disorderly conduct. The sausage whacking was broadcast repeatedly, but Block ignored the controversy, accepting Simon's apology. When he returned to Miller Park later in the season, Simon bought Italian sausages for a section of fans. Block was recognised by the National Hot Dog and Sausage Council with a certificate of bravery. 'I'm proud of it,' Block said. 'I didn't even know there was a hot dog council.'

– K.P.

10 Really Unusual Medical Conditions

'Nothing is too wonderful to be true' – Michael Faraday

1. ART ATTACK
   Fine art can really make you sick. Or so says Dr Graziella Magherini, author of *The Stendhal Syndrome*. She has studied more than 100 tourists in Florence, Italy, who became ill in the presence of great works. Their symptoms include heart palpitations, dizziness and stomach pains. The typical sufferer is a single person between the ages of 26 and 40 who rarely leaves home. Dr Magherini believes the syndrome is a result of jet lag, travel stress, and the shock of an overwhelming sense of the past. 'Very often,' she says, 'there's the anguish of death.' The disorder was named after the nineteenth-century French novelist who became overwhelmed by the frescoes in Florence's Santa Croce Church. Particularly upsetting works of art include Michelangelo's statue of David, Caravaggio's painting of Bacchus, and the concentric circles of the Duomo cupola.

2. HULA-HOOP INTESTINE
   On February 26, 1992, Beijing worker Xu Denghai was hospitalised with a 'twisted intestine' after playing excessively with a Hula-hoop. His was the third such case in the several weeks since a Hula-hoop craze had swept China. The Beijing *Evening News* advised people to warm up properly and avoid Hula-hooping immediately after eating.

3. CARROT ADDICTION
   In its August 1992 issue, the highly respected *British Journal of Addiction* described three unusual cases of carrot dependence.

One 40-year-old man had replaced cigarettes with carrots. He ate as many as five bunches a day and thought about them obsessively. According to two Czech psychiatrists, when carrots were withdrawn, he and the other patients 'lapsed into heightened irritability'.

4. CUTLERY CRAVING
The desire to eat metal objects is comparatively common. Occasionally there is an extreme case, such as that of 47-year-old Englishman Allison Johnson. An alcoholic burglar with a compulsion to eat silverware, Johnson has had 30 operations to remove strange things from his stomach. In 1992, he had eight forks and the metal sections of a mop head lodged in his body. He has repeatedly been jailed and then released, each time going immediately to a restaurant and ordering lavishly. Unable to pay, he would then tell the owners to call the police, and eat cutlery until they arrived. Johnson's lawyer said of his client, 'He finds it hard to eat and obviously had difficulty going to the lavatory.'

5. DR STRANGELOVE SYNDROME
Officially known as Alien Hand Syndrome, this bizarre neurological disorder afflicts thousands of people. It is caused by damage to certain parts of the brain, and causes one of a person's hands to act independently of the other and of its owner's wishes. For example, the misbehaving hand may do the opposite of what the normal one is doing: if a person is trying to button a shirt with one hand, the other will follow along and undo the buttons. If one hand pulls up trousers, the other will pull them down. Sometimes the hand may become aggressive – pinching, slapping or punching the patient; in at least one case, it tried to strangle its owner. Says neurologist Rachelle Doody, 'Often a patient will sit on the hand, but eventually it gets loose and starts doing everything again.'

6. MUD WRESTLER'S RASH
Twenty-four men and women wrestled in calf-deep mud at the University of Washington. Within 36 hours, 7 wrestlers were covered with patches of 'pus-filled red bumps similar to pimples', and the rest succumbed later. Bumps were on areas not covered by bathing suits – one unlucky victim had wrestled in the nude. The dermatitis palastraie limosae, or 'muddy wrestling rash', may have been caused by manure-tainted mud.

7. ELECTRIC PEOPLE
According to British paranormalist Hilary Evans, some people are 'upright human [electric] eels, capable of generating

charges strong enough to knock out streetlights and electronic equipment'. Cases of 'electric people' date back to 1786; the most famous is that of 14-year-old Angelique Cottin, whose presence caused compass needles to gyrate wildly. To further investigate this phenomenon, Evans founded SLIDE, the Street Lamp Interference Data Exchange.

8. MARY HART EPILEPSY
The case of Dianne Neale, 49, appeared in the *New England Journal of Medicine*. In a much-publicised 1991 incident, Neale apparently suffered epileptic seizures at hearing the voice of *Entertainment Tonight* co-host Mary Hart. Neale experienced an upset stomach, a sense of pressure in her head, and confusion. Laboratory tests confirmed the abnormal electrical discharges in her brain, and Neale held a press conference to insist that she was not crazy and resented being the object of jokes. She said she bore no hard feelings toward Hart, who apologised on the air for the situation.

In another bizarre case, the theme from the show *Growing Pains* brought 27-year-old Janet Richardson out of a coma. She had been unresponsive for five days after falling out of bed and hitting her head, until, according to her sister, the TV theme 'woke her up'.

9. FOREIGN ACCENT SYNDROME
There are about 50 recorded cases of foreign accent syndrome, in which people who have suffered strokes or other injuries adopt a new accent. For example, Tiffany Roberts of Florida suffered a stroke and then began speaking with an English accent. She even adopted such Anglicisms as 'bloody' and 'loo'. Ms Roberts had never been to Great Britain, and was not a fan of British television shows.

Perhaps the oddest case concerned a Norwegian woman who fell into a coma after being hit on the head by shrapnel during an air raid in 1941. When she woke up, she spoke with a thick German accent. She was then ostracised by her neighbours.

10. UNCOMBABLE HAIR SYNDROME
Also known as 'hair felting', this condition causes hair to form a tangled mass. In a case reported in 1993 in the *Archives of Dermatology*, a 39-year-old woman's hair fell out and was replaced by dry, coarse, curly hair which was so tangled that it was impossible to comb. It lacked knots, kinks or twists that would explain the tangling. The hairs themselves were strangely shaped: the

cross-sections were triangular, grooved, or shaped like kidneys instead of circular. The usual solution to the condition is to cut off the solidified mass of hair. In one case, a woman from Indiana wanted to keep her hair, having spent 24 years growing it. After two and a half months of lubricating her hair with olive oil and separating the strands with knitting needles, her hair returned to normal.

– C.F.

10 Famous Insomniacs

1. MARLENE DIETRICH, actress
Dietrich said that the only thing that lulled her to sleep was a sardine-and-onion sandwich on rye.

2. AMY LOWELL, poet
Whenever she stayed in a hotel, Lowell would hire five rooms – one to sleep in, and empty rooms above, below, and on either side, in order to guarantee quiet.

3. W.C. FIELDS, actor
The aging Fields resorted to unusual methods to go to sleep. He would stretch out in a barber's chair (he had always enjoyed getting haircuts) with towels wrapped around him, until he felt drowsy. Sometimes he could only get to sleep by stretching out on his pool table. On his worst nights, he could only fall asleep under a beach umbrella being sprinkled by a garden hose. He told a friend that 'somehow a moratorium is declared on all my troubles when it is raining'.

4. ALEXANDRE DUMAS, author
Dumas suffered from terrible insomnia, and after trying many remedies, he was advised by a famous doctor to get out of bed when he couldn't sleep. He began to take late-night strolls, and eventually started to sleep through the night.

5. JUDY GARLAND, actress
As a teenager, Garland was prescribed amphetamines to control her weight. As the years went by she took so many that she sometimes stayed up three or four days running. She added sleeping pills to her regime, and her insomnia and addiction increased. She eventually died of a drug overdose.

6. TALLULAH BANKHEAD, actress
Bankhead suffered from severe insomnia. She hired young homosexual 'caddies' to keep her company, and one of their

most important duties was to hold her hand until she drifted off to sleep.

7. FRANZ KAFKA, author
   Kafka, miserable with insomnia, kept a diary detailing his suffering. For October 2, 1911, he wrote, 'Sleepless night. The third in a row. I fall asleep soundly, but after an hour I wake up, as though I had laid my head in the wrong hole.'

8. THEODORE ROOSEVELT, US president
   His insomnia cure was a shot of cognac in a glass of milk.

9. GROUCHO MARX, comic actor
   Marx first began to have insomnia when the stock market crashed in 1929 and he lost $240,000 in 48 hours. When he couldn't sleep, he would phone people up in the middle of the night and insult them.

10. MARK TWAIN, author
    An irritable insomniac, Twain once threw a pillow at the window of his bedroom while he was a guest in a friend's house. When the satisfying crash let in what he thought was fresh air, he fell asleep at last. In the morning he discovered that he had broken a glass-enclosed bookcase.

14 Healthy Insomnia Cures

Do not use these cures without consulting your health practitioner, as every body is different.

1. DRINK A CUP OF CAMOMILE TEA, unless you have an allergy to plants in the ragwort family.
2. TAKE THE DIETARY SUPPLEMENT MELATONIN. In the UK Melatonin is a prescription drug; in America it is available at wholefood stores and pharmacies. It is widely considered an effective and safe sleep aid.
3. TAKE THE AMINO ACID GABA. This safe sleep aid can cause some people to itch the way the B-vitamin Niacin does. Most people, however, find Gaba very soothing.
4. A MUG OF HOT MILK WITH HONEY AND/OR A FEW DROPS OF BRANDY. Though health experts argue, this is a time-honoured remedy which may be effective because it is so comforting.

5. TO NAP OR NOT TO NAP? In certain countries, like Mexico and Italy, napping is a part of life, and seems to be healthy. In America, napping is often regarded as weak or lazy. Naps are usually recommended to be not over two hours maximum, and if you do nap, the important thing is that it be regular.
6. DOZE, REST AND MEDITATE. If you can't fall asleep, these practices are highly restorative for our brains and bodies.
7. MORNING AND EVENING RITUALS. Do you like to read when you wake up, or before bed? Sew buttons? Play solitaire? Whatever you do, it has to be regular.
8. TAKE CALCIUM, MAGNESIUM AND POTASSIUM. These sleep aids, found at pharmacies and wholefood stores, are both soothing and can stop 'restless leg syndrome', which keeps millions of people awake. You can also rub organic balms into your legs.
9. AVOID STIMULANTS SUCH AS TEA AND COFFEE IN THE EVENING – unless: you're used to an after-dinner coffee and it doesn't bother you. Never disrupt a schedule that works.
10. FIND OUT IF YOU HAVE SLEEP APNOEA. Overweight people, or those with sinus problems, may have 'sleep apnoea', a term describing cessation of breath during the night, usually accompanied by heavy snoring. Consult your health practitioner, because there are cures and sleep apnoea prevents you from getting the levels of REM sleep we all need to function healthily.
11. EAT POTATOES, WARM OR ROOM TEMPERATURE, BEFORE BED. Many studies show this to be a wonderful insomnia cure, as are a single candy or pasta. Other studies argue that one should not eat anything three hours before sleep.
12. USE WHITE NOISE. Boxes are available that produce what is called 'white noise', said to be highly effective for some. Alternatively, tapes of tides or soft sounds of nature can send you to sleep.
13. AVOID ANY STRENUOUS EXERCISE THREE HOURS BEFORE BED. Studies have shown that this is the wrong time for aerobic exercise, and will keep you awake.
14. DON'T GO TO SLEEP WITH AN ARGUMENT UNSETTLED. American comedienne Phyllis Diller is often credited with this bit of wisdom, but in truth it is as old as the hills. Do all you

can to make up your fight before sleeping, or at least one of you is likely to have insomnia or even nightmares.

29 Activities and the Calories They Consume

	Activity	Calories per hour
1.	Making mountains out of molehills	500
2.	Running around in circles	350
3.	Wading through paperwork	300
4.	Pushing your luck	250
5.	Eating crow	225
6.	Flying off the handle	225
7.	Jumping on the bandwagon	200
8.	Spinning your wheels	175
9.	Adding fuel to the fire	150
10.	Beating your head against the wall	150
11.	Climbing the walls	150
12.	Jogging your memory	125
13.	Beating your own drum	100
14.	Dragging your heels	100
15.	Jumping to conclusions	100
16.	Beating around the bush	75
17.	Bending over backwards	75
18.	Grasping at straws	75
19.	Pulling out the stoppers	75
20.	Turning the other cheek	75
21.	Fishing for compliments	50
22.	Hitting the nail on the head	50
23.	Pouring salt on a wound	50
24.	Swallowing your pride	50
25.	Throwing your weight around (depending on your weight)	50–300
26.	Passing the buck	25
27.	Tooting your own horn	25
28.	Balancing the books	23
29.	Wrapping it up at day's end	12

Source: *Bulletin*, Columbus Industrial Association, July 11, 1977

Chapter 5

11 EXAMPLES OF UNUSUAL ANIMAL MATING HABITS

10 ANIMALS THAT HAVE EATEN HUMANS

13 PLACES WITH MORE SHEEP THAN HUMANS

4 PLACES WITH MORE PIGS THAN HUMANS

AVERAGE ERECT PENIS LENGTHS FOR 10 SPECIES

THE CAT CAME BACK: 9 CATS WHO TRAVELLED LONG DISTANCES TO RETURN HOME

18 CHILDREN WHO MAY HAVE LIVED WITH WILD ANIMALS

THE DAY OF EXTINCTION FOR 8 BIRDS

8 EXAMPLES OF STRANGE ANIMAL BEHAVIOUR

MAXIMUM RECORDED LIFESPAN OF 58 ANIMALS

7 EXTINCT ANIMALS THAT ARE NO LONGER EXTINCT

11 LARGE ANIMALS DISCOVERED BY WESTERN SCIENCE SINCE 1900

5 OF THE WORLD'S MOST OFT-SIGHTED LAKE AND SEA MONSTERS

5 PIECES OF ADVICE ON HOW TO SURVIVE AN ENCOUNTER WITH A BEAR

10 MOST INTELLIGENT BREEDS OF DOG

10 LEAST INTELLIGENT BREEDS OF DOG

Animals

© G. R. Guy

PENGUINS MATING – see p.126

11 Examples of Unusual Animal Mating Habits

1. PENGUINS

   Penguins prefer to be 'married', but they suffer long separations due to their migratory habits. When reunited, a pair will stand breast to breast, heads thrown back, singing loudly, with outstretched flippers trembling. Two weeks after a pair is formed, their union is consummated. The male makes his intentions known by laying his head across his partner's stomach. They go on a long trek to find privacy, but the actual process of intercourse takes only three minutes. Neither penguin will mate again that year.

   The male Adele penguin must select his mate from a colony of more than a million, and he indicates his choice by rolling a stone at the female's feet. Stones are scarce at mating time because many are needed to build walls around nests. It becomes commonplace for penguins to steal them from one another. If she accepts this gift, they stand belly to belly and sing a mating song.

2. HIPPOPOTAMI

   Hippos have their own form of aromatherapy. Hippos attract mates by marking territory, urinating and defecating at the same time. Then, an enamoured hippo will twirl its tail like a propellor to spread this delicious slop in every direction. This attracts lovers, and a pair will begin foreplay, which consists of playing by splashing around in the water before settling down to business.

3. THE MALE UGANDA KOB

   Exhaustion is the frequent fate of the male Uganda kob, an African antelope. Like many species of birds and mammals, the kob roams in a social group until the mating season, when the dominant male establishes a mating territory, or lek. But the females decide which territory they wish to enter and then pick the male they think most attractive. He then mates with all the females until he is too weak to continue (usually due to lack of food) and is replaced by another.

4. SQUID

   Squid begin mating with a circling nuptial dance. Teams of squid revolve around across a 'spawning bed' 200 metres in diameter. At daybreak they begin having sex and continue all day long – they only take a break so the female can drive down and deposit eggs. When she returns to the circle, the two go at it again. As twilight falls, the pair go offshore to eat and rest. At the first sign of sunlight, they return to their spot and do it all over again. This routine can last up to two weeks, ensuring a healthy population of squid.

5. PORCUPINES

The answer to one of our oldest jokes: 'How do porcupines do it?' 'Veeery carefully!' is not quite true. The truth is more bizarre than dangerous. Females are only receptive for a few hours a year. As summer approaches, young females become nervous and very excited. Next, they go off their food, and stick close by the males and mope. Meanwhile the male becomes aggressive with other males, and begins a period of carefully sniffing every place the female of his choice urinates, smelling her all over. This is a tremendous aphrodisiac. While she is sulking by his side, he begins to 'sing'.

When he is ready to make love, the female runs away if she's not ready. If she is in the mood, they both rear up and face each other, belly-to-belly. Then, males spray their ladies with a tremendous stream of urine, soaking their loved one from head to foot – the stream can shoot as far as 7 feet.

If they're not ready, females respond by 1) objecting verbally 2) hitting with front paws like boxers 3) trying to bite 4) shaking off the urine. When ready, they accept the bath. This routine can go on for weeks. Six months after the beginning of courtship, the female will accept any male she has been close to. The spines and quills of both go relaxed and flat, and the male enters from behind. Mating continues until the male is worn out. Every time he tries to stop, the female wants to continue. If he has given up, she chooses another partner, only now *she* acts out the male role. To 'cool off', females engage in the same courtship series, step-by-step, in reverse order.

It is advised never to stand close to a cage that contains courting porcupines.

6. GEESE

Two male geese may form a homosexual bond and prefer each other's company to any female's. Sometimes, however, a female may interpose herself between them during such a courtship, and be quickly fertilised. They will accept her, and weeks later the happy family of three can be seen attending to its tiny newborn goslings.

7. WHITE-FRONTED PARROTS
These birds, native to Mexico and and Central America, are believed to be the only species besides humans to kiss. Before actually mating, male and female will lock their beaks and gently flick their tongues together. If kissing is satisfying for both parties, the male boldly takes the next step, by regurgitating his food for his girlfriend, to show his love. White-fronted parrots also share parenting, unlike many other species. When the female lays her one egg, both parents take turns incubating it. When the baby hatches, the couple feed and care for their offspring together.

8. GRASSHOPPERS
Why are grasshoppers so noisy? It's because they're singing to woo their partners. They have as many as 400 distinct songs, which they sing during their courtship and mating cycles. Some males have a different song for each distinct mating period – for example, there may be a flirting song, then a mating song.

9. SEAGULLS
Lesbian mating is practised by between 8% and 14% of the seagulls on the Santa Barbara islands, off the California coast. Lesbian gulls go through all the motions of mating, and they lay sterile eggs. Homosexual behaviour is also known in geese, ostriches, cichlid fish, squid, rats and monkeys.

10. RED-SIDED GARTER SNAKES
These snakes are small and poisonous, and live in Canada and the Northwestern United States. Their highly unusual mating takes place during an enormous orgy. Twenty-five thousand snakes slither together in a large den, eager to copulate. In that pile, one female may have as many as 100 males vying for her. These 'nesting balls' grow as large as two feet high. Now and then a female is crushed under the heavy mound – and the males are so randy that they continue to copulate, becoming the only necrophiliac snakes!

11. LYNX SPIDERS
When a male lynx spider feels the urge, he will capture his beauty in his web and wrap her in silk. Offering her this elegant meal (the silken web) is his way of wooing. When the mood is right, the female, distracted by her feast, will allow her suitor to mount her and begin mating. Oblivious, she ignores him and enjoys her supper.

10 Animals That Have Eaten Humans

1. BEARS
The North American bear, although smaller and less aggressive than the grizzly, can be deadly and has been responsible for many harmful attacks on humans. In 1963, when the Alaskan blueberry crop was poor, hungry black bears attacked at least four people, one of whom they killed.

2. CROCODILES
Estuarine crocodiles are the most prolific man-eaters on earth, killing approximately 2,000 people a year. On the night of February 19, 1945, they were responsible for the most devastating animal attack on human beings in recorded history. British troops had trapped 1,000 Japanese infantrymen, many of whom were wounded, in a swampy area in the Bay of Bengal. The noise of gunfire and the smell of blood attracted hundreds of crocodiles, and by evening the British could hear terrible screams. The following morning, only 20 Japanese were found alive.

3. GIANT SQUID
The giant squid is the most highly developed of the invertebrates. Its eyes are almost exact replicas of human eyes. It has 10 arms, and its body can reach up to 65 feet in length. Often confused with the octopus, which attacks humans only when threatened, the giant squid is a carnivorous predator. One notable incident occurred on March 25, 1941, when the British ship *Britannia* sank in the Atlantic Ocean. As a dozen survivors clung to their lifeboat, a giant squid reached its arms around the body of a man and pulled him below. Male squid sometimes eat the female after mating.

4. KOMODO DRAGON
The world's largest lizard, the Komodo dragon can reach 10 feet in length and weigh more than 300 pounds. They are the top predators on the handful of Indonesian islands where they live. Their prey normally consists of deer, wild goats and pigs, but they will eat anything they can catch, including the occasional human. Komodo dragons devour their prey completely, including the bones. All that was left of a French tourist killed in 1986 was his blood-stained shoes. All that was left of a German tourist eaten in 1988 was his mangled glasses.

5. **LEOPARDS**
Considered one of the most dangerous animals to hunt, the leopard is quick and stealthy and is seldom observed. In the central provinces of India, leopards have been known to invade native huts to find their prey. One, known as the Panawar man-eater, is reputed to have killed 400 people. It was shot in 1910 by Jim Corbett, who also killed the Champawat man-eating tigress the following year.

6. **LIONS**
Like tigers, lions do not usually attack humans. Man-eating lions usually hunt in prides, or groups, although occasionally single lions and pairs have become man-eaters. In October 1943, a lone lion was shot in the Kasama District of what is now Zambia after it had killed 40 people.

7. **PUMA (MOUNTAIN LION)**
Pumas have been known to catch prey seven to eight times their own size: a 100-lb female has been seen killing an 800-lb bull elk. In recent years, as people have built subdivisions in the mountains of the Western US, attacks by pumas on humans have exploded. Since 1970, there have been more than 40 attacks, at least 7 of them fatal. In 1994, two female joggers in California were killed and partly consumed by female pumas.

8. **PYTHON**
Pythons are quite capable of killing people, and several such incidents have been reported since they became a trendy pet in the 1990s. However, most reports of pythons actually eating humans have proven untrue. A picture circulating on the internet of a boy allegedly recovered from a python's digestive tract is a hoax. However, there is at least one credible report. In 1992, a group of children playing in a mango plantation near Durban, South Africa, was attacked by a 20-foot rock python, which swallowed one of them. Craig Smith, the owner of a snake park, declared, 'I've dealt with a few cases like this and I always dispel them as absolute rubbish. But in my opinion this one did happen.'

9. **SHARKS**
Of the 200 to 250 species of shark, only 18 are known to be dangerous to humans. The most notable are the great white, the mako, the tiger, the white-tipped, the Ganges River, and the hammerhead. The best-known of all individual 'rogue' shark

attacks occurred on July 12, 1916. Twelve-year-old Lester Stilwell was swimming in Matawan Creek, New Jersey, 15 to 20 miles inland, when he was attacked by a great white shark. Both he and his would-be rescuer were killed. In 10 days four people were killed over a 60-mile stretch of the New Jersey coast. Two days after the last attack, an 8½ foot great white was netted just 4 miles from the mouth of the creek. According to the Florida Museum of Natural History, between 1670 and 2003 there were 833 confirmed unprovoked shark attacks in the United States, 52 of which were fatal.

10. TIGERS
A tigress known as the Champawat man-eater killed 438 people in the Himalayas in Nepal between 1903 and 1911. Tigers do not usually hunt humans, unless the animals are old, or injured, or have become accustomed to the taste of human flesh.

Note: AND TWO WHO WOULD NOT
While it is almost certain that wolves have preyed on human beings at some time in history, there are no confirmed reports of unprovoked attacks on humans by North American wolves. Likewise, there are no confirmed reports of piranha-caused deaths. Observers in the river regions of northeastern South America do report that many natives have lost fingers, toes or penny-sized chunks of flesh while bathing in piranha-infested waters. A school of piranhas can strip a wounded alligator of flesh in five minutes, but they are generally sluggish in their movements.

– D.L. & C.F.

13 Places With More Sheep Than Humans

		Sheep	Humans
1.	Australia	98,200,000	19,731,000
2.	Sudan	47,000,000	33,610,000
3.	New Zealand	39,250,000	3,875,000
4.	Mongolia	11,797,000	2,594,000
5.	Uruguay	9,780,000	3,415,000
6.	Mauritania	8,700,000	2,893,000
7.	Turkmenistan	6,000,000	4,867,000
8.	Ireland	4,828,500	3,956,000

9.	Namibia	2,370,000	1,987,000
10.	Falkland Islands	690,000	3,000
11.	Iceland	470,000	290,000
12.	Faeroe Islands	68,100	46,000
13.	Montserrat	4,700	4,000

World Sheep Population: 1,024,039,610

Source: Food and Agriculture Organization of the United Nations, FAOSTAT, 2003

4 Places With More Pigs Than Humans

		Pigs	Humans
1.	Denmark	12,984,944	5,364,000
2.	Samoa	201,000	178,000
3.	Wallis and Futuna Islands	29,000	14,000
4.	Tuvalu	13,200	10,000

World Pig Population: 956,016,932
Source: Food and Agriculture Organization of the United Nations, FAOSTAT, 2003

Average Erect Penis Lengths for 10 Species

Animal	Average erect penis length
1. Humpback whale	10 ft
2. Elephant	5–6 ft
3. Bull	3 ft
4. Stallion	2 ft 6 in.
5. Rhinoceros	2 ft
6. Pig	18–20 in.
7. Man	6 in.
8. Gorilla	2 in.
9. Cat	¾ in.
10. Mosquito	1/100 in.

Source: Leigh Rutledge, *The Gay Book of Lists* (Boston: Alyson Publication, 1987)

The Cat Came Back: 9 Cats Who Travelled Long Distances to Return Home

1. SUGAR – 1,500 miles
   Sugar, a two-year-old part-Persian, had a hip deformity that made her uncomfortable during car travel. Consequently, she was left behind with a neighbour when her family left Anderson, California, for Gage, Oklahoma. Two weeks later, Sugar disappeared. Fourteen months later, she turned up in Gage on her old owner's doorstep – having travelled 100 miles a month to reach a place she had never been. The case was investigated in person by the famous parapsychologist J.B. Rhine, who observed Sugar and interviewed witnesses.

2. MINOSCH – 1,500 miles
   In 1981 Mehmet Tunc, a Turkish 'guest worker' in Germany, went home with his cat and family for a vacation. At the Turkish border, Minosch disappeared. Sixty-one days later, back on the island of Sylt, in northern Germany, the family heard a faint scratching at the door. It was a bedraggled Minosch.

3. SILKY – 1,472 miles
   Shaun Philips, and his father, Ken, lost Silky at Gin Gin, about 200 miles north of Brisbane, Australia. That was in the summer of 1977. On March 28, 1978, Silky turn up at Mr Philips's house in a Melbourne suburb. According to his owner, 'he was as thin as a wisp and stank to high heavens'.

4. HOWIE – 1,200 miles
   In 1978, this three-year-old Persian walked home from the Gold Coast in Queensland, Australia, to Adelaide – a trip that took a year. Said his owner, Kirsten Hicks, 15, 'although its white coat was matted and filthy and its paws were sore and bleeding, Howie was actually purring'.

5. RUSTY – 950 miles
   Rusty distinguished himself by setting an American all-time speed record for a cat return. In 1949 this ginger tom travelled from Boston, Massachusetts, to Chicago, Illinois, in 83 days. It is speculated that he hitched rides on cars, lorries and trains.

6. NINJA – 850 miles
Brent Todd and his family moved from Farmington, Utah, to Mill Creek, a suburb of Seattle, Washington, in April, 1996, taking with them their eight-year-old tomcat, Ninja. After a week, Ninja jumped over the fence of the new yard and disappeared. More than a year later, on May 25, 1997, Ninja turned up on the porch of the Todds' former home in Farmington, waiting to be let inside and fed. He was thin and scraggly, but his distinctive caterwaul was recognised by the Todds' former neighbours, Marilyn and John Parker. Mrs Parker offered to send Ninja back to the Todds, but they decided to let him stay.

7. ERNIE – 600 miles
In September 1994, Ernie jumped from the truck of Chris and Jennifer Trevino while it was travelling 60 mph down the highway 600 miles west of their home. A week later, Ernie showed up at the Trevinos' home in Victoria, Texas. When Mrs Trevino called the cat by name, he came forward and rubbed his face against Mr Trevino's leg.

8. GRINGO – 480 miles
The Servoz family lost their pet tom, Gringo, from their home in Lamarche-sur-Seine, France, in December 1982. The following July they learned that the cat had moved to the French Riviera. Wishing to escape the cold winter, he had made the journey south in a week and appeared at their summer home, where neighbours took care of him.

9. MUDDY WATER WHITE – 450 miles
On June 23 or 24, 1985, Muddy Water White jumped out of a van driven by his owner, Barbara Paule, in Dayton, Ohio. Almost exactly three years later, he returned to his home in Pennsylvania. 'He came and just flopped down like he was home,' said Mrs Paule. She fed him for three days before realising he was Muddy Water White, an identification that was confirmed by the local vet.

18 Children Who May Have Lived With Wild Animals

1.-2. ROMULUS AND REMUS (8th century BC)
Twin brothers Romulus and Remus were allegedly raised by a wolf after being abandoned in the countryside by their uncle. A number of years later they were rescued by a shepherd, and

they went on to found the city of Rome in 753 BC. Scholars long considered their childhood adventures to be mythical, but recent studies of children known to have lived with animals have demonstrated that they could well be an element of truth to the Romulus and Remus legend.

3. HESSIAN WOLF-BOY (1344)
In 1344, hunters in the German Kingdom of Hesse captured a boy between 7 and 12 years of age who had been living in the wild. Wolves had brought him food and dug holes to shelter him at night. The boy ran on all fours and had an extraordinary ability to leap long distances. Treated as a freak by his human captors, he died shortly after his return to civilization because of an enforced diet of cooked food.

4. LITHUANIAN BEAR-BOY (1661)
In 1661, in a Lithuanian forest, a party of hunters discovered a boy living with a group of bears. The hunters captured him even though he resisted by biting and clawing them. Taken to Warsaw, Poland, and christened Joseph, the boy continued to eat raw meat and graze on grass. Although he never dropped the habit of growling like a bear, Joseph acquired a limited vocabulary and became the servant of a Polish nobleman.

5. IRISH SHEEP-BOY (1672)
In 1672 a 16-year-old boy was found trapped in a hunter's net in the hills of southern Ireland. Since running away from his parents' home as a young child, the boy had lived with a herd of wild sheep. He was healthy and muscular even though he ate only grass and hay. After his capture he was taken to the Netherlands, where he was cared for in Amsterdam by Dr Nicholas Tulp. The boy never learned human speech, but continued to bleat like a sheep throughout his life.

6. FRAUMARK BEAR-GIRL (1767)
In 1767 two hunters captured a girl who attacked them after they shot her bear companion in the mountains near the village of Fraumark, Hungary. The tall, muscular 18-year-old girl had lived with bears since infancy. Later she was locked up in an asylum in the town of Karpfen because she refused to wear clothes or eat anything but raw meat and tree bark.

7. WILD BOY OF AVEYRON (1800)
In 1800 hunters captured a 17-year-old boy who had lived alone in the forest of Aveyron, France, since he was an infant. Given

the name Victor, the boy was not happy living in civilised society and repeatedly tried to escape. He also growled and gnashed his teeth at first, but later became adjusted to being with humans. When he died at the age of 40, he had learned only three words.

8. DINA SANICHAR (1867)
In 1867, a hunting party found a seven-year-old boy living with wolves in a cave in the jungles of Bulandshahr, India. Taken to the Sekandra Orphanage near Agra and given the name Dina Sanichar, the boy refused to wear clothes and sharpened his teeth by gnawing on bones. For 28 years he lived at the orphanage, but he never learned to talk. In 1895 he died of tuberculosis aggravated by the one human habit he had adopted – smoking tobacco.

9. WILLIAM MILDIN (1883)
An intriguing but not fully substantiated case is that of Englishman William Milding, the 14th Earl of Streatham. (One authority believes the name of this child was actually William Russell.) Shipwrecked on the West African coast at the age of 11 in 1868, Mildin lived with apes for 15 years before being discovered and returned to England. Mildin may have inspired Edgar Rice Burroughs to create his most famous character – Tarzan of the Apes.

10.-11. AMALA AND KAMALA (1920)
In October 1920, the Reverend J.A.L. Singh captured two girls, one about three years old and the other about five, who had lived with a pack of wolves near the village of Midnapore, India. Named Amala and Kamala by Singh, the girls were mute except for occasional growling sounds, walked on all fours and loved to eat raw meat. After a year in civilization, Amala died. Kamala eventually acquired a 45-word vocabulary before her death in 1929.

12. TARZANCITO (1933)
In December 1933, a woodcutter captured a boy about five years of age in the jungles of Ahuachapan Province in El Salvador. The boy, nicknamed 'Tarzancito', had lived alone since infancy, subsisting on a diet of wild fruit and raw fish. Newspaper correspondent Ernie Pyle, who met Tarzancito, reported that when the boy first returned to human society, he communicated by howling and frequently attacked and bit people. Eventually Tarzancito learned to talked and adjusted to human life.

13. CACHARI LEOPARD-BOY (1938)

In 1938 an English sportsman found an eight-year-old boy living with a leopard and her cubs in the north Cachar Hills of India. The boy, who had been carried off by the leopard five years earlier, was returned to his family of peasant farmers. Although nearly blind, he could identify different individuals and objects by his extremely well-developed sense of smell.

14. MISHA DEFONESCA (1945)

When she was seven years old, Misha's mother and father were seized by Nazis. She was hidden in a safe house, but, worried that she might be turned over the Germans, she ran off and lived in the wild. For the next four years, as World War II raged, Defonesca wandered through Europe, covering more than 3,000 miles. During this time she lived on raw berries, raw meat and food stolen from farmhouses. On occasion, she lived with packs of wolves. She later recalled: 'In all my travels, the only time I ever slept deeply was when I was with wolves . . . The days with my wolf family multiplied. I have no idea how many months I spent with them, but I wanted it to last forever – it was far better than returning to the world of my own kind . . . Those were the most beautiful days I had ever experienced.'

15. SAHARAN GAZELLE BOY (1960)

In September, 1960, Basque poet Jean Claude Armen discovered and observed a boy who was approximately eight years old living with a herd of gazelles in the desert regions of the Western Sahara. For two months Armen studied the boy, whom he speculated was the orphaned child of some nomadic Saharan Moorish family. The boy travelled on all fours, grazed on grass dug roots, and seemed to be thoroughly accepted by the gazelles as a member of the herd. Since the boy appeared happy, Armen left him with his gazelle family. American soldiers attempted to capture the boy in 1966 and 1970, but without success.

16. SHAMDEO THE WOLF BOY (1972)

This boy was taken to the Catholic mission at Sultanpur, a town in Punjab, India, by a man who allegedly had found him living in a forest with wolves. The boy, estimated to be three or four years old at the time, was covered with matted hair and had calluses on his elbows, palms, and knees. According to Father Joseph de Souza, Shamdeo learned to stand upright in five months, and within two years he was doing chores around the mission. He communicated by sign language. Father Joseph also noted that the boy no longer caught and ate live chickens, but he was still drawn by the scent of blood. That Shamdeo actually lived with wolves has not been authenticated.

17. JOHN SSEBUNYA (1991)
In 1991, Ugandan villagers treed and captured a little boy living with a pack of monkeys. One of the villagers identified the child as John Ssebunya, who had fled the village three years earlier when his father had murdered his mother and then disappeared. John was adopted by Paul and Molly Wasswa, who ran an orphanage. Several experts who studied John were convinced that John really had lived with monkeys. When left with a group of monkeys, he approached them from the side with open palms in classic simian fashion. He also had an unusual lopsided gait and pulled his lips back when he smiled. He tended to greet people with a powerful hug, the way that monkeys greet each other. After some time in the orphanage, John learned to talk and to sing. In 1999, he visited Great Britain as part of the Pearl of Africa Children's Choir. That same year, he was the subject of a BBC documentary, *Living Proof*.

18. BELLO OF NIGERIA (1996)
In 1996, a boy about two years of age was found by hunters living with chimps in the Folgore forest in Nigeria. He was taken to the Maliki Torrey children's home where the staff named him Bello. Mentally and physically disabled, with a misshapen forehead, sloping right shoulder and protruding chest, he was apparently abandoned by his parents, members of the nomadic Fulari tribe. When he first arrived at the home, Bello walked like a chimp, moving on his hind legs and dragging his feet on the ground. As of 2002, he still could not speak, but made chimp-like noises.

– R.J.F. & C.F.

The Day of Extinction for 8 Birds

1. GREAT AUK, 3 JUNE, 1844
The great auk was a large, flightless bird which lived in the Arctic regions of the North Atlantic. It was the first bird known as a 'penguin' and, when explorers from the northern hemisphere came across the similar but unrelated species in the Antarctic, they transferred the name to the new bird. The last recorded breeding place of the great auk was Eldey Island, off the coast of Iceland. At the beginning of June 1844, three men,

part of an expedition funded by an Icelandic bird collector called Carl Siemsen, landed on the island. They found and killed two auks among other birds gathered on the island's cliffs and took away an egg, which was later sold to an apothecary in Rykjavik for £9. There has since been no confirmed sighting of a great auk on Eldey Island or anywhere else.

2. LABRADOR DUCK, DECEMBER 12, 1872
A small black and white duck indigenous to North America, the Labrador was considered to be a strong and hardy species, and its decline is still mysterious. The duck bred on the east coast of Canada but flew as far south as Philadelphia in the summer. Hunting no doubt contributed to its demise. The last reported Labrador duck was shot down over Long Island in 1872.

3. GUADALUPE ISLAND CARCARA, DECEMBER 1, 1900
A large brown hawk with a black head and grey striped wings, the caracara was last seen alive and collected by R.H. Beck in 1900. One of the few cases where a bird was deliberately exterminated, the caracara was poisoned and shot by goatherds, who thought it was killing the kids in their herds.

4. PASSENGER PIGEON, SEPTEMBER 1, 1914
These brownish-gray pigeons were once so numerous that a passing flock could darken the sky for days. As recently as 1810, an estimated 2 billion pigeons were sighted in one flock. But massive hunting by settlers and a century of forest destruction eliminated the passenger and its native forest habitat. In 1869, 7,500,000 pigeons were captured in a single nesting raid. In 1909, a $1,500 reward was offered for a live nesting pair, but no one could be found. Martha, the last of the passenger pigeons, died of old age in 1914 in the Cincinnati Zoo.

5. CAROLINA PARAKEET, FEBRUARY 21, 1918
The striking green and yellow Carolina parakeet was once common in the forests of the eastern and southern US, but because of the widespread crop destruction it caused, farmers hunted the bird to extinction. The last Carolina parakeet, an old male named Incas, died in the Cincinnati Zoo. The zoo's general manager believed it died of grief over the loss of Lady Jane, its mate of 30 years, the previous summer.

6. HEATH HEN, MARCH 11, 1932
An east coast US relative of the prairie chicken, the heath hen was once so common around Boston that servants sometimes

stipulated before accepting employment that heath hen not be served to them more than a few times a week. But the bird was hunted to extinction, and the last heath hen, alone since December 1928, passed away in Martha's Vineyard at the age of eight, after the harsh winter 1932.

7. EULER'S FLYCATCHER, SEPTEMBER 26, 1955
Known only from two specimens and one sighting, Euler's flycatcher was an 8½-inch olive and dusky yellow bird. The flycatcher was believed by James Bond (the authority of Caribbean birds, not Ian Fleming's 007) to have perished on Jamaica in 1955 during Hurricane Janet.

8. DUSKY SEASIDE SPARROW, JUNE 18, 1987
This sparrow was once common in the marshes of Merritt Island, Florida, and along the nearby St John's River. In the 1960s, Merritt Island was flooded to deal with the mosquito problem at the Kennedy Space Center, while the marshes along the St John's were drained for highway construction. Pesticides and pollution also contributed to the bird's demise. In 1977, the last five dusky seaside sparrows were captured. Unfortunately, they were all male, with no female to perpetuate the species. The five were relocated to Disney World's Discovery Island to live out their last days. The last one, an aged male blind in one eye, named Orange Band, died ten years later.

– D.L.

8 Examples of Strange Animal Behaviour

1. GENTLE CROCODILES
Nile crocodiles, although physically and morally capable of killing humans, are tender guardians of their own babies. Newborn crocodiles average 28 cm (11 inches) in length and weigh 100 grams (3½ ounces) – tempting prey for a wide range of predators. To protect them when they emerge from their shells, a mother crocodile delicately picks up the hatchlings with her deadly jaws and slips them into a pouch inside her mouth. Then she carries the chirping babies to the water where they are greeted by a roaring chorus from the adult males.

2. **TRANSFORMER FROGS**
The female gastric brooding frog (Rheobatrachus silus), which flourished in Queensland, Australia, until its recent extinction, swallowed her fertilised eggs, transformed her stomach into a uterus, carried the developing tadpoles in her stomach, and then gave birth to fully formed young through her mouth.

3. **FARMER ANTS**
Aphids produce a sugary excrement, which has come to be known as honeydew, by licking the leaves and stems on which it has fallen. But some ant species have learned to gather the aphids into their nests, feed them, and then when the ants are hungry, to stroke the aphids with their feelers so that they produce the honeydew, which the ants then drink fresh.

4. **INCESTUOUS MITES**
The female mite known as Histiostoma murchiei creates her own husband from scratch. She lays eggs that turn into adults without needing to be fertilised. The mother then copulates with her sons within three of four days of laying the eggs, after which the sons die rather quickly.

5. **NON-NURTURING CUCKOOS**
Female cuckoos deposit their eggs in the nests of other birds, who then incubate the eggs and raise the offspring until they are able to fly away on their own. Curiously, each individual cuckoo mother chooses the same species to adopt all of her children and is able to lay eggs that resemble the eggs of the foster family.

6. **CODEPENDENT ANGLER FISH**
As soon as they mature sexually, male angler fish begin a desperate search to find a mate in the dark water 6,000 feet below the surface. As soon as they locate likely prospects, certain species of angler fish attach themselves to the females – literally. The male latches on to the much larger female and never lets go for the rest of his life. In fact, their vascular systems become united and the male becomes entirely dependent on the female's blood for nutrition. In exchange, the male provides the female with sperm.

7. **CHILD-LABOURING ANTS**
Several species of tree ants in Southeast Asia have evolved a bizarre method for building their nests. While one brigade of ants holds together two leaves, another brigade grabs hold of ant larvae and squeezes out of their young bodies a sticky thread that is used to hold together the edges of the leaves.

8. TORTURING, MURDEROUS WASPS
Ichneumon wasps are the sort of beings that inspire horror films. At the worst, an ichneumon mother picks a victim, usually a caterpillar, and injects her eggs into the host's body. Often she also injects a poison that paralyses the victim without killing it. When the eggs hatch, the wasp larvae begin eating the caterpillar. Because a dead caterpillar would be useless to developing wasps, they contrive to keep the unfortunate victim alive as long as possible by eating its fatty deposits and digestive organs first and saving the heart and central nervous system for last.

Maximum Recorded Lifespan of 58 Animals

1.	Tortoise	188 years
2.	Lake Sturgeon	152 years
3.	Human	122 years, 5 months
4.	Fin Whale	116 years
5.	Blue Whale	110 years
6.	Humpback Whale	95 years
7.	Elephant (African)	80 years
8.	Turtle (eastern box)	75 years
9.	Parrot (African grey)	73 years
10.	Alligator	66 years
11.	Horse	62 years
12.	Chimpanzee	59 years, 5 months
13.	Orangutan	59 years
14.	Eagle (eastern imperial)	56 years
15.	Seal (Baikal)	56 years
16.	Hippopotamus	54 years, 4 months
17.	Gorilla	54 years
18.	Camel	50 years
19.	Grizzly Bear	50 years
20.	Rhinoceros (Indian)	49 years
21.	Brown Bear	47 years
22.	Condor (California)	45 years
23.	Goldfish	43 years
24.	Hyena (spotted)	41 years, 1 month
25.	Boa constrictor	40 years, 3 months
26.	Vulture	39 years
27.	Polar Bear	38 years, 2 months
28.	Giraffe	36 years, 4 months

29. Dolphin	35 years
30. Rhinoceros (Sumatran)	35 years
31. Cat	34 years
32. Ant (queen)	30 years
33. Kangaroo (red)	30 years
34. Panda (giant)	30 years
35. Dog	29 years, 6 months
36. Lion	29 years
37. Porcupine (Old World)	27 years, 4 months
38. Tiger	26 years, 4 months
39. Wombat	26 years, 1 month
40. Aardvark	24 years
41. Sheep	24 years
42. Jaguar	22 years
43. Raccoon	20 years, 7 months
44. Frog	20 years
45. Koala	20 years
46. Porcupine (normal)	20 years
47. Vampire Bat	19 years, 6 months
48. Pigeon	18 years, 6 months
49. Rabbit	18 years
50. Duck-billed Platypus	17 years
51. Guinea Pig	14 years, 10 months
52. Hedgehog	14 years
53. Shrew (non-human)	12 years
54. Hamster	10 years
55. Gopher (eastern pocket)	7 years, 2 months
56. Anchovy	7 years
57. Partridge	6 years, 3 months
58. Mole	5 years

Primary Source: Max Planck Institute web site http://www.demogr.mpg.de/; also *Longevity Records: Life Spans of Mammals, Birds, Amphibians, Reptiles, and Fish*, by James R. Carey and Debra S. Judge

7 Extinct Animals That Are No Longer Extinct

1. CAHOW
   This ocean-wandering bird nested exclusively on the islets of Bermuda. Also known as the Bermuda petrel, the last of the cahows was believed to have been killed during the famine of

1615, when British colonists built cook-fires into which the unwary cahows flew by the thousand. On January 8, 1951, the cahow was rediscovered by Bermuda's conservation officer, David Wingate. Under his protection, the existing 18 birds were encouraged to breed, and now number more than 150.

2. DIBBLER

A marsupial mouse, the dibbler was listed as extinct in 1884. In 1967 an Australian naturalist hoping to trap live honey possums, caught instead a pair of dibblers. The female of the captured pair soon produced a litter of eight, and they were then bred in captivity.

3. DWARF LEMUR

The last known dwarf lemur was reported in 1875, and was regarded as extinct. Then in 1966 the small tree-dwelling marsupial was once again seen, near the city of Mananara, Madagascar.

4. MOUNTAIN PYGMY POSSUM

This small marsupial was considered to have been extinct for 20,000 years until Dr Kenneth Shortman caught one in the kitchen of his skiing lodge, Mount Hothan, in southeast Australia in 1966. Three more of the tiny possums were discovered in 1970.

5.-6. TARPAN and AUROCHS

A primeval forest horse of central Asia and long extinct, the tarpan was recreated by brothers Lutz and Heinz Heck, curators of the Berlin and Munich zoos, respectively. By selective crossbreeding of Polish primitive horses with Swedish Gotlands, Icelandic ponies and Polish Konik mares, they created a strain of wild horse identical in appearance to what we know of the mouse-gray tarpan. The first colt was born on May 22, 1933. By this same method, the aurochs, a European wild ox which died out in Poland in 1627, have also been duplicated.

7. WHITE-WINGED GUAN

A flower-eating South American bird, the guan was thought extinct for a century until sighted in September of 1977. An American ornithologist and his Peruvian associate located four of the pheasant-sised birds in remote northwestern Peru.

– D.L.

11 Large Animals Discovered by Western Science Since 1900

In 1812, the 'Father of Paleontology', Baron Georges Cuvier, rashly pronounced that 'there is little hope of discovering a new species' of large animals and that naturalists should concentrate on extinct fauna. In 1819 the American tapir was discovered, and since then a long list of 'new' animals has disproved Cuvier's dictum.

1. OKAPI
   By saving a group of Congolese Pygmies from a German showman who wanted to take them to the 1900 Paris Exhibition, Sir Harry Johnston gained their trust. He then began hearing stories about the okapi, a mule-sized animal with zebra stripes. In 1901, Sir Harry sent a whole skin, two skulls and a detailed description of the okapi to London, and it was found that the okapi had a close relationship to the giraffe. In 1919, the first live okapi were brought out of the Congo River basin, and in 1941, the Stanleyville Zoo witnessed the first birth of an okapi in captivity. The okapis, striking in appearance, are now rare but popular attractions at the larger, more progressive zoological parks of the world.

2. MOUNTAIN NYALA
   First discovered in the high mountains of southern Ethiopia in 1910, the mountain nyala remains a relatively unknown species. The male has gently twisting horns almost 4 ft long and can weigh up to 450 lb. The coat is a majestically greyish-brown, with white vertical stripes on the back. After it was described by Richard Lydekker, the eminent British naturalist, it was ruthlessly hunted by field biologists and trophy seekers through some of the most inhospitable terrain in existence. The mountain nyala lives in the Arussi and Bale mountains at heights above 9,000 ft, where the sun burns hotly in the day and the night temperatures fall to freezing. Its existence is presently threatened by illegal hunting.

3. PYGMY HIPPOPOTAMUS
   Karl Hagenbeck, a famous German animal dealer, established a zoological garden near Hamburg that was the prototype of the modern open-air zoo. In 1909, Hagenbeck send German explorer Hans Schomburgk to Liberia to check on rumours about a 'giant black pig'. After two years of jungle pursuit, Schomburgk finally spotted the animal 30 ft in front of him. It was big, shiny and

black, but the animal was clearly related to the hippopotamus, not the pig. Unable to catch it, he went home to Hamburg empty-handed. In 1912, Hans Schomburgk returned to Liberia, and to the dismay of his critics, came back with five live pygmy hippos. A full-grown pygmy hippopotamus weighs only about 400 lb, a tenth of the weight of the average adult hippopotamus.

4. KOMODO DRAGON
These giant monitor lizards are named for the rugged volcanic island of Komodo, part of the Lesser Sunda Islands of Indonesia. Unknown to science until 1912, the Komodo dragon can be up to 12 ft long and weigh over 350 lb. The discovery of the giant lizard was made by an airman who landed on Komodo island and brought back incredible stories of monstrous dragons eating goats, pigs and even attacking horses. At first no one believed him, but then the stories were confirmed by Major P.A. Ouwens, director of the Buitenzorg Botanical Gardens in Java, who offered skins and photographs as proof. Soon live specimens were caught and exhibited. The world's largest living lizard is now a popular zoo exhibit.

5. CONGO PEACOCK
Some animal discoveries are made in museums. In 1913, the New York Zoological Society sent an unsuccessful expedition to the Congo in an attempt to bring back a live okapi. Instead one of the team's members, Dr James P. Chapin, brought back some native headdresses with curious long reddish-brown feathers striped with black. None of the experts could identify them. In 1934, Chapin, on another of his frequent visits to the Congo, noticed similar feathers on two stuffed birds at the Tervueren Museum. They were labelled 'Young Indian Peacocks', but Chapin immediately knew that was not what they were. A mining company in the Congo had donated them to the museum and labelled them 'Indian peacocks', but Chapin soon discovered that they were a new species. The following year he flew down to the Congo and brought back seven birds. Chapin confirmed them as the first new bird genus discovered in 40 years. They were not peacocks at all, but pheasants. The Congo peacock is now commonly found in European and North American zoos.

6. KOUPREY
The kouprey is a large wild ox that was found along the Mekong River in Cambodia and Laos and has been the source of much

controversy. It first came to the attention of Western scientists in 1936, when it showed up as a hunting trophy in the home of a French vet. The following year, the director of the Paris Vincennes Zoo, Professor Achille Urbain, went to northern Cambodia and reported that a new wild ox, unlike the gaur and the banteng, was to be seen in Cambodia. Other naturalists felt he was wrong and suggested that the kouprey might be just a hybrid of the gaur and the banteng. Finally, in 1961, a detailed anatomical study of the kouprey proved it to be so different from the area's other wild oxen that it might belong in a new genus, although many scientists continue to insist that it does not. Urbain's 1937 discovery was upheld. The Vietnam War was responsible for the death of many koupreys. A 1975 New York Zoological Society expedition was unable to capture any, although they did see a herd of 50. The kouprey has not been observed by scientists since 1988, although kouprey skulls occasionally show up at local markets. It is now considered critically endangered.

7. COELACANTH
This 5-ft-long, 127-lb, large-scaled, steel-blue fish was brought up in a net off South Africa in December 1938. The huge fish crawled around on deck for three hours before it died. The only problem was that the coelacanth was supposed to have been extinct for 60 million years. Ms M. Courtenay-Latimer and ichthyologist James Smith of Rhodes University, South Africa, identified the coelacanth after it was already dead and had begun to decay. Professor Smith then began years of searching for a second living coelacanth and was finally rewarded in December 1952, when a fishing trawler off the Comoro island of Anjouan, near Africa's east coast, brought up an excellent specimen. Dr Smith was soon shocked to learn that the local inhabitants of the Comoros had been catching and eating the 'living fossils' for generations.

8. BLACK-FACED LION TAMARIN MONKEY
Brazilian scientists found the black-faced lion tamarin monkey in June 1990 on the island of Superagui, along Brazil's heavily populated Atlantic coast, where less than 5% of the country's original Atlantic forest still remains. The amazing discovery led biologist Dr Russell Mittermeier, president of Conservation International, to say, 'It's almost like finding a major new species in a suburb of Los Angeles.' The monkey has a lion-like head and a gold coat. Its face, forearms and tail are black.

Prior to its discovery, there were only three known species of the lion tamarin monkey. It is estimated that fewer than two dozen of the new primate species exist. In 1992, two years after this species' discovery, another new species of monkey, the Maues marmoset, was found in Brazil – this time in a remote part of the Amazon rain forest. First spotted near the Maues River, a tributary of the Amazon, by Swiss biologist Marco Schwarz, the tiny monkey has a pink koala-like face and faint zebra-like stripes.

9. SAO LA
According to British biologist John MacKinnon, who discovered the sao la in May 1992, the mammal 'appears to be a cow that lives the life of a goat'. Skulls, horns and skins of the sao la were found by MacKinnon in the Vu Quang Nature Reserve, a pristine 150,000-acre rain forest in northwestern Vietnam near the Laotian border. Known to the local Vietnamese as a 'forest goat', the sao la – also called the Vu Quang ox – weighs about 220 lb. Smaller than a cow but larger than a goat, the mammal has a dark brown shiny coat with white markings on its face. It has dagger-like straight horns about 20 in. long and two-toed concave hooves that enable it to manoeuvre through slippery and rugged mountain areas. Scientists did not see a live example of the new species until June 1994, when a four-month-old female calf was captured. Unfortunately the calf, and another adolescent sao la that was subsequently captured, died in October 1994; both from an infection of the digestive system. Despite the illegality of hunting and trapping soa la, by 1998 their population was estimated at just 120–150, and they are threatened with extinction. This is partly due to the bounties offered local hunters by TV crews and scientists trying to capture or view live specimens of this popular species.

10. GIANT MUNTJAC DEER
Muntjacs, or barking deer, are a common food in Vietnam. But in April 1994, the World Wildlife Fund and the Vietnamese Ministry of Forestry announced that a new species of the mammal – the giant muntjac deer – was discovered in Vu Quang Nature Reserve, the same rain forest where the sao la had been found two years earlier. One and a half times larger than other muntjacs, the deer weighs about 100 lb and has 8-in. antlers that are bowed inward. It has a reddish coat and large canine teeth. A live animal was captured in Laos by a team of

researchers working for the Wildlife Conservation Society, and in August 1997 another mountjac, the Truong Son or dwarf muntjac, was located in the Vu Quang Nature Reserve. Weighing only 30 lb, it has black fur and extremely short antlers. It is expected that other new species of animals will be found in the Vu Quang Nature Reserve, which miraculously survived bombing and herbicide spraying during the Vietnam War. British biologist John MacKinnon calls the area 'a corner of the world unknown to modern science' and 'a biological gold mine'.

11. BONDEGEZOU
This large, black and white whistling tree kangaroo was first described by zoologist Dr Tim Flannery in 1995. The local Moni tribe in West Papua (Irian Jaya) on the island of New Guinea had long revered the bondegezou as their ancestor.

– L.C. & C.O.M.

5 of the World's Most Oft-Sighted Lake and Sea Monsters

1. NESSIE – THE LOCH NESS MONSTER
'Nessie', the world-famous serpent-like creature of Loch Ness, Scotland, was first photographed in 1933, after decades of rumours that something odd lived in the lake. Since then, 'Nessie-watching' has become an international sport, and there now exist a variety of photographs, an official Loch Ness Monster Fan Club and numerous theories. One of the most popular theories is that the snake-like neck and lizard-like head point to this beast being one of a race of as many as 30 remaining pleiosaurs, a type of dinosaur previously believed to be extinct. However, Loch Ness could not provide sustenance for a pleiosaur, and other theories are hotly debated. Nay-sayers believe all the photos to be no more than bark, driftwood and seaweed. The latest theory, proposed by cryptozoologist Jon Downes, is that Nessie is actually a European eel, grown to an enormous size. Occasionally, these eels become sterile and lose their biological imperative to move from a lake to the Sargasso Sea and breed – thus they are called 'eunuch eels'. Downes proposes that there is something in the waters of Loch Ness and nearby lakes that causes this condition. These eels can cross long distances on land, which might account for the numerous out-of-water sightings.

2. CHAMP – THE MONSTER OF LAKE CHAMPLAIN
This creature apparently lives in a lake which knifes from New York to Canada. Only a few photographs and videos of 'Champ' exist. However, a 1977 photo, taken by one Sandra Mansi, is considered the most impressive photo of any sea or lake 'monster'. Ms Mansi was taking a leisurely drive with her family along the lake when she saw a disturbance in the water. She 'saw the head come up . . . then the neck, then the back'. Her fiancé began to scream, 'Get the kids out of the water!' Sandra had the nous to take a picture, which she tucked away in the family album for four years until it was published in the *New York Times*. Since then, over 130 further sightings have been reported. Books, seminars and arguments followed, and many strongly believe Ms Mansi took a photo of a piece of driftwood. Arguing against this is her statement that 'the mouth was open when it came up and water came out'. Champ is most often seen in early mornings in summer.

3. OGOPOGO
Canada is said to be home to numerous famous lake monsters. There are usually several sightings a year of the Ogopogo, rumoured to live in the Okanagan Lake in British Columbia. Author Mary Moon lists hundreds of sightings, beginning in the late 1700s. The creature is 30–50 ft long (9–15 m.), with an undulating, serpent-like body, a long, thin neck, and a rather horse-like head. It is reputed to swim extremely fast, appearing as several humps, or arches, on the surface. Native American legends tell of the Ogopogo attacking humans, and some swimmers in the lake have disappeared without a trace.

4. THE KRAKEN
Sea monster lore includes myths of giant squid, the most famous of which is the terrifying Kraken, the subject of Norse myth and a poem by Tennyson – 'There hath he lain for ages and will lie Battening upon huge sea worms in his sleep'. Modern scientists speculate that the Kraken is actually a school of giant squid breaking the surface, or several schools, fanning out together.

5. CADBOROSAURUS – 'CADDY AND AMY'
Cadboro Bay in British Columbia supposedly sports a pair of aquatic reptiles nicknamed 'Caddy' and 'Amy'. Caddy's overall length is estimated at 40–70 ft (12–20 m.). There have been more than 50 years of sightings, beginning in the 1940s, continuing with at least half a dozen a year. In 1946 sightings were so common that a plan developed to catch one of the creatures and put it on

display in Vancouver's swimming pool; happily, Caddy and Amy's friends vetoed the idea. In 1994, Dr Ed Bousfield published a book about Caddy – *Cadborosaurus – Survivor from the Deep*.

5 Pieces of Advice on How to Survive an Encounter With a Bear

The following situations may occur anywhere in bear country. This recommended behaviour is generally advised, but is no guarantee of averting a mishap. Above all, remain calm and give the bear the opportunity to learn that your intentions are not hostile.

1. NEVER RUN
   Do not run. Bears can run faster than 30 miles (50 kilometers) per hour – even faster than Olympic sprinters. Running can elicit a chase response from otherwise nonaggressive bears.

2. AN UNAWARE BEAR
   If the bear is unaware of you, detour quickly and quietly away from it. Give the bear plenty of room, allowing it to continue undisturbed.

3. AN AWARE BEAR
   If the bear is aware of you but has not acted aggressively, back away slowly, talking in a calm, firm voice while slowly waving your arms. Bears that stand up on their hind legs are usually just trying to identify you, and are not threatening.

4. AN APPROACHING BEAR
   Do not run; do not drop your pack. A pack can help protect your body in case of an attack. To drop a pack may encourage the bear to approach people for food. Bears occasionally make 'bluff charges', sometimes coming to within ten feet of a person before stopping or veering off. Stand still until the bear stops and has moved away, then slowly back off. Climbing trees will not protect you from black bears, and may not provide protection from grizzlies.

5. IF A BEAR TOUCHES YOU
   If a grizzly bear does actually make contact with you, curl up in a ball, protecting your stomach and neck, and play dead. If the attack is prolonged, however, change tactics and fight back vigorously. If it is a black bear, do not play dead; fight back.

Source: Denali National Park and Preserve, Denali Park, Alaska

10 Most Intelligent Breeds of Dog

In *The Intelligence of Dogs* (New York: The Free Press, 1994), Stanley Coren ranked breeds of dogs for working intelligence. The rankings were based on questionnaires completed by 199 obedience judges from the American and Canadian Kennel Clubs.

1. Border Collie
2. Poodle
3. German Shepherd
4. Golden Retriever
5. Doberman Pinscher
6. Shetland Sheepdog
7. Labrador Retriever
8. Papillon
9. Rottweiller
10. Australian Cattle Dog

10 Least Intelligent Breeds of Dog

1. Afghan Hound
2. Basenji
3. Bulldog
4. Chow Chow
5. Borzoi
6. Bloodhound
7. Pekingese
8. Mastiff
9. Beagle
10. Basset Hound

Source: *The Intelligence of Dogs* Stanley Coren (New York: The Free Press, 1994)

Chapter 6

THE 11 MOST UNUSUAL OBJECTS SOLD ON EBAY

20 VERY ODD JOBS

4 UNFORTUNATE PRODUCT NAMES AND 1 HONOURABLE MENTION

12 LIBRARIANS WHO BECAME FAMOUS IN OTHER FIELDS

15 FAMOUS PEOPLE WHO WORKED IN BED

EARLY CAREERS OF 6 SELF-MADE BILLIONAIRES

Work and Money

MICROSOFT CORPORATION, 1978 – see p.165

The 11 Most Unusual Objects Sold on eBay

1. Gulf Jet Stream – $4.9 million (the most expensive item sold on the site)
2. Lady Thatcher's handbag – £103,000
3. Max the Mammoth (prehistoric skeleton) – £61,000
4. Joanna Lumley's Ferrari – £35,000
5. Decommissioned nuclear bunker – £14,000
6. A date with Penny Smith (GMTV presenter) – £9,000
7. David Beckham's Range Rover – £24,000
8. Ronan Keating's leather trousers – £5,000
9. FA Cup Final football medal Bradford City 1911 – £26,201
10. Jamie Oliver's scooter – £7,600
11. Wedding dress (modelled by ex-husband – the highest viewed item in the history of eBay – over 17 million) – £2,125

20 Very Odd Jobs

1. ANT CATCHER
   Digs up live ants for use in plastic ant farms.

2. BONE CRUSHER
   Tends the machine that crushes animal bones that are used in the manufacture of glue.

3. BONER
   Inserts stays (bones or steels) into prepared pockets of women's foundation garments, such as corsets or brassieres.

4. BOTTOM BLEACHER
   Applies bleaching liquid to bottom of leather outsoles of lasted shoes, using brush or cloth, to lighten colour outsoles.

5. BRAIN PICKER
   Places animal head on a table or on hooks in a slaughterhouse, splits the skull, and picks out the brains

6. CHICK SEXER
   Inserts a light to examine the sex organs of chicks, then separates the males from the females. A university degree in chick sexing is offered in Japan.

7. EGG SMELLER
   Smells eggs after they are broken open to check for spoilage.

8. **FINGER WAVER**
Hairdresser who sets waves in with fingers.

9. **HOOKER INSPECTOR**
Inspects cloth in a textile mill for defects by using a hooking machine which folds the cloth.

10. **IMPREGNATOR**
Tends vacuum or pressure tank that impregnates powdered-metal parts with lubricating oil or molten plastic.

11. **LEGEND MAKER**
Arranges and mounts letters, logos, and numbers on paper backing to make signs and displays

12. **MASHER**
Operates cooker and mashing tub to combine cereal and malt in the preparation of beer.

13. **MOTHER REPAIRER**
Repairs metal phonograph record 'mother' by removing dirt and nickel particles from sound-track grooves. Records are mass-produced by being pressed by the metal mother record.

14. **PRUNE WASHER**
Tends machine that washes prunes preparatory to canning, packaging, or making speciality foods.

15. **QUEEN PRODUCER**
Raises queen bees.

16. **REEFER ENGINEER**
Operates refrigeration or air-conditioning equipment aboard ships.

17. **SLIME-PLANT OPERATOR**
Tends agitation tanks that mix copper or slime and acid solution preparatory to precipitation of copper.

18. **SNIFFER**
Sniffs people's body parts to test the effectiveness of foot and underarm deodorants.

19. **SUCKER-MACHINE OPERATOR**
Tends machine that automatically forms lollipops of specified shape on ends of wooden sticks.

20. TOE PUNCHER
 Tends toe-punching machine that flattens toe seams of knitted seamless socks.

– E.N. & The Eds

4 Unfortunate Product Names and 1 Honourable Mention

A corporate or product name can symbolise more than intended, especially when that name is used in other lands. Today's multinational markets require sensitivity to other cultures, as many companies have learned the hard way.

1. GROS JOS
 Hunt-Wesson introduced its Big John products in Canada before realising that the name, which translated to *Gros Jos*, was French-Canadian slang for 'big breasts'. However, sales did not suffer from this translation.

2. PINTO
 The Ford Pinto suffered image problems when it went on sale in Brazil – *pinto* is Portuguese slang for 'small male genitals'. For Brazilian buyers, Ford changed the name to Corcel, which means 'horse'.

3. BITE THE WAX TADPOLE
 When Coca-Cola expanded into China in the 1920s, the company chose Chinese characters which, when pronounced, would sound like the English name for the drink. Those particular Chinese letters, though, actually translated to 'bite the wax tadpole' or 'wax-flattened mare'. The company now uses characters that mean 'good mouth, good pleasure' or 'happiness in the mouth'.

4. PLEDGE
 The Johnson Company retained the American name of the wax product when it was introduced in the Netherlands. Unfortunately, in Dutch it means 'piss', making it difficult for shoppers to ask for Pledge. The product survived because most Dutch retail stores converted to self-service.

HONOURABLE MENTION
The Yokohama Rubber Company was forced to withdraw hundreds of tyres from the sultanate of Brunei when Islamic authorities complained that the tread design resembled the word for Allah.

12 Librarians Who Became Famous in Other Fields

1. DAVID HUME (1771–76)
   British philosopher, economist, and historian, Hume spent the years 1752–57 as librarian at the Library of the Faculty of the Advocates at Edinburgh, where he wrote his *History of England*.

2. CASANOVA (GIOVANNI GIACOMO CASANOVA DE SEINGALT, 1725–98)
   At the climax of his career in 1785, the inestimable womanizer began 13 years as librarian for Count von Waldstein in the chateau of Dux in Bohemia.

3. AUGUST STRINDBERG (1849–1912)
   The Swedish author of the classic drama *Miss Julie* was made assistant librarian at the Royal Library in Stockholm in 1874.

4. POPE PIUS XI (Achille Ambrogio Damiano Ratti, 1857–1939)
   After 19 years as a member of the College of Doctors of the Ambrosian Library in Milan, he was appointed chief librarian. In 1911 he was asked to reorganize and update the Vatican Library. From 1922 until his death in 1939, the former librarian served as pope.

5. MARCEL DUCHAMP (1887–1968)
   Before launching his art career, Duchamp worked as a librarian at the Bibliotheque Sainte-Genevieve in Paris.

6. BORIS PASTERNAK (1890–1960)
   After the Russian Revolution, the future author of *Doctor Zhivago* was employed by the library of the Soviet Commisariat of Education.

7. ARCHIBALD MACLEISH (1892–1982)
   Playwright, poet, lawyer, assistant secretary of state, winner of three Pulitzer prizes, and a founder of the United Nations Educational, Scientific and Cultural organization (UNESCO), MacLeish was appointed by President Franklin D. Roosevelt as librarian of Congress in 1939 for five years.

8. MAO TSE TUNG (1893–1973)
   In 1918 he worked as an assistant to the chief librarian of the University of Beijing. Overlooked for advancement, he decided to get ahead in another field and eventually became chairman of the Chinese Communist party.

9. J. EDGAR HOOVER (1895–1972)
His first job as a young man was that of messenger and cataloguer in the Library of Congress.

10. JORGE LUIS BORGES (1899–1986)
After his father's death in 1938, Borges (who later became Argentina's most famous author) started his first regular job, as an assistant in a small municipal library in Buenos Aires. In 1946, he was fired for signing an anti-Peron manifesto. After Juan Peron was overthrown in 1955, Borges was named director of the National Library of Argentina.

11. PHILIP LARKIN (1922–85)
The English poet, author of *The Whitsun Weddings* (1964) and *High Windows* (1974) spent his entire working life as a university librarian, at the University of Leicester (1946–50), Queen's University, Belfast (1950–55) and at the Brynmor Jones Library in the University of Hull (1955–85).

12. JOHN BRAINE (1922–86)
British author of *Room at the Top* (1957), Braine worked as assistant librarian at Bingley Public Library (1940–51), branch librarian at Northumberland Country Library (1954–56) and branch librarian at West Riding of Yorks Country Library (1956–57).

– S.S. & C.F.

15 Famous People Who Worked in Bed

1. KING LOUIS XI (1423–83)
This French King was ugly, fat and sickly but also ruthless and clever, earning the title of the 'universal spider'. He introduced the custom of the *lit de justice* ('bed of justice'), a ceremonial appearance of the monarch, in bed, before *le parlement* with the princes of the realm on stools, the greater officials standing, and the lesser ones kneeling. No one is sure exactly why he began the practice, but it caught on and lasted until the French Revolution. Fontenelle, a critic of Louis XV, was asked on the eve of the Revolution, 'What, sir, is a "bed of justice"?' He replied, 'It is the place where justice lies asleep.'

2. **LEONARDO DA VINCI (1452–1519)**
Leonardo earned a unique fame as an artist and scientist, and according to his *Notebooks*, he spent some time each night 'in bed in the dark to go over again in the imagination the main outlines of the form previously studied . . . it is useful in fixing things in the memory'.

3. **CARDINAL DE RICHELIEU (1585–1642)**
In the last year of his life, the diabolically clever and scheming cardinal took to his bed and stayed there because of his rapidly deteriorating health. This did not prevent him from working – he directed his highly efficient secret police in exposing the treasonous machinations of the youthful royal favourite Cinq-Mars. Nor did it hinder the peripatetic cardinal from travelling – his servants carried him about in his bed, and if the door of the house he wanted to stay in was too narrow, they would break open the walls.

4. **THOMAS HOBBES (1588–1679)**
Hobbes, the great British political philosopher, was renowned for his mathematical approach to natural philosophy and found bed a comfortable and handy place to work on his formulas. He wrote the numbers on the sheets and, when he ran out of room, on his thighs. He wrote his 1661 *Dialogue on Physics or On the Nature of Air* entirely in bed. Hobbes also sang in bed because (according to Aubrey's *Brief Lives*) 'he did believe it did his lungs good, and conduced much to prolong his life'.

5. **HENRY WADSWORTH LONGFELLOW (1807–82)**
Throughout his life Longfellow suffered from periodic bouts of severe insomnia. Out of desperation he decided to put his sleepless nights to some good use, and he began to write poetry in bed – including his 1842 classic 'The Wreck of the Hesperus'.

6. **MARK TWAIN (1835–1910)**
Twain loved the luxurious comfort of writing in bed and there composed large portions of *Huckleberry Finn, The Adventures of Tom Sawyer* and *A Connecticut Yankee in King Arthur's Court*. He seems to have been the first person to point out that working in bed must be a very dangerous occupation, since so many deaths occur there.

7. **IGNACE FANTIN-LATOUR (1836–1904)**
Best known for his portrait groups, especially *Homage á Delacroix*, this French painter worked in bed out of necessity

when he could not afford wood for a fire. William Gaunt, in *The Aesthetic Adventure*, describes him propped up in bed, 'Shivering, mournful, persistent . . . in a threadbare overcoat, a top hat over his eyes and a scarf round his mouth, balancing a candle on the edge of his drawing board and sketching with numbed, gloved hand.'

8. ROBERT LOUIS STEVENSON (1850–94)
For years Stevenson was wracked by coughing spells caused by tuberculosis, and consequently he wrote most of *Kidnapped* and *A Child's Garden of Verses* in bed at his home in Bournemouth, England. Bed sometimes brought him inspiration in the form of dreams. One night his subconscious mind spun 'a fine bogey tale', as he called it, based on a real-life criminal he had read about. Stevenson's dream became *Dr Jekyll and Mr Hyde*.

9. EDITH WHARTON (1862–1937)
Pulitzer Prize-winning author (*Age of Innocence*, 1920) Edith Wharton wrote primarily about the upper class into which she was born. Her perspective on the good life was no doubt sharpened by her works habits – she wrote in the mornings, finding inspiration in the comfort of her bed. So accustomed was she to this routine that she once suffered a fit of hysterics because her hotel room bed did not face the light, so she could work.

10. MARCEL PROUST (1871–1922)
Bundled in sweaters, a hot-water bottle at his feet, the French author worked to refine his series of novels called *A la Recherche du Temps Perdu* ('Remembrance of Things Past') while lying virtually flat in bed in a cork-lined room. He had all the necessities within arm's reach – more than a dozen pens (if he dropped one, he refused to pick it up because of dust), all of his notes, notebooks and manuscripts; even fumigation powder, which he believed helped his asthma. In spite of all his precautions, he died of pneumonia at the age of 51.

11. WINSTON CHURCHILL (1874–1965)
Churchill loved to lie abed in comfort while dictating letters and going through the boxes of official state papers for several hours each morning. Although he much preferred to write his books while standing up, declining health in his later years forced him to write and correct most of *The Second World War* and *History of the English Speaking Peoples* in bed.

12. MAE WEST (1892–1980)
The legendary sex queen with the hourglass figure was famous for her *double-entendre* lines. She wrote several of her own screenplays, including *Diamond Lil*, and in 1959 she published her autobiography, *Goodness Had Nothing to Do With It*. She did all her writing in bed, she reported, noting that 'Everybody knows I do my best work in bed.'

13. MAMIE EISENHOWER (1896–1979)
While in the White House, First Lady Mamie Eisenhower did away with an office but not with the office routine. She held bedside conferences, dictated to her secretary, paid the bills and signed letters while ensconced in her pink-ruffled bed.

14. F. SCOTT FITZGERALD (1896–1940)
During the last two years of his life, while writing *The Last Tycoon*, Fitzgerald found that he could work longer hours by staying in bed. He'd retire to bed with a dozen Coca-Colas (which had replaced alcohol in his drinking habits), prop himself up on pillows, and using a lapboard, he'd work for about five hours a day. A fatal heart attack prevented him from completing *The Last Tycoon*.

15. HUGH HEFNER (1926–)
It seems appropriate that a man who made his fortune in sex should have done so in bed. For decades, Hefner controlled the Playboy empire from a massive bed in his Chicago mansion, where he stayed awake for 60-hour stretches, fuelled by amphetamines and Pepsi.

– R.W.S. & The Eds

Early Careers of 6 Self-made Billionaires

1. WARREN BUFFETT (1930–)
Growing up the son of a US Representative from Nebraska, Buffett was an energetic paperboy for the *Washington Post*, covering several routes simultaneously. He also retrieved lost golf balls from a suburban course and sold them. When he was 11 years old, he and his sister began playing the stock market on a modest scale. A year later, he published a horse-racing handicapping sheet, and, while in high school, he and a fellow student were partners in a small pinball machine business that grossed $50 a week.

As a business undergraduate (he earned a BS from the University of Nebraska and an MBA from Columbia), Buffett studied with Benjamin Graham, who taught students to seek out undervalued stocks and wait patiently for them to rise. After Buffett formed his own investment fund, he scored one of his first big coups by following Graham's advice. In 1963, shares of American Express were selling cheaply because the company, then the victim of a major swindle, was considered near bankruptcy by many on Wall Street. Buffett, noticing that customers in Omaha shops and restaurants were using their American Express cards just as much as before the scandal had broken, ignored the Wall Street gossip and bought 5 per cent of the company's stock. Over the next five years, the value of the stock quintupled. Buffett's fortune has since grown to $42 billion.

2. MICHAEL DELL (1965–)

When he was 12 years old, Dell used the money he earned working at a Chinese restaurant to start a stamp collection. He then made $2,000 re-selling the stamps through mail order. By the time he was 16, he had saved enough money to buy an Apple computer. He used the computer in his next business venture, selling subscriptions to the *Houston Post*. Reasoning that many new subscribers would be people setting up new households, such as newlyweds, he obtained lists of marriage licence applicants from local courthouses. Then, using the computer, he sent out personalised letters with subscription offers. He earned $17,000, which he used to buy his first BMW.

Dell's parents wanted Michael to become a doctor. When he entered the University of Texas in 1983, he obliged his parents by enrolling in pre-med courses. But he began a new business on the side – selling computers. Operating out of his dorm room, he bought remaindered IBM and IBM-clone computers from local dealers, upgraded them, and sold them both door-to-door and through mail order. When his parents found out, they were upset and asked him to quit. A compromise was reached: Dell would put his business on hold until he finished the school year; if sales during his summer break weren't good, he would return to school. During the last month of his break, Dell sold $180,000-worth of computers. He dropped out of college, set up shop in Austin, Texas, and achieved sales of $6 million in his first year. He soon pioneered the concept of 'direct selling' to customers, which established computer companies had resisted in the belief that buyers of expensive equipment would not be willing to make a purchase without a hands-on inspection. Dell Computers grew into the third-largest computer seller in the United States and Michael Dell's net worth is now $13 billion.

3. BILL GATES (1955–)
Gates attended Lakeside School, a private Seattle establishment with rigorous academic standards. In 1967, the school's mothers' club used the proceeds of a rummage sale to buy a digital training terminal that was linked by phone to a computer at a local company. Gates was hooked immediately and, with three like-minded friends, formed the Lakeside Programming Group and hung out at the computing centre day and night. Gates and his friends were so enamoured of computers that they rummaged through the rubbish bins at the nearby Computing Centre Corporation (CCC), looking for scraps of paper left by the programmers. After searching for errors in the company's programs, the group produced a 300–page manual, *The Problem Report Book*, that landed them on the CCC payroll. Later, the members of the Lakeside Programming Group formed their own company, Traf-O-Data, to sell a traffic monitoring program. Within a year, Traf-O-Data had earned $20,000, but business fell off when customers learned that Gates, the company president, was only 14 years old. During his senior year of high school, Gates was permitted to suspend his studies to accept a position as a programmer for TRW.

In 1975, Gates, who had enrolled at Harvard as a pre-law major, and Paul Allen, a former member of the Lakeside Programming Group who was working for Honeywell, set about designing software programs for the Altair 8800, the first commercially available microprocessor. They contacted the president of MITS, the manufacturer of the Altair, and told him they had successfully adapted the computer language BASIC for the Altair, even though they had yet to begin. When the president asked to see their program, they started working day and night in Gates's dorm room. Although neither Gates nor Allen had ever seen the Altair 8800 first hand, their program worked and became the industry standard for the next six years. Gates dropped out of Harvard to form Microsoft with Allen. The company was so successful that Gates became a self-made billionaire at 31. He is now the world's second richest man, worth $46 billion (the world's richest man is Ingvar Kamprad, Swedish founder of IKEA).

4. STEVE JOBS (1955–)
While he was in high school, Jobs attended lectures at the Hewlett-Packard electronics plant in Palo Alto, California. One day he phoned William Hewlett, the company president, and asked for parts to build a frequency counter for a school project. Hewlett not only complied, he also gave Jobs a summer job.

In college, Jobs teamed up with his future partner in Apple Computers, Stephen Wozniak, to sell 'blue boxes' that allowed people to illegally make free long-distance calls. Jobs supplied the parts, Wozniak provided the labour, and they sold hundreds of the devices for $150 each in University of California dorms and through a friend in Beverly Hills. After dropping out of Reed College, Jobs landed a job as a technician at Atari. One of his first tasks was engineering on the computer game Breakout. When Jobs was unable to meet the deadline, he asked Wozniak for help. 'Steve wasn't able to design anything that complex,' said Wozniak later. 'I designed the game thinking that he was going to sell it to Atari for $700 and that I would receive $350. It wasn't until years later that I learned that he had actually sold the game for $7,000.' Jobs used the money he received to travel to India, searching for spiritual enlightenment. Back in the United States, he spent time at an Oregon farm commune. After returning to California in 1975, he met up with Wozniak again and suggested that they start their own computer company. To raise the $1,000 they needed, Wozniak sold his prized HP-65 calculator while Jobs sold his VW van. The Apple Computer company set up shop in the Jobs family garage. Their Apple II was the first computer designed for home use and set off the personal computer revolution. Although Jobs had a contentious relationship with Apple – he was forced out of the company in the late 1980s, then brought back in 1998 – the company remains the centre of his $2 billion fortune.

5. ROSS PEROT (1930–)
Perot got his first job at the age of six, working for his father, a cotton dealer and horse trader, breaking horses to the saddle for a dollar or two apiece. At 12, he worked out a deal with the *Texarkana Gazette* by which he would establish a paper route in the city's predominately black slum area and in return would receive 70 per cent, rather than the standard 30 per cent, of subscription fees collected. Setting out on horseback at 3:30 each morning. Perot covered 20 miles a day and was soon earning $40 a week.

After high school, he attended Texarkana Junior College for a year before obtaining an appointment to the US Naval Academy in 1949. Although Perot loved the navy, he was less than enamoured of the promotion and seniority systems, and so decided not to sign on for another hitch. While serving aboard the aircraft carrier *Leyte*, Perot had been invited by an IBM executive to look him up after his discharge. Perot did so, and got a job selling computers. During his fifth year at IBM, he sold his entire quota for the year before January was over, and was promoted to a desk job at the corporation's Dallas office. While there, Perot became convinced that there was a market for a company that would design, instal and operate processing systems on a contract basis. He left his IBM job to strike out on his own, and, on his 32nd birthday, used $1,000 of savings to found Electronic Data Systems. Perot's net worth is now $3.8 billion.

6. SAM WALTON (1918–92)

After graduating from the University of Missouri with a BA in economics in 1940, Walton took his first job in retailing – as a JC Penny sales trainee. A few years later, Sam and his brother James became franchisees of the Ben Franklin variety store chain. As franchisees (the brother eventually ran 15 stores in Arkansas and Missouri), Sam Walton travelled throughout the eastern and midwestern United States and noticed that the large retail chains always placed their stores in or near large cities. Walton felt that smaller towns could successfully support a large retailer, but he received no encouragement from Ben Franklin's management when he brought up the idea. Undaunted, Walton launched the project himself, and in 1962 opened the first Wal-Mart in Rogers, Arkansas. Although the chain struggled early on – David Glass, who later became Wal-Mart's CEO, called the second Wal-Mart 'the worst retail store I had ever seen' – by 1991, Wal-Mart had passed Sears as America's largest retailer and Walton was worth more that $8 billion.

– C.F.

Chapter 7

22 MEMORABLE KISSES

7 CELEBRITY COUPLES MARRIED THREE WEEKS OR LESS

RUDOLPH VALENTINO'S 10 ATTRIBUTES OF THE PERFECT WOMAN

23 FAMOUS PEOPLE'S THOUGHTS ABOUT MARRIAGE

HOW 10 FAMOUS PEOPLE MET THEIR MATES

12 FOODS CLAIMED TO BE APHRODISIACS

6 POSITIONS FOR SEXUAL INTERCOURSE – IN ORDER OF POPULARITY

6 INCESTUOUS COUPLES OF THE BIBLE

MEMBERS OF SOCIETY: PRESERVED SEX ORGANS OF 4 FAMOUS MEN

Sex, Love and Marriage

THE MTV CELEBRITY KISSFEST, 2003 – see p.174

22 Memorable Kisses

1. THE KISS OF LIFE
   It was a kiss from God that infused the 'spirit of life' into man, according to the account of Genesis (2:7). God is said to have formed Adam from slime and dust and then breathed a rational soul into him. This concept of divine insufflation, which surfaces frequently in religious teachings, is often viewed through the kiss metaphor.

2. THE BETRAYAL KISS OF JUDAS (c.AD29)
   As told in the New Testament, Judas Iscariot used the kiss as a tool of betrayal around AD29, when he embraced Jesus Christ in the Garden of Gethsemane. Jewish leaders under the high priest Caiaphas had paid Judas 30 pieces of silver to identify Jesus. With a kiss, Judas singled him out. Jesus was arrested; charged with blasphemy and condemned to death.

3. THE KISS THAT AWAKENED SLEEPING BEAUTY (17th century)
   In the classic fairy tale 'Sleeping Beauty', it is with a kiss that the handsome prince awakens the enchanted princess. This kiss first appeared in Charles Perrault's version of 1697, 'La Belle au bois dormant'. But in fact, 'Sleeping Beauty' dates back to two earlier romances. 'Perceforest' and 'Pentamerone'. In those stories, the handsome prince finds the sleeping beauty, falls in love with her, rapes her and leaves.

4. THE KISS THAT COST THOMAS SAVERLAND HIS NOSE (1837)
   In 1837, at the dawn of the Victorian era in Great Britain, Thomas Saverland attempted to kiss Caroline Newton in a light-hearted manner. Rejecting Saverland's pass, Miss Newton not so lightheartedly bit off part of his nose. Saverland took Newton to court, but she was acquitted. 'When a man kisses a woman against her will,' ruled the judge, 'she is fully entitled to bite his nose, if she so pleases.' 'And eat it up,' added a barrister.

5. *THE KISS* BY FRANÇOIS AUGUSTE RODIN (1886)
   One of the most renowned sculptures in the Western world is *The Kiss*, sculpted by French artist François Auguste Rodin in 1886. Inspired by Dante, the figure of two nude lovers kissing brought the era of classical art to an end. Rodin described *The Kiss* as 'complete in itself and artificially set apart from the surrounding world'.

6. **THE FIRST KISS RECORDED ON FILM (1896)**
The first kiss ever to be recorded in a film occurred in Thomas Edison's *The Kiss*, between John C. Rice and May Irwin in April 1896. Adapted from a short scene in the Broadway comedy *The Widow Jones*, *The Kiss* was filmed by Raff and Gammon for nickelodeon audiences. Its running time was less than 30 seconds.

7. **THE MOST OFTEN KISSED STATUE IN HISTORY (late 1800s)**
The figure of Guidarello Guidarelli, a fearless sixteenth-century Italian soldier, was sculpted in marble by Tullio Lombardo (c. 1455–1532) and displayed at the Academy of Fine Arts in Ravenna, Italy. During the late 1800s a rumour started that any woman who kissed the reclining, armour-clad statue would marry a wonderful gentleman. More than five million superstitious women have since kissed Guidarelli's cold marble lips. Consequently, the soldier's mouth has acquired a faint reddish glow.

8. **THE MOVIE WITH 191 KISSES (1926)**
In 1926 Warner Brothers Studios starred John Barrymore in *Don Juan*. During the course of the film (2 hours, 47 minutes), the amorous adventurer bestows a total of 191 kisses on a number of beautiful señoritas – an average of one every 53 seconds.

9. **THE LONGEST KISS ON FILM (1941)**
The longest kiss in movie history is between Jane Wyman and Regis Toomey in the 1941 production of *You're in the Army Now*. The Lewis Seiler comedy about two vacuum-cleaner salesmen features a scene in which Toomey and Wyman hold a single kiss for 3 minutes and 5 seconds (or 4% of the film's running time).

10. **THE VJ-DAY KISS (1945)**
When the news of Japan's surrender was announced in New York City's Times Square on August 14, 1945, *Life* photojournalist Alfred Eisenstaedt photographed a jubilant sailor clutching a nurse in a back-bending passionate kiss to vent his joy. The picture became an icon of the cathartic celebration that erupted over the end of the war. Over the years, at least three nurses and ten sailors claimed to be the people in the photo. Since Eisenstaedt had lost his notes and negatives by the time the claimants came forward, he was never able to say definitively who was in the photo.

11. THE KISS AT L'HÔTEL DE VILLE (1950)
A famous 1950 photograph of a young couple kissing on the streets of Paris – 'Le Baiser de l'Hôtel de Ville' – found itself under an international media spotlight when, four decades after the picture was taken, the photo became a commercial success, drawing out of the woodwork dozens of people who claimed to have been the photo's unidentified kissers. The black-and-white snapshot – originally taken for *Life* magazine by Robert Doisneau as part of his series on the Parisian working class – made Doisneau wealthy when, between 1986 and 1992, it became a bestseller through poster and postcard reprints. Among those who subsequently identified themselves as the kissers were Denise and Jean-Louis Lavergne, who sued Doisneau for $100,000 after he rejected their claim. They lost their case when it was determined, in 1993, that the kissers were actually two professional models (and real-life lovers), Françoise Bornet and Jacques Cartaud.

12. THE FIRST INTERRACIAL KISS ON US TELEVISION (1968)
NBC's *Star Trek* was the first programme to show a white man kissing a black woman. In the episode 'Plato's Children', aliens with psychic powers force Captain Kirk (William Shatner) to kiss Lt. Uhura (Nichelle Nichols).

13. THE MAJORCA, SPAIN, KISS-IN (1969)
In 1969 an effort was made to crack down on young lovers who were smooching in public in the town of Inca on the island of Majorca. When the police chief began handing out citations that cost offenders 500 pesetas per kiss, a group of 30 couples protested by staging a kiss-in at the harbour at Cala Figuera. Following a massive roundup by police, the amorous rebels were fined 45,000 pesetas for their defiant canoodling and then released.

14. THE HOMOSEXUAL KISS IN *SUNDAY, BLOODY SUNDAY* (1971)
One cinema kiss that turned heads among the movie-going public was between two male actors, Peter Finch and Murray Head, in the 1971 film *Sunday, Bloody Sunday*. The British tale of a bisexual love triangle included a medium close-up shot of this kiss in a scene originally planned to have featured only an embrace from afar. Director John Schlesinger commented that Finch and Head 'were certainly less shocked by the kiss than the technicians on the set were. When Finch was asked about the scene by somebody on TV, he said, "I did it for England."'

15. THE KISS OF HUMILITY (1975)
In an unprecedented gesture of humility, Pope Paul VI kissed the feet of Metropolitan Meliton of Chalcedon, envoy of Patriarch Demetrios I, who was head of the Eastern Orthodox Church, during a Mass at the Sistine Chapel in Rome in 1975. The two men were commemorating the tenth anniversary of the lifting of excommunications that the churches of Constantinople and Rome had conferred on each other during the eleventh century. Taken aback by the pontiff's dramatic action, Meliton attempted to kiss the pope's feet in return but the pope prevented him from doing so. Meliton instead kissed his hand.

16. THE KISS THAT DIDN'T HAPPEN (1975)
King Faisal of Saudi Arabia was engaged in discussions with the Kuwait oil minister when the king's nephew, Prince Faisal ibn Mussad Abdel Aziz, burst into the office unannounced. The king stood and, assuming that the prince wished to offer him holy greetings for Mohammed's birthday, lowered his head and waited for the traditional kiss. It never arrived. Instead the prince fired a bullet into the king's head, and another into his neck, killing him.

17. THE KISS THAT COST $1,260 (1977)
Ruth van Herpen visited an art gallery in Oxford, England, in 1977 and kissed a painting by American artist Jo Baer, leaving red lipstick stains on the $18,000 work. Restoration costs were reported to be as much as $1,260. Appearing in court, van Herpen explained, 'I only kissed it to cheer it up. It looked so cold.'

18. THE KISS THAT CAUSED A CENSORSHIP DEBATE (1978)
The first kiss to reach the movie screen in India was between actor Shashi Kapoor and actress Zeenat Aman in the 1978 film *Love Sublime*. This landmark kiss, a product of new film guidelines, triggered a nationwide debate over censorship. Kapoor felt that the increased creative freedom would only add logic to Indian love stories and result in less cinema violence. Chief minister and film actor M.G. Ramachandran called for a mass protest, labelling the kissing scenes 'an insult'.

19. THE FIRST LESBIAN KISS ON AMERICAN COMMERCIAL TELEVISION (1991)
The first visible kiss between two women on an American network television series took place in 1991 on the show *L.A. Law*, when Michelle Greene kissed Amanda Donohoe. However,

it was a later kiss, on the March 1, 1994, ABC-TV broadcast of the situation comedy *Roseanne* that caused a sensation. In a controversial scene well-publicised in the press, guest star Mariel Hemingway kisses series star Roseanne Arnold on the mouth. The kiss occurs in a 'gay bar' setting, and Hemingway portrays a lesbian stripper whose kiss causes Roseanne to question her own sensibilities. The episode (whose script originally included a second kiss between two additional women) became the subject of much high-profile bickering between ABC executives and series producers Tom and Roseanne Arnold during the weeks prior to its airing. Up to the eleventh hour, the very inclusion of the kiss appeared to remain in question, prompting protests by gay rights organizations. ABC finally let the kiss happen, but added a viewer warning at the start of the episode. The first lesbian kiss on British TV was broadcast two years later, on Christmas Eve 1993, when *Brookside*'s Beth (Anna Friel) and Margaret (Nicola Stephenson), shared an eight-second smooch.

20. THE SEXUAL HARASSMENT KISS (1996)
Six-year-old Johnathan Prevette, a first-grader at Southwest Elementary School in Lexington, North Carolina, kissed a classmate on the cheek. A teacher saw the September 19, 1996, incident and reported it to the school principal, Lisa Horne, who punished Johnathan by keeping him from attending an ice cream party and ordering him to spend a day in a disciplinary programme. But Johnathan's mother called a local radio talk show, word of the incident spread and within six months the US Department of Education had rewritten its sexual harassment guidelines to omit kisses by first graders. For the record, Johnathan said that the girl asked him for a kiss.

21. THE MTV CELEBRITY KISSFEST (2003)
For the opening number of the 2003 MTV Video Music Awards, Britney Spears and Christina Aguilera sang Madonna's 1984 hit 'Like a Virgin' while wearing white wedding gowns. As the music segued into Madonna's latest hit 'Hollywood', Madonna stepped out of a wedding cake wearing a tuxedo. What followed was a drag show of sorts with Madonna playing the groom and Britney and Christina the virginal brides. The performance climaxed with a French kiss between Madonna and Britney and then between Madonna and Christina. The kisses overshadowed the awards themselves and were front-page news around the world.

22. BIG BROTHER IN BAHRAIN (2004)
Bahrain-based MBC-TV attempted to introduce a Middle Eastern version of the voyeuristic reality show 'Big Brother' to Arabic-speaking audiences. A few minutes into the first episode, Abdel Hakim of Saudi Arabia kissed Kawthar of Tunisia. This ran so counter to cultural tradition that public protests broke out and the show was cancelled after only two weeks.

– D.B.

7 Celebrity Couples Married Three Weeks or Less

1. RUDOLPH VALENTINO (Actor) and JEAN ACKER (Actress) – 6 HOURS
Married November 5, 1919, Hollywood's smouldering Great Lover was locked out on his wedding night by his lovely bride. His first marriage lasted less than six hours.

2. ZSA ZSA GABOR (Professional celebrity) and FELIPE DE ALBA (Socialite) – 1 DAY
After surviving her one-day marriage, Gabor commented, 'I'm a wonderful housekeeper. Whenever I leave a man, I keep his house.'

3. JEAN ARTHUR (Actress) and JULIAN ANKER (Nice Jewish boy) – 1 DAY
Before she gained fame in such films as *Mr Deeds Goes to Town*, *Mr Smith Goes to Washington* and *Shane*, Arthur fell in love with 'a nice Jewish boy' named Julian Anker because 'he looked like Abraham Lincoln'. They married on a whim, but both sets of parents were horrified and the couple filed for annulment the following day.

4. BRITNEY SPEARS (Singer) and JASON ALEXANDER (Childhood friend) – 2 DAYS
Pop superstar Britney Spears was married for 48 hours to an old Kentwood, Louisiana buddy. The marriage took place in Las Vegas at the Little White Wedding Chapel. The bride wore a baseball cap and torn jeans. Both were 22 years old, and claimed they were not intoxicated at the time. Said the groom, 'It was just crazy, man. We said, "Let's do something wild. Let's get married, for the hell of it."' Spears made no comment. Calling it 'a mistake', the couple had a judge annul the marriage, which took two hours.

5. GLORIA SWANSON (Actress) and WALLACE BEERY (Actor) – 3 WEEKS
Married in Hollywood in March, 1916, Swanson and Beery separated three weeks later. Said Beery: 'She wanted the fancy life – to put on airs and all of that. Me, I like huntin' and fishin' and the simple life.' Said Swanson: 'I wanted to have a baby and Wally didn't want that responsibility.'

6. GERMAINE GREER (Writer/Feminist) and PAUL DE FEU (Model) – 3 WEEKS
The first male nude centrefold model for the London edition of *Cosmopolitan* magazine, De Feu lured Greer into marriage in May 1968. However, in Greer's words, 'The marriage lasted three weeks. Three weekends, to be precise.'

7. DREW BARRYMORE (Actress) and JEFFREY THOMAS (Welsh barman) – 3 WEEKS
In 1994, the pair was married for three weeks. Barrymore later admitted that she was trying to help Thomas obtain a green card to stay in the United States.

Rudolph Valentino's 10 Attributes of the Perfect Woman

Idolised as the great lover of the screen in the 1920s, Rudolph Valentino starred in such romantic epics as *The Sheik*, *Blood and Sand* and *The Eagle*. His death in 1926 caused worldwide hysteria, several suicides, and riots at his funeral. Each year, on the anniversary of his death, hundreds of the faithful gather at his burial-site to pay tribute.

1. Fidelity
2. The recognition of the supreme importance of love
3. Intelligence
4. Beauty
5. A sense of humour
6. Sincerity
7. An appreciation of good food
8. A serious interest in some art, trade or hobby
9. An old-fashioned and wholehearted acceptance of monogamy
10. Courage

Source: Cleveland Amory, *Vanity Fair* (Copyright © 1926, 1954 by The Condé Nast Publications Inc.)

23 Famous People's Thoughts About Marriage

1. 'Marriage, *n.* The state or condition of a community consisting of a master, a mistress and two slaves, making in all, two.'
   – *Ambrose Bierce*

2. 'A man may be a fool and not know it – but not if he is married.'
   – *H.L. Mencken*

3. 'For a while we pondered whether to take a vacation or get a divorce. We decided that a trip to Bermuda is over in two weeks, but a divorce is something you always have.'
   – *Woody Allen*

4. *Heinrich Heine bequeathed his estate to his wife on the condition that she marry again, because, according to Heine,* 'There will be at least one man who will regret my death.'

5. 'American women expect to find in their husbands a perfection that English women only hope to find in their butlers.'
   – *W. Somerset Maugham*

6. 'I've only slept with the men I've been married to. How many women can make that claim?' – *Elizabeth Taylor*

7. 'Take it from me, marriage isn't a word – it's a sentence.'
   – *King Vidor*

8. 'Marriage is like a cage; one sees the birds outside desperate to get in, and those inside equally desperate to get out.'
   – *Michel de Montaigne*

9. 'I don't think I'll get married again. I'll just find a woman I don't like and give her a house.' – *Lewis Grizzard*

10. 'There's only one way to have a happy marriage and as soon as I learn what it is I'll get married again.' – *Clint Eastwood*

11. 'The only charm of marriage is that it makes a life of deception necessary for both parties.' – *Oscar Wilde*

12. 'By all means marry; if you get a good wife, you'll be happy. If you get a bad one, you'll become a philosopher.' – *Socrates*

13. 'Marriage is neither heaven nor hell; it is simply purgatory.'
   – *Abraham Lincoln*

14. 'It destroys one's nerves to be amiable every day to the same human being.' – *Benjamin Disraeli*

15. 'It is not a lack of love, but a lack of friendship that makes unhappy marriages.' – *Friedrich Nietzsche*

16. 'She has buried all her female friends; I wish she would make friends with my wife.' – *Martial*

17. 'Wives are people who feel they don't dance enough.' – *Groucho Marx*

18. 'If you want to sacrifice the admiration of many men for the criticism of one, go ahead, get married.' – *Katharine Hepburn*

19. 'Married men live longer than single men. But married men are a lot more willing to die.' – *Johnny Carson*

20. 'Sex when you're married is like going to a 7-Eleven. There's not as much variety, but at three in the morning, it's always there.' – *Carol Leifer*

21. 'Sex in marriage is like medicine. Three times a day for the first week. Then once a day for another week. Then once every three or four days until the condition clears up.' – *Peter De Vries*

22. 'My wife and I were happy for twenty years. Then we met.' – *Rodney Dangerfield*

23. 'Only choose in marriage a woman whom you would choose as a friend if she were a man.' – *Joseph Joubert*

Primary source: *A Curmudgeon's Garden of Love*, compiled and edited by Jon Winokur (copyright © 1991 by Jon Winokur. Reprinted by permission of the author.)

How 10 Famous People Met Their Mates

1. JOHN LENNON and YOKO ONO
According to biographers, avant-garde artist Ono pursued Lennon relentlessly. At the time they met, she was showing her work at London's Indica Gallery. Lennon saw the show, which impressed him, but did not respond immediately to her advances, which included pleas for sponsorship of her art, hanging around outside his door, and bombarding him with

notes. Eventually the couple divorced their respective spouses and married in 1969 on the Rock of Gibraltar.

2. OLIVER HARDY and VIRGINIA LUCILLE JONES
Jones was a script girl on *The Flying Deuces*, starring Laurel and Hardy. One day on the set, she tripped over a rolled-up carpet, struck her head on the arc light, and was taken to the hospital. While she was unconscious, Hardy was struck by her beauty. He courted her by sending flowers and notes to the hospital. They were married in 1940.

3. OZZY OSBOURNE and SHARON ADREN
Heavy-metal rocker Osbourne met his wife-to-be when she was working as a receptionist for her father, a London music agent. He walked into her office barefoot, with a tap dangling from his neck, and sat on the floor. 'I was terrified,' she recalled. The couple wed two years later, in 1981, and had three children together. The Osbournes subsequently became beloved MTV stars as the world watched their vivid family life unfolding on the small screen.

4. RUTH WESTHEIMER and MANFRED 'FRED' WESTHEIMER
The diminutive sex therapist met her third husband on a ski trip in the Catskills in 1966. Her boyfriend, Hans, was six feet tall, and an uncomfortable match on the ski-lift T-bar. At the top she told Hans, 'I'm going up with that short man,' pointing to the five-foot Westheimer. They married less than a year later. Westheimer sometimes called his wife 'my skiing accident'.

5. THE DUKE OF WINDSOR and MRS WALLIS SIMPSON
The Duke of Windsor was introduced to Mrs Wallis Simpson – the woman for whom he eventually gave up the throne – at a house party. He asked whether she missed American central heating. She replied, 'I'm sorry, sir, but you disappoint me . . . Every American woman that comes to your country is always asked the same question. I had hoped for something more original from the Prince of Wales.'

6. PAMELA ANDERSON and TOMMY LEE
Baywatch actress Anderson met the Motley Crue drummer at a New Year's party. 'He sat with me and kept licking my face,' she recalled. 'When I left, he was begging me for my phone number. I said no way. But then I gave him my number because

he was interesting.' After a five-day courtship at the resort of Cancun, Mexico, the couple was wed on the beach.

7. JULIE ANDREWS and BLAKE EDWARDS
Their romance began after Andrews heard that movie director Edwards had described her as 'so sweet she probably has violets between her legs'. Amused by this remark, she sent him a bunch of violets and a note. They soon began dating and were married in 1969.

8. SAMUEL BECKETT and SUZANNE DESCHEVAUX-DUMESNIL
Avant-garde playwright Beckett had been stabbed by a pimp and was discovered bleeding in the street by Deschevaux-Dumesnil. She found help and visited him in the hospital. After his release, they moved in together, married and were together 28 years, until his death in 1989.

9. TINA BROWN and HAROLD EVANS
Brown, the future editor of *Vanity Fair* and *The New Yorker*, was a 22-year-old Oxford co-ed when she decided to meet Evans, the 47-year-old editor of the venerable *Times* of London. Brown camped outside Evans's door and refused to move until he agreed to see her. Four years later, Evans divorced his wife and married Brown.

10. DOLLY PARTON and CARL DEAN
On her first day in Nashville in 1964, Parton took a suitcase of dirty clothes to a launderette. Dean drove by and honked his truck's horn at the pretty blonde. Parton cheerfully waved back, and he stopped. They chatted, began dating, and fell in love. After Dean got out of the army two years later, he and Parton married.

The Eds and C.F.

12 Foods Claimed to be Aphrodisiacs

1. ASPARAGUS
Asparagus contains a diuretic that increases the amount of urine excreted and excites the urinary passages. The vegetable is rich in potassium, phosphorus, and calcium – all necessary for maintenance of a high energy level. However, it also contains aspartic acid, which neutralises excess amounts of ammonia in one's body and may cause apathy and sexual uninterest.

2. CAVIAR
In addition to being nutritious (30% protein), caviar has been considered an aphrodisiac because of its obvious place in the reproductive process. All fish and their by-products have been linked to the myth of Aphrodite, the goddess of love who was born from the foam of the sea.

3. EEL
Eel, like most fish, is rich in phosphorus and has an excitant effect on the bladder. In addition to its general associations with the aphrodisiac effect of fish, it has probably been favoured as an aphrodisiac because of its phallic appearance.

4. GARLIC
Both Eastern and Western cultures have long regarded garlic as an aphrodisiac. The Greeks and Romans sang its praises and oriental lovers claimed to be towers of strength because of eating it.

5. GINSENG
The Chinese call ginseng the 'elixir of life' and have used it for more than 5,000 years. Although medical opinion is sharply divided as to its merits, Russian experiments claim that ginseng increases sexual energy and has a general healing and rejuvenating influence on the body.

6. GREEN M&MS
Mars, who make M&Ms, have consistently denied that green M&Ms have any effect on the libido. Nobody is sure how the rumour started, but in 1996 Mars ran an ad in which comedian Dennis Miller asks a female green M&M, 'Is it true what they say about the green ones?'

7. HONEY
Honey is highly nutritious and rich in minerals, amino acids, enzymes and B-complex vitamins. Galen, Ovid and Sheikh Nefzawi, author of *The Perfumed Garden*, believed that honey has outstanding aphrodisiac powers.

8. LOBSTER
The lobster has been described as an amatory excitant by many writers, including Henry Fielding in *Tom Jones*. In addition, it shares the Aphrodite-derived power attributed to all seafood.

9. OYSTERS
Oysters are one of the most renowned aphrodisiac foods. Like other seafoods, they are rich in phosphorus. Although they are

not a high source of energy, oysters are easily digestible. Among the eminent lovers who have vouched for oysters was Casanova, who called them 'a spur to the spirit and to love'.

10. PEACHES
'Venus owns this tree . . . the fruit provokes lust . . .' wrote herbalist Nicholas Culpeper. The Chinese considered the fruit's sweet juices symbolic of the effluvia of the vagina, and both the Chinese and Arabs regard its deep fur-edged cleft as symbolic of the female genitalia. A 'peach house' was once a common English slang term for a brothel.

11. TOMATOES
When they were first brought from South America to Europe, tomatoes were thought to be the forbidden fruit of Eden. They were also celebrated as a sexual stimulant and nicknamed 'love apples'.

12. TRUFFLES
Truffles, the expensive underground fungi, are similar to oysters in that they are composed mostly of water and are rich in protein. Rabelais, Casanova, George Sand, Sade, Napoleon and Mme Pompadour are a few of the many notables who have praised the truffle's aphrodisiac powers. An ancient French proverb warns: 'Those who wish to lead virtuous lives should abstain from truffles.'

– R.H.

6 Positions for Sexual Intercourse – In Order of Popularity

Gershon Legman, an American who wrote about sex, calculated that there are more than 4 million possible ways for men and women to have sexual intercourse with each other. Most of these 'postures', as he called them, are probably variations on the six main positions that Alfred C. Kinsey used as categories in the questionnaires on sexual habits which were the basis for his Kinsey Reports in 1948 and 1953.

The *Kama Sutra*, a Hindu love manual written sometime between AD300 and 540, lists many imaginative and acrobatic variations on these positions – for example, the Bamboo Cleft, the Crab, the Wild Boar; some *Kama Sutra* experts suggest that people try out difficult positions in the water first. Chinese pillow books, written more than

400 years ago, show more feasible positions with titles like 'Two Dragons Exhausted by Battle' and name the parts of the body equally poetically – the penis is called the 'jade stem' and the clitoris, the 'pearl on the jade step'.

According to these sources, interpretations of ancient art, and anthropological studies, humans have changed their preference rankings of sexual positions – the 'missionary' (man-on-top) position, overwhelmingly the number-one choice of the Americans Kinsey studied, was not that high on the lists of ancient Greeks and Romans, primitive tribes, or many other groups.

The advantages and disadvantages of each position are taken from Albert Ellis's *The Art and Science of Love* and from *Human Sexual Inadequacy* by William H. Masters and Virginia E. Johnson.

1. MAN ON TOP
   To many people this is the only position considered biologically 'natural', though other primates use the rear-entry position almost exclusively. Called the 'missionary' position because it was introduced to native converts – who liked to make fun of it – by Christian missionaries who regarded other positions as sinful.
   Advantage: Allows face-to-face intimacy, deep thrusting by male, pace setting by male.
   Disadvantage: Does not allow good control for the premature ejaculator, or freedom of movement for the woman.
   Chances for conception: Good.

2. WOMAN ON TOP
   Shown in ancient art as most common position in Ur, Greece, Rome, Peru, India, China and Japan. Roman poet Martial portrayed Hector and Andromache in this position. Generally avoided by those at lower educational levels, according to Kinsey, because it *seems* to make the man less masculine, the woman less feminine.
   Advantages: Allows freedom of movement for women, control for premature ejaculators, caressing of female by male. Most often results in orgasm for women. Good when the man is tired.
   Disadvantage: Too acrobatic for some women.
   Chances for conception: Not good.

3. SIDE BY SIDE
   From Ovid, a poet of ancient Rome: 'Of love's thousand ways, a simple way and with the least labour, this is: to lie on the right side, and half supine withal.'

Advantage: Allows manipulation of clitoris, freedom of movement for man and woman. Good for tired or convalescent people, and premature ejaculators, as well as pregnant women.
Disadvantage: Does not allow easy entry.
Chances for conception: Okay.

4. REAR ENTRANCE
Frequently used by 15 per cent of married women. Favoured by primates and early Greeks. Rejected by many Americans because of its 'animal origins' and lack of face-to-face intimacy.
Advantages: Allows manual stimulation of clitoris. Exciting for men who are turned on by female buttocks. Good for pregnant women, males with small penises, women with large vaginas.
Disadvantages: Does not allow easy entry or face-to-face intimacy. Penis tends to fall out.
Chances for conception: Good.

5. SITTING
According to Kinsey, learned by many while 'making out' in back seats of cars.
Advantages: Allows clitoral contact with male body, free movement, intimacy. Good for male who wants to hold off orgasm, pregnant women.
Disadvantage: Does not allow vigorous thrusting. Sometimes tiring. Penetration may be too deep.
Chances for conception: Poor.

6. STANDING
Has echoes of a 'quickie' against an alley wall with a prostitute, therefore exciting. Indian lotus position: each stands on one leg, wraps other around partner.
Advantage: Allows caressing. Exciting, can flow from dancing, taking shower.
Disadvantage: Does not allow much thrusting. Entry difficult, particularly when one partner is taller than the other. Tiring. Not good for pregnant women.
Chances for conception: Poor.

– A.E.

6 Incestuous Couples of the Bible

1.-2. LOT and HIS DAUGHTERS
After the destruction of Sodom and Gomorrah, the only survivors, Lot and his two virgin daughters, lived in a cave.

One night the daughters plied their father with wine, and the elder daughter seduced Lot in order to 'preserve the seed of [their] father'. The following night they got him drunk again, and the younger daughter took her turn. Lot apparently had no memory of the events, although nine months later his daughters gave birth to two sons, Moab and Ben-ammi. (Gen. 19:30–38)

3. ABRAHAM and SARAH
Abraham and Sarah had the same father but different mothers. Sarah married her half-brother in Ur, and they remained together until she died, at the age of 127. (Gen. 20:12)

4. NAHOR and MILCAH
Abraham's brother, Nahor, married his niece, the daughter of his dead brother Haran and the sister of Lot. (Gen. 11:27, 29)

5. AMRAM and JOCHEBED
Amram married his father's sister, and Aunt Jochebed bore him two sons, Aaron and Moses. (Exod. 6:20)

6. AMNON and TAMAR
Amnon raped his half-sister Tamar and was murdered in revenge two years later by Tamar's full brother Absalom. (II Sam. 13:2, 14, 28–29)

Members of Society: Preserved Sex Organs of 4 Famous Men

1. NAPOLEON BONAPARTE
When the exiled former emperor of France died of stomach cancer on May 5, 1821, on the remote island of St Helena, a postmortem was held. According to Dr C. MacLaurin, 'his reproductive organs were small and apparently atrophied. He is said to have been impotent for some time before he died'. A priest in attendance obtained Napoleon's penis. After a secret odyssey of 150 years, the severed penis turned up at Christie's Fine Art Auctioneers in London around 1971. The one-inch penis, resembling a tiny sea horse, an attendant said, was described by the auction house as 'a small dried-up object'. It was put on sale for £13,300, then withdrawn from bidding. Shortly afterward, the emperor's sex organ (along with bits of his hair and beard) was offered for sale in Flayderman's Mail Order Catalogue. There were no buyers. In 1977 Napoleon's

penis was sold to an American urologist for about $3,800. Today Napoleon's body rests in the crypt at the Invalides, Paris – sans penis.

2. GRIGORI RASPUTIN
In 1968, in the St Denis section of Paris, an elderly White Russian female émigré, a former maid in czarist St Petersburg and later a follower and lover of the Russian holy man Rasputin, kept a polished wooden box, 18 in. by 6 in. in size, atop her bedroom bureau. Inside the box lay Rasputin's penis. It 'looked like a blackened, overripe banana, about a foot long, and resting on a velvet cloth', reported Rasputin biographer Patte Barham. In life this penis, wrote Rasputin's daughter Maria, measured 'a good 13 inches when fully erect'. According to Maria's account, in 1916, when Prince Felix Yussupov and his fellow assassins attacked Rasputin, Yussupov first raped him, and then fired a bullet into his head, wounding him. As Rasputin fell, another young nobleman pulled out a dagger and 'castrated Grigori Rasputin, flinging the severed penis across the room'. One of Yussupov's servants, a relative of Rasputin's lover, recovered the penis and turned the severed organ over to the maid. She in turn fled to Paris with it.

3. JOHN DILLINGER
One of the controversial legends of the twentieth century concerns the disposition of bank robber and badman John Dillinger's private parts. When Dillinger was shot to death by the FBI in front of a Chicago cinema in 1934, his corpse was taken to the morgue for dissection by forensic pathologists. The gangster's penis – reported as 14 in. flaccid, 20 in. erect – was supposedly amputated by an overenthusiastic pathologist. After that, many people heard that the penis had been seen (always by someone else) preserved in a showcase at the Smithsonian Institution. Since the publication of *The Book of Lists 1*, the authors have received a great number of letters asking if the story of Dillinger's pickled penis is true. The editors called the Smithsonian to prove the story myth or fact and museum curators denied any knowledge of such an exhibit. Tour guides at the museum believe that years ago, many people mistakenly entered the building next door to the Smithsonian thinking it was part of the same complex; it was, however, a different museum altogether – the Medical Museum of the Armed Forces Institute of Pathology – and it housed gruesome displays of diseased and oversized body parts, including penises and testes,

as well as pictures of victims of gunshot wounds. It was here some visitors claimed they had seen Dillinger's giant penis. The collection has since been moved to the Walter Reed Army Medical Centre, but its operators also deny that Dillinger's organ has ever been one of its displays.

4. ISHIDA KICHIZO

Kichizo, a well-known Tokyo gangster, and his mistress, a young Japanese geisha named Abe Sada, were involved in a long, passionate sadomasochistic love affair. He enjoyed having her try to strangle him with a sash cord as she mounted him. Kichizo could make love to Abe Sada only at intervals, because he was married and had children. She hated their separations and suggested they run away or commit suicide together. On the night of May 18, 1936, fearing he was going to leave her forever, she started to play their strangling game, then really strangled him to death. Taking a butcher knife, she cut off Kichizo's penis and testicles, wrapped them in his jacket, and placed the bundle in a loincloth she tied around her kimono. Abe Sada fled her geisha house, but the police eventually caught her and confiscated the penis. She was tried for her crime, found guilty and sentenced to jail. She languished in prison for eight years, all through WWII, until the American army of occupation moved into Tokyo. The Americans released all Japanese political prisoners – including Abe Sada, by mistake. In 1947 an 'aging but vivacious' Abe Sada owned a bar near Tokyo's Sumida River. A sensational film, *In the Realm of the Senses*, was made about the affair, which made dear Abe and dead Kichizo – and his penis – legend in Japan.

– I.W.

Chapter 8

15 UNUSUAL STOLEN OBJECTS

18 STUPID THIEVES AND 3 DISHONOURABLE MENTIONS

20 UNDERWORLD NICKNAMES

22 CASES OF ANIMALS AND INSECTS BROUGHT BEFORE THE LAW

8 TRIAL VERDICTS THAT CAUSED RIOTS

WITTICISMS OF 9 CONDEMNED CRIMINALS

29 UNUSUAL LAWSUITS

Crime

MAFIA BOSS JOSEPH AIUPPA – IRONICALLY THEY CALLED HIM 'HA HA' – **see p.199**

15 Unusual Stolen Objects

1. GEORGE WASHINGTON'S WALLET
One hundred and ninety-one years after his death in 1799, George Washington's battered wallet was stolen from an unlocked case in the Old Barracks Museum in Trenton, New Jersey. The wallet was later returned to police. In a separate incident in 1986, a lock of Washington's hair was taken from a museum in France. Five years later it was recovered, along with a lock of hair belonging to the Marquis de Lafayette, by French police during a raid on a drug dealer's hideout.

2. BULL SEMEN
In October 1989, $10,000 worth of frozen bull semen and embryos was taken from the dairy building at California Polytechnic University in San Luis Obispo, California. The embryos were later found, but despite a $1,500 reward, the semen was never recovered.

3. CHURCH PULPIT
On August 2, 1992, congregation leaders of the first missionary Baptist Church in Houston, Texas, voted to oust their pastor, the Reverend Robert L. White. The Reverend White retaliated by loading most of the church's property into three cars, a pickup, and a 14–foot-long-U-haul truck. Included in his haul were furniture, an organ, curtains, speakers, amplifiers and even the pulpit. He left behind the church's piano because it was still being paid for.

4. HALF A HUMAN HEAD
Jason Paluck, a premedical student at Adelphi University, was arrested in May 1992 after his landlord discovered half of a human head in a plastic bag while evicting Paluck from his Mineola, New York, apartment. Paluck admitted that he had taken the head from one of his classes.

5. KATEY SAGAL'S PUSH-UP BRA
On the night of April 30, 1992, Jim B., a 24-year-old art student in Los Angeles, drove into Hollywood to observe the fires and looting that followed the acquittal of four police officers in the beating of Rodney King. Jim B. joined the crowd looting Frederick's of Hollywood, the famous purveyor of exotic lingerie. He headed straight for their lingerie museum, intent on grabbing Madonna's bustier. It had already been stolen, so Jim B. settled for Ava Gardner's bloomers and a push-up bra worn

by Katey Sagal on the television comedy *Married . . . With Children*. A couple of days later, a repentant Jim B. handed over the stolen items to the Reverend Bob Frambini, the pastor at the Church of the Blessed Sacrament, who returned them to Frederick's. Madonna's bustier is still on the missing list. However, she did donate a replacement in exchange for a donation to a charity that provides free mammograms for the poor.

6. TWENTY-FOOT INFLATABLE CHICKEN
To mark the March 1990 debut of a new franchise in Sherman Oaks, California, the El Pollo Loco fast-food chain installed a 20-foot inflatable rubber chicken in front of the restaurant. Two weeks later, it was stolen. 'Don't ask me what someone would do with it,' said Joe Masiello, director of operations for Chicken Enterprises, Ltd. 'If you put it in your yard, someone would notice it.' The restaurant's owners offered a reward of 12 free chicken combos for its return, but the thieves didn't bite.

7. BUTTONS
Felicidad Noriega, the wife of Panamanian dictator Manuel Noriega, was arrested in a Miami-area shopping mall in March 1992. She and a companion eventually pleaded guilty to stealing $305-worth of buttons, which they had removed from clothes in a department store.

8. FIFTEEN-TON BUILDING
In August 1990, businessman Andy Barrett of Pembroke, New Hampshire, reported the unexpected loss of an unassembled 15-ton prefabricated structure, complete with steel girders and beams 35 feet long and 3 feet thick.

9. SACRED CHIN
St Anthony's jawbone and several teeth were taken from a basilica in Padua, Italy, in October 1991, but were later found near Rome's international airport at Fiumicino.

10. VINTAGE AEROPLANE
Israeli Air Force Reserve Major Ishmael Yitzhaki was convicted in February 1992 of stealing a WWII Mustang fighter plane and flying it to Sweden, where he sold it for $331,000. He had managed to remove the plane from the Air Force museum by saying it needed painting.

11. GENE KELLY'S LAMPPOST
Bryan Goetzinger was part of the labour crew that cleared out the Metro-Goldwyn-Mayer film company vaults when MGM

ceded its Culver City, California, lot to Lorimar Telepictures, in 1986. Among the items scheduled to be dumped was the lamppost that Gene Kelly swung on in the Hollywood musical classic *Singin' in the Rain*. Goetzinger took the lamppost home and installed it in the front yard of his Hermosa Beach home. Four years later it was stolen. It was never recovered.

12. MARY'S LITTLE LAMB
A life-size statue of Mary's famous little lamb was erected in Sterling, Massachusetts, the hometown of Mary Sawyer, who was the inspiration for the nursery rhyme written in 1830 by Sarah J. Hale. During the night of June 30, 1990, the unfortunate lamb was stolen from the town commons. Fortunately, it was later returned.

13. FAKE BISON TESTICLES
In celebration of the 2001 World Championships in Athletics, the host city of Edmonton, Canada, erected statues of bison, painted in colours representing the competing nations. Twenty of the statues were vandalised, with thieves removing the testicles from the bison. Although two vandals were caught red-handed in August, police considered the remaining cases unsolved. Ric Dolphin, chairman of the project that erected the statues, suggested that if the vandals were caught, 'Let the punishment fit the crime.'

14. CABIN
Kay Kugler and her husband B.J. Miller bought 40 acres in California's El Dorado County and erected a 10-by-20-foot prefabricated cabin on the property, which they used as a vacation home. In July 2003, they arrived at their property to discover that the cabin was gone. In their absence, someone had stolen the cabin, a shed, a generator, an antique bed, a well pump and a 2,600-gallon water tank.

15. CONDOM MACHINE
Keith Bradford, 34, drank three beers at the Irish Tavern in Waterford, Michigan, in November, 1994, headed into the men's room and ripped a condom machine from the wall. Numerous witnesses saw him walking away with the machine, so the police followed him home and recovered the machine, 48 condoms and 127 quarters.

18 Stupid Thieves and 3 Dishonourable Mentions

1. SHOWING OFF HIS BOOTY
Charles Taylor of Wichita, Kansas, was arrested for robbing a shoe store at knifepoint and stealing a $69 pair of size 10½ tan hiking boots on December 18, 1996. At his trial three months later, Taylor arrogantly rested his feet on the defence table. He was wearing a pair of size 10½ tan hiking boots. The judge, James Fleetwood was incredulous. 'I leaned over and stared,' he later said. 'Surely nobody would be so stupid as to wear the boots he stole to his trial.' But it turned out that one person was that stupid. Taylor was convicted of aggravated robbery and sent back to jail in his stocking feet.

2. WRONG PLACE, WRONG TIME
On November 29, 1978, David Goodhall and two female accomplices entered a home supplies shop in Barnsley, South Yorkshire, intending to engage in a bit of shoplifting. After stuffing a pair of curtains into a plastic carrier bag, the threesome attempted to leave by separate exits. However, they were apprehended immediately by several store detectives. Goodhall and his cohorts had failed to notice that the shop, at that very moment, was hosting a convention of store detectives.

3. CHECKING OUT
Eighteen-year-old Charles A. Meriweather broke into a home in Northwest Baltimore on the night of November 22–23, 1978, raped the woman who lived there, and then ransacked the house. When he discovered she had only $11.50 in cash, he asked her 'How do you pay your bills?'

   She replied, 'By cheque' and he ordered her to write out a cheque for $30. Then he changed his mind and upped it to $50.

   'Who shall I make it out to?' asked the woman, a 34-year-old government employee.

   'Charles A. Meriweather,' said Charles A. Meriweather, adding, 'It better not bounce or I'll be back.'

   Meriweather was arrested several hours later.

4. JUST REWARD
Every night, Mrs Hollis Sharpe of Los Angeles took her miniature poodle, Jonathan, out for a walk so that he could do his duty. A responsible and considerate citizen, Mrs Sharpe always brought along with her a newspaper and a plastic bag to clean

up after him 'You have to think of your neighbours,' she explained. On the night of November 13, 1974, Jonathan had finished his business and Mrs Sharpe was walking home with the bag in her right hand when a mugger attacked her from behind, shoved her to the ground, grabbed her plastic bag, jumped into a car, and drove off with the spoils of his crime. Mrs Sharpe suffered a broken arm, but remained good-humoured about the incident. 'I only wish there had been a little more in the bag,' she said.

5. A MINOR DETAIL
Edward McAlea put on a stocking mask, burst into a jewellery store in Liverpool, and pointed a revolver at the three men inside. 'This is a stick up,' he said. 'Get down.' None of them did, since all of them noticed the red plastic stopper in the muzzle of McAlea's toy gun. After a brief scuffle, McAlea escaped, but not before he had pulled off his mask. The jeweller recognised him as a customer from the day before, and McAlea was apprehended.

6. KEEP THE CHANGE
In 1977, a thief in Southampton, England, came up with a clever method of robbing the cash register at a local supermarket. After collecting a basket full of groceries, he approached the checkout area and placed a £10 note on the counter. The grocery clerk took the bill and opened the cash register, at which point the thief snatched the contents and ran off. It turned out to be a bad deal for the thief, since the till contained only £4.37 and the thief ended up losing £5.63.

7. THE WELD-PLANNED ROBBERY
On the night of August 23–24, 1980, a well-organised gang of thieves began their raid on the safe of the leisure-centre office in Chichester, Sussex, by stealing a speedboat. Using water skis to paddle across the lake, they picked up their equipment and paddled on to the office. However, what they thought were cutting tools turned out to be welding gear, and they soon managed to seal the safe completely shut. The next morning it took the office staff an hour to hammer and chisel the safe open again.

8. STUCK FOR LIFE
There is a whole sub-genre of stupid thieves who get stuck while trying to sneak into buildings through chimneys and air vents that turn out to be narrower at the bottom than at the top.

However, none has quite met the fate that befell Calvin Wilson of Natchez, Mississippi. A burglar with a criminal record, Wilson disappeared in 1985. The following year, a body found on the banks of the Mississippi River was identified – incorrectly, as it turned out – as that of Wilson. Fifteen years later, in January 2001, masons renovating a historic building in Natchez discovered a fully-clothed skeleton in the chimney. Lying next to the skeleton was a wallet belonging to Calvin Wilson. Adams County sheriffs theorised that Wilson had tried to enter the building, which was then a gift shop, through the chimney, fallen in head first and become stuck in the chimney, unable to call for help.

9. WHO WAS THAT MASKED MAN?
Clive Bunyan ran into a store in Cayton, near Scarborough, England, and forced the shop assistant to give him £157 from the till. Then he made his getaway on his motorbike. To hide his identity, Bunyan had worn his full-face helmet as a mask. It was a smooth successful heist, except for one detail. He had forgotten that across his helmet, in inch-high letters, were the words, 'Clive Bunyan – Driver'. Bunyan was arrested and ordered to pay for his crime by doing 200 hours of community service.

10. BURGLARY BY THE NUMBER
Terry Johnson had no trouble identifying the two men who burgled her Chicago apartment at 2.30 am on August 17, 1981. All she had to do was write down the number on the police badge that one of them was wearing and the identity number on the fender of their squad car. The two officers – Stephen Webster, 33, and Tyrone Pickens, 32 – had actually committed the crime in full uniform, while on duty, using police department tools.

11. THE WORST LAWYER
Twenty-five-year-old Marshall George Cummings, Jr., of Tulsa, Oklahoma, was charged with attempted robbery in connection with a purse-snatching at a shopping centre on October 14, 1976. During the trial the following January, Cummings chose to act as his own attorney. While cross-examining the victim, Cummings asked, 'Did you get a good look at my face when I took your purse?' Cummings later decided to turn over his defence to a public defender, but it was too late. He was convicted and sentenced to 10 years in prison.

12. SAFE AT LAST

On the night of June 12, 1991, John Meacham, Joseph Plante and Joe Laattsch were burgling a soon-to-be demolished bank building in West Covina, California, when Meacham came upon an empty vault. He called over his accomplices and invited them inside to check out the acoustics. Then he closed the vault door so they could appreciate the full effect. Unfortunately, the door locked. Meacham spent 40 minutes trying to open it, without success. Finally he called the fire department, who called the police. After seven hours, a concrete-sawing firm was able to free the locked-up robbers, after which they were transported to another building they could not get out of.

13. BIG MOUTH

Dennis Newton was on trial in 1985 for armed robbery in Oklahoma City. Assistant District Attorney Larry Jones asked one of the witnesses, the supervisor of the store that had been robbed, to identify the robber. When she pointed to the defendant, Newton jumped to his feet, accused the witness of lying, and said, 'I should have blown your –ing head off!' After a moment of stunned silence, he added, 'If I'd been the one that was there.' The jury sentenced Jones to 30 years in prison.

14. INCONVENIENCE STORE

In December 1989, three 15-year-old boys stole a car in Prairie Village, Kansas, and stopped off at the nearest convenience store to ask directions back to Missouri. Except that it wasn't a convenience store – it was a police station. At the same moment, a description of the stolen vehicle was broadcast over the police station public address system. The car thieves tried to escape, but were quickly apprehended.

15. WRONG FENCE

Stephen Le and two juvenile companions tried to break into a parked pickup truck in Larkspur, California, on the night of September 27, 1989. But the owner caught them in the act, chased them, and hailed a police car. Le and one of his friends climbed a fence and ran. It soon became apparent that they had chosen the wrong fence – this one surrounded the property of San Quentin prison. The suspects were booked for investigation of auto burglary and trespassing on state property, although charges were never filed. 'Nothing like this has ever happened here before,' said Lieutenant Cal White. 'People just don't break into prison every day.'

16. BIRDBRAINED THIEVES
During a midnight raid in May 1997, thieves climbed a 6-ft fence at the home of Bob Hodgson in Ryton, near Gateshead, Tyne and Wear. They broke open two locks and stole 40 homing pigeons worth £1,000. It was a clever, well-organised robbery – except for one minor problem: homing pigeons fly home. That is exactly what all but the eight youngest pigeons did.

17. RETURNING TO THE SCENE OF THE CRIME
While training to become a military police officer, US Army Private Daniel Bowden was taught how criminals commit bank robberies. As it turned out, Bowden was not a very good student. In May 1997, he robbed a federal credit union in Fort Belvoir, Virginia, making away with $4,759 in cash. The following week, Bowden, who had not worn a mask during the commission of his crime, returned to the same bank and tried to deposit the money into his own personal account. He was immediately recognised by a teller, who alerted the military police.

18. SHOOTING HIMSELF IN THE FOOT
In February 2004, Carlos Henrique Auad of Petropolis, Brazil, broke into a bar near his home and stole a television set. A few nights later, Auad tried to break into the same bar through the roof. This time, carrying a gun, he slipped and fell and shot himself in the right foot. Auad went straight home, but failed to notice that he left a trail of blood that led right to his door. He was arrested by police who found the television set.

DISHONOURABLE MENTIONS

1. STUPID DRUG DEALER
Alfred Acree Jr was sitting in a van in Charles City, Virginia, on April 7, 1993, with three friends and at least 30 small bags of cocaine. When sheriff's deputies surrounded the van, Acree raced into a dark, wooded area by the side of the road. He weaved in and out of the trees in an attempt to evade his pursuers. He thought he had done a pretty good job – and was amazed when the deputies caught him (and found $800 worth of cocaine in his pockets). What Acree had forgotten was that he was wearing LA Tech sneakers that sent out a red light every time they struck the ground. While Acree was tiring himself zigzagging through the forest, the sheriffs were calmly following the blinking red lights.

2. STUPID DRUG TRAFFICKERS

Drug traffickers Edward Velez and José Gonzales were transporting 2 lb of methamphetamine by aeroplane on the night of December 7, 1994. They had planned to land at a small airport in Turlock, California, but Velez, the pilot, miscalculated and touched down at a different airport 20 miles away. Unfortunately for Velez and Gonzalez, the airport was part of the Castle Air Force Base, where air force pilots were practicing night touch-and-go landings. Security police intercepted the plane as soon as it landed.

3. STUPID TERRORIST

In early 1994 an Islamic fundamentalist group in Jordan launched a terrorist campaign that included attacks against secular sites such as video stores and supermarkets that sold liquor. During the late morning of February 1, Eid Saleh al Jahaleen, a 31-year-old plumber, entered the Salwa Cinema in the city of Zarqa. The cinema was showing soft-core pornographic films from Turkey. Jahaleen, who was apparently paid $50 to plant a bomb, had never seen soft-core porn and became entranced. When the bomb went off, he was still in his seat. Jahaleen lost both legs in the explosion.

20 Underworld Nicknames

1. FRANK 'THE DASHER' ABBANDANDO

A prolific hit man for Murder, Inc. – organised crime's enforcement arm in the 1930s – and with some 50 killings to his credit, Frank Abbandando once approached a longshoreman on whom there was a 'contract'. Abbandando fired directly into his victim's face, only to have the weapon misfire. The chagrined executioner dashed off, circling the block so fast that he came up behind his slowly pursuing target, and this time Abbandando managed to shoot him dead, picking up his moniker in the process.

2. TONY 'JOE BATTERS' ACCARDO

Tough Tony Accardo was a Chicago syndicate boss for many decades. Accardo, who prided himself on never having spent a day in jail, was sometimes called 'Joe Batters', harking back to his earlier days of proficiency with a baseball bat when he was one of Al Capone's most dedicated sluggers.

3. **JOSEPH 'HA HA' AIUPPA**
An old-time Capone muscle-man, Joseph Aiuppa rose to become the Mafia boss of Cicero III. Because he was a notorious scowler not given to smiling, he was called 'Ha Ha'.

4. **ISRAEL 'ICEPICK WILLIE' ALDERMAN**
This Minneapolis gangster liked to brag about the grotesque murder method that earned him his nickname. Israel Alderman (also known as 'Little Auldie' and 'Izzy Lump Lump') ran a second-storey speakeasy where he claimed to have committed 11 murders. In each case he deftly pressed an icepick through his victim's eardrum into the brain; his quick technique made it appear that the dead man had merely slumped in a drunken heap on the bar. 'Icepick Willie' would laughingly chide the corpse as he dragged it to a back room, where he dumped the body down a coal chute leading to a truck in the alley below.

5. **LOUIS 'PRETTY' AMBERG**
Louis Amberg, the underworld terror of Brooklyn from the 1920s to 1935 – when he was finally rubbed out – was called 'Pretty' because he may well have been the ugliest gangster who ever lived. Immortalised by Damon Runyon in several stories as the gangster who stuffed his victims into laundry bags, Amberg was approached when he was 20 by Ringling Brothers Circus, which wanted him to appear as the missing link. 'Pretty' turned the job down but often bragged about the offer afterwards.

6. **MICHAEL 'UMBRELLA MIKE' BOYLE**
Business agent of the mob-dominated electrical workers union in Chicago in the 1920s, Michael J. Boyle gained the title of 'Umbrella Mike' because of his practice of standing at a bar on certain days of the week with an unfurled umbrella. Building contractors deposited cash levies into this receptacle and then magically were not beset by labour difficulties.

7. **LOUIS 'LEPKE' BUCHALTER**
Louis Buchalter – who died in the electric chair in 1944 – was the head of Murder, Inc. He was better known as 'Lepke', a form of 'Lepkeleh'. This was the affectionate Yiddish diminutive, meaning 'Little Louis', that his mother had used. Affectionate, 'Lepke' was not. As one associate once said, 'Lep loves to hurt people.'

8. 'SCARFACE' AL CAPONE
Al Capone claimed that the huge scar on his cheek was from a WWI wound suffered while fighting with the lost battalion in France, but actually he was never in the armed service. He had been knifed while working as a bouncer in a Brooklyn saloon-brothel by a hoodlum named Frank Galluccio during a dispute over a woman. Capone once visited the editorial offices of William Randolph Hearst's Chicago *American* and convinced that paper to stop referring to him as 'Scarface Al'.

9. VINCENT 'MAD DOG' COLL
Vincent 'Mad Dog' Coll was feared by police and rival gangsters alike in the early 1930s because of his utter disregard for human life. Once he shot down several children at play while trying to get an underworld foe. When he was trapped in a phone booth and riddled with bullets in 1932 no one cried over his death, and police made little effort to solve the crime.

10. JOSEPH 'JOE ADONIS' DOTO
Racket boss Joseph Doto adopted the name of 'Joe Adonis' because he considered his looks the equal of Aphrodite's famous lover.

11. CHARLES 'PRETTY BOY' FLOYD
Public enemy Charles Arthur Floyd hated his nickname, which was used by prostitutes of the Midwest whorehouses he patronised, and in fact he killed at least two gangsters for repeatedly calling him 'Pretty Boy'. When he was shot down by FBI agents in 1934, he refused to identify himself as 'Pretty Boy' Floyd and with his dying breath snarled, 'I'm Charles Arthur Floyd!'

12. CHARLIE 'MONKEY FACE' GENKER
For several decades after the beginning of the twentieth century a mainstay of the Chicago whorehouse world, Charlie 'Monkey Face' Genker achieved his moniker not simply for a countenance lacking in beauty but also for his actions while employed by Mike 'de Pike' Heitler (a piker because he ran a 50-cent house). 'Monkey Face' matched the bounciness of his jungle cousins by scampering up doors and peeking over the transoms to get the girls and their customers to speed things up.

13. JAKE 'GREASY THUMB' GUZIK
A long-time devoted aide to Al Capone, Jake Guzik continued until his death in 1956 to be the payoff man to the politicians

and police for the Chicago mob. He often complained that he handled so much money he could not get the inky grease off his thumb. This explanation of the 'Greasy Thumb' sobriquet was such an embarrassment to the police that they concocted their own story, maintaining that Jake had once worked as a waiter and gained his nickname because he constantly stuck his thumb in the soup bowls.

14. 'GOLF BAG' SAM HUNT
Notorious Capone mob enforcer 'Golf Bag' Sam Hunt was so called because he lugged automatic weapons about in his golf bag to conceal them when on murder missions.

15. ALVIN 'KREEPY' KARPIS
Bank robber Alvin Karpis was tabbed 'Kreepy' by fellow prison inmates in the 1920s because of his sallow, dour-faced looks. By the time he became public enemy No. 1 in 1935, Karpis's face had become even creepier thanks to a botched plastic surgery job which was supposed to alter his appearance.

16. GEORGE 'MACHINE GUN' KELLY
Somehow a blundering bootlegger named George R. Kelly became the feared public enemy 'Machine Gun' Kelly of the 1930s. His criminally ambitious wife, Kathryn, forced him to practise with the machine gun she gave him as a birthday present, while she built up his reputation with other criminals. However, Kelly was not a murderer, nor did he ever fire his weapon in anger with intent to kill.

17. CHARLES 'LUCKY' LUCIANO
Charles Luciano earned his 'Lucky' when he was taken for a ride and came back alive, although a knife wound gave him a permanently drooping right eye. Luciano told many stories over the years about the identity of his abductors – two different criminal gangs were mentioned as well as the police, who were trying to find out about an impending drug shipment, but the most likely version is that he was tortured and mutilated by the family of a cop whose daughter he had seduced. Luciano parlayed his misfortune into a public-relations coup, since he was the one and only underworld figure lucky enough to return alive after being taken for a one-way ride.

18. THOMAS 'BUTTERFINGERS' MORAN
The acknowledged king of the pickpockets of the twentieth century, Thomas 'Butterfingers' Moran picked his first pocket

during the 1906 San Francisco earthquake and his last in 1970 at 78, some 50,000 pockets in all. He could, other practitioners acknowledged rather jealously, 'slide in and out of a pocket like pure butter'.

19. LESTER 'BABY FACE' NELSON
The most pathological public enemy of the 1930s, Lester Gillis considered his own name as non-macho and came up with 'Big George' Nelson instead – a ridiculous alias considering the fact that he was just 5 ft 4 in. tall. He was called 'Baby Face' Nelson behind his back and in the press, which constantly enraged him.

20. BENJAMIN 'BUGSY' SIEGEL
Alternately the most charming and the most vicious of all syndicate killers, Benjamin Siegel could thus be described as being 'bugs'. However, no one called him 'Bugsy' to his face, since it caused him to fly into a murderous rage. His mistress, Virginia Hall, likewise clobbered newsmen who called her man by this offensive sobriquet.

– C.S.

22 Cases of Animals and Insects Brought Before the Law

There has been a long and shocking tradition of punishing, excommunicating and killing animals for real or supposed crimes. In medieval times, animals were even put on the rack to extort confessions of guilt. Cases have been recorded and documented involving such unlikely creatures as flies, locusts, snakes, mosquitoes, caterpillars, eels, snails, beetles, grasshoppers, dolphins and most larger mammals. In seventeenth-century Russia, a goat was banished to Siberia. The belief that animals are morally culpable is happily out of fashion – but not completely, for even now, these travesties and comedies occasionally occur.

1. CANINE CONVICT NO. C2559
Rarely in American history has an animal served a prison term. Incredibly, it happened as recently as 1924, in Pike County, Pennsylvania. Pep, a male Labrador retriever, belonged to neighbours of Governor and Mrs Gifford Pinchot. A friendly dog, Pep unaccountably went wild one hot summer day and killed Mrs Pinchot's cat. An enraged Governor Pinchot presided over an immediate hearing and then a trial.

Poor Pep had no legal counsel, and the evidence against him was damning. Pinchot sentenced him to life imprisonment. The no doubt bewildered beast was taken to the state penitentiary in Philadelphia. The warden, also bewildered, wondered whether he should assign the mutt an ID number like the rest of the cons. Tradition won out, and Pep became No. C2559. The story has a happy ending: Pep's fellow inmates lavished him with affection, and he was allowed to switch cellmates at will. The prisoners were building a new penitentiary in Graterford, Pennsylvania, and every morning the enthusiastic dog boarded the bus for work upon hearing his number called. When the prison was completed, Pep was one of the first to move in. In 1930, after six years in prison (42 dog years), Pep died of old age.

2. THE RISING COST OF AIR TRAVEL.
In Tripoli in 1963, 75 carrier pigeons received the death sentence. A gang of smugglers had trained the birds to carry bank notes from Italy, Greece and Egypt into Libya. The court ordered the pigeons to be killed because 'They were too well trained and dangerous to be let loose.' The humans were merely fined.

3. TOO MUCH MONKEY BUSINESS
In 1905 the law against public cigarette smoking was violated in South Bend, Indiana. A showman's chimpanzee puffed tobacco in front of a crowd and was hauled before the court, where he was convicted and fined.

4. IT'S A DOG'S LIFE
In 1933 four dogs in McGraw, New York, were prosecuted to the full extent of the law for biting six-year-old Joyce Hammond. In a full hearing before an audience of 150, their lawyer failed to save them from execution by the county veterinarian. Proclaimed justice A.P. McGraw: 'I know the value of a good dog. But this is a serious case . . . The dogs are criminals of the worst kind.'

5. A HOOF FOR A HOOF
The Wild West custom of killing a horse responsible for the death of a human was re-enacted by a group of Chicago gangsters in 1924. When the infamous Nails Morton died in Lincoln Park after being thrown from a riding horse, his buddies in Dion O'Banion's gang sought revenge. They kidnapped the animal from its stable at gunpoint and took it to the scene of the crime, where they solemnly executed it.

6. **YOU REALLY GOT A HOLD ON ME**
In 1451 in Lausanne, a number of leeches were brought into an ecclesiastical court. We can only imagine their distress as they listened to the reading of a document demanding that they leave town. When the tenacious leeches stuck to their guns they were exorcised by the bishop-court.

7. **DOGGED BY THE LAW**
'Perverts transformed their stables into harems', wrote a French author in his legal history of the province of Lorraine. For centuries, bestiality was a regularly prosecuted crime, and as recently as 1940 a man was burned at the stake in Pont-à-Mousson, France, with three cows. The case of Guillaume Guyart in 1606 contains a surreal twist. Guyart was sentenced to be hanged and burned for sodomy; his accomplice, a female dog, was to be knocked on the head and burned along with him. When Guyart managed to escape, the court decreed that his property be confiscated to pay for the costs of the trial. If the criminal were not caught, the judges ruled, the sentence would be carried out – a painting of Guyart would be hung from the scaffold. There is no record of the ultimate fate of the man or the dog.

8. **THE BARNYARD BORDELLO**
Puritan clergyman Cotton Mather left a rare account of an American buggery case. He wrote, 'on June 6, 1662, at New Haven, there was a most unparallelled wretch, one Potter by name, about 60 years of age, executed for damnable Beastialities [sic]'. Potter, it seems, began sodomising animals at the age of 10 and never stopped. At the same time, he was a devout churchgoer noted for his piety and for being 'zealous in reforming the sins of other people'. The man's wife, Mather wrote, 'had seen him confounding himself with a bitch ten years before; and he had excused himself as well as he could, but conjured her to keep it secret'. Potter then hanged the animal, presumably as an apology to his wife. Eventually, the law caught up with him, and he went to the gallows preceded by a cow, two heifers, three sheep and two sows. Watching his concubines die one by one, Potter was in tears by the time he approached the scaffold.

9. **I'M NOT THAT KIND OF GIRL**
In Vanvres, France, in 1750, Jacques Ferron was caught in the act of love with a she-ass and sentenced to hang. Normally, his

partner would have died as well – but members of the community took an unprecedented step. They signed a petition that they had known the she-ass for four years, that she had always been well behaved at home and abroad and had never caused a scandal of any kind. She was, they concluded, 'in all her habits of life a most honest creature'. As the result of this intervention, Ferron was hanged for sodomy, and the she-ass was acquitted.

10. JUVENILE DELINQUENTS?

The vast majority of prosecuted animals were pigs. In the Middle Ages they were frequently left unwatched, and they often harmed small children. Once arrested, they were usually placed in solitary confinement in the same jail with human criminals, registered as 'so-and-so's pig', and publicly hanged with all the formality of a typical medieval execution. In the annals of animal crime, there are many famous pig cases. One of the most fully documented and most unusual occurred in Savigny, France, in 1457. A sow and her six piglets were accused of 'willfully and feloniously' murdering a five-year-old boy, Jean Martin. Found guilty, the sow was eventually hanged by its hind legs from the gallows. But the matter was not so simple: were the six piglets – who had been found stained with blood at the scene of the crime – also guilty? Their owner, Jean Bailly, was asked to post bail for them until a second trial and to take the accused back into his custody. Bailly said he didn't have the money, and furthermore, refused to make any promises about the piglets' future good behaviour. Three weeks later 'the six little porklets' went to court. Because of their youth and the lack of firm evidence of their guilt, the court was lenient. The piglets were given to a local noblewoman; Bailly did not have to pay, and the porklets could hold their heads high.

11. AN IMPORTANT RULING

A significant pig case occurred in 1846 in Pleternica, Slavonia – it was one of the first times an animal's owner bore responsibility for damages. A pig ate the ears of a one-year-old girl and was given the usual death sentence. Its owner was sentenced to labour in order to provide a dowry for the earless girl, so that, despite her loss, she might someday find a husband.

12. MONKEYING AROUND

As recently as January 23, 1962, an animal was called into the court-room. Makao, a young cercopithecoid monkey, escaped from his master's apartment in Paris and wandered into an empty studio nearby. He bit into a tube of lipstick, destroyed some expensive knick-knacks and 'stole' a box that was later recovered – empty. The victims of Makao's pranks filed a complaint stating that the box had contained a valuable ring. The monkey's owner contended before the judge that his pet could not possibly have opened such a box. Makao was ordered to appear in court, where he deftly opened a series of boxes. His defence ruined, Makao's master was held liable for full damages.

13. A HAPPY TAIL
In 1877 in New York City, Mary Shea, a woman of Celtic origin, was bitten on the finger by Jimmy, an organ-grinder's monkey. Mary demanded retribution, but the judge said he could not commit an animal. Miffed, Mary stormed out of the courtroom, snarling, 'This is a nice country for justice!' The monkey, who was dressed in a scarlet coat and velvet cap, showed his appreciation: he curled his tail around the gas fixture on the judge's desk and tried to shake hands with him. The police blotter gave this record of the event: '*Name*: Jimmy Dillio. *Occupation*: Monkey. *Disposition*: Discharged'.

14. HARD-BOILED CRIMINAL
One of the most celebrated animal trials was that of the rooster in Basel, Switzerland, which was accused in 1474 of laying an egg (without a yolk no less). It was a widely held belief that such eggs could be hatched by witches in league with Satan, giving birth to deadly winged snakes. The accused cock was in a tight spot, and even his defence attorney did not argue that the charges were false. He did argue that his client had no pact with the devil and that laying an egg was an unpremeditated and involuntary act. The judges were not impressed, and after a lengthy trial it was decided that the rooster was possessed by Satan. The bird and the egg were burned at the stake before a huge crowd. The subject was being debated more than 200 years later, in 1710, when a Frenchman presented a paper before the Academy of Sciences stating that yolkless eggs were merely the occasional products of an ailing hen.

15. WOMEN AND CHILDREN FIRST
In Stelvio, Italy, in 1519, field mice (referred to in a German account as *Lutmäusse* – they may have been moles) were

accused of damaging crops by burrowing. They were granted a defence attorney, Hans Grienebner, so that they could 'show cause for their conduct by pleading their exigencies and distress'. He claimed that his clients were helpful citizens who ate harmful insects and enriched the soil. The prosecutor, Schwartz Mining, argued that the damage they caused was preventing local tenants from paying their rents. The judge was merciful. Though he exiled the animals, he assured them of safe conduct 'and an additional respite of 14 days to all those which are with young, and to such as are yet in their infancy'.

16. PUTTING THE BITE ON THE LANDLORD

In the 1700s, an order of Franciscan friars in Brazil was driven to despair by the termites which were devouring not only the food and furniture, but also the very walls of the monastery. The monks pleaded with the bishop for an act of excommunication, and an ecclesiastical trial was held. When the accused defiantly failed to appear in court, they were appointed a lawyer. He made the usual speech about how all God's creatures deserved to eat, and he praised his clients' industry, which he said was far greater than that of the friars. Further, he argued that the termites had occupied the land long before the monks. The lengthy trial overflowed with complicated legal speeches and much passionate quoting of authorities. In the end, it was decided that the monks should give the termites their own plot of land. The judge's order was read aloud to the termite hills. According to a monk's document dated January, 1713, the termites promptly came out of the hills and marched in columns to their new home. Woodn't you know it?

17. A CAT-ASTROPHIC RULING

It was an ancient Breton belief that tomcats had to be killed before reaching the age of seven, or they would kill their masters. One morning a farmer of Pleyben was found dead in his bed, his throat slit. The local judge had already arrested two servants, when the herdsman noticed the household cat in front of the hearth. Proclaiming, 'I for one know who the culprit is!' the herdsman pulled the following stunt: he tied a string to the dead man's wrist, ran the other end through a window, and gave it a tug from outside – thus 'shaking' the corpse's arm. Right in front of the judge, the tomcat calmly approached his 'revived' master in order to finish him off properly. The guilty cat was burned alive.

18. WHAT'S A MAYOR TO DO?

In Ansbach, Germany, in 1685, it was reported that a vicious wolf was ravaging herds and devouring women and children. The beast was believed to be none other than the town's deceased mayor, who had turned into a werewolf. A typical politician, the wolf/mayor was hard to pin down, but was finally captured and killed. The animal's carcass was then dressed in a flesh-coloured suit, a brown wig, and a long grey-white beard. Its snout was cut off and replaced with a mask of the mayor. By court order, the creature was hanged from a windmill. The weremayor's pelt was then stuffed and displayed in a town official's cabinet, to serve forever as proof of the existence of werewolves.

19. THE CRUEL DEATH OF 'FIVE-TON MARY'

There are ancient records of the hangings of bulls and oxen, but there is only one known case of the hanging of an elephant – it happened in Erwin, Tennessee, on September 13, 1916. The Sparks Circus was stationed in Kingsport, Tennessee, when Mary, a veteran circus elephant, was being ridden to water by an inexperienced trainer, Walter Eldridge. On the way, Mary spotted a watermelon rind and headed for this snack. When Eldridge jerked hard on her head with a spear-tipped stick, Mary let out a loud trumpet, reached behind her with her trunk, and yanked the trainer off her back. Mary dashed Eldridge against a soft-drink stand and then walked over and stepped on his head. A Kingsport resident came running and fired five pistol shots into the huge animal. Mary groaned and shook but did not die – in fact, she performed in that night's show. The next day the circus moved to Erwin, where 'authorities' (no one is sure who) decreed that Mary should die on the gallows, to the great sorrow of her friends in the circus. She was taken to the Clinchfield railroad yards, where a large crowd was gathered. A 7/8-in. chain was slung around her neck, and a 100-ton derrick hoisted her 5 ft in the air. The chain broke. The next chain held, and Mary died quickly. Her 5-ton corpse was buried with a steam shovel.

20. FREE SPEECH

Carl Miles exhibited Blackie, his 'talking' cat, on street corners in Augusta, Georgia, and collected 'contributions'. Blackie could say two phrases: 'I love you' and 'I want my momma'. In 1981, the city of Augusta said the enterprise required a business licence and a fee, which Miles refused to pay. He sued the city council, arguing that the fee impinged on the cat's right to free speech. The judge actually heard Blackie say 'I love you' in court. However, he ruled that the case was not a free speech issue. Since Blackie was charging money for his speech, the city was entitled to their fee. Miles paid $50 for the licence and Blackie went back to work. He died in 1992 at the age of 18.

21. LAST-MINUTE ESCAPE

On September 30, 1982, Tucker, a 140-lb bull mastiff, ran into a neighbour's yard and attacked the neighbour's black miniature poodle, Bonnie. Tucker's owner, Eric Leonard, freed the poodle from Tucker's mouth, but the poodle had received critical injuries and died. A district court in Augusta, Maine, ruled that Tucker was a danger to other dogs and should be killed by intravenous injection. Leonard appealed to the Maine Supreme Court, but it upheld the lower court's ruling. In 1984, two days before his scheduled execution, the 'National Doggie Liberation Front' removed Tucker from the shelter where he was being held. What happened to Tucker is unknown.

22. DEATH-ROW DOG

The long arm of the law almost took the life of a 110-lb Akita named Taro, who got into trouble on Christmas Day of 1990. Owned by Lonnie and Sandy Lehrer of Haworth, New Jersey, Taro injured the Lehrers' ten-year-old niece, but how the injury occurred was in dispute. Police and doctors who inspected the injury said the dog bit the girl's lower lip. The Lehrers said the child provoked the dog and that while protecting himself, Taro scratched her lip. Taro had never before hurt a human being, but he had been in three dogfights and had killed a dog during one of the fights. A panel of local authorities ruled that Taro fell under the state's vicious-dog law and sentenced the Akita to death. A three-year legal nightmare ensued as the Lehrers fought their way through municipal court, superior court, a state appeals court, and finally the New Jersey Supreme Court. While the legal battle raged on, Taro remained on death row at Bergen County Jail in Hackensack, where he was kept in a climate-controlled cell and was allowed two exercise walks a day. By the time his execution day neared, the dog had become an international celebrity. Animal rights activist and former actress Brigitte Bardot pleaded for clemency; a businessman from Kenya raised money to save the dog. Thousands of animal lovers wrote to the Lehrers and offered to adopt the dog. Even the dog's jailer and the assemblyman behind the vicious-dog law interceded on behalf of Taro. But when the courts failed to free the dog, the final verdict fell to Governor Christine Todd Whitman. Although the governor did not exactly pardon the Akita, she agreed to release him on three conditions: Taro would be exiled from New Jersey; Taro must have new owners; Taro's new owners, or the Lehrers, must assume all financial liability for the dog's future actions. The Lehrers agreed, and the dog was released in February 1994, after spending three years in jail. The Lehrers subsequently found a new home for Taro in Pleasantville, New York. When all the costs of the canine death-row case were added up, the total exceeded $100,000. Taro died of natural causes in 1999.

– A.W. & C.O.M.

8 Trial Verdicts That Caused Riots

1. THE DREYFUS AFFAIR (1894–1906)
The conviction of a Jewish army officer for high treason in 1894 unleashed a tidal wave of anti-Semitism and popular unrest in France. Alfred Dreyfus, the son of a manufacturer who lived in Alsace, a region annexed by Germany in 1871, had achieved the rank of captain and was the only Jew on the general staff when he was accused of selling military secrets to the Germans. On the basis of forged and falsified evidence, he was court-martialled and sentenced to life imprisonment on Devil's Island, the notorious prison of French Guiana. His trial polarised French society into two groups – the 'revisionists' (liberals and anticlericals) and the 'nationalists' (the army and the Catholic Church). Friendship and family ties were broken over the case, duels were fought, strikes occurred, and street fights broke out, bringing France to the verge of civil war. Novelist Émile Zola was convicted of criminal libel for writing a newspaper article that accused the authorities of framing Dreyfus. Retried in 1899 – and again found guilty by the army – Dreyfus was pardoned by the president of France that year, but he was not restored to his former rank until 1906.

2. MME CAILLAUX (JULY 28, 1914)
In July 1914, the wife of France's minister of finance was tried for the murder of Gaston Calmette, the editor of *Le Figaro*. Lacking any legal means to stop Calmette's personal and professional attacks upon her husband, Henriette Caillaux had purchased a pistol, presented herself at the editor's office, and

shot him to death. During her nine-day trial she wept copiously and was subject to fainting spells, especially when her prenuptial love letters from the then-married Caillaux were read in open court. After the verdict of acquittal was announced on July 28, pandemonium broke out in the courtroom and in the streets of Paris, reflecting the widespread feeling that power and wealth had subverted justice. Coincidentally, that very day Austria-Hungary declared war on Serbia, swallowing up the Caillaux verdict in the general onrush towards WWI.

3. SACCO AND VANZETTI (1921–27)
In 1921 two Italian-born anarchists were convicted, on the basis of disputed evidence, of murdering a guard and a paymaster in a South Braintree, Massachusetts, payroll robbery. The six-year legal battle for the life of shoemaker Nicola Sacco and his friend Bartolomeo Vanzetti, a fishmonger, became an international *cause célèbre*. There were general strikes in South America, massive demonstrations in Europe, and protest meetings in Asia and Africa to affirm a worldwide belief in their innocence. Despite new evidence, the trial judge refused to reopen the case, sending Sacco and Vanzetti to the electric chair on August 23, 1927, and sparking a new wave of riots all over the world. In the US, important people and public facilities were placed under armed guard as a precaution, while thousands of mourners conducted the martyrs to their final resting place.

4. THE SCOTTSBORO BOYS (1931–50)
Nine black youths, aged 13–19, were charged with the 'rape' of two white prostitutes who had been riding the rails with them. Hurriedly tried and convicted in the Alabama town of Scottsboro, all but the youngest boy received a death sentence in 1931. The case attracted the attention of the Communist party, and workers throughout the US soon demonstrated – at Communist instigation – against the convictions of the 'Scottsboro boys'. In Dresden, Germany, the US consulate was stoned by a crowd of Communist youths. In New York City's Harlem, 1,500 protestors led by Communists left so many signs and banners after their march that two dump trucks were needed to haul the refuse away. The US Supreme Court twice ordered retrials, citing the inadequacy of defence counsel and the exclusion of black citizens from southern juries. The Scottsboro boys were retried three times in all. It was 1950 before the last one – middle-aged by then – was released.

5. THE MARIA HERTOGH CUSTODY CASE (December 11, 1950)
Maria Hertogh was born in 1937 in Indonesia to Dutch Roman Catholic parents. When the Japanese invaded in WWII they interned Maria's parents. During this time, Che Amirah and her husband looked after Maria. She was renamed Nadra and raised as a Muslim. Later, the Amirahs moved to the British colony of Malaysia. After the war, Maria's parents tried to find her but were unable to locate her until 1949. Adeline Hertogh went to court to claim custody of Maria. A Singapore court ruled that Maria should be returned to her natural parents. After the verdict was announced, Maria cried, 'Amirah is my mother. She has loved me, cared for me and brought me up.' Che Amirah then appealed and the verdict was reversed in July 1950. In August, 13-year old Maria married a 22-year-old teacher in a Muslim ceremony. Meanwhile, the custody case was again appealed. The court ruled that Maria's father had never consented to have the Amirahs raise the girl and that the Hertoghs should therefore have custody. The court also annulled Maria's marriage. While Che Amirah appealed this latest verdict, authorities decided to place Maria in the care of a convent. Newspaper pictures of Maria in a Christian convent aroused the antipathy of Singapore's Muslim population. On December 11 the court rendered its final decision, dismissing Amirah's appeal and confirming the Hertoghs' custody of Maria. After the verdict was announced, crowds of Muslims outside the courthouse started rioting. By the time British military police regained control of the streets 3 days later, 18 people had been killed and 173 injured.

6. THE CHICAGO SEVEN (1969–70)
The case of the Chicago Seven, spawned in street rioting during the 1968 Democratic national convention in Chicago, triggered a renewed round of protest after the jury verdict was delivered in 1970. The trial itself was chaotic: Black Panther leader Bobby Seale had to be bound and gagged to keep him quiet, and the wife of Yippie leader Abbie Hoffman warned the judge that she would dance on his grave. The seven defendants were acquitted of conspiracy, but five of them received maximum sentences (five years plus fines and court costs) for their intent to incite a riot. The 'jury of the streets' registered its immediate disapproval: some 5,000 marchers protested the verdict in Boston, 3,000 assembled in Chicago, and in Washington, DC more than 500 demonstrators convened in front of the Watergate residence of

US Attorney General John Mitchell. Students at the University of California in Santa Barbara burned down a local bank in protest, prompting Governor Ronald Reagan to threaten further antiriot prosecutions.

7. THE DAN WHITE CASE (1979)
At his trial for the murders of San Francisco Mayor George Moscone and Supervisor Harvey Milk, Dan White claimed as a mitigating circumstance that he ate too much junk food. A former policeman and a member of the city's board of supervisors (he was elected with the slogan, 'Crime is number one with me'), White had resigned from the board, then changed his mind. Angered by the mayor's refusal to reappoint him, he shot Moscone and Milk, leader of the city's large gay population, on November 27, 1978. White had suffered from depressions that were compounded by his overconsumption of Twinkies, his attorney argued. On May 21, 1979, when the jury returned a verdict of involuntary manslaughter due to 'diminished capacity' – which meant the possibility of parole in five years – the huge gay community and their supporters rioted in the streets of San Francisco, torching 12 police cars and causing $1 million-worth of property damage. As one gay leader announced, 'Society is going to have to deal with us not as nice little fairies, who have hairdressing salons, but as people capable of violence.' White committed suicide in 1985.

8. THE RODNEY KING BEATING TRIAL (April 29–30, 1992)
In the early morning hours of March 3, 1991, motorist Rodney King was stopped by Los Angeles police officers following a three-mile high-speed chase. According to the arrest reports filed later, King refused orders to exit the car, then put up such a struggle that officers had to use batons and stun guns to subdue him. However, unknown to the police, the entire incident had been filmed by a nearby resident, and the video told a different story. On the tape, King appeared to offer little resistance as several officers kicked and beat him to the ground, while a dozen of their colleagues looked on. Public outrage led to a grand jury investigation that indicted four officers – Theodore J. Briseno, Stacey C. Koons, Laurence M. Powell, and Timothy E. Wind – for assault and the use of excessive force. Because of the massive publicity, when the trial opened on March 4, 1992, it had been moved from Los Angeles to suburban Simi Valley. The prosecution presented several witnesses who testified that the officers – particularly Powell –

were 'out of control'. However, defence attorney Michael Stone insisted, 'We do not see an example of unprovoked police brutality. We see, rather, a controlled application of baton strikes for the very obvious reason of getting this man into custody.' The jury clearly agreed. On April 29 they returned not-guilty verdicts for all the defendants. The verdict rocked Los Angeles. Within hours, the city erupted in rioting that left 58 people dead and caused $1 billion in damages.

– C.D. & C.F.

Witticisms of 9 Condemned Criminals

1. GEORGE APPEL (electrocuted in 1928)
   As he was being strapped into the electric chair Appel quipped, 'Well, folks, you'll soon see a baked Appel.'
2. JESSE WALTER BISHOP (gassed in 1979)
   The last man to die in Nevada's gas chamber, Bishop's final words were, 'I've always wanted to try everything once . . . Let's go!'
3. GUY CLARK (hanged in 1832)
   On the way to the gallows the sheriff told Clark to speed up the pace. Clark replied, 'Nothing will happen until I get there.'
4. JAMES DONALD FRENCH (electrocuted in 1966)
   Turning to a newsman on his way to the electric chair, French helpfully suggested, 'I have a terrific headline for you in the morning: "French Fries".'
5. ROBERT ALTON HARRIS (gassed in 1992)
   The last person to die in the gas chamber at San Quentin, Harris issued a final statement through the prison warden that stated, 'You can be a king or a street-sweeper, but everybody dances with the Grim Reaper.' The quote was inspired by a line from the film *Bill and Ted's Bogus Journey*.
6. WILLIAM PALMER (hanged in 1856)
   As he stepped onto the gallows Palmer looked at the trapdoor and exclaimed, 'Are you sure it's safe?'
7. SIR WALTER RALEIGH (beheaded in 1618)
   Feeling the edge of the axe soon to be used on him, Raleigh said, ''Tis a sharp remedy but a sure one for all ills.'

8. JAMES W. RODGERS (shot in 1960)
Asked if he had a last request, Rodgers stated, 'Why yes – a bulletproof vest.'

9. FREDERICK CHARLES WOOD (electrocuted in 1963)
Sitting down in the electric chair Wood said, 'Gentlemen, you are about to see the effects of electricity upon wood.'

29 Unusual Lawsuits

1. PRAY FOR RAIN
In hopes of ending a drought in upstate New York in the 1880s, a Presbyterian minister named Duncan McLeod organized a mass prayer session to take place on a Saturday in August. At noon people throughout the area stopped their activities and prayed for rain. By one o'clock clouds had appeared; by two a gusty wind was blowing; by three the temperature had dropped 20°, and by four a thunderstorm had arrived. The storm, which dropped almost two inches of rain, washed out a bridge and completely destroyed a barn, which burned to the ground after being struck by lightning.
As it happened, the barn belonged to Phineas Dodd, the only farmer in Phelps, New York, who had refused to join the collective prayer. Many thought that Dodd had been a victim of divine justice, but Dodd had other ideas: when he heard that Reverend McLeod was accepting congratulations for having ended the drought, he sued the minister for $5,000 to cover the damages to his property. The minister was put in a difficult situation: after repeatedly telling his followers that God had answered their prayers, he could hardly back down and say that the storm was just a coincidence. Fortunately for McLeod, his lawyer was able to convince the judge that the mass prayers had requested only rain and that the thunder and lightning had been a bonus provided by God and for which McLeod and his parishioners were not responsible.

2. A TIGHT SQUEEZE
In the spring of 1888, actress Lillian Russell starred on Broadway in the play *The Queen's Mate*. When producer James Duff decided to take the show on the road, he insisted that

Russell wear silk tights in one scene, as she had in New York. Russell refused, saying that what was acceptable in New York might be considered scandalous in smaller cities. She also claimed that theatres out West were draughty and that she might catch cold. While cynics gossiped that Russell's reluctance was due to recent weight gains (she was now 5 ft 6 in. and 165 lb), Duff took the issue to court. The judge turned out to be a gallant fellow who ruled in Lillian Russell's favour, observing that her figure was a national asset that needed to be protected at all costs.

3. THE KABOTCHNICKS SPEAK ONLY TO GOD
The elite status of the Cabot family of New England is summarised in the old ditty:

Here's to the city of Boston,
The land of the bean and the cod,
Where the Lowells speak only to the Cabots,
And the Cabots speak only to God.

In August 1923, the Cabots received a bit of a jolt when Harry and Myrtle Kabotchnick of Philadelphia filed a petition to have their last name changed to Cabot. Immediate objections were raised by several prominent members of the Cabot family as well as by The Pennsylvania Society of the Order of Founders and Patriots of America. However, Judge Audendried ruled in favour of the Kabotchnicks, and a new branch was grafted onto the Cabot family tree.

4. A CABLE CAR NAMED DESIRE
The case of Gloria Sykes caused a sensation in San Francisco throughout the month of April 1970. A devout Lutheran and college graduate from Dearborn Heights, Michigan, the 23-year-old Sykes had been involved in a cable car accident. The Hyde Street cable car lost its grip and plunged backwards, throwing Sykes against a pole. She suffered two black eyes and several bruises, but worst of all, claimed her lawyer, she was transformed into a nymphomaniac. Although she had had sex back in Michigan, she became insatiable after the accident and once engaged in sexual intercourse 50 times in five days. This inconvenience caused her to sue the Municipal Railway for $500,000 for physical and emotional injuries. The jury of eight woman and four men was basically sympathetic and awarded Sykes a judgment for $50,000.

5. **SUING A FOREIGN PRINCE**
In 1971 Gerald Mayo filed suit in Pennsylvania at the US district court against Satan and his servants, claiming they had placed obstacles in his path which caused his downfall. On December 3, Mayo's complaint was denied on the grounds that the defendant did not reside in Pennsylvania.

6. **THE LOUISIANA PURCHASE RIP-OFF**
In 1976, Cecilia M. Pizzo filed suit in New Orleans to nullify the Louisiana Purchase, which had doubled the size of the United States in 1803. Pizzo claimed that neither Napoleon nor Thomas Jefferson had the authority to make the deal and that the 8-million-acre parcel still belonged to Spain. Judge Jack M. Gordon ruled that although it might be true that only the French Parliament and the US Congress had had the legal right to engage in negotiations, the fact was that Pizzo had filed her suit 167 years too late, since the statute of limitations on such cases is only six years.

7. **SHARPER THAN A SERPENT'S TOOTH IS A THANKLESS CHILD**
In April 1978, 24-year-old Tom Hansen of Boulder, Colorado, sued his parents, Richard and Shirley, for 'parental malpractice'. Young Hansen claimed that his parents had done such a bad job of rearing him that he would be forced to seek psychiatric care for the rest of his life. He asked $250,000 in medical expenses and $100,000 in punitive damages. In explaining his reasons for filing the suit, Hansen said it was an alternative to his desire to kill his father: 'I felt like killing my father for a long time. I guess I found a more appropriate way of dealing with it.' The suit was subsequently dismissed by the District Court and later by the Colorado Court of Appeals.

8. **STANDING UP FOR THE STOOD UP**
Tom Horsley, a 41-year-old accountant from Campbell, California, was quite upset in May 1978, when his date for the night, 31-year-old waitress Alyn Chesselet of San Francisco, failed to show up. He was so upset, in fact, that he sued her for 'breach of oral contract'. His lawyer explained that Mr Horsley is 'not the type of man to take standing up lying down'. Horsley asked for $38 in compensation: $17 for time lost at his hourly wage of $8.50, $17 in travel expenses, and $4 in court costs. Chesselet, in her defence, said she had attempted to call Horsley about her change in plans, which was due to having to work an

extra shift, but he had already left his office. Judge Richard P. Figone ruled against Horsley, who remained philosophical. 'I feel good about the whole thing,' he said. 'It raised people's consciousness about this problem . . .There's too much of this thing, broken dates. It shows people are not sincere.'

9. THE MISPLACED CORPSE
Beatrice Daigle, 73, of Woonsocket, R.I., filed a $250,000 suit when she learned that she had been praying at the wrong grave for 17 years. After her husband died on January 28, 1961, The Church of the Precious Blood in Woonsocket sold Mrs Daigle a plot at St John the Baptist Cemetery in Bellingham, Massachusetts. Mrs Daigle visited the grave frequently to pray for the repose of her dead husband's soul. On April 26, 1978, workers opened the grave in order to move Mr Daigle's body to another plot and discovered instead the body of a woman, Jeanne Champagne. Three more graves had to be dug up before Mr Daigle's body was located. Mrs Daigle, who was present at the exhumation, suffered 'severe emotional trauma and distress' because of the mistake. In November 1979 the case was dismissed.

10. DEMON LIQUOR
On February 5, 1979, Woodrow W. Bussey filed a $2 million suit in Oklahoma County District Court claiming that the Adolph Coors Co. and a local tavern had caused him to become an alcoholic by failing to warn him that the 3.2-proof beer served in Oklahoma is actually an intoxicating beverage. Bussey said that Coors beer had done irreparable damage to his brain, 'pickling his mind' and preventing him from thinking clearly. In 1988 Bussey, reacting to the reparations paid to Japanese-Americans who were interned during World War II, sued the United States government for uprooting his Cherokee ancestors during the 1838 forced march known as the Trail of Tears.

11. EXTRASENSORY PAIN
Martha Burke's twin sister, Margaret Fox, was one of the 580 people killed in the plane disaster at Tenerife in the Canary Islands on March 27, 1977. Consequently, Mrs Burke sued Pan American – not for the wrongful death of her sister, but for her own injuries, which she sustained because of the 'extrasensory empathy' which is common among identical twins. At the moment of the collision, Mrs Burke, sitting at her home in Fremont, California, suffered burning sensations in her chest and stomach and a feeling of being split.

On February 21, 1980, Federal Court Judge Robert Ward ruled against Burke, explaining that legally she had to be physically present at the accident to collect damages.

12. THE POORLY TRAINED SPY
Maria del Carmen y Ruiz was married to one of Fidel Castro's intelligence chiefs when, in 1964, she was approached by the CIA in Cuba and asked to be a spy. She worked diligently at her new job, but in January 1969 she was caught by Cuban counterintelligence agents and sentenced to 20 years in prison. After serving 8½ years, she became the first convicted American spy to be released from Cuban custody. In May 1980 Ruiz, now remarried and known as Carmen Mackowski, sued the CIA for inadequate training. She also charged that the CIA had misled her into believing that if she was detected, they would arrange for her immediate release. US District Court Judge Dickinson Debevoise of Trenton, New Jersey, ruled in favor of the CIA because, as one newspaper put it, federal judges 'do not have authority to intervene in CIA employment matters that might result in the release of intelligence information'.

13. X-RATED SHRUBBERY
In September 1980, in La Jolla, California, the 'Grand Old Man of Divorce Law', John T. Holt and his wife, Phyllis, filed suit against their neighbours, William and Helen Hawkins. The Holts claimed that the Hawkins had trimmed their hedges into obscene shapes. The Holts named 20 other neighbours as co-conspirators. They asked $250,000 in punitive damages and demanded removal of trees and hedges that had been shaped 'to resemble phallic symbols'. The case was finally dismissed in January 1982.

14. THE WANDERING BELLY-BUTTON
Virginia O'Hare, 42, of Poughkeepsie, New York, filed a malpractice suit against plastic surgeon Howard Bellin after her navel ended up two inches off-centre following surgery in November 1974, to give her 'a flat sexy belly'. Dr Bellin had previously performed successful operations on O'Hare's nose and eyelids. Bellin argued that O'Hare's navel (which was later returned to its proper position by another plastic surgeon) had only been misplaced by a half inch, which he called 'not cosmetically unacceptable'. In May 1979, a State Supreme Court jury awarded O'Hare $854,219, including $100,000 for pain and

suffering, $4,219 for the corrective surgery, and $750,000 for loss of earnings. Not surprisingly, Dr Bellin appealed the verdict but later agreed to pay Mrs O'Hare $200,000.

15. THE MUMMY'S CURSE
Police officer George E. La Brash, 56, suffered a stroke on September 23, 1979, while guarding the 3,300-year-old golden mask of King Tutankhamun when it was on display in San Francisco. La Brash claimed that he was a victim of the famous Curse of King Tut, which had caused the sudden death of numerous people involved in the 1923 discovery of Tut's tomb. For this reason he contended that the stroke was job-related and that he was entitled to $18,400 in disability pay for the eight months of his recuperation. On February 9, 1982, Superior Court Judge Richard P. Figone denied La Brash's claim.

16. LOSS OF PARANORMAL POWERS
Penny Pellito of Miramar, Florida, filed a personal-injury lawsuit against the Hollywood Home Depot hardware store after she was struck in the head by three eight-foot planks while shopping in April 1987. Pellito claimed that the accident caused her to lose the unusual ability to block out pain. Although witnesses testified to having witnessed a doctor saw Pellito's toe bone without benefit of anaesthesia before the accident, a jury rejected her claim. They also decided that she was 80% responsible for the accident, but they did award her $1,200 for normal physical damages.

17. SPRINTING TO THE COURTS
On August 28, 1988, the world-championship cycling road race, held in Robse, Belgium, came down to a sprint between Steve Bauer of Canada and 1984 world champion Claude Criquielion of Belgium. But a mere 75 m. from the finish line the two crashed, allowing Maurizio Fondriest of Italy to snatch an unexpected victory. In a case without precedent in professional cycling, Criquielion sued Bauer for assault and asked for more than $1.5 million in damages. Criquielion alleged that Bauer had swerved in front of him and elbowed him, thus denying him the glory and financial rewards that come with a world championship. The case dragged though the courts, but finally, three and a half years later, a Belgian judge ruled in favour of Bauer.

18. ACTING LIKE AN ASS
Former sex symbol Brigitte Bardot has devoted her post-film career years to promoting the rights of animals. Among the

members of her personal menagerie in St Tropez, France, were a 32-year-old mare named Duchesse and a young donkey named Mimosa. In the summer of 1989, Bardot invited her neighbour's donkey, a three-year-old male named Charley, to graze alongside Duchesse and Mimosa. When Charley began to display a sexual interest in Duchesse, Bardot feared that if Charley were allowed to have his way with the elderly mare, it might prove fatal to her. So she called in her vet and had Charley castrated. Charley's owner, Jean-Pierre Manivet, was out of town at the time. When he returned to St Tropez, he was outraged by what had happened. Manivet sued Bardot, claiming that Charley had really been interested in Mimosa, not Duchesse. Bardot countersued, alleging that the bad publicity had harmed her reputation. Both suits were eventually rejected by the courts.

19. LACK OF FORESIGHT

In 1982, Charles Wayne Brown of Newton, Iowa, was struck in the right eye by a golf ball stroked by car salesman Bill Samuelson. The accident caused permanent damage to Brown's eye. Brown sued Samuelson for failing to yell 'fore' before he hit the ball. The case was dismissed in 1984.

20. COKE ISN'T IT

Amanda Blake of Northampton, Massachusetts, had been working for Coca-Cola Bottling Company for eight years when, in 1985, Coca-Cola discovered that she had fallen in love with and become engaged to David Cronin, who worked for Pepsi. Blake was ordered to break off her engagement, persuade Cronin to quit his job, or quit herself. She refused, and was fired for 'conflict of interest'. Black sued Coca-Cola for damages and won a settlement worth several hundred thousand dollars.

21. THE BIG SPIN

On December 30, 1985, Doris Barnett of Los Angeles appeared on television to try her luck at the California lottery's Big Spin. Barnett spun the lottery wheel and watched as her ball settled into the $3 million slot. Show host Geoff Edwards threw his hands in the air and shouted 'Three million dollars!' Barnett's children rushed out of the audience and joined her in celebration, whooping and jumping for joy. Then Edwards tapped Barnett on the shoulder and turned her attention back to the wheel. The ball had slipped out of the $3 million slot and into the $10,000 slot. Edwards explained that lottery rules required the ball to stay in the slot for five seconds. Barnett was hustled offstage, but she did not go meekly. She sued the California lottery. In 1989, after watching endless videos of other contestants being declared winners in less than five seconds, a jury awarded Barnett the $3 million, as well as an extra $400,000 in damages for emotional trauma. But the California lottery didn't go meekly either: they refused to pay. Eventually, though, 'a mutually satisfactory settlement' was reached, with the agreement that the amount not be made public.

22. NERDS NOT ALLOWED

Two cases filed in Los Angeles challenged the right of fashionable nightclubs to deny entrance to would-be patrons because they are not stylishly dressed. In the first case, settled in 1990, Kenneth Lipton, an attorney specialising in dog-bite cases, was barred from entering the Mayan nightclub because a doorman judged his turquoise shirt and baggy olive pants to be 'not cool'. Owners of the club were forced to pay Lipton and three companions $1,112 in damages. The following year, the California State Department of Alcoholic Beverage Control won its suit against Vertigo, another trendy club that refused admittance to those people they claimed had no fashion sense. Administrative law judge Milford Maron ruled that Vertigo would lose its license if it continued to exclude customers based on a discriminatory dress code and the whim of doormen. Vertigo's owners chose to close the club in December 1992.

23. FALSE PREGNANCY

'World's Oldest Newspaper Carrier, 101, Quits Because She's Pregnant', read the headline in a 1990 edition of the *Sun*, a supermarket tabloid. The accompanying article, complete with a photograph of the sexually active senior, told the story of a newspaper carrier in Stirling, Australia, who had to give up her job when a millionaire on her route impregnated her. The story was totally false. Stirling, Australia, didn't even exist. But, as it turned out, the photo was of a real, living person – Nellie Mitchell, who had delivered the Arkansas *Gazette* for 50 years. Mitchell wasn't really 101 years old – she was only 96, young enough to be humiliated when friends and neighbours asked her when her baby was due. Mitchell sued the *Sun*, charging invasion of privacy and extreme emotional distress. John Vader, the editor of the *Sun*, admitted in court that he had chosen the picture of Mitchell because he assumed she was dead. Dead people cannot sue. A jury awarded Mitchell $850,000 in punitive damages and $650,000 in compensatory damages. In 1993 a federal district court judge reduced the amount of compensatory damages to $150,000.

24. A HARD CASE
On the surface, Plaster Caster v. Cohen was just another lawsuit concerning disputed property. What made the case unusual was the nature of the property. In 1966, Cynthia Albritton was, in her own words, 'a teen-age virgin dying to meet rock stars'. She was also a student at the University of Illinois. When her art teacher gave her an assignment to make a plaster cast of 'something hard', she got an idea. She began approaching visiting rock groups and asking if she could make plaster casts of their penises. She had no problem finding girlfriends to help her prepare her models. At first she used plaster of paris, then a combination of tinfoil and hot wax, before settling on an alginate product used for tooth and jaw moulds. Her project gained underground notoriety and she changed her name to Cynthia Plaster Caster. In 1970 her home in Los Angeles was burgled, so she gave 23 of her rock members to music publisher Herb Cohen for safekeeping. Cohen refused to return them, claiming they were a payoff for a business debt owed him by Frank Zappa, who had employed Plaster Caster. In 1991 Plaster Caster filed suit against Cohen, who countersued. Two years later a Los Angeles superior court ruled in favour of Cynthia Plaster Caster, who regained control of her 'babies', including Jimi Hendrix, Anthony Newley, Eric Burdon and Eddie Brigati.

25. BOTTOM LINES
Krandel Lee Newton, a street artist in Dallas's West End, thought he had a pretty good thing going. Unlike other street artists, Newton specialised in drawing people's rear ends. He even registered a trademark for his business: Butt Sketch. Then in 1992 along came another street artist, Mark Burton, who decided to add rear-end sketches to his repertoire. Burton called his business Fanny Sketch. Newton filed a federal lawsuit accusing Burton of threatening his business. The suit was settled out of court when Burton agreed to stop using the name Fanny Sketch and to refrain from engaging in any act which could cause the public to confuse his work with Mr. Newton's 'customartistry services'.

26. ROTTHUAHUAS
Canella, a Rottweiler living in Key Largo, Florida, was in heat and her owner, Kevin Foley, had plans to mate her with 'an

acceptable male' and then sell the litter. But before he could do so, a neighbouring Chihuahua named Rocky sneaked onto Foley's property and engaged Canella. Rocky and Canella were caught in the act, both by Foley, who snapped a photo of the incident, and by an animal control officer who happened to be passing by and stopped to watch the unusual coupling. A month later Foley learned that Canella was pregnant. He terminated the pregnancy by hysterectomy and sued Rocky's owner, Dayami Diaz. On November 1, 1993, Monroe County judge Reagan Ptomey ruled in favour of Foley and ordered Diaz to pay him $2,567.50.

27. DAMAGED BY BARRY MANILOW
It was with some reluctance that Arizona Court of Appeals Judge Philip Espinosa accompanied his wife to a Barry Manilow concert on the fateful night of December 23, 1993. Not a Manilow fan to begin with, he nonetheless expected an endurable evening of 'soft, amplified music'. Instead he found himself sitting through the loudest concert he had ever attended. It was so loud, in fact, that Espinosa was left with a constant and permanent ringing in his ears. He sued Manilow and others responsible for damages. The case was settled out of court in 1997 when Manilow agreed to donate $5,000 to an ear disorder association.

28. BREASTLASH
In honour of his impending wedding, Paul Shimkonis' friends threw a bachelor party for him at the Diamond Dolls topless club in Clearwater, Florida. As part of the show, he was asked to lean back in a chair with his eyes closed while dancer Tawny Peaks danced around him. In the words of the lawsuit that Shimkonis filed a year and a half later, 'Suddenly, without warning and without Plaintiff's consent, (the dancer) jumped on the Plaintiff, forcing her very large breasts into his face, causing his head to jerk backwards.' Shimkonis, a physical therapist, suffered head and neck injuries, incurred major medical bills and still couldn't turn his head to the right. Finally, on June 29, 1998, he filed suit against Diamond Dolls, asking $15,000 to cover his medical expenses and as compensation for 'loss of capacity for the enjoyment of life'. The case was brought before television's 'The People's Court' with former New York City mayor Ed Koch presiding. A female court officer examined Peaks' 69HH breasts in chambers and reported that although they were 20 per cent silicone, they were soft and 'not as dense

as Plaintiff described'. Koch ruled in favour of Tawny Peaks and the club. Peaks had her breasts reduced in 1999 and in 2005 put one of the implants up for sale on eBay: 'Somebody might bid on it. It's like the first boob to be sued over in a lawsuit,' she said. The infamous implant sold for $16,766.00 to Internet casino company GoldenPalace.com.

Surprising as it may seem, Shimkonis v. Peaks was not the only lawsuit to arise from a 1996 breast attack. In an unrelated case in Belleview, Illinois, Bennie Casson sued dancer Busty Heart (Susan Sykes) and P.T.'s Show Club in Sauget after he was assaulted by Heart's 88-inch breasts during a performance.

29. FLYING GLADIS

Australian mega-star Dame Edna Everage (a.k.a. Barry Humphries) made a point of ending her public performances by tossing dozens of gladioli with cut stems into the audience. Unfortunately, at the end of a show in Melbourne in April 2000, the stem of one of Dame Edna's gladis hit singing teacher Gary May in the left eye. May, who was taken away in an ambulance, sued for 40,000 Australian dollars, but later reached an out-of-court settlement.

Chapter 9

15 ACTORS WHO BECAME POLITICIANS

THE 10 WORST LIVING DICTATORS

13 DEPOSED DICTATORS . . . AFTER THE FALL

11 COMMANDERS KILLED BY THEIR OWN TROOPS

10 LARGEST ARMS EXPORTERS

10 LARGEST ARMS IMPORTERS

THE 10 MEN WHO CONQUERED THE MOST MILES

PERCENTAGE OF WOMEN IN 30 NATIONAL LEGISLATURES

9 UNUSUAL DISASTERS

11 ALTERNATIVE GUNMEN IN THE ASSASSINATION OF JOHN F. KENNEDY

18 SECRET ARMIES OF THE CIA

War, Politics and World Affairs

KIM JONG IL – see p.231

15 Actors Who Became Politicians

1. HELEN GAHAGAN DOUGLAS
A Broadway star, Gahagan moved to Hollywood after marrying film actor Melvyn Douglas. Her brief movie career was highlighted by her leading role in the cult classic *She* (1935). After several years' involvement in Democratic Party politics, she was elected to Congress in 1944 and served three terms. Gahagan Douglas ran for the US Senate in California in 1950, facing up-and-coming right-winger Richard Nixon. Nixon scared voters by calling her 'red hot' and 'pink right down to her underwear' and by insinuating that she had slept with President Truman. Nixon won the election and went on to further political success. Gahagan Douglas never ran for office again.

2. CLINT EASTWOOD
In 1986, the star by then of such films as *A Fistful of Dollars* (1964), *Dirty Harry* (1971) and *Sudden Impact* (1983), Eastwood took time off from his film career to serve two years as mayor of Carmel, California (pop. 4,800). Elected on a pro-development platform in 1986, Eastwood nonetheless stopped greedy developers from buying the 22-acre Mission Ranch by buying it himself for $5 million.

3. JOSEPH ESTRADA
Known as the 'Filipino Ronald Reagan' because he starred in so many B movies, Estrada built his reputation by playing the role of the common man fighting the system. Elected mayor of San Juan, a suburb of Manila, Estrada moved on to become the only senator without a college degree. In 1992 he was elected vice-president of the Philippines. Estrada was elected president of the Philippines in 1998. In 2000, he was impeached by the Philippine Congress on charges of corruption and bribery. He resigned on January 20, 2001, in the face of a bloodless 'people's revolt'. He has since served time in prison for perjury.

4. FRED GRANDY
Although he has appeared on Broadway and in the movies, Grandy, a Harvard graduate, is best known for his portrayal of Gopher in the TV series *The Love Boat* (1977–86). In 1986 he returned to his earlier interest in politics, winning election from Sioux City, Iowa, to the US House of Representatives. A Republican, Grandy describes himself as a 'knee-jerk moderate'.

5. GLENDA JACKSON
Jackson won two Academy Awards for her performances in *Women in Love* (1970) and *A Touch of Class* (1972). Running as a Labour Party candidate, the bricklayer's daughter won election to Parliament in 1992 in the Hampstead and Highgate constituencies of north London and has since had a committed career as an MP.

6. BEN JONES
Best known for his portrayal of the mechanic Cooter Davenport in *The Dukes of Hazzard*, Jones, a Georgia Democrat, won election to the US Congress in 1988. He was re-elected in 1990, but in 1992 he was defeated in the Democratic Party primary.

7. SHEILA KUEHL
Kuehl played Zelda Gilroy in the TV series *The Many Loves of Dobie Gillis* from 1959 to 1963. After the series ended she went to law school and became an attorney specialising in feminist issues. In 1994 she was elected speaker pro tem of the California State Assembly, the first woman to hold that position. In 2000 she was elected to the State Senate. Kuehl was the first openly gay or lesbian politician to be elected to the California legislature.

8. MELINA MERCOURI
The star of *Never on Sunday* (1959), Mercouri entered Greek politics as soon as democracy was restored in 1974. A member of the Pan-Hellenic Socialist movement, she was elected to Parliament in 1977 and has represented the working-class district of Piraeus ever since. She also served as minister of culture from 1981 until 1990. In 1990 she ran for mayor of Athens, but was defeated.

9. ALESSANDRA MUSSOLINI
No one was surprised or upset when the beautiful niece of actress Sophia Loren became a film actress herself, appearing in such films as *White Sister* (1973) and *A Special Day* (1977). But she did cause a stir when, at the age of 30, she followed in the footsteps of her grandfather, dictator Benito Mussolini, by entering politics. In 1992 she was elected to Parliament as the representative of the neo-Fascist party from Naples.

10. N.T. RAMA RAO
Known as the 'Saffron Caesar' because he usually appeared in an orange costume, Rama Rao, the star of more than 300 Indian films, capitalised on his widespread popularity to enter

politics. He rose to become chief minister of Andhra Pradesh state. After leaving office, he remained the leader of the Telegu Desam Party, and in 1991, at the age of 69, he was arrested in the midst of a hunger strike to protest at an attack on his house by supporters of the ruling Congress Party.

11. RONALD REAGAN
Reagan was a movie actor, a president of the Screen Actors' Guild, and a Democrat-turned-Republican. When he announced that he planned to run for governor of California in 1966, studio head Jack Warner commented, 'No, no, no! Jimmy Stewart for governor, Ronald Reagan for best friend.' When he won the election, Reagan was asked what he planned to do when he took office. 'I don't know,' he replied, 'I've never played a governor.' Reagan was re-elected in 1970 and later served two terms as President of the United States (1981–89). Nevertheless, he never lost his basic actor's mentality. At the 1987 economic summit in Venice, Reagan startled the leaders of the world's industrial nations by showing up with cue cards, not just for important meetings, but even at an informal cocktail party.

12. ARNOLD SCHWARZENEGGER
The bodybuilder-turned-actor rose to stardom in such films as *Conan the Barbarian* (1982) and *The Terminator* (1984). By the end of the 1980s, he was Hollywood's top action hero. After he married into the Kennedy clan (his wife, broadcast journalist Maria Shriver, is the daughter of Eunice Kennedy Shriver), speculation grew about a possible political career. He saw his chance in 2003, when Republicans launched a drive to recall California's Democratic Governor Gray Davis from office. In true Hollywood fashion, Schwarzenegger announced his candidacy on August 7, 2003, to Jay Leno on *The Tonight Show*. Two months later, California voters chose to oust Davis and replace him with Schwarzenegger.

13. ILONA STALLER
Hungarian-born pornographic film star Ilona Staller, better known by her stage name, Cicciolina, was elected to the Italian Parliament in 1987. A member of the Radical Party and the Party of Love, Staller represented her Rome constituency until retiring in 1992.

14. FRED THOMPSON
A veteran character actor, Thompson had prominent roles in the movies *The Hunt for Red October* (1990) and *In the Line of*

Fire (1993). A Republican from Tennessee, he was elected to the US Senate in 1994. In the fall of 2002 Thompson joined the cast of the NBC series *Law and Order*, becoming the first serving US senator with a regular television acting job. He left the Senate when his term ended in January of 2003.

15. JESSE VENTURA
Jesse 'The Body' Ventura first emerged as a star in the World Wrestling Federation. He parlayed that fame into a movie career, appearing with Arnold Schwarzenegger in *Predator* (1987) and with Sylvester Stallone in *Demolition Man* (1993). In 1998 he was elected Governor of Minnesota as the candidate of the upstart Reform Party. He drew fire from critics for appearing as a TV commentator for the short-lived XFL (Extreme Football League) and being a celebrity referee at a WWF event while still in office. He served one term, choosing not to run for re-election in 2002.

– D.W. & C.F.

The 10 Worst Living Dictators

1. KIM JONG IL, North Korea
In power since 1994.
There has been so much discussion about Kim Jong Il's development of nuclear weapons that it has tended to deflect attention from the fact that Kim's government represses its own people more completely than any other dictatorship in the world. Each year, the human-rights group Freedom House ranks every country according to its level of political rights and civil liberties. North Korea is the only nation to earn the worst possible score for 31 years in a row. According to the organisation Reporters Without Borders, North Korea also ranks in last place in its international index of press freedom. The US Committee for Human Rights in North Korea estimates that 150,000 Koreans perform forced labour in prison camps created to punish alleged political dissidents and their family members, as well as North Koreans who fled the country to China but were forced back by the Chinese government.

Although Kim Jong Il, who inherited leadership from his father, Kim Il Sung, is often portrayed as being crazy, he is actually a clever and efficient manipulator of his people. He is also the author of the books *On the Art of the Cinema* and *On the Art of Opera*.

2. THAN SHWE, Burma
In power since 1992.
General Than Shwe has survived a power struggle to emerge as the sole leader of Burma's military dictatorship. Because Than Shwe represents the hard-line faction, his rise has turned an already awful human rights situation even worse. Burma has more child soldiers than any nation in the world and the Burmese regime continues to kidnap normal citizens and force them to serve as porters for the military in various conflicts against non-Burmese ethnic groups. In 1990 the party of Nobel Peace Prize winner Aung San Suu Kyi won 80% of the vote in an open election. The military cancelled the results. Suu Kyi has spent most of the ensuing years under house arrest. On May 31, 2003 hired thugs attacked Suu Kyi's motorcade, killing several of her supporters and arresting dozens of others including Suu Kyi herself. She has since been returned to house arrest. Unlike most dictators, Than Shwe is not a public figure, preferring to work behind the scenes. Consequently, even the Burmese people know little about him. Than Shwe has promised new elections . . . in four or five years.

3. HU JINTAO, China
In power since 2002.
Trained as a hydraulic engineer, Hu Jintao joined the Communist Party in 1964 and spent the next 38 years slowly moving his way up the Party hierarchy. Along the way he proved himself to be quiet, efficient and willing to do whatever was necessary to promote his own advancement. While serving as Party Secretary of Tibet, he did not hesitate to administer martial law and to oversee the killing of unarmed demonstrators. Now that he is General Secretary of the Communist Party of China, Hu, although not all-powerful, is the leader of an unusually repressive regime. Apologists point to China's economic liberalisation and claim that the Chinese human rights situation is better than it used to be. However, the Communist Party still controls all media and uses 40,000 'Internet security agents' to monitor online use. More than 200,000 Chinese are serving 're-education' sentences in labour camps and China performs 4,000 executions a year, more than all the other nations of the world combined, and many of them for non-violent crimes.

4. ROBERT MUGABE, Zimbabwe
In power since 1980.
Robert Mugabe began his reign with widespread domestic and international support. After leading a successful anti-colonial

war of liberation, he was elected independent Zimbabwe's first president. But over the years he has displayed increasingly dictatorial tendencies. According to Amnesty International, in 2002 alone, Mugabe's government killed or tortured 70,000 people. Unemployment is above 70% and inflation 500%. Mugabe has been accused of blocking the delivery of food aid to groups and areas that support the main opposition party. He has continued to hold elections, but has restricted the opposition's ability to campaign and has shut down media that do not support him. When opposition leader Morgan Tsvangirai won 42% of the vote anyway, Mugabe had him arrested and charged with treason. As his support has slipped, Mugabe has played the race card, confiscating farms owned by white people and turning them over to his supporters.

5. CROWN PRINCE ABDULLAH, Saudi Arabia
   In power since 1995.
   Crown Prince Abdullah has been the acting leader of Saudi Arabia since his half-brother, King Fahd, suffered a stroke in 1995. Saudi Arabia is one of the only nations that holds no elections whatsoever. The royal family has promised municipal elections in the coming year, but has not announced if women will be allowed to vote. In fact, it is forbidden for unrelated Saudis of the opposite sex to appear in public together, even inside a taxi. Women are not allowed to testify on their own behalf in divorce proceedings and, in all court cases, the testimony of one man is equal to that of two women. According to the US State Department, Saudi Arabia continues to engage in arbitrary arrest and torture. During a human rights conference in October '95, Saudi authorities arrested non-violent protesters who were calling for freedom of expression, and some were later flogged, which is the normal punishment for alleged political and religious offences. Under pressure from world opinion, the government announced that people living in Saudi Arabia may practise religions other than Sunni Islam, as long as they do so privately, inside their homes. In one of the more unusual manifestations of control, the religious police forbade children from playing with Barbie dolls, which they dubbed 'Jewish dolls' that are 'symbols of decadence of the perverted West'.

6. TEODORO OBIANG NGUEMA, Equatorial Guinea
   In power since 1979.
   This tiny West African nation (pop. 500,000) was a forgotten dictatorship until major reserves of oil were discovered in 1995.

Since then, US oil companies have poured billions of dollars into the country. Although the per capita annual income is $4,472, 60% of Equatoguineans live on less than $1 a day. The bulk of the oil income goes directly to President Obiang, who has declared that 'there is no poverty in Guinea'. Rather, 'the people are used to living in a different way'. In July, state radio announced that Obiang is 'in permanent contact with the Almighty', and that 'He can decide to kill without anyone calling him to account and without going to Hell.' There is no public transport, no newspapers and only 1% of government spending goes to health care. Nonetheless, the US government reopened its embassy in October after it had been closed for eight years as a protest against human rights abuses. When asked why so much of his nation's oil revenue is deposited directly into his personal account at the Riggs Bank in Washington, DC, Obiang explained that he keeps total control of the money in order to 'avoid corruption'.

7. OMAR AL-BASHIR, Sudan
In power since 1989.
Sudan, the largest country in Africa, is in the midst of a complex 20-year civil war that has claimed the lives of 2 million people and uprooted another 4 million. Al-Bashir seized power in a military coup and immediately suspended the constitution, abolished the legislature and banned political parties and unions. He has tried to negotiate a peace agreement with the main rebel group, but he insists that the nation be ruled according to Islamic Shari'a law, even in southern Sudan, where the people are Christian and animist. Meanwhile, his army has routinely bombed civilians and tortured and massacred non-Arabs, particularly in the oil-producing areas of the south. Sudanese troops have also kidnapped southerners and subjected them to slavery. Al-Bashir has also been accused of 'engineering famine' in regions that oppose him. He has a long history of providing sanctuary for a wide range of terrorists, only to turn against them. He turned over the notorious Carlos the Jackal to France in exchange for financial and military aid and, in 1996, he tried unsuccessfully to sell Osama bin Laden to the US government.

8. SAPARMURAT NIYAZOV, Turkmenistan
In power since 1990.
Since taking charge of this former Soviet republic in central Asia, Niyazov has developed the world's most extreme personality cult,

challenged only by that of Kim Jong Il. Niyazov's picture appears on all Turkmen money, there are statues of him everywhere and he renamed the month of January after himself. His book, *Rukhnama* (Book of the Soul), is required reading in all schools at all levels and all government employees must memorise passages in order to keep their jobs. Niyazov rules without opposition. As he once put it, 'There are no opposition parties, so how can we grant them freedom?' In the past year, Niyazov has cracked down on religious and ethnic minorities, including Russians, and has refused to issue exit visas for families or for women under the age of 35. He has imprisoned political dissidents and subjected them to Stalinist-style show trials and public confessions. The Turkmen constitution requires retirement at the age of 70, but in August Niyazov ensured his own rule by creating a 2,507-member People's Council which unanimously elected him Lifetime Chairman.

9. FIDEL CASTRO, Cuba
In power since 1959.
The world's longest-reigning dictator, Fidel Castro took advantage of the world's preoccupation with the war in Iraq in March and April of 2003 to carry out his biggest round-up of non-violent dissidents in more than a decade. He arrested 75 human rights activists, journalists and academics, and sent them to prison for an average of 19 years. Cuba remains a one-party state with all power in the hands of Castro. The courts are controlled by the executive branch – in other words, Castro, who has traditionally blamed all of his country's problems, economic and social, on the United States.

10. KING MSWATI III, Swaziland
In power since 1986.
Swaziland (pop. 1.2 million) is the last remaining absolute monarchy in Africa. Mswati III ascended to the throne when he turned 18, four years after the death of his father. Because Mswati had been educated in England, it was thought that he would modernise his kingdom. However, he has shown a liking for certain Swazi traditions. On September 15, 2002 he watched thousands of girls and young women dance bare-breasted in the annual Reed Dance and then chose one to be his tenth wife (his father had 100 wives). The girl's mother filed a lawsuit against the king, charging him with abducting her daughter. Mswati, who rules by decree, then announced that the Swazi courts were forbidden from issuing rulings that limited the king's power. In

an attempt to appease international opinion, Mswati approved the drafting of a new constitution to replace the one that his father had suspended 30 years earlier. However, the new constitution bans political parties, allows the death penalty for any criminal offence and provides for the reintroduction of debtors' prisons.

13 Deposed Dictators . . . After the Fall

1. IDI AMIN, Uganda
Amin seized power in 1971 and launched a reign of terror that led to the deaths of an estimated 300,000 people. Deposed in 1979, Amin was offered asylum in Saudi Arabia, with all living expenses paid. In 1989 he tried to return to Uganda using a false passport. He got as far as the Congo, where he was recognised and arrested and then sent back to Saudi Arabia. Amin died in 2003 at the age of 78. Ugandan president Yoweri Museveni vetoed a suggestion to give Amin a state funeral in order to win votes in his home region: 'I would not bury Amin. I will never touch Amin. Never. Not even with a long spoon.'

2. JEAN-BEDEL BOKASSA, Central African Republic
Bokassa seized power in 1965. In 1976 he declared himself emperor and a year later staged an elaborate coronation celebration that used up one-fourth of the nation's annual earnings. He was overthrown in 1979, but not before he had committed a series of horrible outrages, including ordering the massacre of schoolchildren who refused to buy uniforms made in a factory owned by Bokassa's wife. After he was ousted, he lived lavishly in Paris. Then, incredibly, he returned to the CAR, where he was arrested upon arrival and charged with murder and cannibalism. He was convicted of the former charge and was kept in 'comfortable confinement' in the capital city of Bangui. Bokassa was set free in 1993, when General Andre Kolingba, the country's latest dictator, ordered all the nation's convicts released. He died in 1996.

3. JEAN-CLAUDE DUVALIER, Haiti
When longtime Haitian dictator François 'Papa Doc' Duvalier died in 1971, the mantle of power passed to his 19-year-old son Jean-Claude, better known as 'Baby Doc', who also inherited

the dreaded Tonton Macoutes secret police. Baby Doc was finally forced out of office in 1986 after widespread protest and flown out of the country on a US Air Force plane. Baby Doc and his wife, Michelle, not content with stuffing an Air Haiti cargo plane with plunder, bumped 11 passengers off their escape flight – including Michelle's grandparents – to make room for more loot. The Duvaliers settled on the French Riviera and spent millions of dollars a year before divorcing in 1990.

4. ERICH HONECKER, East Germany
As head of East German security, Honecker supervised the construction of the Berlin Wall in 1961. Ten years later he assumed leadership of the Communist Party. Among his more odious acts was ordering all border area to be mined and equipped with automatic shooting devices. With the fall of Communism in 1989, Honecker was put under house arrest. In 1991 he was flown from a Soviet military hospital near Berlin to Moscow itself. However, on July 29, 1992, the 79-year-old Honecker was expelled from the Chilean embassy where he had sought refuge and was flown back to Berlin to face charges of corruption and manslaughter. Because he was diagnosed as dying from liver cancer, Honecker was allowed to leave for Chile in January 1993. He died on May 29, 1994.

5. SADDAM HUSSEIN, Iraq
Saddam Hussein took power in 1979. A ruthless dictator, he used poison gas during his eight-year war with neighbouring Iran and to suppress rebellions by his country's Kurdish minority. He managed to survive despite losing the first Gulf War with a United States-led coalition in 1991. In 2003, the United States led a 'pre-emptive' war against Iraq. As Baghdad swiftly fell, Saddam disappeared. He remained elusive until December 13, 2003, when US forces found Saddam in a 6-ft deep hole on a farm outside his hometown of Tikrit. He offered no resistance, telling the American soldiers in English, 'My name is Saddam Hussein. I am the president of Iraq and I want to negotiate.' At the time of writing Saddam is being held in Baghdad, awaiting trial on war crimes and other charges. In February of 2004, French lawyer Jacques Vergez became Saddam's attorney and declared his intent to call officials from the US and other Western powers to the stand to demonstrate their complicity in Saddam's acts.

6. MENGISTU HAILE MARIAM, Ethiopia
Mengistu was a member of the military junta that ousted Haile Selassie in 1974. By 1977 Mengistu had consolidated his personal power. While the Ethiopian people were suffering through a series of droughts and famines, Mengistu concentrated on brutally suppressing his opponents. Bodies of political prisoners who had been tortured to death were displayed in public and shown on television. Mengistu's ability to beat back various secessionist armies finally failed, and on May 21, 1991, he resigned and fled the country. He settled in Zimbabwe, where he was welcomed by that country's dictator, Robert Mugabe.

7. MOBUTU SESE SEKO, Congo
After taking power in 1965, Mobutu amassed a huge fortune through economic exploitation and corruption, leading some observers to dub the government a 'kleptocracy'. He stole more than half of the $12 billion in aid that Congo (formerly Zaire) received from the International Money Fund during his 32-year reign, saddling the country with a crippling debt. On May 18, 1997 Mobutu fled the country as rebel forces led by Laurent Kabila seized the capital. For his exile, Mobutu could choose between luxury residences in Morocco, South Africa, France, Belgium, Spain and Portugal. The wine collection at his castle in Portugal was worth an estimated $23 million. Mobutu didn't have much time to enjoy his ill-gotten luxuries: he died on September 7, 1997, of prostate cancer.

8. MANUEL NORIEGA, Panama
Noriega was raised in a poor family of Colombian background. Something of an ugly duckling, he found his place in the military. He rose rapidly to become head of Panama's intelligence service. In 1983 he took command of the national army and, with it, the nation. A devious manipulator who played all sides, Noriega cooperated with the US government and the CIA while at the same time making huge profits from drug trafficking, money laundering and racketeering. When Noriega refused to abide by the results of a free election, President George Bush Sr ordered the invasion of Panama, and troops seized Noriega and brought him back to Miami to stand trial. He was convicted and sentenced to 40 years in prison. In December 1992 US District Court Judge William Hoeveler declared Noriega a prisoner of war, entitled to the rights guaranteed by the third Geneva Convention. He will be eligible for parole in 2006, although the

Panamanian government has sought his extradition because in 1995 he was tried in absentia and found guilty of murder.

9. AUGUSTO PINOCHET, Chile
As commander-in-chief of Chile's armed forces, Pinochet led the 1973 coup that overthrew the elected government of Salvador Allende. For the next 17 years he ruled Chile with an iron fist, suspending parliament and ordering the abduction and murder of 2,000 political opponents. He did, however, agree to democratic elections in 1988, which he lost. In 1990 he stepped down as president, but retained control of the armed forces, a position that he still holds. Pinochet was arrested in Great Britain in 1998 and held under house arrest while the British government considered extradition requests from four countries. During his house arrest, he lived at Wentworth, an exclusive estate outside London, at a cost of $10,000 per month. In May of 2000 he was returned to Chile on medical grounds. He was then arrested in Chile, with more than 200 charges filed against him. In 2002 all charges were dropped after the Chilean Supreme Court declared Pinochet unfit to stand trial.

10. POL POT, Cambodia
Pol Pot was one of the few modern dictators whose genocidal policies were so horrible that they rivalled those of Adolf Hitler. As leader of the notorious Khmer Rouge, Pol Pot launched a four-year reign of terror (1975–79) that turned Cambodia into one large forced-labour camp and led to the deaths of an estimated 1 million people. When Vietnamese forces finally drove the Khmer Rouge from power in 1979, Pol Pot and his followers set up shop in Thailand and northern Cambodia, where, with the encouragement of the government of the United States, he continued to be supported by the governments of China and Thailand. As late as 1996, Pol Pot was still executing Khmer Rouge opponents. He finally died of heart failure on April 15, 1998.

11. ALFREDO STROESSNER, Paraguay
Stroessner seized power in a 1954 military coup and held on for over 34 years, thus setting a record as the longest-ruling head of state in the western hemisphere. He was finally deposed in February 1989. He flew to exile in Brazil with one of his sons, while the rest of his family moved to Miami. In April 2004 the Paraguayan government paid compensation to 34 victims of Stroessner's repression.

12. SUHARTO, Indonesia
Shortly after seizing the presidency in a 1965 coup, Suharto launched an anti-Communist and anti-Chinese campaign that killed at least 500,000 people. In 1975 the Indonesian army invaded the former Portuguese colony of East Timor and killed 200,000 people – more than a quarter of the island's population. Despite these genocides, the US supported Suharto as an anti-Communist throughout the Cold War. The recession that hit East Asia in 1997 sent the Indonesian economy into free-fall. As increasing numbers of demonstrators took to the streets, Suharto was forced out of office in May of 1998. In April of 2000, Suharto was put on trial for misappropriating $571 million from various charities that he controlled. However, in September, a panel of judges dismissed the charges, concluding that Suharto, who had suffered several strokes, was medically unfit to stand trial. They also lifted a house arrest that had been imposed on Suharto. The decisions led to rioting in the streets. Unable to prosecute Suharto himself, Indonesian authorities arrested his son, Tommy, and convicted him of murder.

13. CHARLES TAYLOR, Liberia
In 1989 Taylor launched a revolt against the Liberian government, beginning 14 years of near-constant civil war. In 1997 Taylor was elected president, drawing 75% of the vote from a populace hoping his election would end the warfare. Taylor's regime became increasingly repressive and brutal. He was notorious for using child soldiers, organised into 'Small Boy Units'. Even as civil war resumed in Liberia, Taylor participated in conflicts in nearby Guinea, Côte d'Ivoire and Sierra Leone. His soldiers were repeatedly accused by human rights groups of widespread looting, rape, torture, forced labour and summary killings. By 2003 Taylor controlled little but the downtown of the Liberian capital, referred to derisively by rebels as the 'Federal Republic of Central Monrovia'. On August 11, 2003 Taylor accepted an asylum offer from Nigeria and fled Liberia, taking along $1 billion, emptying the national treasury. As Taylor settled into a luxury villa in the Nigerian city of Calabar, a United Nations tribunal indicted him on charges of committing war crimes in Sierra Leone. Although the Nigerian journalists' union and bar association have both called for Taylor to be handed over to Sierra Leone, Nigerian president Olusegun Obasanjo has said he will not extradite the former warlord.

– D.W. & C.F.

11 Commanders Killed by Their Own Troops

1. COL. JOHN FINNIS (1804–57), English
On the morning of May 10, 1857, in Meerut, India, Colonel Finnis, commander of the 11th Native Regiment of the British Indian Army, was informed that his troops had occupied the parade grounds and were in a state of mutiny. He mounted his horse, rode to the parade ground and began lecturing his troops on insubordination. The inflamed Indian soldiers – known as sepoys – promptly fired a volley at Finnis and killed him. This violent action triggered the Sepoy (or Indian) Mutiny.

2. CAPT. YEVGENY GOLIKOV (d. 1905), Russian
On June 13, 1905, the crew of the Russian cruiser *Potemkin* mutinied after an unsuccessful protest challenging the quality of meat served on the ship. Captain Golikov, the ship's commander, was seized by the mutineers and flung overboard. This incident was dramatised in the classic film *Battleship Potemkin* (1925), directed by Sergei Eisenstein.

3. KING GUSTAVUS II (1594–1632), Swedish
In 1632, at the Battle of Lützen during the Thirty Years' War, King Gustavus Adolphus was shot in the back while leading his cavalry in a charge against the Catholic armies of the Holy Roman Empire. Who actually killed him remains an unanswered question. However, many historical authorities insist that Gustavus must have been killed by one of his own men, if not accidentally, then intentionally by a traitor.

4.-5. LT. RICHARD HARLAN and LT. THOMAS DELLWO (d. 1971), US
In the early morning hours of March 16, 1971, an enlisted man at the US Army base in Bienhoa, Vietnam, cut a hole through the screen covering a window in the officers' quarters and threw a fragmentation grenade inside. Two lieutenants – Richard Harlan and Thomas Dellwo – were killed. Private Billy Dean Smith was arrested and court-martialled for the crime but was later declared innocent. The real murderer was never found.

6. GEN. THOMAS 'STONEWALL' JACKSON (1824–63), American (Confederate)
On the night of May 2, 1863, at the Battle of Chancellorsville during the American Civil War, Confederate General Thomas

'Stonewall' Jackson went on a scouting mission ahead of his lines in order to find a way to attack the rear of the Union forces. When he returned, Jackson was fired upon by a North Carolina Confederate regiment that thought he and his staff were Yankee cavalrymen. He died eight days later.

7. CAPT. LASHKEVITCH (d. 1917), Russian
On March 12, 1917, in Petrograd (now St Petersburg), Russian soldiers of the Volynsky Regiment refused to fire on street demonstrators and, instead, shot their commanding officer, Captain Lashkevitch. This marked a major turning point in the Russian Revolution, because after killing Lashkevitch, the Volynsky Regiment – the first Russian unit to mutiny – joined the revolutionary forces.

8. COL. DAVID MARCUS (1901–48), US
In 1948, US Army Colonel David Marcus resigned his post at the Pentagon and enlisted in the newly formed Israeli Army. On the night of June 10, 1948, after overseeing the construction of a relief road from Tel Aviv to besieged Jerusalem during the Israeli war for independence, Marcus was shot and killed while urinating in a field. One of his own sentries had mistaken him for an Arab because he had a bed sheet wrapped around him.

9. NADIR SHAH (1688–1747), Persian
A Turkish tribesman who became a Persian general and then head of the Persian Empire, Nadir Shah was a highly successful conqueror who defeated the Afghans, Mongols, Indians and Turks. In 1747 Nadir's own military bodyguard murdered him. His death met with widespread approval in Persia because of the harshness and cruelty of his rule.

10. CPL PAT TILLMAN (d. 2004), US
Tillman, a member of the Arizona Cardinals football team, gave up a lucrative contract extension to join the US Army in 2002. On April 22, 2004, Tillman was killed while leading a team of Army Rangers up a hill in southeastern Afghanistan to knock out enemy fire that had pinned down other soldiers. The army posthumously awarded him the Silver Star, its third-highest honour. One month later, the army announced that Tillman had been killed by fellow Americans in a 'friendly fire' accident.

11. CAPT. PEDRO DE URZÚA (d. 1561), Spanish
In 1559 Captain Pedro de Urzúa led an expedition of Spanish soldiers from coastal Peru across the Andes to the Amazon

Basin in search of El Dorado. Two years later, while still searching unsuccessfully for gold, de Urzúa was killed by his own men when they mutinied under the leadership of Lope de Aguirre. De Urzúa's death and the fate of the mutineers was depicted in the 1973 movie *Aguirre, Wrath of God*.

– R.J.F.

10 Largest Arms Exporters

		$ Millions (US) (1998–2002)
1.	USA	37,723
2.	Russia	20,741
3.	France	8,312
4.	Germany	4,954
5.	UK	4,811
6.	Ukraine	2,673
7.	Italy	1,787
8.	China	1,561
9.	Netherlands	1,520
10.	Belarus	1,142

Source: Stockholm International Peace Research Institute (SIPRI Yearbook 2002)

10 Largest Arms Importers

		Millions of US Dollars (1998-2002)	Major Supplier
1.	China	8,818	Russia (93%)
2.	Taiwan	6,822	USA (71%)
3.	India	4,824	Russia (81%)
4.	Turkey	4,688	USA (60%)
5.	Saudi Arabia	4,360	USA (66%)
6.	Greece	3,958	USA (47%)
7.	South Korea	3,445	USA (64%)
8.	Egypt	3,251	USA (91%)
9.	United Kingdom	3,116	USA (82%)
10.	Israel	3,033	USA (74%)

Source: Stockholm International Peace Research Institute (SIPRI Yearbook 2002)

The 10 Men Who Conquered the Most Miles

1. GENGHIS KHAN (1162–1227)
From 1206 to 1227 Mongol chieftain, Genghis Khan, conquered approximately 4,860,000 square miles. Stretching from the Pacific Ocean to the Caspian Sea, his empire included northern China, Mongolia, southern Siberia and central Asia.

2. ALEXANDER THE GREAT (356–323BC)
From 334 to 326BC the Macedonian king, Alexander the Great, conquered approximately 2,180,000 square miles. His empire included the southern Balkan peninsula, Asia Minor, Egypt and the entire Near East, as far as the Indus River.

3. TAMERLANE (1336?–1405)
From 1370 to 1402 the Islamic Turkicised Mongol chieftain, Tamerlane, conquered approximately 2,145,000 square miles. His empire included most of the Near East, from the Indus River to the Mediterranean Sea, and from the Indian Ocean north to the Aral Sea.

4. CYRUS THE GREAT (600?–529BC)
From 559 to 539BC the Persian king, Cyrus the Great, conquered approximately 2,090,000 square miles. He conquered the Median Empire, Babylonia, Assyria, Syria, Palestine, the Indus Valley and southern Turkestan.

5. ATTILA (406?–453)
From 433 to 453 Attila, the king of the Huns and the Scourge of God, conquered approximately 1,450,000 square miles. Although he failed in his attempt to conquer Gaul, Attila ruled an empire encompassing central and eastern Europe and the western Russian plain.

6. ADOLF HITLER (1889–1945)
From 1933 to the autumn of 1942 Nazi dictator, Adolf Hitler, conquered 1,370,000 square miles, all of which he lost within three years. Hitler's Third Reich included most of continental Europe and extended from the English Channel to the outskirts of Moscow, and from North Africa to Norway.

7. NAPOLEON BONAPARTE (1769–1821)
From 1796 to the height of his power in 1810 Napoleon Bonaparte conquered approximately 720,000 square miles.

Napoleon's Grand Empire included France, Belgium, Holland, Germany, Poland, Switzerland and Spain.

8. MAHMUD OF GHAZNI (971?–1030)
From 997 to 1030 Mahmud, the Muslim sultan and Afghan king of Ghazni, conquered 680,000 square miles. His Near Eastern empire extended from the Indian Ocean north to the Amu Darya River, and from the Tigris River east to the Ganges River in India.

9. FRANCISCO PIZARRO (1470?–1541)
From 1531 to 1541 Spanish adventurer, Francisco Pizarro, conquered 480,000 square miles. Employing treachery and assassination, and taking advantage of internal discord, he subjugated the Inca Empire, which extended from Ecuador south through the Andes to Bolivia.

10. HERNANDO CORTES (1485–1547)
From 1519 to 1526 Hernando Cortes, commanding a small Spanish military expedition, conquered 315,000 square miles. Defeating the Aztecs, he seized central and southern Mexico and later subjugated Guatemala and Honduras to Spanish rule.

– R.J.F.

Percentage of Women in 30 National Legislatures

The Inter-Parliamentary Union, an international organisation that works to foster representative government and world peace, reports that women are appallingly under-represented in their national parliaments. Although women account for more than 50% of the world's population, in 2004 the number of female legislators stood at only 15.6%. The figures below are for March 2004. (The IPU can be contacted at www.ipu.org or by writing to 5, Chemin du Pommier/ Case postale 330/ CH-1218 Le Grand-Saconnex/ Geneva, Switzerland.)

THE 10 NATIONS WITH THE HIGHEST PERCENTAGE OF WOMEN IN THEIR LEGISLATURES . . .

1.	Sweden	45.3%
2.	Rwanda	45.0
3.	Denmark	38.0
4.	Finland	37.5

5.	Norway	36.4
6.	Cuba	36.0
7.	Costa Rica	35.1
8.	Netherlands	35.1
9.	Belgium	33.9
10.	Germany	31.4
. . . COMPARED TO 20 OTHERS		
11.	Argentina	30.7
12.	Spain	30.5
13.	Mozambique	30.0
14.	New Zealand	28.3
15.	Vietnam	27.3
16.	Canada	23.6
17.	Mexico	21.2
18.	Pakistan	20.8
19.	Nicaragua	20.7
20.	China	20.2
21.	United Kingdom	17.3
22.	Israel	15.0
23.	United States	14.0
24.	Syria	12.0
25.	France	11.7
26.	India	9.3
27.	Russia	8.0
28.	South Korea	5.5
29.	Kuwait	0.0
30.	Saudi Arabia	0.0

Source: 'Women in National Parliaments: World Classification', Inter-Parliamentary Union.

9 Unusual Disasters

1. ST PIERRE SNAKE INVASION
Volcanic activity on the 'bald mountain' towering over St Pierre, Martinique, was usually so inconsequential that no one took seriously the fresh steaming ventholes and earth tremors during April 1902. By early May, however, ash began to rain down continuously, and the nauseating stench of sulphur filled the air. Their homes on the mountainside made uninhabitable, more than 100 fer-de-lance snakes slithered down and invaded the mulatto quarter of St Pierre. The 6-ft long serpents killed 50 people and innumerable animals

before they were finally destroyed by the town's giant street cats. But the annihilation had only begun. On May 5, a landslide of boiling mud spilled into the sea, followed by a tsunami that killed hundreds and, three days later, May 8, Mt Pelee finally exploded, sending a murderous avalanche of white-hot lava straight toward the town. Within three minutes St Pierre was completely obliterated. Of its 30,000 population, there were only two survivors.

2. THE SHILOH BAPTIST CHURCH PANIC

Two thousand people, mostly black, jammed into the Shiloh Baptist Church in Birmingham, Alabama, on September 19, 1902, to hear an address by Booker T. Washington. The brick church was new. A steep flight of stairs, enclosed in brick, led from the entrance doors to the church proper. After Washington's speech, there was an altercation over an unoccupied seat, and the word 'fight' was misunderstood as 'fire'. The congregation rose as if on cue and stampeded for the stairs. Those who reached them first were pushed from behind and fell. Others fell on top of them until the entrance was completely blocked by a pile of screaming humanity 10 ft high. Efforts by Washington and the churchmen down in the front to induce calm were fruitless, and they stood by helplessly while their brothers and sisters, mostly the latter, were trampled or suffocated to death. There was neither fire – nor even a real fight – but 115 people died.

3. THE GREAT BOSTON MOLASSES FLOOD

On January 15, 1919 the workers and residents of Boston's North End, mostly Irish and Italian, were out enjoying the noontime sun of an unseasonably warm day. Suddenly, with only a low rumble of warning, the huge cast-iron tank of the Purity Distilling Company burst open and a great wave of raw black molasses, two storeys high, poured down Commercial Street and oozed into the adjacent waterfront area. Neither pedestrians nor horse-drawn wagons could outrun it. Two million gallons of molasses, originally destined for rum, engulfed scores of people – 21 men, women and children died of drowning or suffocation, while another 150 were injured. Buildings crumbled, and an elevated train track collapsed. Those horses not completely swallowed up were so trapped in the goo they had to be shot by the police. Sightseers who came to see the chaos couldn't help but walk in the molasses. On their way home they spread the sticky substance throughout the city.

Boston smelled of molasses for a week, and the harbour ran brown until summer.

4. THE PITTSBURGH GASOMETER EXPLOSION
A huge cylindrical gasometer – the largest in the world at that time – located in the heart of the industrial centre of Pittsburgh, Pennsylvania, developed a leak. On the morning of November 14, 1927 repairmen set out to look for it – with an open-flame blowlamp. At about 10 o'clock they apparently found the leak. The tank, containing 5 million cu. ft of natural gas, rose in the air like a balloon and exploded. Chunks of metal, some weighing more than 100 lb, were scattered great distances, and the combined effects of air pressure and fire left a square mile of devastation. Twenty-eight people were killed and hundreds were injured.

5. THE GILLINGHAM FIRE 'DEMONSTRATION'
Every year the firemen of Gillingham, Kent, would construct a makeshift 'house' out of wood and canvas for the popular fire-fighting demonstration at the annual Gillingham Park fête. Every year, too, a few local boys were selected from many aspirants to take part in the charade. On July 11, 1929 nine boys – aged 10 to 14 – and six firemen costumed as if for a wedding party climbed to the third floor of the 'house'. The plan was to light a smoke fire on the first floor, rescue the 'wedding party' with ropes and ladders, and then set the empty house ablaze to demonstrate the use of the fire hoses. By some error, the real fire was lit first. The spectators, assuming the bodies they saw burning were dummies, cheered and clapped, while the firemen outside directed streams of water on what they knew to be a real catastrophe. All 15 people inside the house died.

6. THE EMPIRE STATE BUILDING CRASH
On Saturday morning, July 28, 1945, a veteran Army pilot took off in a B-25 light bomber from Bedford, Massachusetts, headed for Newark, New Jersey, the co-pilot and a young sailor hitching a ride were also aboard. Fog made visibility poor. About an hour later, people on the streets of midtown Manhattan became aware of the rapidly increasing roar of a plane and watched with horror as a bomber suddenly appeared out of the clouds, dodged between skyscrapers, and then plunged into the side of the Empire State Building. Pieces of plane and building fell like hail. A gaping hole was gouged in the 78th floor, one of the

plane's two engines hurtled through seven walls and came out the opposite side of the building, and the other engine shot through an elevator shaft, severing the cables and sending the car plummeting to the basement. When the plane's fuel tank exploded, six floors were engulfed in flame, and burning gasoline streamed down the sides of the building. Fortunately, few offices were open on a Saturday and only 11 people – plus the three occupants of the plane – died.

7. THE TEXAS CITY CHAIN REACTION EXPLOSIONS
On April 15, 1947 the French freighter *Grandcamp* docked at Texas City, Texas, and took on some 1,400 tons of ammonium nitrate fertiliser. That night a fire broke out in the hold of the ship. By dawn, thick black smoke had port authorities worried because the Monsanto chemical plant was only 700 ft away. As men stood on the dock watching, tugboats prepared to tow the freighter out to sea. Suddenly a ball of fire enveloped the ship. For many it was the last thing they ever saw. A great wall of flame radiated outward from the wreckage, and within minutes the Monsanto plant exploded, killing and maiming hundreds of workers and any spectators who had survived the initial blast. Most of the business district was devastated, and fires raged along the waterfront, where huge tanks of butane gas stood imperilled. Shortly after midnight, a second freighter – also carrying nitrates – exploded, and the whole sequence began again. More than 500 people died, and another 1,000 were badly injured.

8. THE BASRA MASS POISONING
In September 1971 a shipment of 90,000 metric tons of seed grain arrived in the Iraqi port of Basra. The American barley and Mexican wheat – which had been chemically treated with methylmercury to prevent rot – were sprayed a bright pink to indicate their lethal coating, and clear warnings were printed on the bags – but only in English and Spanish. Before they could be distributed to the farmers, the bags were stolen from the docks and the grain was sold as food to the starving populace. The Iraqi government, embarrassed at its criminal negligence or for other reasons, hushed up the story, and it was not until two years later that an American newsman came up with evidence that 6,530 hospital cases of mercury poisoning were attributable to the unsavoury affair. Officials would admit to only 459 deaths, but total fatalities were probably more like 6,000, with another 100,000 suffering such permanent effects as blindness, deafness and brain damage.

9. THE CHANDKA FOREST ELEPHANT STAMPEDE
In the spring of 1972 the Chandka Forest area in India – already suffering from drought – was hit by a searing heat wave as well. The local elephants, who normally were no problem, became so crazed by the high temperatures and lack of water that the villagers told authorities they were afraid to venture out and to farm their land. By summer the situation had worsened. On July 10, the elephant herds went berserk and stampeded through five villages, leaving general devastation and 24 deaths in their wake.

– N.C.S.

11 Alternative Gunmen in the Assassination of John F. Kennedy

According to the Warren Commission, Lee Harvey Oswald was the lone assassin in the killing of President Kennedy. However, a large majority of the public believes that the assassination was the result of a conspiracy. The CIA, the FBI, the Mafia, the military, pro-Castro Cubans and anti-Castro Cubans have all been cited as possible forces behind the scenes. Among the people accused of doing the actual shooting are the following:

1. LUCIEN SARTI and TWO CORSICAN HITMEN
According to jailed French mobster Christian David, Kennedy was shot by three Corsican assassins. David named the deceased Sarti as one of the gunmen and offered to reveal the identities of the others if he was given his freedom. According to David, the two unnamed assassins were in buildings to the rear of the President, while Sarti fired from the grassy knoll in front of the motorcade. The British television documentary *The Men Who Killed Kennedy* identified Sarti as the man in a police uniform apparently firing a rifle on the grassy knoll visible in a computer-enhanced enlargement of a photo taken by Mary Moorman at the moment of the fatal shot.

2. CHARLES V. HARRELSON
Harrelson – the father of actor Woody Harrelson – has been serving a life sentence since 1979 for murdering federal judge John H. Wood Jr. During a six-hour stand-off before his arrest, Harrelson held a gun to his head and confessed to shooting Kennedy. He later retracted the statement, saying he had been high on cocaine at the time.

3. 'CARLOS' and OTHERS
Minister Raymond Broshears reported that David Ferrie – a bizarre individual often suspected of involvement in the assassination who had ties to Oswald, the CIA and the Mafia – would, after getting drunk, often talk about his role in the conspiracy. Ferrie reportedly said his job was to wait in Houston for two gunmen, one of them a Cuban exile Ferrie referred to as Carlos, and then fly them on the second leg of an escape route that was to take the assassins to South Africa via South America. Ferrie told Broshears the plan fell apart when the assassins, flying in a light plane, decided to skip the stop in Houston and press on to Mexico. They allegedly died when their plane crashed near Corpus Christi, Texas.

4. LUIS ANGEL CASTILLO
According to assassination researcher Penn Jones, Castillo has stated under hypnosis that 'he was on the parade route with a rifle that day . . . [with] instructions to shoot at a man in a car with red roses'. Jackie Kennedy was the only person in the motorcade with red roses; all the other women had been given yellow Texas roses.

5. ELADIO DEL VALLE and LORAN HALL
According to 'Harry Dean' (the 'war name' of a man who claims to be a former CIA agent), as quoted by W.B. Morris and R.B. Cutler in *Alias Oswald*, the assassins were anti-Castro activists Hall and del Valle, who were hired by the John Birch Society. Although Hall says he was at his home in California on November 22, 1963, he allegedly told the *Dallas Morning News* in 1978 that, a month before the assassination, right-wing activists working with the CIA tried to recruit him for a plot to kill Kennedy. As for del Valle, he died under suspicious circumstances in 1967. Del Valle, who was being searched for as a possible witness in the Clay Shaw conspiracy trial, was discovered shot through the heart and with his head split open by a machete.

6. 'BROTHER-IN-LAW' and 'SLIM'
In 1992 Kerry Thornley appeared on the television show *A Current Affair* and said he had been part of a conspiracy to kill President Kennedy. His co-conspirators were two men he called 'Brother-in-Law' and 'Slim'. Thornley also denied having been responsible for framing Oswald, whom Thornley had befriended in the Marines: 'I would gladly have killed Kennedy, but I

would never have betrayed Oswald.' He added, 'I wanted [Kennedy] dead. I would have shot him myself.' Thornley has also claimed that he and Oswald were the products of a genetic engineering experiment carried out by a secret neo-Nazi sect of eugenicists called the Vril Society, and that the two of them had been manipulated since childhood by Vril overlords.

7. JEAN RENE SOUTRE
Soutre, a terrorist in the French Secret Army Organisation, is believed by some researchers to have been recruited by the CIA to serve as an assassin. According to CIA documents obtained under the Freedom of Information Act by researcher Mary Ferrell, French intelligence reported that Soutre was in Fort Worth on the morning of November 22, 1963, and in Dallas that afternoon. Soutre was picked up by US authorities in Texas within 48 hours of the assassination and expelled from the country.

8. ROSCOE WHITE, 'SAUL' and 'LEBANON'
In 1990 Ricky White claimed his father Roscoe, a Dallas police officer, had been one of President Kennedy's assassins. According to Ricky, a detailed description of the conspiracy could be found in Roscoe's diary, which had disappeared after it was taken by the FBI for inspection. Two other gunmen, referred to in the diary only by the code names 'Saul' and 'Lebanon', were also involved. In addition, Roscoe's widow, Geneva, told journalist Ron Laytner that she had overheard Roscoe and Jack Ruby plotting to kill Kennedy, adding, 'We at first thought the assassination was more Mob [but later realised] it was more CIA.' Fifteen years before Ricky and Geneva White went public, Hugh McDonald, in *Appointment in Dallas*, identified one of the killers as a professional assassin known as Saul. McDonald claimed to have tracked down Saul, who admitted to having been paid $50,000 to shoot the President. Saul claimed to have fired from the Dallas County Records Building – which was also described in Roscoe White's diary as one of the locations the assassins had shot from. Despite these similarities, there are some inconsistencies in the plots described by McDonald and Ricky White. Most notably, Roscoe White in his diary and Saul in his meeting with McDonald each allegedly claimed to have fired the fatal shot.

9. GEORGE HICKEY JR
According to Bonar Menninger's book *Mortal Error* – based on 25 years of research by ballistics expert Howard Donahue – Kennedy was accidentally killed by Hickey, a secret service

agent in the car behind the presidential limo. According to this theory, when Oswald began shooting, Hickey reached for his rifle and slipped off the safety. As he tried to stand in the backseat of the car to return fire, he lost his balance and accidentally pulled the trigger, firing the shot that killed the President. Hickey himself had told the Warren Commission that he did not even pick up his rifle until after the fatal shot.

10. FRANK STURGIS and OPERATION 40
Marita Lorenz, a CIA operative who had been Fidel Castro's mistress, told the *New York Daily News* in 1977 that she had accompanied Lee Harvey Oswald and an assassination squad to Dallas a few days before Kennedy was killed. She identified her companions on the trip as CIA operative (and future Watergate burglar) Frank Sturgis and four Cuban exiles: Orlando Bosch, Pedro Diaz Lang and two brothers named Novis. The men were members of 'Operation 40', a group of about 30 anti-Castro Cubans and their American advisors originally formed by the CIA in 1960 for the Bay of Pigs invasion. Lorenz later stated that Sturgis had been one of the actual gunmen and that he told her after the assassination, 'You could have been part of it – you know, part of history. You should have stayed. It was safe. Everything was covered in advance. No arrests, no real newspaper investigation. It was all covered, very professional.' Sturgis denies that there is any truth to Lorenz's story. However, he once said that the FBI questioned him about the assassination right after it happened, because, the agents said, 'Frank, if there's anybody capable of killing the President of the United States, you're the guy who can do it.'

11. JAMES FILES and CHARLES NICOLETTI
In 1996 Files claimed that he and Nicoletti, a Mafia hitman, had been on the grassy knoll at Dealey Plaza and that they had both shot President Kennedy at the same time. Files said that he was paid $30,000 and had orders not to hit Jacqueline Kennedy. He added that Nicoletti took his order from Sam 'Momo' Giancana, who in turn answered to Anthony 'Big Tuna' Accardo. Since all three mobsters were murdered between 1975 and 1977, there was no one to corroborate Files's story. The FBI dismissed the story, noting that Files is now serving a 50-year sentence in Illinois for murdering a policeman and thus had little to lose by 'confessing' while gaining his 15 minutes of fame.

– C.F.

18 Secret Armies of the CIA

1. UKRAINIAN PARTISANS
From 1945 to 1952 the CIA trained and aerially supplied Ukrainian partisan units which had originally been organised by the Germans to fight the Soviets during WWII. For seven years, the partisans, operating in the Carpathian Mountains, made sporadic attacks. Finally, in 1952, a massive Soviet military force wiped them out.

2. CHINESE BRIGADE IN BURMA
After the Communist victory in China, Nationalist Chinese soldiers fled into northern Burma. During the early 1950s, the CIA used these soldiers to create a 12,000-man brigade which made raids into Red China. However, the Nationalist soldiers found it more profitable to monopolise the local opium trade.

3. GUATEMALAN REBEL ARMY
After Guatemalan president Jacobo Arbenz legalised that country's Communist party and expropriated 400,000 acres of United Fruit banana plantations, the CIA decided to overthrow his government. Guatemalan rebels were trained in Honduras and backed up with a CIA air contingent of bombers and fighter planes. This army invaded Guatemala in 1954, promptly toppling Arbenz's regime.

4. SUMATRAN REBELS
In an attempt to overthrow Indonesian president Sukarno in 1958, the CIA sent paramilitary experts and radio operators to the island of Sumatra to organise a revolt. With CIA air support, the rebel army attacked but was quickly defeated. The American government denied involvement even after a CIA B-26 was shot down and its CIA pilot, Allen Pope, was captured.

5. KHAMBA HORSEMEN
After the 1950 Chinese invasion of Tibet, the CIA began recruiting Khamba horsemen – fierce warriors who supported Tibet's religious leader, the Dalai Lama – as they escaped into India in 1959. These Khambas were trained in modern warfare at Camp Hale, high in the Rocky Mountains near Leadville, Colorado. Transported back to Tibet by the CIA-operated Air America, the Khambas organised an army numbering at its peak some 14,000. By the mid-1960s the Khambas had been abandoned by the CIA but they fought on alone until 1970.

6. **BAY OF PIGS INVASION FORCE**
In 1960 CIA operatives recruited 1,500 Cuban refugees living in Miami and staged a surprise attack on Fidel Castro's Cuba. Trained at a base in Guatemala, this small army – complete with an air force consisting of B-26 bombers – landed at the Bay of Pigs on April 17, 1961. The ill-conceived, poorly planned operation ended in disaster, since all but 150 men of the force were either killed or captured within three days.

7. **L'ARMÉE CLANDESTINE**
In 1962 CIA agents recruited Meo tribesmen living in the mountains of Laos to fight as guerrillas against Communist Pathet Lao forces. Called l'Armée Clandestine, this unit – paid, trained and supplied by the CIA – grew into a 30,000-man force. By 1975 the Meos – who had numbered a quarter million in 1962 – had been reduced to 10,000 refugees fleeing into Thailand.

8. **NUNG MERCENARIES**
A Chinese hill people living in Vietnam, the Nungs were hired and organised by the CIA as a mercenary force, during the Vietnam War. Fearsome and brutal fighters, the Nungs were employed throughout Vietnam and along the Ho Chi Minh Trail. The Nungs proved costly since they refused to fight unless constantly supplied with beer and prostitutes.

9. **PERUVIAN REGIMENT**
Unable to quell guerrilla forces in its eastern Amazonian provinces, Peru called on the US for help in the mid-1960s. The CIA responded by establishing a fortified camp in the area and hiring local Peruvians who were trained by Green Beret personnel on loan from the US Army. After crushing the guerillas, the elite unit was disbanded because of fears it might stage a coup against the government.

10. **CONGO MERCENARY FORCE**
In 1964, during the Congolese Civil War, the CIA established an army in the Congo to back pro-Western leaders Cyril Adoula and Joseph Mobutu. The CIA imported European mercenaries and Cuban pilots – exiles from Cuba – to pilot the CIA air force, composed of transports and B-26 bombers.

11. **THE CAMBODIAN COUP**
For over 15 years the CIA had tried various unsuccessful means of deposing Cambodia's left-leaning Prince Norodom Sihanouk, including assassination attempts. However, in March 1970 a

CIA-backed coup finally did the job. Funded by US tax dollars, armed with US weapons and trained by American Green Berets, anti-Sihanouk forces called Kampuchea Khmer Krom (KKK) overran the capital of Phnom Penh and took control of the government. With the blessing of the CIA and the Nixon administration, control of Cambodia was placed in the hands of Lon Nol, who would later distinguish himself by dispatching soldiers to butcher tens of thousands of civilians.

12. KURD REBELS
During the early 1970s the CIA moved into eastern Iraq to organise and supply the Kurds of that area, who were rebelling against the pro-Soviet Iraqi government. The real purpose behind this action was to help the Shah of Iran settle a border dispute with Iraq favourably. After an Iran–Iraq settlement was reached, the CIA withdrew its support from the Kurds, who were then crushed by the Iraqi Army.

13. ANGOLA MERCENARY FORCE
In 1975, after years of bloody fighting and civil unrest in Angola, Portugal resolved to relinquish its hold on the last of its African colonies. The transition was to take place on November 11, with control of the country going to whichever political faction controlled the capital city of Luanda on that date. In the months preceding the change, three groups vied for power: the Popular Movement for the Liberation of Angola (MPLA), the National Front for the Liberation of Angola (FNLA) and the National Union for the Total Independence of Angola (UNITA). By July 1975 the Marxist MPLA had ousted the moderate FNLA and UNITA from Luanda, so the CIA decided to intervene covertly. Over $30 million was spent on the Angolan operation, the bulk of the money going to buy arms and pay French and South African mercenaries, who aided the FNLA and UNITA in their fight. Despite overwhelming evidence to the contrary, US officials categorically denied any involvement in the Angolan conflict. In the end, it was a fruitless military adventure, for the MPLA assumed power and controls Angola to this day.

14. AFGHAN MUJAHEDIN
Covert support for the groups fighting against the Soviet invasion of Afghanistan began under President Jimmy Carter in 1979, and was stepped up during the administration of Ronald Reagan. The operation succeeded in its initial goal, as the Soviets were forced to begin withdrawing their forces in 1987.

Unfortunately, once the Soviets left, the US essentially ignored Afghanistan as it collapsed into a five-year civil war followed by the rise of the ultra-fundamentalist Taliban. The Taliban provided a haven for Osama bin Laden and al-Qaeda, the perpetrators of the 9/11 terrorist attacks in 2001.

15. SALVADORAN DEATH SQUADS
As far back as 1964 the CIA helped form ORDEN and ANSESAL, two paramilitary intelligence networks that developed into the Salvadoran death squads. The CIA trained ORDEN leaders in the use of automatic weapons and surveillance techniques, and placed several leaders on the CIA payroll. The CIA also provided detailed intelligence on Salvadoran individuals later murdered by the death squads. During the civil war in El Salvador from 1980 to 1992, the death squads were responsible for 40,000 killings. Even after a public outcry forced President Reagan to denounce the death squads in 1984, CIA support continued.

16. NICARAGUAN CONTRAS
On November 23, 1981, President Ronald Reagan signed a top secret National Security Directive authorising the CIA to spend $19 million to recruit and support the Contras, opponents of Nicaragua's Sandinista government. In supporting the Contras, the CIA carried out several acts of sabotage without the Congressional intelligence committees giving consent – or even being informed beforehand. In response, Congress passed the Boland Amendment, prohibiting the CIA from providing aid to the Contras. Attempts to find alternate sources of funds led to the Iran-Contra scandal. It may also have led the CIA and the Contras to become actively involved in drug smuggling. In 1988 the Senate Subcommittee on Narcotics, Terrorism, and International Operations concluded that individuals in the Contra movement engaged in drug trafficking; that known drug traffickers provided assistance to the Contras; and that 'there are some serious questions as to whether or not US officials involved in Central America failed to address the drug issue for fear of jeopardizing the war effort against Nicaragua'.

17. HAITIAN COUPS
In 1988 the CIA attempted to intervene in Haiti's elections with a 'covert action program' to undermine the campaign of the eventual winner, Jean-Bertrand Aristide. Three years later, Aristide was overthrown in a bloody coup that killed more than

4,000 civilians. Many of the leaders of the coup had been on the CIA payroll since the mid-1980s. For example, Emmanuel 'Toto' Constant, the head of FRAPH, a brutal gang of thugs known for murder, torture and beatings, admitted to being a paid agent of the CIA. Similarly, the CIA-created Haitian National Intelligence Service (NIS), supposedly created to combat drugs, functioned during the coup as a 'political intimidation and assassination squad.' In 1994 an American force of 20,000 was sent to Haiti to allow Aristide to return. Ironically, even after this, the CIA continued working with FRAPH and the NIS. In 2004 Aristide was overthrown once again, with Aristide claiming that US forces had kidnapped him.

18. VENEZUELAN COUP ATTEMPT
On April 11, 2002 Venezuelan military leaders attempted to overthrow the country's democratically-elected left-wing president, Hugo Chavez. The coup collapsed after two days, as hundreds of thousands of people took to the streets and as units of the military joined with the protestors. The administration of George W. Bush was the only democracy in the western hemisphere not to condemn the coup attempt. According to intelligence analyst Wayne Madsen, the CIA had actively organised the coup: 'The CIA provided Special Operations Group personnel, headed by a lieutenant colonel on loan from the US Special Operations Command at Fort Bragg, North Carolina, to help organise the coup against Chavez.'

R.J.F. & C.F.

Chapter 10

11 MUSEUMS OF LIMITED APPEAL

14 OF THE STRANGEST THINGS FOUND IN LONDON TRANSPORT'S LOST PROPERTY OFFICE

THE 7 WONDERS OF THE ANCIENT WORLD

THE 15 LEAST POPULOUS INDEPENDENT NATIONS

5 PLACES WITH UNLIKELY NAMES

13 POSSIBLE SITES FOR THE GARDEN OF EDEN

23 CASES OF BIZARRE WEATHER

15 SHIPWRECK SURVIVAL TIPS

Travel

Courtesy of and © the Icelandic Phallological Museum
(www.ismennt.is/not/phallus/ens.htm)

BLUE WHALE EXHIBIT AT THE ICELANDIC PHALLOLOGICAL MUSEUM – see p.264

11 Museums of Limited Appeal

1. THE MUSEUM OF BAD ART (580 High St, Dedham, MA, USA; www.glyphs.com/moba/)
   Founded in 1993, MOBA is located in the basement of the Dedham Community Theater eight miles south of Boston. Its motto is 'Art too bad to be ignored'. Although the bulk of the collection has been acquired at thrift shops, many of the finest pieces were fished out of rubbish bins.

2. STRIPTEASE MUSEUM (29053 Wild Road, Helendale, CA, USA; www.exoticworldusa.org/)
   Officially titled Exotic World Burlesque Hall of Fame and Museum, it is the domain of former exotic dancer Dixie Evans, whose speciality was imitating Marilyn Monroe. Items on display include breakaway sequinned gowns, tasselled panties, and Gypsy Rose Lee's black velvet shoulder cape.

3. THE MÜTTER MUSEUM (College of Physicians of Philadelphia, 19 South 22nd St, Philadelphia, PA, USA; www.collphyphil.org/ muttpg1.shtml)
   This stunning collection of medical oddities and instruments includes the Chevalier Jackson collection of foreign bodies removed from the lungs and bronchi, the Sappey collection of mercury-filled lymphaticus, the B.C. Hirot pelvis collection and medical tools from Pompeii. Individual items include Florence Nightingale's sewing kit; the joined liver of Chang and Eng, the original Siamese twins; bladder stones removed from US Chief Justice John Marshall; a piece of John Wilkes Booth's thorax; a wax model of a six-inch horn projecting from a woman's forehead; a cheek retractor used in a secret operation on President Grover Cleveland, as well as the cancerous tumour that was removed from his left upper jaw.

4. THE DOG COLLAR MUSEUM (Leeds Castle, Maidstone, Kent, ME17 1PL, United Kingdom; http://www.leeds-castle.com/content/ visiting_the_castle/dog_collar_museum/.html)
   Housed in the Gate Tower of Leeds Castle, the museum features medieval and ornamental dog collars spanning four centuries. Included are numerous spiked collars designed for dogs used in hunting and bull- and bear-baiting.

5. KIM IL SUNG GIFT MUSEUM (Mount Myohyang, North Korea)
   Housed in a 120-room, 6-storey temple north of Pyongyang, the

museum is home to 90,000 gifts that have been given to Kim Il Sung, the late dictator of Communist North Korea and to his son, Kim Jong Il, the current dictator. Included are Nicolae Ceausescu's gift of a bear's head mounted on a blood-red cushion, a Polish machine gun and a rubber ashtray from China's Hwabei Tyre factory. Twenty rooms are devoted to gifts given to Kim's son, Kim Jong Il, including an inlaid pearl and abalone box from the Ayatollah Khomeini and a pen set from the chairman of the Journalist Association of Kuwait.

6. ANTIQUE VIBRATOR MUSEUM (603 Valencia, San Francisco, CA 94110, USA; http://www.goodvibes.com/museum.html)
   The museum has collected more than 100 vibrators going back to 1869. Antique models include a hand-crafted wooden vibrator that works like an egg-beater and another that advertises 'Health, Vigour and Beauty' to users. The museum's collection is displayed in Good Vibrations, a sex-toy emporium.

7. AMERICAN ACADEMY OF OTOLARYNGOLOGY MUSEUM (One Prince St, Alexandria, VA 22314-3357, USA; http://www.entnet.org/ museum/index.cfm)
   Devoted to the world of head and neck surgery, the museum displays special exhibits dealing with such topics as the history of the hearing aid and the evolution of tracheotomies. The diseases of famous people are examined, including Oscar Wilde's ear infections and Johannes Brahms's sleep apnoea. The giftshop sells holiday decorations in the shape of ear trumpets.

8. SULABH INTERNATIONAL MUSEUM OF TOILETS (Mahavir Enclave, Palm Dabri Marg, New Delhi, India; www.sulabhtoiletmuseum.org)
   The Sulabh International Social Service Organization was created to bring inexpensive but environmentally safe sanitation to poor, rural areas. On the grounds of their headquarters, they have built an indoor and outdoor museum that presents the history of toilets around the world. One panel reprints poetry relating to toilets and another gives examples of toilet humour from around the world.

9. BRITISH LAWNMOWER MUSEUM (106–114 Shakespeare Street, Southport, Lancashire, PR8 5AJ, United Kingdom)
   The museum includes 400 vintage and experimental lawnmowers, highlighting the best of British technological ingenuity. Of particular interest are the 1921 ATCO Standard 9 Blade, a

solar-powered robot mower, and unusually fast or expensive mowers.

10. MARIKINA CITY FOOTWEAR MUSEUM (Manila, Philippines)
Former Philippine first lady Imelda Marcos, the world's most notorious shoe collector, donated the collection that made possible the opening of this footwear museum on February 16, 2001. The displays at the museum include several hundred of the pairs of shoes left behind at the presidential palace when Imelda and her husband Ferdinand fled the country in disgrace in 1986. Other shoes at the museum were donated by local politicians and film stars.

11. ICELANDIC PHALLOLOGICAL MUSEUM (Hedinsbraut 3a, 640 Húsavík, Iceland)
The world's only museum for genitalia, the Icelandic Phallological Museum contains more than 218 preserved penises, as well as specimens that have been pressed into service as purses, walking sticks and pepper pots. The museum's holdings represent nearly all of Iceland's land and sea mammals, with the 47 whale specimens making for the most impressive viewing. As yet, the museum has no human specimen, but an elderly man has pledged his privates in a legally-binding letter of donation.

14 of the Strangest Things Found in London Transport's Lost Property Office

1. 2½ hundredweight of sultanas/currants
2. Lawn mower
3. Breast implants
4. Theatrical coffin
5. Stuffed eagle
6. 14-ft boat
7. Divan bed
8. Park bench
9. Garden slide
10. Jar of bull's sperm
11. Urn of ashes
12. Dead bats in container

13. Vasectomy kit
14. Two human skulls in a bag

The 7 Wonders of the Ancient World

Who created one of the earliest and most enduring of all lists, a list that arbitrarily named the seven most spectacular sights existing in the world 150 years before the birth of Jesus Christ? The list was created by a most respected Byzantine mathematician and traveller named Philon. In a series of arduous trips, Philon saw all of the western civilised world there was to see in his time, and then he sat down and wrote a short but widely circulated paper entitled *De Septem Orbis Spectaculis* (The Seven Wonders of the World).

1. THE GREAT PYRAMID OF CHEOPS (Egypt)
   Begun as a royal tomb in c. 2600BC, standing in splendour 2,000 years before any of the other Seven Wonders were built, this largest of Egypt's 80-odd pyramids is the only Wonder to have survived to this day. Located outside Cairo, near Giza, the burial tomb of King Cheops was made up of 2.3 million blocks of stone, some of them 2½ tons in weight. The height is 481 ft, the width at the base 755 ft on each side, large enough to enclose London's Westminster Abbey, Rome's St Peter's and Milan's and Florence's main cathedrals.

2. THE HANGING GARDENS OF BABYLON (Iraq)
   They were not hanging gardens, but gardens on balconies or terraces. When Nebuchadnezzar brought home his new wife, a princess from Medes, she pined for the mountains and lush growth of her native land. To please her, in 600BC the king started to build a man-made mountain with exotic growths. Actually it was a square climbing upward, each densely planted with grass, flowers and fruit trees, irrigated from below by pumps manned by slaves or oxen. Inside and beneath the gardens, the queen held court amid the vegetation and artificial rain. Due to the erosion of time and influx of conquerors, the Hanging Gardens had been levelled and reduced to wilderness when Pliny the Elder visited them before his death in AD79.

3. THE STATUE OF ZEUS AT OLYMPIA (Greece)
   The multicoloured Temple of Zeus, in the area where the Greek Olympic Games were held every fourth year, contained the magnificent statue of Zeus, king of the gods. Sculptured by Phidias (who had done Athena for the Parthenon) some time

after 432BC, the statue was 40 ft high, made of ivory and gold plates set on wood. Zeus, with jewels for eyes, sat on a golden throne, feet resting on a footstool of gold. Ancients came from afar to worship at the god's feet. A Greek writer, Pausanias, saw the statue intact as late as second century AD. After that it disappeared from history, probably the victim of looting armies and fire.

4. THE TEMPLE OF DIANA AT EPHESUS (Turkey)
Summing up his Seven Wonders, Philon chose his favourite: 'But when I saw the temple at Ephesus rising to the clouds, all these other wonders were put in the shade.' The temple, a religious shrine built after 350BC, housed a statue of Diana, goddess of hunting, symbol of fertility. The kings of many Asian states contributed to the construction. The temple, 225 ft wide and 525 ft long, was supported by 127 marble columns 60 ft high. St Paul, in the New Testament, railed against it, being quoted as saying that 'the temple of the great goddess Diana should be despised, and her magnificence should be destroyed, whom all Asia and the world worshippeth'. The craftsmen of the temple disagreed: 'And when they heard these sayings, they were full of wrath, and cried out saying, "Great is Diana of the Ephesians" '. Ravaged and brought down by invaders, the temple was rebuilt three times before the Goths permanently destroyed it in AD262. In 1874, after 11 years of digging, the English archaeologist J.T. Wood unearthed fragments of the original columns.

5. THE TOMB OF KING MAUSOLUS AT HALICARNASSUS (Turkey)
King Mausolus, conqueror of Rhodes, ruled over the Persian province of Caria. His queen, Artemisia, was also his sister. When he died in 353BC, he was cremated and his grieving widow drank his ashes in wine. As a memorial to him, she determined to build the most beautiful tomb in the world at Halicarnassus, now called Bodrum. She sent to Greece for the greatest architects and sculptors, and by 350BC the memorial was complete. There was a rectangular sculptured marble tomb on a platform, then 36 golden-white Ionic columns upon which sat an architrave, which in turn held a pyramid topped by a bronzed chariot with statues of Mausolus and Artemisia. The monument survived 1,900 years, only to tumble down in an earthquake. What remains of it today is the word 'mausoleum'.

6. THE COLOSSUS OF RHODES ON THE ISLE OF RHODES (in the Aegean Sea)
   To celebrate being saved from a Macedonian siege by Ptolemy I, the Rhodians, between 292 and 280BC, erected a mammoth statue to their heavenly protector, the sun-god Apollo. Chares, who had studied under a favourite of Alexander the Great, fashioned the statue. The nude Colossus was 120 ft tall, with its chest and back 60 ft around, built of stone blocks and iron and plated with thin bronze. It did not stand astride the harbour, with room for ships to pass between the legs, but stood with feet together on a promontory at the entrance to the harbour. In 224BC it was felled by an earthquake. It lay in ruins almost 900 years. In AD667 the Arabs, who controlled Rhodes, sold the 720,900 lb of broken statue for scrap metal to a Jewish merchant. When the merchant hauled his purchase to Alexandria, he found that it required 900 camel loads.
7. THE LIGHTHOUSE ON THE ISLE OF PHAROS (off Alexandria, Egypt)
   On orders of Ptolemy Philadelphus, in 200BC, the architect Sostratus of Cnidus constructed a pharos or lighthouse such as the world had not seen before. Built on a small island off Alexandria, the tiers of the marble tower – first square, then round, each with a balcony – rose to a height of 400 ft. At the summit a huge brazier with an eternal flame was amplified by a great glass mirror so that the fire could be seen 300 miles out at sea. Half the lighthouse was torn down by occupying Arabs, who hoped to find gold inside the structure. The rest of the structure crashed to the ground when an earthquake struck in 1375.

– I.W.

The 15 Least Populous Independent Nations

		Population
1.	Tuvalu	11,468
2.	Nauru	12,809
3.	Palau	20,016
4.	San Marino	28,503
5.	Monaco	32,270
6.	Liechtenstein	33,436
7.	Saint Kitts and Nevis	38,836

8.	Marshall Islands	57,738
9.	Antigua and Barbuda	68,320
10.	Dominica	69,278
11.	Andorra	69,865
12.	Seychelles	80,832
13.	Grenada	89,357
14.	Kiribati	100,798
15.	Federated States of Micronesia	108,155

Source: US Census Bureau, International Data Base, April 30, 2004

5 Places with Unlikely Names

1. CAPE OF GOOD HOPE
   When the Portuguese explorer Bartholomeu Dias rounded the southern tip of Africa in 1488, he found the seas so rough he called it the Cape of Storms. This epithet was hardly likely to encourage traffic through this new gateway to India, so Portugal's King John II called it the Cape of Good Hope.

2. GREENLAND
   Known by a singularly inappropriate epithet, this great, snow-covered island is a tenth-century example of false advertising. Eric the Red hoped to attract settlers from the more clement Iceland.

3. NOME
   A classic geographical mistake, 'Nome' was miscopied from a British map of Alaska on which '? Name' had been written around 1850.

4. PACIFIC OCEAN
   Magellan had the remarkable luck of crossing this ocean without encountering a storm, so he called it *Mar Pacifico* – 'the calm sea'. The Pacific in fact produces some of the roughest storms in the world.

5. SINGAPORE
   This word derives from the Sanskrit for 'city of the lion'. Its exact origin is a mystery, since lions are not indigenous to the region.

– R.K.R.

13 Possible Sites for the Garden of Eden

'And the Lord God planted a garden eastward in Eden . . . And a river went out of Eden to water the garden; and from thence it was parted and became into four heads. The name of the first is Pison: that is it which compasseth the whole land of Havilah, where there is gold; And the gold of that land is good: there is bdellium and the onyx stone. And the name of the second river is Gihon: the same is it that compasseth the whole land of Ethiopia. And the name of the third river is Kiddekel: that is it which goeth toward the east of Assyria. And the fourth river is Euphrates.'

– *Genesis 2:8–14*

1. SOUTHERN IRAQ
Many biblical scholars believe that the Garden of Eden, the original home of Adam and Eve, was located in Sumer, at the confluence of the Euphrates and Tigris (or Hiddekel) rivers in present-day Iraq. They presume that the geographical references in Genesis relate to the situation from the ninth to the fifth centuries BC and that the Pison and Gihon were tributaries of the Euphrates and Tigris which have since disappeared. In fact, they may have been ancient canals.

2. EASTERN TURKEY
Other students of the Bible reason that if the four major rivers flowed *out* of the garden, then the garden itself must have been located far north of the Tigris–Euphrates civilization. They place the site in the mysterious northland of Armenia in present-day Turkey. This theory presumes that Gihon and Pison may not have been precise geographical designations, but rather vague descriptions of faraway places.

3. NORTHERN IRAN
British archeologist David Rohl claimed that Eden is a lush valley in Iran, located about 10 miles from the modern city of Tabriz. Rohl suggests that the Gihon and Pison are the Iranian rivers Araxes and Uizhun. He also identifies nearby Mt Sahand, a snow-capped extinct volcano, as the prophet Ezekiel's Mountain of God.

4. ISRAEL
There are those who say that the garden of God must have been in the Holy Land and that the original river that flowed into the

garden *before* it split into four separate rivers must have been the Jordan, which was longer in the days of Genesis. The Gihon would be the Nile, and Havilah would be the Arabian Peninsula. Some supporters of this theory go further, stating that Mt Moriah in Jerusalem was the heart of the Garden of Eden and that the entire garden included all of Jerusalem, Bethlehem and Mt Olivet.

5. EGYPT
Supporters of Egypt as the site of the Garden of Eden claim that only the Nile region meets the Genesis description of a land watered, not by rain, but by a mist rising from the ground, in that the Nile ran partially underground before surfacing in spring holes below the first cataract. The four world rivers, including the Tigris and Euphrates, are explained away as beginning far, far beyond the actual site of Paradise.

6.-7. EAST AFRICA and JAVA
Since Adam and Eve were the first humans, and since the oldest human remains have been found in East Africa, many people conclude that the Garden of Eden must have been in Africa. Likewise, when archaeologists discovered the remains of *Pithecanthropus* in Java in 1891, they guessed that Java was the location of the Garden of Eden.

8. SINKIANG, CHINA
Tse Tsan Tai, in his work *The Creation, the Real Situation of Eden, and the Origin of the Chinese* (1914), presents a case for the garden being in Chinese Turkestan in the plateau of eastern Asia. He claims that the river that flowed through the garden was the Tarim, which has four tributaries flowing eastwards.

9. LEMURIA
In the mid-nineteenth century a theory developed that a vast continent once occupied much of what is now the Indian Ocean. The name Lemuria was created by British zoologist P.L. Sclater in honour of the lemur family of animals, which has a somewhat unusual range of distribution in Africa, southern India and Malaysia. Other scientists suggested that Lemuria was the cradle of the human race; thus it must have been the site of the Garden of Eden.

10. PRASLIN ISLAND, SEYCHELLES
General Charles 'Chinese' Gordon supported the theory that Africa and India used to be part of one massive continent.

While on a survey expedition for the British government in the Indian Ocean, he came upon Praslin Island in the Seychelles group. So enchanted was he by this island, and by its Vallée de Mai in particular, that he became convinced that this was the location of the original Garden of Eden. The clincher for Gordon was the existence on Praslin of the coco-de-mer, a rare and exotic tree, which is native to only one other island of the Seychelles and which Gordon concluded was the tree of the knowledge of good and evil.

11. MARS
In his book *The Sky People*, Brinsley Le Poer Trench argues that not only Adam and Eve but Noah lived on Mars. He states that the biblical description of a river watering the garden and then parting into four heads is inconsistent with nature. Only canals can be made to flow that way, and Mars, supposedly, had canals. So the Garden of Eden was created on Mars as an experiment by Space People. Eventually the north polar ice cap on Mars melted, and the descendants of Adam and Eve were forced to take refuge on Earth.

12. GALESVILLE, WISCONSIN, USA
In 1886 the Rev. D.O. Van Slyke published a small pamphlet that expounded his belief that Eden was the area stretching from the Allegheny Mountains to the Rocky Mountains and that the Garden of Eden was located on the east bank of the Mississippi River between La Crosse, Wisconsin, and Winona, Minnesota. When the Deluge began, Noah was living in present-day Wisconsin, and the flood carried his ark eastward until it landed on Mt Ararat.

13. JACKSON COUNTY, MISSOURI, USA
While travelling through Davies County, Missouri, Mormon church founder Joseph Smith found a stone slab that he declared was an altar that Adam built shortly after being driven from the Garden of Eden. Declaring, 'This is the valley of God in which Adam blessed his children', Smith made plans to build a city called Adam-ondi-Ahram at the site. The Garden of Eden itself, Smith determined, was located 40 miles south, near the modern-day city of Independence.

23 Cases of Bizarre Weather

1. NEW ENGLAND'S DARK DAY
The sun did rise in New England on May 19, 1780, but by midday the sky had turned so dark that it was almost impossible to read or conduct business, and lunch had to be served by candlelight. The phenomenon was noted as far north as Portland, Maine, and as far south as northern New Jersey. General George Washington made mention of the spectacle in his diary. At Hartford, Connecticut, there was great fear that the Day of Judgement had arrived, and at the state legislature a motion was made to adjourn. Calmer heads prevailed and when the sky cleared the following day, it was generally concluded that the problem had been caused by smoke and ash from a fire 'out West'.

2. THUNDER AND LIGHTNING DURING SNOWSTORM
During the night of February 13, 1853, the residents of Mt Desert Island, Maine, were frightened by the freak attack of a thunderstorm during a snowstorm. Bolts of purple lightning flashed to the ground and balls of fire entered homes, injuring several people. Fortunately, no one was killed.

3. GIANT SNOWFLAKES
Huge snowflakes, 15 in. across and 8 in. thick, fell on the Coleman ranch at Fort Keogh, Montana, on January 28, 1887. The size of the flakes, which were described as being 'bigger than milk pans', was verified by a mail carrier who was caught in the storm.

4. TURTLE HAIL
Included in a severe hailstorm in Mississippi on May 11, 1894, was a 6-in.-by-8-in. gopher turtle, which fell to the ground, completely encased in ice, at Bovina, east of Vicksburg.

5. SUDDEN TEMPERATURE RISE
On February 21 1918, the temperature in Granville, North Dakota, rose 83° Fahrenheit in 12 hours – from -33° Fahrenheit (-36.3° Celsius) in the early morning to 50° Fahrenheit (10° Celsius) in the late afternoon.

6. FOURTH OF JULY BLIZZARD
Patriotic celebrants were stunned in 1918 when a major blizzard swept across the western plains of the United States, disrupting Fourth of July festivities in several states.

Independence Day began with the usual picnics and parties, but in the afternoon the temperature dropped suddenly and rain began to fall, followed by hail, snow and gale-force winds.

7. HEAVIEST SNOWFALL
On April 5 and 6, 1969 68 in. (172.7 cm) of snow fell on Bessans, France, in only 19 hours.

8. SLOWEST HAIL
On April 24, 1930, at 2:30 p.m., hail began to fall at Hinaidi, Iraq, at the remarkably slow speed of 9 mph. A clever observer was able to determine the speed by timing the fall of several specimens against the side of a building.

9. GREATEST TEMPERATURE FLUCTUATION
The most bizarre temperature changes in history occurred at Spearfish, South Dakota, on January 22, 1943. At 7.30 am the thermometer read -4° Fahrenheit. However, by 7.32 am the temperature had risen 45°, to 49° Fahrenheit. By 9.00 am the temperature had drifted up to 54° Fahrenheit. Then, suddenly, it began to plunge, 58° in 27 minutes, until, at 9.27 am, it had returned to -4° Fahrenheit.

10. MOST RAIN IN ONE MINUTE
The most rain ever recorded in one minute was 1.5 in. (2.68 cm) at Barot on the Caribbean island of Guadeloupe on November 26, 1970.

11. CURIOUS PRECIPITATION AT THE EMPIRE STATE BUILDING
While rain was falling in the street in front of the Empire State Building on November 3, 1958, guards near the top of the building were making snowballs.

12. POINT RAINFALL
An extreme case of localised rainfall occurred the night of August 2, 1966, one and a half miles northeast of Greenfield, New Hampshire. Robert H. Stanley reported that rain began to fall at 7.00 pm, reaching great intensity from 7.45 pm until 10.15 pm. When he awoke the next morning, Mr Stanley found that his rain gauge had filled to the 5.75-in. (14.6 cm) mark. However, Stanley's neighbour three-tenths of a mile (483 m.) away had collected only one-half in. (1.27 cm) in his rain gauge. Walking around the area, Stanley discovered that the heavy rainfall was limited to no more than one half-mile (805 m.) in any direction.

Another strange case of point rainfall took place on November 11, 1958, in the backyard of Mrs R. Babington of Alexandria, Louisiana. Although there were no clouds in the sky, a misty drizzle fell over an area of 100 sq. ft (9.3 sq. m.) for two and a half hours. Mrs Babington called a local reporter, who confirmed the phenomenon. The Shreveport weather bureau suggested the moisture had been formed by condensation from a nearby air conditioner, but their theory was never proved.

13. SNOW IN MIAMI
At 6:10 a.m. on January 19, 1977 West Palm Beach reported its first snowfall ever. By 8:30 a.m. snow was falling in Fort Lauderdale, the farthest south that snow had ever been reported in Florida. The snow continued south to Miami, and some even fell in Homestead, 23 miles south of Miami International Airport. The cold wave was so unusual that heat lamps had to be brought out to protect the iguanas at Miami's Crandon Park Zoo.

14. HIGHEST TEMPERATURE
On September 13, 1922 the temperature in Azizia, Libya, reached 136.4° Fahrenheit (58° Celsius) – in the shade.

15. LOWEST TEMPERATURE
On July 21, 1983 the thermometer at Vostok, Antarctica, registered -128.6° Fahrenheit (-89.2° Celsius). Vostok also holds the record for consistently cold weather. To reach an optimum temperature of 65 degrees Fahrenheit (18.3° Celsius), Vostok would require 48,800 'heating degree days' a year. By comparison, Fairbanks, Alaska, needs only 14,300.

16. EXTREME TEMPERATURES
Temperatures in Verkhoyansk, Russia, have ranged from 98° Fahrenheit (37° Celsius) down to 90.4° Fahrenheit (-68° Celsius), a variance of 188.4° Fahrenheit (105° Celsius).

17. LONGEST HOT SPELL
Marble Bar, Western Australia, experienced 160 consecutive days of 100° Fahrenheit (37.8° Celsius) temperatures from October 31, 1923 to April 7, 1924.

18. THE RAINIEST DAY
On March 16, 1952 73.62 in. (187 cm) of rain – more than 6 ft – fell at Cilaos on Réunion Island east of Madagascar. Another 24 in. (60.96 cm) fell during the 24 hours surrounding March 16.

19. **MOST RAIN IN 15 DAYS**
    Cherrapunji, Assam, India, received 189 in. (226.06 cm) of rain between June 24 and July 8, 1931. Back in 1861, Cherrapunji received 366.14 in. (930 cm) of rain in one month and 905.12 in. (2400 cm) for the calendar year.

20. **NO RAIN**
    The driest place on Earth is Arica, Chile, in the Atacama Desert. No rain fell there for more than 14 years, between October 1903 and December 1917. Over a 59-year period, Arica averaged three-hundredths of an inch (.76 mm) of rain a year.

21. **SNOWIEST DAY**
    The largest snowfall in a 24-hour period was 75.8 in. (192.5 cm) – more than 6 ft – recorded at Silver Lake, Colorado, on April 14-15, 1921.

22. **SNOWIEST SEASON**
    Paradise Ranger Station on Mt Rainier in Washington State recorded 1,122 in. (2,850 cm) of snow in 1971–72. Their average is 582 in. (1,478 cm).

23. **CHAMPION HURRICANE**
    Hurricane John, which flourished in August and September of 1994, was notable for two reasons. It lasted for all or part of 31 days, making it the longest-lived tropical storm on record. It also crossed over the International Date Line twice, changing its name from Hurricane John to Typhoon John and back to Hurricane John.

15 Shipwreck Survival Tips

This list is from Yann Martel's Man Booker prize-winning novel, *Life of Pi*.

1. Always read instructions carefully
2. Do not drink urine. Or sea water. Or bird blood.
3. Do not eat jellyfish. Or fish that are armed with spikes. Or that have parrot-like beaks. Or that puff up like balloons.
4. Pressing the eyes of fish will paralyse them.
5. The body can be a hero in battle. If a castaway is injured, beware of well-meaning but ill-founded medical treatment. Ignorance is the worst doctor, while rest and sleep are the best nurses.

6. Put up your feet at least five minutes every hour.
7. Unnecessary exertion should be avoided. But an idle mind tends to sink, so the mind should be kept occupied with whatever light distraction may suggest itself. Playing card games, Twenty Questions and I Spy With My Little Eye are excellent forms of simple recreation. Community singing is another sure-fire way to life the spirits. Yarn spinning is also highly recommended.
8. Green water is shallower than blue water.
9. Beware of far-off clouds that look like mountains. Look for green. Ultimately, a foot is the only good judge of land.
10. Do not go swimming. It wastes energy. Besides, a survival craft may drift faster than you can swim. Not to mention the danger of sea life. If you are hot, wet your clothes instead.
11. Do not urinate in your clothes. The momentary warmth is not worth the nappy rash.
12. Shelter yourself. Exposure can kill faster than thirst or hunger.
13. So long as no excessive water is lost through perspiration, the body can survive up to 14 days without water. If you feel thirsty, suck a button.
14. Turtles are an easy catch and make for excellent meals. Their blood is a good, nutritious, salt-free drink; their flesh is tasty and filling; their fat has many uses; and the castaway will find turtle eggs a real treat. Mind the beak and the claws.
15. Don't let your morale flag. Be daunted, but not defeated. Remember: the spirit, above all else, counts. If you have the will to live, you will. Good luck!

(Note that urine has on occasion been found to have positive health properties in emergency situations – The Eds.)

Chapter 11

28 GREAT BEGINNINGS TO NOVELS

10 POETS AND HOW THEY EARNED A LIVING

32 CURIOUS HISTORIES AND ESOTERIC STUDIES FROM THE LIBRARY OF *THE PEOPLE'S ALMANAC*

8 UNLIKELY HOW-TO BOOKS

THE ORIGINAL TITLES OF 28 FAMOUS BOOKS

THE BOOKSELLER'S 9 GREAT MODERN SURPRISE BESTSELLERS

28 BAD REVIEWS OF FAMOUS WORKS

11 INCREDIBLE LIPOGRAMS

MARGARET ATWOOD'S 10 ANNOYING THINGS TO SAY TO WRITERS

ROALD DAHL'S 5 BOOKS TO TAKE TO A NEW PLANET

HENRY MILLER'S 10 GREATEST WRITERS OF ALL TIME

IRVING WALLACE'S 9 FAVOURITE AUTHORS

BRIAN ALDISS'S 10 FAVOURITE SCIENCE FICTION NOVELS

WILL SELF'S 9 BOOKS THAT PROVE FACT IS STRANGER THAN FICTION

BRIAN ENO'S 18 MIND-CHANGING BOOKS

SIR CHRISTOPHER BLAND'S 10 BEST REFERENCE BOOKS

JOYCE CAROL OATES'S 14 FAVOURITE AMERICAN AUTHORS

ELMORE LEONARD'S 11 FAVOURITE NOVELS

WILLIAM S. BURROUGHS' 10 FAVOURITE NOVELS

12 LAST LINES OF NOVELS

Literature

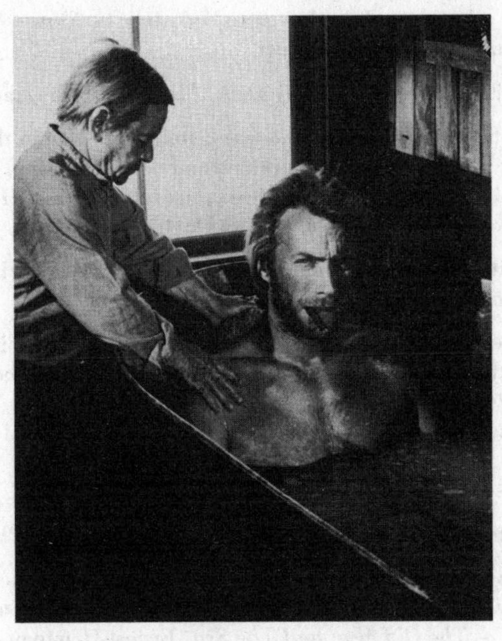

EXTRACTED FROM THE BOOK *MOVIE STARS IN BATH TUBS* BY JACK SCAGNETTI (1975). DOES EXACTLY WHAT IT SAYS ON THE TIN – **see p.290**

28 Great Beginnings to Novels

1. 'Somewhere in La Mancha, in a place whose name I do not care to remember, a gentleman lived not long ago, one of those who has a lance and ancient shield on a shelf and keeps a skinny nag and a greyhound for racing.' *Don Quixote*, Miguel de Cervantes, 1605

2. 'For a long time I used to go to bed early.' – *Remembrance of Things Past*, Marcel Proust

3. 'Call me Ishmael.' – *Moby-Dick, The Whale*, Herman Melville

4. 'Mr Sherlock Holmes, who was usually very late in the mornings, save upon those not infrequent occasions when he was up all night, was seated at the breakfast table.' – *The Hound of the Baskervilles*, Sir Arthur Conan Doyle

5. 'Lolita, light of my life, fire of my loins.' – *Lolita*, Vladimir Nabokov

6. 'Whether I shall turn out to be the hero of my own life, or whether that station will be held by anybody else, these pages must show.'
– *The Personal History of David Copperfield*, Charles Dickens

7. 'She was so deeply imbedded in my consciousness that for the first year of school I seem to have believed that each of my teachers was my mother in disguise.' – *Portnoy's Complaint*, Philip Roth

8. 'He was an old man who fished alone in a skiff in the Gulf Stream and he had gone eighty-four days now without taking a fish.' – *The Old Man and The Sea*, Ernest Hemingway

9. 'Last night I dreamt I went to Manderley again.' – *Rebecca*, Daphne du Maurier

10. 'Many years later, as he faced the firing squad, Colónel Aureliano Buendía was to remember that distant afternoon when his father took him to discover ice.' – *One Hundred Years of Solitude*, Gabriel García Marquez

11. 'It was a queer, sultry summer, the summer they electrocuted the Rosenbergs, and I didn't know what I was doing in New York.' – *The Bell Jar*, Sylvia Plath

12. 'It is a truth universally acknowledged, that a single man in possession of a good fortune must be in want of a wife.' – *Pride and Prejudice*, Jane Austen

13. 'The past is a foreign country: they do things differently there.' – Prologue, *The Go-Between*, L.P. Hartley

14. 'Maman died today. Or yesterday maybe, I don't know.' – *The Stranger*, Albert Camus

15. 'It was love at first sight. The first time Yossarian saw the chaplain he fell madly in love with him.' – *Catch-22*, Joseph Heller

16. 'All happy families are alike; each unhappy family is unhappy in its own way.' – *Anna Karenina*, Leo Tolstoy

17. 'Tom!' – *The Adventures of Tom Sawyer*, Mark Twain

18. ' "Christmas won't be Christmas without any presents," grumbled Jo, lying on the rug.' – *Little Women*, Louisa May Alcott

19. '3 May. Bistritz. Left Munich at 8:35 p.m., on 1st May, arriving at Vienna early next morning; should have arrived at 6:46, but train was an hour late.' – *Dracula*, Bram Stoker

20. 'Someone must have been telling lies about Joseph K., for without having done anything wrong he was arrested one fine morning.'
– *The Trial*, Franz Kafka

21. 'When he was nearly thirteen my brother Jem got his arm badly broken at the elbow.' – *To Kill a Mockingbird*, Harper Lee

22. 'Amerigo Bonasera sat in New York Criminal Court Number 3 and waited for justice; vengance on the men who had so cruelly hurt his daughter, who had tried to dishonor her.' – *The Godfather*, Mario Puzo

23. 'In eighteenth-century France there lived a man who was one of the most gifted and abominable personages in an era that knew no lack of gifted and abominable personages.' – *Perfume*, Patrick Suskind

24. 'It was a bright cold day in April, and the clocks were striking thirteen.' – *1984*, George Orwell

25. 'If you really want to hear about it, the first thing you'll probably want to know is where I was born, and what my lousy childhood was like, and how my parents were occupied and all before they had me, and all that David Copperfield kind of crap, but I don't feel like going into it, if you want to know the truth.' – *Catcher in the Rye*, J.D. Salinger

26. 'It was about eleven o'clock in the morning, mid-October, with the sun not shining and a look of hard wet rain in the clearness of the foothills. I was wearing my powder-blue suit, with dark blue shirt, tie and display handkerchief, black brogues, black wool socks with dark blue clocks on them. I was neat, clean, shaved and sober, and I didn't care who knew it. I was everything the well-dressed private detective ought to be.' – *The Big Sleep*, Raymond Chandler
27. 'People are afraid to merge on freeways in Los Angeles.' – *Less Than Zero*, Brett Easton Ellis
28. 'All nights should be so dark, all winters so warm, all headlights so dazzling.' – *Gorky Park*, Martin Cruz Smith

– The Eds & S.C.B.

10 Poets and How They Earned a Living

1. WILLIAM BLAKE (1757–1827), English poet and artist
Trained as an engraver, Blake studied art at the Royal Academy but left to earn a living engraving for booksellers. For a few years he was a partner in a print-selling and engraving business. He then worked as an illustrator, graphic designer and drawing teacher. It became increasingly hard for Blake to earn a living. He had a patron but lived essentially in poverty and obscurity, occasionally receiving an art commission. Blake was later recognised as one of England's finest engravers and most remarkable poet.

2. ROBERT BURNS (1759–96), Scottish poet
Raised on a farm in Ayrshire, Burns was a full-time labourer on the land at the age of 15. He tried to become a surveyor, but ill health forced him to give up. Next he lived with relatives who ran a flax-dressing business, until their shop burned down. Farming barely paid his bills, so Burns published *Poems, Chiefly in the Scottish Dialect* in 1786 to get money for passage to Jamaica, where he had a job offer as an overseer. The book was so successful that he used the money to visit Edinburgh instead. Returning to the farm, Burns took a job as a tax inspector, trying unsuccessfully to juggle three occupations. He lost the farm, but moved to Dumfries and continued as a tax inspector and poet.

3. **JOHN KEATS (1795–1821), English poet**
Keats was trained as a surgeon and apothecary in Edmonton, and later moved to London to work as a dresser in a hospital. For a year or so Keats had his own surgeon/apothecary practice, and at the same time began publishing his poetry. His first major work, *Poems*, appeared in 1817, and that year he gave up medicine for the literary life. Charles Armitage Brown became his patron, providing him with a house in Hampstead, outside London.

4. **WALT WHITMAN (1819–92), American poet**
Whitman had a chequered career in newspaper work, starting as a printer's assistant and eventually becoming an editor in New York throughout the 1840s. After ten years he gave up journalism for carpentry and verse. During the Civil War, Whitman moved to Washington, DC, took a job in the paymaster's office, and spent his spare time nursing the wounded. In 1865 he became a clerk at the Department of the Interior's Bureau of Indian Affairs, but was soon fired for being the author of the scandalous *Leaves of Grass*. He then clerked in the attorney general's office until a paralytic stroke forced him to retire in 1873.

5. **ARTHUR RIMBAUD (1854–91), French poet**
Rimbaud's lover Paul Verlaine supported him for a while in Paris; after their separation, Rimbaud lived in London, working at various menial jobs until poverty or ill health or both caused his return to France. In 1876 he joined the Dutch colonial army and went to Indonesia, but deserted and again returned to France. From there he joined a circus en route to Scandinavia; went to Cyprus as a labourer and later as a builder's foreman; and finally gave up his wandering in Harar, Ethiopia. There he worked for a coffee exporter, and later tried (unsuccessfully) to become an independent arms dealer. In 1888 he was managing a trading post, dealing in coffee, ivory, arms and possibly slaves.

6. **WALLACE STEVENS (1879–1955), American poet**
After leaving Harvard University without a degree, Stevens was a reporter for the *New York Herald Tribune* for a year. He then attended New York University Law School, passed the bar in 1904, and for the next 12 years practised law in New York. In 1916 he joined the legal department of the Hartford Accident and Indemnity Company in Connecticut; by 1934 he was vice-president of the company.

7. **WILLIAM CARLOS WILLIAMS (1883–1963), American poet**
Williams earned a medical degree from the University of Pennsylvania in 1906, interned at a hospital in New York City, and for a year did postgraduate work in paediatrics at the University of Leipzig in Germany. He established a medical practice in his home town of Rutherford, New Jersey, in 1910, and until the mid-1950s maintained both a medical and a literary career. An appointment to the chair of poetry at the Library of Congress in 1952 was withdrawn because of Williams's radical politics. He spent his last 10 years lecturing at many American universities.

8. **PABLO NERUDA (1904–73), Chilean poet**
In recognition of his poetic skills, the Chilean government awarded Neruda with a non-paying position as Chile's consul in Burma in 1927. Eventually he graduated to a salaried office, serving in Ceylon, the Dutch East Indies, Argentina and Spain. With the outbreak of the Spanish Civil War in 1936, Neruda, without waiting for orders, declared Chile on the side of the Spanish republic. He was recalled by the Chilean government and later reassigned to Mexico. In 1944 he was elected to the national senate as a member of the Communist Party. He later served as a member of the central committee of the Chilean Communist Party and as a member of the faculty of the University of Chile.

9. **ALLEN GINSBERG (1921–97), American poet**
In 1945, while suspended from Columbia University for a year, Ginsberg worked as a dishwasher in a Times Square, New York, restaurant, as a merchant seaman and a reporter for a newspaper in New Jersey. He returned to Columbia and graduated with a BA in literature in 1948. Far more influential was his off-campus friendship with a number of figures in the future Beat movement, including Jack Kerouac, Neal Cassady and William S. Burroughs. In 1949 Ginsberg was arrested for letting one of the friends, Herbert Huncke, use his apartment to store some stolen property. For his sentence, Ginsberg was committed to a psychiatric hospital for eight months. Upon his release, he went home to Patterson, New Jersey, to live with his father. After a few years, Ginsberg completely changed his lifestyle. He moved to San Francisco and led a life of middle-class respectability. He had a high-paying job in market research, a live-in girlfriend and an upscale apartment. He was also miserable and began seeing a therapist. 'The doctor kept asking me,

"What do you want to do?" Finally I told him – quit. Quit the job, my tie and suit, the apartment on Nob Hill. Quit it and go off and do what I wanted, which was to get a room with Peter [Orlovsky], and devote myself to writing and contemplation, to Blake and smoking pot, and doing whatever I wanted.' Ginsberg wrote a memo to his boss explaining how his position could be eliminated and then he left. In 1955, shortly after devoting himself to poetry, he created a sensation with the first public reading of his poem 'Howl', an event considered the birth of the Beat revolution. Ginsberg and his partner, Orlovsky, were able to live off Ginsberg's royalties, money Ginsberg earned at poetry readings and disability cheques Orlovsky received as a Korean War veteran.

10. MAYA ANGELOU (1928–), American poet and memoirist
In her youth, Angelou worked as a cook and a waitress, and as the first black female fare-collector with the San Francisco Streetcar Company. In the 1950s she became a nightclub performer, specialising in calypso songs and dances. She also performed in *Porgy and Bess* on a 22-country tour of Europe and Africa organised by the US State Department in 1954 and 1955. During the 1960s Angelou was northern coordinator of Dr Martin Luther King Jr's Southern Christian Leadership Council, associate editor of an English-language newspaper in Cairo, features editor of a paper in Ghana and assistant administrator at the University of Ghana. She acted in Jean Genet's play *The Blacks*, wrote songs for B.B. King, wrote and produced educational television series, and acted on Broadway (for one night in 1973) and on television – as Kunta Kinte's grandmother in *Roots*, in 1977. In 1972 she wrote the script for *Georgia, Georgia*, the first original screenplay by a black woman to be produced. She continues to be a popular lecturer, as well as a university professor.

32 Curious Histories and Esoteric Studies from the Library of *The People's Almanac*

1. *MANUALE DI CONVERSAZIONE: ITALIANO-GROENLANDESE* by Ciro Sozio and Mario Fantin. Bologna, Italy: Tamari Editori, 1962.
One of the least-used dictionaries in the world, this slim 62-page

booklet translates Italian into the language of the Greenland Eskimos. Collectors of obscure dictionaries will also appreciate Vladimir Marku's seminal work *Fjalori I Naftës* (1995), which translates 25,000 oil industry-related terms from English into Albanian.

2. *STURGEON HOOKS OF EURASIA* by Géza de Rohan-Csermak. Chicago: Aldine Publishing Co., 1963.
An important contribution to the history of fishhooks. Some of the chapter titles: II. 'The Character of Sturgeon Hooks'; IV. 'Hooks in Eastern Europe'; and VII. 'Life Story of Hooks of the Samolov Type'.

3. *THE EVOKED VOCAL RESPONSE OF THE BULLFROG: A STUDY OF COMMUNICATION BY SOUND* by Robert R. Capranica. Cambridge, MA.: The MIT Press, 1965.
This monograph details the responses of caged bullfrogs to the recorded sound of mating calls of 34 kinds of frogs and toads. The author's academic career was made possible by a fellowship awarded by Bell Telephone Laboratories.

4. *WHY BRING THAT UP?* by Dr J. F. Montague. New York: Home Health Library, 1936.
A guide to and from seasickness by the medical director of the New York Intestinal Sanitarium.

5. *CLUCK!: THE TRUE STORY OF CHICKENS IN THE CINEMA* by Jon-Stephen Fink. London: Virgin Books, 1981.
At last, a fully illustrated filmography of every movie in which a chicken – living, dead or cooked – appears. Films in which the words 'chicken', 'hen' or 'rooster' are mentioned are also included.

6. *ON THE SKULL AND PORTRAITS OF GEORGE BUCHANAN* by Karl Pearson. Edinburgh: Oliver and Boyd, 1926.
Buchanan, one of Scotland's greatest scholars and historians, died in poverty in 1582. This publication was part of a series which included *Phrenological Studies of the Skull and Endocranial Cast of Sir Thomas Browne of Norwich* by Sir Arthur Keith and *The Relations of Shoulder Blade Types to Problems of Mental and Physical Adaptability* by William Washington Graves.

7. *COMMUNISM, HYPNOTISM, AND THE BEATLES* by David A. Noebel. Tulsa, OK.: Christian Crusade, 1979.
This 15-page diatribe contends that the Beatles were agents of

communism, sent to America to subvert its youth through mass hypnosis 'The Beatles' ability to make teenagers take off their clothes and riot is labouratory tested and approved', states Noebel. He supports his theory with no less than 168 footnotes.

8. *CAMEL BRANDS AND GRAFFITI FROM IRAQ, SYRIA, JORDAN, IRAN, AND ARABIA* by Henry Field. Baltimore, MD: American Oriental Society, 1952.
The publication of this study was made possible by the generosity of an anonymous donor.

9. *ICE CARVING PROFESSIONALLY* by George P. Weising. Fairfield, CT., 1954.
An excellent textbook by a master ice sculptor. Weising gives instructions for carving such items as Tablets of the Ten Commandments Delivered by Moses (for bar mitzvahs); Rudolph, the Red-Nosed Reindeer; and the Travellers Insurance Company Tower in Hartford, CT.

10. *THE ONE-LEG RESTING POSITION (NILOTENSTELLUNG) IN AFRICA AND ELSEWHERE* by Gerhard Lindblom. Stockholm: Statens Ethnografiska Museum, 1949.
A survey of cultures in which people commonly rest while standing by placing one foot on or near the knee of the other leg. Contains 15 photographs from Africa, Sri Lanka, Romania, Australia and Bolivia, as well as a fold-out locator map of Africa.

11. *DIRT: A SOCIAL HISTORY AS SEEN THROUGH THE USES AND ABUSES OF DIRT* by Terence McLaughlin. New York: Stein and Day, 1971.
Readers who are drawn to dirty books might also enjoy *Smut: An Anatomy of Dirt* by Christian Engnensberger (New York: Seabury, 1972); *The Kingdom of Dust* by J. Gordon Ogden (Chicago: Popular Mechanics, 1912); and *All About Mud* by Oliver R. Selfrige (Reading, MA: Addison-Wesley, 1978).

12. *BIRDS ASLEEP* by Alexander F. Skutch. Austin: University of Texas Press, 1989.
A detailed and surprisingly readable study by an ornithologist resident in Costa Rica. A 12-page bibliography is included for serious students. Less pacific readers might prefer *Birds Fighting* by Stuart Smith and Erik Hosking (London: Faber and Faber, 1955), which includes numerous photos of real birds attacking stuffed birds.

13. *KNIGHT LIFE: JOUSTING IN THE UNITED STATES* by Robert L. Loeffelbein. Lexington Park, MD: Golden Owl, 1977.
A fully illustrated account of the history of jousting tournaments in the United States, with emphasis on modern contests, records, rules and heroes.

14. *HOW TO CONDUCT A MAGNETIC HEALING BUSINESS*, by A.C. Murphy. Kansas City, MO: Hudson-Kimbery, 1902.
A nuts-and-bolts account including advertising tips and postal rules and regulations, as well as discussion of such difficult topics as 'Should a lady healer employ a gentleman assistant?'

15. *I DREAM OF WOODY* by Dee Burton. New York: William Morrow, 1984.
Burton presents the cases of 70 people from New York and Los Angeles who have dreamed about Woody Allen. Fans of books on people who dream about famous people will also want to track down *Dreams about H.M. the Queen* by Brian Masters (Frogmore, St Albans, Herts: Mayflower, 1973), a collection of dreams about Queen Elizabeth II and other members of the British royal family; *I Dream of Madonna* by Kay Turner (San Francisco: Collins, 1993); *Dreams of Bill* by Judith Anderson-Miller and Bruce Joshua Miller (New York: Citadel Press, 1994), a collection of dreams about Bill Clinton; and *Dreaming of Diana: The Dreams Diana, Princess of Wales, Inspired* by Rita Frances (London: Robson Books, 1998).

16. *LITTLE-KNOWN SISTERS OF WELL-KNOWN MEN* by Sarah G. Pomeroy. Boston: Dana Estes, 1912.
A review of the lives of eight little-known sisters, including Sarianna Browning, Sarah Disraeli and Sophia Thoreau, as well as two known sisters of English writers, Dorothy Wordsworth and Mary Lamb.

17. *THE ROYAL TOUCH: SACRED MONARCHY AND SCROFULA IN ENGLAND AND FRANCE* by Mark Bloch. London: Routledge and Kegan Paul, 1973.
This book, written in 1923, examines the unusual custom of curing the disease of scrofula, a form of tuberculosis, by being touched by the King of France or the King of England. The practice died out after 1825.

18. *LUST FOR FAME: THE STAGE CAREER OF JOHN WILKES BOOTH* by Gordon Samples. Jefferson, NC: McFarland, 1982.
A biography that ignores Booth's assassination of Abraham

Lincoln and deals instead, for 234 pages, with his career as an actor, which continued until four weeks before he killed the President of the United States.

19. *THE HISTORY AND ROMANCE OF ELASTIC WEBBING* by Clifford A. Richmond. Eastampton, MA: Easthampton News Company, 1946.
A lively account of the birth and growth of the elastic webbing industry in the nineteenth century. In the words of the author, once a man has 'got the smell of rubber in his nostrils . . . he either stays with rubber or is thereafter ever homesick to get back into the rubber industry'.

20. *CANADIAN NATIONAL EGG LAYING CONTESTS* by F.C. Elford and A.G. Taylor. Ottawa: Department of Agriculture, 1924.
A report of the first three years of the Canadian national egg laying contests, from 1919 to 1922, as well as a preliminary contest held on Prince Edward Island in 1918–19. The work consists almost entirely of charts comparing production and costs by owner, bird and year. In 1921–22 one of the birds belonging to Lewis N. Clark of Port Hope, Ontario, produced 294 eggs.

21. *THE DIRECTION OF HAIR IN ANIMALS AND MAN* by Walter Kidd. London: Adam and Charles Black, 1903.
In his preface, Dr Kidd states, 'No doubt many of the phenomena here described are intrinsically uninteresting and unimportant.' However, if you have ever yearned for a book that analyses the direction in which hair grows on lions, oxen, dogs, apes, tapirs, humans, asses, anteaters, sloths, and other animals, you won't be disappointed.

22. *A STUDY OF SPLASHES* by A.M. Worthington. London: Longmans, Green and Co., 1908.
This pioneering classic makes use of 197 photographs to help answer the question 'What actually happens when a drop falls and splashes?' Worthington's book was considered so valuable to students of physics that it was reissued as recently as 1963.

23. *THE QUICK BROWN FOX* by Richard G. Templeton Jr. Chicago: At the Sign of the Gargoyle, 1945.
Thirty-three examples of sentences that include all twenty-six letters of the English alphabet. Included are classics such as 'The quick brown fox jumps over the lazy dog' and 'Pack my

bags with five dozen liquor jugs', as well as the less well-known 'The July sun caused a fragment of black pine waxe to ooze on the velvet quilt' and 'Very careful and exact knowledge should be emphasized in adjudging a quadrant.'

24. *PAINTINGS AND DRAWINGS ON THE BACKS OF NATIONAL GALLERY PICTURES* by Martin Davies. London: National Gallery Publications, 1946.
A rare opportunity to view the flip side of 42 famous works of art.

25. *EARLY UNITED STATES BARBED WIRE PATENTS* by Jesse S. James. Maywood, CA: Self-published, 1966.
A definitive listing of 401 barbed wire patents filed between the years 1867 and 1897.

26. *MOVIE STARS IN BATHTUBS*, by Jack Scagnetti. Middle Village, NY: Jonathan David Publishers, 1975.
One hundred and fifty-six photographs of movie stars in bathtubs. There are also numerous shots of actors, actresses and animals in showers and steambaths.

27. *AMERICA IN WAX* by Gene Gurney. New York: Crown Publishers, 1977.
A complete guidebook to wax museums in the United States, with 678 illustrations, including Brigitte Bardot, Nikita Khrushchev and the Battle of Yorktown.

28. *THE GENDER TRAP* by Chris Johnson and Cathy Brown with Wendy Nelson. London: Proteus, 1982.
The autobiography of the world's first transsexual parents. Chris and Cathy began life as Anne and Eugene. Anne was a social worker who wished she was a man; Eugene was a Kung Fu instructor who wished he was a woman. They fell in love, Anne gave birth to a baby girl, Emma, and then Anne and Eugene switched sexes. Anne, now Chris, became Emma's father and Eugene, now Cathy, took over the role of mother.

29. *SELL YOURSELF TO SCIENCE* by Jim Hogshire. Port Townsend, WA: Loompanics Unlimited, 1992.
The subtitle says it all: *The Complete Guide to Selling Your Organs, Body Fluids, Bodily Functions, and Being a Human Guinea Pig*. If you are reasonably healthy, but have no job skills, this is the book for you. Hogshire explains how to earn $100 a day as a subject for drug studies and other scientific experiments, and how to sell your blood, sperm, hair, breast milk and bone marrow.

30. *THE LIFE AND CUISINE OF ELVIS PRESLEY* by David Adler. New York: Crown, 1993.
In exquisite detail, Adler traces the evolution of what Elvis ate from the time he was a baby (corn bread soaked in buttermilk) through his years in the army, Las Vegas, Hollywood and Graceland, and finally the bingeing that weakened his health. Elvis gobbled a dozen honey doughnuts in a cab before a visit to the White House and once ate five chocolate sundaes for breakfast before passing out. Included are recipes for fried squirrel, peanut butter and American cheese sandwich, and Elvis's last supper, which was actually ice cream and cookies.

31. *THE ALIEN ABDUCTION SURVIVAL GUIDE: HOW TO COPE WITH YOUR ET EXPERIENCE*, by Michelle LaVigne. Newberg, OR: Wild Flower Press, 1995.
Unlike most books that deal with alien abduction, LaVigne's treatise is a practical guide that helps abductees control their fear and 'take control' of the experience. The author smashes various myths such as 'the ETs have no lips, and do not open their mouths', 'all ETs who are called greys are grey' and 'the ETs have long tentacle-like fingers covered with suction cups, similar to those found on an octopus'.

32. *PIE ANY MEANS NECESSARY: THE BIOTIC BAKING BRIGADE COOKBOOK*. Oakland/Edinburgh: AK Press, 2004.
The BBB presents the history of pie-throwing as a political act and includes several recipes for easy-to-throw pies. Also included are photographs of such celebrities as Bill Gates and Clare Short being pied.

8 Unlikely How-To Books

1. *How to Be Happy Though Married* by 'A Graduate in the University of Matrimony'. London: J. Fisher Unwin, 1895.

2. *How to Rob Banks Without Violence* by Roderic Knowles. London: Michael Joseph, 1972.

3. *How to Shit in the Woods* by Kathleen Meyer. Berkeley, CA: Ten Speed Press, 1989.

4. *How to Become a Schizophrenic* by John Modrow. Everett, WA: Apollyon Press, 1992.

5. *How to Speak With the Dead: A Practical Handbook* by 'Sciens'. New York: E.P. Dutton, 1918.

The author is identified as also having written 'recognised scientific text-books'.

6. *How to Start Your Own Country* by Erwin S Strauss. Port Townsend, WA: Loompanics Unlimited, 1984.
7. *How to Avoid Huge Ships* by Captain John W. Trimmer. Seattle, WA: Captain John W. Trimmer, 1983.
8. *How to be Pretty Though Plain* by Mrs Humphry. London: James Bowden, 1899.

The Original Titles of 28 Famous Books

1. Original title: *First Impressions*
   Final title: *Pride and Prejudice* (1813)
   Author: Jane Austen
2. Original title: *Mag's Diversions*: also *The Copperfield Disclosures*, *The Copperfield Records, The Copperfield Survey of the World As It Rolled*, and *Copperfield Complete*
   Final title: *David Copperfield* (1849)
   Author: Charles Dickens
3. Original title: *Alice's Adventures Underground*
   Final title: *Alice's Adventures in Wonderland* (1865)
   Author: Lewis Carroll
4. Original title: *All's Well That Ends Well*
   Final title: *War and Peace* (1866)
   Author: Leo Tolstoy
5. Original title: *The Sea-Cook*
   Final title: *Treasure Island* (1883)
   Author: Robert Louis Stevenson
6. Original title: *The Chronic Argonauts*
   Final title: *The Time Machine* (1895)
   Author: H.G. Wells
7. Original title: *Paul Morel*
   Final title: *Sons and Lovers* (1913)
   Author: D.H. Lawrence
8. Original title: *Stephen Hero*
   Final title: *A Portrait of the Artist as a Young Man* (1916)
   Author: James Joyce

9. **Original title:** ***The Romantic Egotist***
Final title: ***This Side of Paradise*** **(1920)**
Author: F. Scott Fitzgerald

10. **Original title:** ***The Village Virus***
Final title: ***Main Street*** **(1920)**
Author: Sinclair Lewis

11. **Original title:** ***Incident at West Egg*****; also** ***Among Ash Heaps and Millionaires*****,** ***Trimalchio in West Egg*****,** ***On the Road to West Egg*****,** ***Gold-Hatted Gatsby*** **and** ***The High-Bounding Lover***
Final title: ***The Great Gatsby*** **(1925)**
Author: F. Scott Fitzgerald

12. **Original title:** ***Fiesta*****; also** ***The Lost Generation*****,** ***River to the Sea*****,** ***Two Lie Together*** **and** ***The Old Leaven***
Final title: ***The Sun Also Rises*** **(1926)**
Author: Ernest Hemingway

13. **Original title:** ***Tenderness***
Final title: ***Lady Chatterley's Lover*** **(1928)**
Author: D.H. Lawrence

14. **Original title:** ***Twilight***
Final title: ***The Sound and the Fury*** **(1929)**
Author: William Faulkner

15. **Original title:** ***Bar-B-Q***
Final title: ***The Postman Always Rings Twice*** **(1934)**
Author: James M. Cain

16. **Original title:** ***Tomorrow Is Another Day*****; also** ***Tote the Weary Load*****,** ***Milestones*****,** ***Jettison*****,** ***Ba! Ba! Black Sheep*****,** ***None So Blind*****,** ***Not in Our Stars*** **and** ***Bugles Sang True***
Final title: ***Gone with the Wind*** **(1936)**
Author: Margaret Mitchell

17. **Original title:** ***The Various Arms*****; also** ***Return to the Wars***
Final title: ***To Have and Have Not*** **(1937)**
Author: Ernest Hemingway

18. **Original title:** ***Something That Happened***
Final title: ***Of Mice and Men*** **(1937)**
Author: John Steinbeck

19. **Original title:** ***Salinas Valley***
Final title: ***East of Eden*** **(1952)**
Author: John Steinbeck

20. Original title: *Interzone*
Final title: *Naked Lunch* (1959)
Author: William S. Burroughs

21. Original title: *Catch-18*
Final title: *Catch-22* (1961)
Author: Joseph Heller

22. Original title: *The Fox*
Final title: *The Magus* (1966)
Author: John Fowles

23. Original title: *A Jewish Patient Begins His Analysis*
Final title: *Portnoy's Complaint* (1969)
Author: Philip Roth

24. Original title: *The Summer of the Shark*; also *The Terror of the Monster* and *The Jaws of the Leviathan*
Final title: *Jaws* (1974)
Author: Peter Benchley

25. Original title: *Before This Anger*
Final title: *Roots: The Saga of an American Family* (1976)
Author: Alex Haley

26. Original title: *The Shine*
Final title: *The Shining* (1977 – altered when King learned that 'shine' was a derogatory term for African Americans, as they are often employed shining shoes; and a black man is a central character in the novel.)
Author: Stephen King

27. Original title: *Harry Potter and the Doomspell Tournament*
Final title: *Harry Potter and the Goblet of Fire* (2000)
Author: J.K. Rowling

28. Original title: *Seven Seas and the Thirteen Rivers*
Final title: *Brick Lane* (2003)
Author: Monica Ali

– R.J.F. & the Eds

The Bookseller's 9 Great Modern Surprise Bestsellers

Founded in 1858, *The Bookseller* is the leading journal of the book industry in the UK.

1. *JONATHAN LIVINGSTONE SEAGULL* by Richard Bach (Turnstone Press, 1970)
   An icky fable about a seagull's quest. No one would go for that, advised several people, including the author's agent ('they're not interested in a talking seagull'). The first US printing was 7,500 copies; the book went on to sell millions, in numerous languages.

2. *THE DAY OF THE JACKAL* by Frederick Forsyth (Hutchinson, 1971)
   Forsyth, a foreign correspondent whose previous book had been an account of the war in Biafra, received numerous rejections for his first thriller, perhaps because publishers did not expect readers to be thrilled by a story of which they knew the outcome (assassin fails to kill de Gaulle). It sold millions, was made into a film and established the career of one of the most successful novelists of our time.

3. *WATERSHIP DOWN* by Richard Adams (Rex Collings, 1972)
   Richard Adams' tale about rabbits first appeared, having been rejected in prototype form by several London publishers, in a print run of just 2,000 copies, from the tiny firm of Rex Collings. In the next 10 years, it sold more than five million copies.

4. *THE COUNTRY DIARY OF AN EDWARDIAN LADY* by Edith Holden (Webb & Bower, 1977)
   A rediscovered, illustrated diary. It became a staple on the bestseller list for years and was responsible for a fashion, now defunct, for prettily illustrated gift books, often using existing texts – *The Illustrated Lark Rise to Candleford* (Century, 1982), for example.

5. *THE F-PLAN* by Audrey Eyton (Penguin, 1982)
   A diet book that sold one million copies. Fibre, which Eyton promoted, is still in vogue; but many other diet trends have supplanted hers. The current bestseller is *The Atkins Diet*.

6. *A BRIEF HISTORY OF TIME* by Stephen Hawking (Bantam Press, 1988)
   It was a book that few people understood. Yet many bought it and it was translated into more than 30 languages. The genius of Hawking's mind, belonging to a body disabled by motor neurone disease, shone out compellingly; and the title, promising illumination in a nutshell, was another strong selling point.

7. *A YEAR IN PROVENCE* by Peter Mayle (Hamish Hamilton, 1989)
   Former adman Mayle's book about his move to the French countryside started out with a print run of 3,000 copies. Not only did it become a bestseller, but it spawned a genre and, possibly, a social trend: the television schedules and bookshelves are awash with the stories of people who have embarked on similar adventures.

8. *HARRY POTTER AND THE PHILOSOPHER'S STONE* by J.K. Rowling (Bloomsbury, 1997)
   Numerous publishers rejected Rowling's first Harry Potter story, because 250-page novels for children were deeply unfashionable. Nor did they warm to the magical and boarding school elements. Whoops.

9. *EATS, SHOOTS & LEAVES* by Lynne Truss (Profile, 2003)
   Autumn 2003 saw publication of autobiographies by David Beckham and by World Cup-winning England rugby captain Martin Johnson, as well as of numerous other blockbusters. They were all outsold by Lynne Truss's little punctuation guide, which went on to be a number one bestseller in the US as well.

28 Bad Reviews of Famous Works

1. *The Monkey Wrench Gang* – Edward Abbey, 1975
   The author of this book should be neutered and locked away forever. – *San Juan County Record*

2. *Les Fleurs Du Mal* – Charles Baudelaire, 1857
   In a hundred years the history of French literature will only mention [this work] as a curio. – Emile Zola, in *Emile Zola*, 1953.

3. *Malloy; Malone Dies; The Unnameable* – Samuel Beckett, 1959 (three novels in one volume)
   The suggestion that something larger is being said about the

human predicament . . . won't hold water, any more than Beckett's incontinent heroes can. – *The Spectator*

4. *Naked Lunch* – William S. Burroughs, 1963
. . . the merest trash, not worth a second look. – *New Republic*

5. *In Cold Blood* – Truman Capote, 1965
One can say of this book – with sufficient truth to make it worth saying: 'This isn't writing. It's research.' – Stanley Kauffmann, *The New Republic*

6. *The Deerslayer* – James Fenimore Cooper, 1841
In one place *Deerslayer*, and in the restricted space of two-thirds of a page, Cooper has scored 114 offences against literary art out of possible 115. It breaks the record. – Mark Twain, *How to Tell a Story and Other Essays*, 1897

7. *An American Tragedy* – Theodore Dreiser, 1925
His style, if style it may be called, is offensively colloquial, commonplace and vulgar. – *The Boston Evening Transcript*

8. *Absalom, Absalom!* – William Faulkner, 1936
The final blowup of what was once a remarkable, if minor, talent.
– Clifton Fadiman, *The New Yorker*

9. *The Great Gatsby* – F. Scott Fitzgerald, 1925
What has never been alive cannot very well go on living. So this is a book of the season only . . . – *New York Herald Tribune*

10. *Madame Bovary* – Gustave Flaubert, 1857
Monsieur Flaubert is not a writer. – *Le Figaro*

11. *The Recognitions* – William Gaddis, 1955
The Recognitions is an evil book, a scurrilous book, a profane, a scatalogical book and an exasperating book . . . what this squalling overwritten book needs above all is to have its mouth washed out with lye soap. – *Chicago Sun Times*

12. *Catch-22* – Joseph Heller, 1961
Heller wallows in his own laughter . . . and the sort of antic behaviour the children fall into when they know they are losing our attention. – Whitey Balliett, *The New Yorker*

13. *The Sun Also Rises* – Ernest Hemingway, 1926
His characters are as shallow as the saucers in which they stack their daily emotions . . . – *The Dial*

14. *For Whom the Bell Tolls* – Ernest Hemingway, 1940
This book offers not pleasure but mounting pain . . . – *Catholic World*

15. *Brave New World* – Aldous Huxley, 1932
A lugubrious and heavy-handed piece of propaganda. – *New York Herald Tribune*

16. *Lives of the English Poets* – Samuel Johnson, 1779–81
Johnson wrote the lives of the poets and left out the poets.
– Elizabeth Barrett Browning, *The Book of the Poets*, 1842

17. *Finnegans Wake* – James Joyce, 1939
As one tortures one's way through *Finnegans Wake* an impression grows that Joyce has lost his hold on human life. – Alfred Kazin, *New York Herald Tribune*

18. *Babbit* – Sinclair Lewis, 1929
As a humorist, Mr Lewis makes valiant attempts to be funny; he merely succeeds in being silly. – *Boston Evening Transcript*

19. *Lolita* – Vladimir Nabokov, 1958
. . . Any bookseller should be very sure that he knows in advance that he is selling very literate pornography. – *Kirkus Reviews*

20. *The Moviegoer* – Walker Percy, 1961
Mr Percy's prose needs oil and a good checkup. – *The New Yorker*

21. *A Midsummer Night's Dream* – William Shakespeare, performed in London, 1662
The most stupid ridiculous play that I ever saw in my life. – Samuel Pepys, *Diary*

22. *Hamlet* – William Shakespeare, 1601
One would imagine this piece to be the work of a drunken savage.
– Voltaire (1768), in *The Works of M. de Voltaire*, 1901

23. *Gulliver's Travels* – Jonathan Swift, 1726
. . . evidence of a diseased mind and lacerated heart. – John Dunlop, *The History of Fiction*, 1814

24. *Anna Karenina* – Leo Tolstoy, 1877
Sentimental rubbish . . . Show me one page that contains an idea.
– *The Odessa Courier*

25. *Breakfast of Champions* – Kurt Vonnegut, 1973
From time to time it's nice to have a book you can hate – it clears the pipes – and I hate this book. – Peter Prescott, *Newsweek*

26. *Leaves of Grass* – Walt Whitman, 1855
Whitman is as unacquainted with art as a hog is with mathematics. – *The London Critic*

27. *The Waves* – Virginia Woolf, 1931
The book is dull. – H.C. Hardwood, *Saturday Review of Literature*

28. *Dictionary* – Samuel Johnson, 1755
. . . the confidence now reposed in its accuracy is the greatest injury to philology that now exists – Noah Webster, letter, 1807

11 Incredible Lipograms

A form of verbal gymnastics, lipograms are written works that deliberately omit a certain letter of the alphabet by avoiding all words that include that letter. 'Lipo' actually means 'lacking' – in this case lacking a letter. An example of a contemporary lipogram is the nursery rhyme, 'Mary Had A Little Lamb', rewritten without the letter s:

Mary had a little lamb
With fleece a pale white hue,
And everywhere that Mary went
The lamb kept her in view;
To academe he went with her,
Illegal, and quite rare;
It made the children laugh and play
To view a lamb in there.

– A. Ross Eckler

1. JACQUES ARAGO – AN A-LESS BOOK
The French author's book *Voyage Autour du Monde Sans la Lettre A* debuted in Paris in 1853. However, 30 years later in another edition, he admitted letting one letter *a* sneak by him in the book – he had overlooked the word *serait*.

2. GYLES BRANDRETH – HAMLET WITHOUT ANY I's
A contemporary British lipogrammarian, Brandreth specialises in dropping a different letter from each of Shakespeare's plays.

All *I*'s were excluded from *Hamlet*, rendering the famous soliloquy: 'To be or not to be; that's the query'. He proceeded to rewrite *Twelfth Night* without the letters *l* and *o*, *Othello* without any *o*'s, and *Macbeth* without any *a*'s or *e*'s.

3. GOTTLOB BURMANN – R-LESS POETRY
Bearing an obsessive dislike for the letter *r*, Burmann not only wrote 130 poems without using that letter, but he also omitted the letter *r* from his daily conversation for 17 years. This practice meant the eccentric 18th-century German poet never said his own last name.

4. A. ROSS ECKLER – LIPOGRAM NURSERY RHYMES
Eckler's speciality is rewriting well-known nursery rhymes such as 'Little Jack Horner', excluding certain letters. His masterpiece was 'Mary Had A Little Lamb', which he re-created in several versions, omitting in turn the letters *s*, *a*, *h*, *e* and *t* (as in the t-less 'Mary Had A Pygmy Lamb').

5. PETER DE RIGA – A LIPOGRAM BIBLE
Summarising the entire Bible in Latin, the sixteenth-century canon of Rheims Cathedral in France omitted a different letter of the alphabet from each of the 23 chapters he produced.

6. TRYPHIODORUS – A LIPOGRAM ODYSSEY
The Greek poet Tryphiodorus wrote his epic poem *Odyssey*, chronicling the adventures of Ulysses, excluding a different letter of the alphabet from each of the 24 books. Thus, the first book was written without alpha, the second book contained no betas, and so on.

7. LOPE DE VEGA CARPIO – 5 NOVELS WITHOUT VOWELS
Also known as Spain's first great dramatist, who reputedly wrote 2,200 plays, this sixteenth-century author wrote five novels that were lipograms. Each book omitted one of the five vowels *a*, *e*, *i*, *o* and *u* in turn.

8. ERNEST VINCENT WRIGHT – NOVEL WITHOUT AN E
Tying down the *e* key on his typewriter to make sure one didn't slip in, Wright, a graduate of MIT, wrote a credible 50,110–word novel, *Gadsby* (1939), totally excluding the most frequently used letter of the English alphabet. 'Try to write a single ten-word sentence without an *e*,' said the Los Angeles *Times*, 'and you will get some idea of the task he set himself.' Wright's novel concerned the effort of a middle-age man named

John Gadsby to make his home town of Branston Hills more progressive and prosperous by turning over its administration to an Organization of Youth. Wright, a 67–year-old Californian, undertook his *e*-less novel to prove such a feat could be done. He wrote the book in 165 days. He employed no tricks, such as coining words or substituting apostrophes for *e*'s. His greatest difficulty, he stated, was in avoiding the use of verbs ending with *ed*, being forced to use 'said' for 'replied' or 'asked', and in avoiding all pronouns such as 'he', 'she' or 'they'. Wright died on the day of his book's publication – but the $3.00 novel remains his monument. Today it sells at rare-book dealers for more than $1,000 a copy, with a jacket.

9. GEORGES PEREC – E-LESS AND E-FULL NOVELS
Perec (1936–82) was a member of the literary group Oulipo (a French acronym for 'workshop of potential literature'), the members of which experimented with constrained writing. Perec's most notable work in this regard is his novel *La Disparation* (1969), written without the letter *e*. It was translated into English, also without *e*'s, by Gilbert Adair under the title *A Void*. Another Perec novel, *Les Revenentes* (1972), is a sort of opposite: the letter *e* is the only vowel used.

10. CHRISTIAN BOK – VOWEL-LESS POETRY
Bok, an experimental Canadian poet, wrote *Eunoia*, a work in which each chapter is missing four of the five vowels. The fourth chapter, for example, does not contain *a*, *e*, *i* or *u*. A sample of the writing from this chapter is: 'Profs from Oxford show frosh who do post-docs how to gloss works of Wordsworth.' *Eunoia* won the Griffin Poetry Prize in 2002 and became one of the best-selling works of Canadian poetry.

11. MARK DUNN – AN INCREASINGLY LIPOGRAMMATIC BOOK
Dunn's *Ella Minnow Pea* (2001) is subtitled 'A Progressively Lipogrammatic Epistolary Fable'. The story concerns a small country that begins to outlaw the use of various letters. As each letter is banned within the story, it is no longer used in the text of the novel.

– L.K.S. & C.F.

Margaret Atwood's 10 Annoying Things to Say to Writers

a) What to say	*b) What writer hears*
1. a) I always wait for your books to come in at the library.	b) I wouldn't pay money for that trash.
2. a) I had to take you in school.	b) Against my will. Or: And I certainly haven't read any of it since! Or: So why aren't you dead?
3. a) You don't look at all like your pictures!	b) Much worse.
4. a) You're so prolific!	b) You write too much, and are repetitive and sloppy.
5. a) I'm going to write a book too, when I can find the time.	b) What you do is trivial, and can be done by any idiot.
6. a) I only read the classics.	b) And you aren't one of them.
7. a) Why don't you write about ______?	b) Unlike the boring stuff you do write about.
8. a) That book by ______ (add name of other writer) is selling like hotcakes!	b)Unlike yours.
9. a) So, do you teach?	b) Because writing isn't real work, and you can't possibly be supporting yourself at it.
10. a) The story of MY life – now THAT would make a good novel!	b) Unlike yours.

Roald Dahl's 5 Books to Take to a New Planet

Born in Llandaff, Wales, in 1916, Roald Dahl served as a Royal Air Force fighter pilot during World War II before becoming a hugely successful writer of novels (*My Uncle Oswald*), short-story collections

(*Someone Like You* and *Kiss, Kiss*), screenplays (the James Bond film *You Only Live Twice*) and highly influential juvenile works (*Charlie and the Chocolate Factory* and *James and the Giant Peach*, which both became highly successful films). Although Dahl was much beloved for his children's books (his preferred form, he said, because 'adults are much too serious for me'), a dysfunctional marriage to Academy Award-winning actress Patricia Neal, as well as accusations of anti-Semitism, have made him a controversial figure since his death in 1990. Dahl contributed this list to *The Book of Lists* in 1983.

1. *Price's Textbook of the Practice of Medicine* (Oxford University Press). Reason: A professional medical textbook covering the description, diagnoses and treatment of virtually every known disease or illness.
2. *The Greater Oxford Dictionary*
3. *The Pickwick Papers* – Charles Dickens
4. A book containing all of Beethoven's piano sonatas
5. Johann Sebastian Bach's B minor Mass

Henry Miller's 10 Greatest Writers of All Time

One of the most controversial and innovative American writers of the twentieth century, Henry Miller was born in New York City on December 26, 1891. He spent much of the 1930s as an expatriate in Paris, where he met Anaïs Nin and wrote his two most famous novels, *Tropic of Cancer* (1934) and *Tropic of Capricorn* (1939). The books were banned for many years in English-speaking countries before being published in the UK in 1963 and the US in 1964, after a landmark obscenity trial. His other works included *Black Spring*, *Colossus of Maroussi* and *The Rosy Crucifixion* trilogy of *Sexus*, *Plexus* and *Nexus*. Henry Miller died in Pacific Palisades, California, on June 7, 1980. He contributed the following list to *The Book of Lists* in 1977.

1. Lao-Tzu
2. François Rabelais
3. Friedrich Nietzsche
4. Rabindranath Tagore
5. Walt Whitman
6. Marcel Proust
7. Ělie Faure

8. Marie Corelli
9. Fyodor Dostoevsky
10. Isaac Bashevis Singer

Élie Faure (1873–1937) was a French art historian who published a five-volume *History of Art* between 1909 and 1921. He had studied medicine and brought a scientific approach to his examinations of art history. London-born Marie Corelli (1855–1924), whose real name was Mary Mackay, wrote 28 books, most of them lurid romances, many dealing with psychic or religious events, and all enormously popular. Critics held her in disdain (once, in retaliation, she refused to send them review copies), but Queen Victoria adored her work. Among Corelli's most widely read books are *The Sorrows of Satan* and *The Murder of Delicia*.

Irving Wallace's 9 Favourite Authors

On June 29, 1990 one of the co-authors of *The Book of Lists*, Irving Wallace, died in Los Angeles at the age of 74. His nearly three dozen books have sold an estimated 200 million copies and have been read by 1 billion people worldwide. He wrote 18 novels, including *The Prize*, *The Man* and *The Word*. Shortly before his death, he compiled a list of his all-time favourite authors.

1. W. Somerset Maugham – *Of Human Bondage*, because of its compelling characterisation, narrative drive, crystal-clear prose; *The Summing Up*, for clarity, cynicism, philosophy; and *The Moon and Sixpence*.
2. F. Scott Fitzgerald – *Tender Is the Night*.
3. Arthur Koestler – *Arrival and Departure* and *Darkness at Noon*.
4. Arthur Conan Doyle – the Sherlock Holmes books; pure pleasure, nothing more. Also, *The Lost World*.
5. James Hilton – *Lost Horizon* and *Without Armor*.
6. Raymond Chandler.
7. Graham Greene.
8. John le Carré – *The Little Drummer Girl*.
9. Nelson De Mille – *Word of Honor* and *By the Rivers of Babylon*.

Brian Aldiss's 10 Favourite Science Fiction Novels

One of the legendary figures in the science fiction genre, Brian W. Aldiss was born in 1925, served with the signal corps in the British

Army, then spent nine years as a bookseller before becoming a full-time writer in 1956. His works include *Frankenstein Unbound*, *Moreau's Other Island* and the groundbreaking *Helliconia* trilogy (*Helliconia Spring*, *Helliconia Summer*, *Helliconia Winter*). His short story 'Supertoys Last All Summer Long' was a long-time dream project for the legendary director Stanley Kubrick, and was eventually filmed after Kubrick's death as *A.I.: Artificial Intelligence* by Steven Spielberg in 2001. A prolific writer, Aldiss lives in Oxford, England, and his most recent novel is *Super-State*, published in 2003.

1. Mary Shelley: *Frankenstein Or, The New Prometheus*
2. Albert Robida: *The Twentieth Century*
3. H.G. Wells: *The Time Machine*
4. H.G. Wells: *The War of the Worlds*
5. Olaf Stapledon: *Star-Maker*
6. Charles Harness: *The Paradox Men*
7. Kurt Vonnegut: *Galapagos*
8. Harry Harrison: *Bill the Galactic Hero*
9. Philip K. Dick: *Martian Timeslip*
10. Robert Holdstock: *Mythago Wood*

Will Self's 9 Books That Prove Fact Is Stranger Than Fiction

1. *Land of Opportunity: One Family's Search for the American Dream in the Age of Crack*, William M. Adler (Atlantic Monthly Pr, 1995)
   The story of the Afro-American family who brought crack cocaine to Detroit in the early 1980s. A staggering portrayal of the ineluctable convergence between addiction and capitalism in Reagan's America. At one point the family ran an entire burnt-out office block in downtown Detroit as a crack house, with different floors assigned to differently priced rocks of crack. Their dealers received MacDonalds-style training.

2. *The Strange Last Voyage of Donald Crowhurst*, Nicholas Tomalin and Ron Hall (Hodder, 1970)
   Crowhurst was the British solo yachtsman who faked his own positions during the 1970 round-the-world yacht race, and then when it became obvious that his subterfuge would be discovered, committed suicide by throwing himself into the sea. In a bizarre echo of the *Marie Celeste*, Crowhurst's boat – *Teignmouth Electron* – was found floating abandoned in the Atlantic, in the

cabin was his increasingly disjointed and surrealistic logbook filled with monomaniacal metaphysical speculation.

3. *Into the Wild*, Jon Krakauer (Villard Books, 1996)
The tale of a teenage American who walked off into the wilds of Alaska and met his end there. Krakauer links this – surprisingly disturbing – account of a bright young man's Tolstoyan rejection of bourgeois comfort to a deep and cogent meditation on isolation and the wilderness.

4. *The Origin of Consciousness and the Breakdown of the Bicameral Mind*, Julian Jaynes (Houghton Mifflin, 1976)
Not strictly speaking facts at all, a theory, but I believe it. Jaynes's view is that some time between the composition of the *Odyssey* and the *Iliad* the human *corpus callosum* was formed and the mind became uni- rather than bicameral. In other words, up until comparatively recently when God or gods 'spoke' to people, they very much heard him, her or them. Developed with startling erudition, this book will make you look at all forms of religious enthusiasm in an altogether new light.

5. *The Man with a Shattered World*, A.R. Luria (Harvard University Press, 1972)
Luria was the pioneering neurosurgeon whose work on the victims of shelling during the Second World War led to startling new insights into the human brain. Because shrapnel wounds tended – where the patient survived at all – to take out localised areas of brain tissue, Luria was able to find an array of individuals with different bits missing. The man of the title had ceased through his injuries to experience the world as a coherent whole. Essential reading for the empiricist, as is Luria's *Mind of a Mnemonist*.

6. *The Mountain People*, Colin Turnbull (Green Apple Books, 1972)
The story of the Ik, an isolated hill tribe in Kenya, who, when their food supply was destroyed by drought, resolved to starve themselves to death rather than migrate. A compelling depiction of the skull beneath the skin of all human communities and a kind of anthro-pological counterpoint to Primo Levi's *If This is a Man*.

7. *Island on the Edge of the World*, Charles MacLean (Simon & Schuster, 1972)
By no means the only book on St Kilda, but to my mind the most readable (along with the original account of the islands written by Martin Martin in the seventeenth century – crazy

name, crazy guy). St Kilda is the micro-archipelago forty miles to the west of the Outer Hebrides, where a community remained almost completely isolated from the rest of the world for seven hundred years. The St Kildans lived almost entirely on seafowl which they harvested from the towering cliffs of their island fastness. They ate seagulls, exported their feathers, made them into shoes, and smeared fulmar oil on their infants' umbilici as part of a pagan ritual. During the nineteenth century steamboat cruises were advertised in Liverpool to visit 'Britain's Modern Primitives'. The islands were finally evacuated in the 1930s. A remarkable story and one that MacLean tells exceptionally well and with considerable sensitivity.

8. *Whoever Fights Monsters*, Robert K. Ressler and Tom Schachtman (St Martin's Press, 1992)
Ressler is the real life FBI agent that Thomas Harris consulted for the writing of his Hannibal Lecter books, and Ressler's character undoubtedly informed his portrayal of Jack Crawford, Clarice Starling *et al.* Ressler was pivotally involved in tracking down most of the serial killers who have preyed on America during the past three decades. His pivotal distinction between 'organised' and 'disorganised' psychopaths makes for unsettling reading if you have poor impulse control and can't keep your desk tidy. But on a more serious note, the minute and detailed accounts of scores of disgusting murders, sexual assaults and dismemberments make this the 'true crime' book to do away with the rest of them.

9. *In the Belly of the Beast: Letters from Prison*, Jack Henry Abbott (Random House, 1981)
Abbott was the murderer who Norman Mailer befriended via correspondence, and who the writer assisted in gaining early release. Tragically Abbott than murdered again, was returned to the 'belly of the beast', and in due course died there. Half of this book consists of the Mailer–Abbott correspondence, the other half is an astonishing philosophic disquisition by a self-taught thinker who absorbed quantities of Marx, Schopenhauer and Nietzsche while serving time in the hardest of federal penitentiaries. I'm not saying that Abbott shapes up as a thinker, but there's no denying the power of his critique or the extraordinary facts of its composition.

Brian Eno's 18 Mind-Changing Books

Brian Eno's career encompasses music, writing, lecturing, teaching and the visual arts. He has released a series of critically acclaimed solo albums and has collaborated with the likes of John Cale, Nico, Robert Fripp, David Bowie and the band James. His award-winning production work spans from Gavin Bryars and Talking Heads to U2 and Laurie Anderson. A pioneer in tape-looping, electronics and other forms of sonic manipulation, with an unusual, strategic approach to music-making, his audio/visual installation work has been shown around the world. Eno has been a Visiting Professor at the Royal College of Art in London and was awarded an Honorary Doctorate in Technology from Plymouth University and Honorary Professorship by the Universität der Künste in Berlin; he is also a founder of The Long Now Foundation. His writings on politics, culture and communications have been widely published, and he is the author of *A Year with Swollen Appendices* published by Faber and Faber in 1996.

1. *Brain of the Firm* – Stafford Beer
   The most approachable book about the self-organising nature of complex systems.
2. *Silence* – John Cage
   Music as philosophy (with lots of Zen wit).
3. *The Evolution of Cooperation* – Robert Axelrod
   How time changes relationships: a message of hope.
4. *The Clock of the Long Now* – Stewart Brand
   Why we need to think long.
5. *Managing the Commons* – Garrett Hardin
   Structural observations about shared resources.
6. *A New Kind of Science* – Stephen Wolfram
   Controversial and exciting new approach to the genesis of complex systems.
7. *Grooming, Gossip and the Evolution of Language* – Robin Fox
   The origins and limits of human community.
8. *The Mystery of Capital* – Hernando de Soto
   Why capitalism can't be planted just anywhere.
9. *Labyrinths* – Jorge Luis Borges
   The ultimate 'what if?' book.

10. *Africa: A Biography of the Continent* – John Reader
The story of Africa beginning 4½ billion BC.

11. *Animal Architecture* – Karl von Frisch
One of the best 'beauty of nature' books, academic jaw-dropper.

12. *Contingency, Irony and Solidarity* – Richard Rorty
A great work of modern pragmatism: the antidote to Derrida.

13. *Peter the Great* – Robert K. Massie
Superb biography of a giant located somewhere between Genghis Khan, Abraham Lincoln and Joseph Stalin.

14. *Roll Jordan Roll, The World the Slaves Built* – Eugene Genovese The unexpected richness and lasting importance of slave culture in America.

15. *Folk Song Style and Culture* – Alan Lomax
An extraordinary theory that singing style is indicative of social structure by the pioneer collector of world music.

16. *The Selfish Gene* – Richard Dawkins
Even if you think you know what this is about, it's worth reading. The atheists' defence.

17. *Democracy in America* – Alexis de Tocqueville
He guessed at the best of it, warned of the worst of it, and was right on both counts.

18. *Guns, Germs and Steel* by Jared Diamond
Compelling account of the physical factors shaping world history.

Sir Christopher Bland's 10 Best Reference Books

Sir Christopher Bland is chairman of British Telecom and former chairman of the BBC (1996–2001). He is also chairman of Canongate Books.

The best reference books are, paradoxically, those you want to read when you don't need to look anything up. They belong by the bath or the lavatory, and are far better companions than the out-of-date magazines or the short works of unfunny humorists normally encountered in either location. With these by your side you can visit nineteenth-century London, drink Chateau Margaux, watch a test match or go to the movies, all without leaving home. Here are my favourites. The first four are essential in every household; the remainder are optional delights.

1. *THE OXFORD ENGLISH DICTIONARY*
   Either the 20-volume edition or, if you are feeling cramped for space, the *Shorter* 2-volume version. A to Zyxt via Dvandra, Mouke, Quemadero and Sequyle.

2. *ENCYCLOPAEDIA BRITANNICA*
   The oldest and most indispensable reference set. Facts historical, political, literary, cultural, scientific and technological in 32 volumes. Essential for answering children's questions and preserving parental reputations for omniscience.

3. *BREWER'S DICTIONARY OF PHRASE AND FABLE*
   Describes the origin of 'to catch a Tartar', 'halcyon days', 'to come a cropper', 'the tortoise and the hare'.

4. *THE OXFORD DICTIONARY OF QUOTATIONS*
   'By necessity, by proclivity and by delight, we all quote' – Emerson. This dictionary provides quotations from Abelard to Zola. And the Emerson extract you've just read.

5. *MOGG'S CAB FARES*
   This nineteenth-century guide to horse-drawn bus, tram and cab fares was the constant companion of Surtees' Soapy Sponge, who read nothing else. Sponge could transport himself to London through fancying himself 'hailing a Turnham Green 'bus . . . wrangling with a conductor for charging him sixpence when there was a pennant flapping at his nose with the words "all the way for threepence".' upon it' or through reciting 'Conduit Street, Astley's Amphitheatre, Bryanston Square, Covent Garden Theatre, Foundling Hospital, Hatton Garden . . .'. No contemporary use.

6. *WISDEN*
   The annual bible for cricket anoraks who like to know the score. Who is the only Nobel Prize-winning author to have appeared in Wisden? This book will tell you.

7. *BURKE'S IRISH LANDED GENTRY*
   Read about the lineage of the McGillicuddy of the Reeks, Captain Blood who attempted to steal the Crown Jewels from the Tower of London, the Knight of Glin and Josephine Bland, Ireland's first woman aviator, who drank whiskey funnelled through an ear-trumpet to sustain her on her maiden flight.

8. *HALLIWELL'S FILM GUIDE*
   Intelligent, opinionated, entertaining reviews of the world's best – and worst – movies, with plots, stars, writers, directors and reliable star ratings. Who directed *Casablanca*, *Brief Encounter*, *Gone with the Wind* or *The Beast from 40,000 Fathoms*? The answer is here.

9. *PARKER'S WINE BUYER'S GUIDE* by Robert M. Parker
   If you cannot afford Chateau Lafite or Petrus, try drinking Parker's adjectives and metaphors. 'Sexy, open-knit, opulent . . . nose of cassis, cedar, spice box and minerals', 'a seamless personality and full body', 'long and lush . . . notes of roasted espresso, crème de cassis, smoke, new saddle leather, graphite and liquorice'. And you won't have a hangover.

10. *REED'S NAUTICAL ALMANAC*
    For the time of high tide at Dover on the 28th of August, the behaviour of tidal streams in the Kyle of Lochalsh, or the best way through the Portland Race.

Joyce Carol Oates's 14 Favourite American Authors

Born in 1938, Joyce Carol Oates had her first book, the short story collection *By the North Gate* (1963), published when she was only 25 years old. At the age of 31, she won the American Book Award for her novel *them* (1969), becoming one of the youngest writers ever to receive the award. A prolific writer, her other novels include *Black Water* (1992), *Zombie* (1995) and *Blonde* (2000), as well as a series of suspense thrillers under the pseudonym Rosamond Smith, along with many works of short fiction, poetry and literary criticism. Oates teaches at Princeton University, and she and her husband Raymond Smith edit the acclaimed literary journal *The Ontario Review*. Her most recent works include a children's book, *Where Is Little Reynard?* (2003), and a short story collection, *I Am No One You Know* (2004).

1. Emily Dickinson
2. Walt Whitman
3. Herman Melville
4. Nathaniel Hawthorne
5. Edgar Allan Poe
6. Henry David Thoreau
7. Henry James

8. William Faulkner
9. Ernest Hemingway
10. William Carlos Williams
11. Mark Twain
12. Willa Cather
13. Robert Frost
14. Flannery O'Connor

Oates notes: This is a purely American list, suggesting, but not fully naming, the wide range and diversity of our native literature. As an American writer with a keen sense of history, I think of myself as having sprung from these nourishing sources, among others. And the list could go on and on . . .

Elmore Leonard's 11 Favourite Novels

Born on October 11, 1925, in New Orleans, Louisiana, Elmore 'Dutch' Leonard began writing novels while working as an advertising executive. His first successes were westerns, including *The Bounty Hunters* (1953) and *Hombre* (1961), before he turned to crime fiction with such bestsellers as *Stick* (1983), *Glitz* (1985) and *Killshot* (1989). Leonard's novels have been the basis for many hit movies, including Barry Sonnenfeld's *Get Shorty* (1995), Quentin Tarantino's *Jackie Brown* (1997) and Steven Soderbergh's *Out of Sight* (1998). His most recent works include his first children's book, *A Coyote's in the House*, and the thriller *Mr Paradise*, both published in 2004. Leonard makes his home outside Detroit, Michigan (the locale for many of his novels).

1. *All Quiet on the Western Front* by Erich Maria Remarque
   The first book that made me want to write, when I was still in grade school.

2. *For Whom the Bell Tolls* by Ernest Hemingway
   A book I studied almost daily when, in 1952, I began to write with a purpose.

3. *A Stretch on the River* by Richard Bissell
   The book that showed me the way I should be writing: not taking it so seriously.

4. *Sweet Thursday* by John Steinbeck
   The book that showed the difference between honest prose and show-off writing.

5. *The Friends of Eddie Coyle* by George V. Higgins
   Twenty years ago George showed how to get into a scene fast.

6. *Paris Trout* by Pete Dexter
   An awfully good writer.

7. *The Heart of the Matter* by Graham Greene
   Especially moving at the time it was written. I like everything he did, from *The Power and the Glory* to *Our Man in Havana*.

8. *The Moviegoer* by Walker Percy
   Walker, the old pro.

9. *Legends of the Fall* by Jim Harrison
   Wonderful prose writer and great poet.

10. *7½ Cents* by Richard Bissell.

11. Collected short stories of Hemingway, Annie Proulx, Raymond Carver and Bobbie Ann Mason
    Have studied and I hope learned from all of them.

William S. Burroughs' 10 Favourite Novels

Born in 1914 in St Louis, Missouri, the rebellious William Seward Burroughs II grew up to be the disinherited heir of the Burroughs Adding Machine Corporation, a multimillion-dollar concern. During a drunken party game in Mexico, he accidentally killed his wife Joan as he aimed for a glass atop her head. Norman Mailer once termed Burroughs 'the only American novelist living today who may conceivably be possessed by genius'. A former private investigator, reporter and exterminator, Burroughs earned a cult following with his novel *Naked Lunch* (1956), a surrealistic account of his experiences as a heroin addict. He wrote or collaborated on more than 35 books, including *Queer* and *Nova Express*. Towards the end of his life, he became a great lover of cats, writing *The Cat Inside*. He died in Lawrence, Kansas, in 1997 at the age of 83. He contributed this list to *The Book of Lists* in 1980.

1. *The Process* by Brion Gysin
2. *The Satyricon* by Petronius
3. *In Youth is Pleasure* by Denton Welch
4. *Two Serious Ladies* by Jane Bowles
5. *The Sheltering Sky* by Paul Bowles

6. *Under Western Eyes* by Joseph Conrad
7. *Journey to the End of the Night* by Louis Ferdinand Céline
8. *Querelle de Brest* by Jean Genet
9. *The Unfortunate Traveller* by Thomas Nashe
10. *The Great Gatsby* by F. Scott Fitzgerald

The Process (1969) by Brion Gysin (1916–86) follows the bizarre adventures of a black American professor travelling across the Sahara Desert. English writer Denton Welch (1915–48) explored an English schoolboy's sexual fears and fantasies in his second novel, *In Youth is Pleasure* (1945). Thomas Nashe (1567–1601), English pamphleteer and dramatist, anticipated the English adventure novel with *The Unfortunate Traveller*.

12 Last Lines of Novels

1. 'It is a far, far better thing that I do, than I have ever done; it is a far, far better rest that I go to, than I have ever known.' – *A Tale of Two Cities*, Charles Dickens

2. 'Yes.' I said. 'Isn't it pretty to think so?' – *The Sun Also Rises*, Ernest Hemingway

3. 'It was not till they had examined the rings that they recognised who it was.' – *The Portrait of Dorian Gray,* Oscar Wilde

4. 'He is a gorilla.' – *Planet of the Apes*, Pierre Boulle

5. 'And however superciliously the highbrows carp, we the public in our heart of hearts all like a success story; so perhaps my ending is not so unsatisfactory after all.' – *The Razor's Edge*, W. Somerset Maugham

6. 'After all, tomorrow is another day.' – *Gone With The Wind*, Margaret Mitchell

7. 'The Martians stared back up at them for a long, long silent time from the rippling water . . .' – *Martian Chronicles*, Ray Bradbury

8. 'Then with a profound and deeply willed desire to believe, to be heard, as she had done every day since the murder of Carlo Rizzi, she said the necessary prayers for the soul of Michael Corleone.' – *The Godfather*, Mario Puzo

9. 'He loved Big Brother.' – *1984*, George Orwell

10. 'And out again, upon the unplumb'd, salt, estranging sea.' – *The French Lieutenant's Woman*, John Fowles

11. 'On the way downtown I stopped at a bar and had a couple of double Scotches. They didn't do me any good. All they did was make me think of Silver Wig, and I never saw her again.' – *The Big Sleep*, Raymond Chandler

12. 'It was the devious-cruising Rachel, that in her retracing search after her missing children, only found another orphan.' – *Moby Dick*, Herman Melville

Chapter 12

23 OBSCURE AND OBSOLETE WORDS

33 NAMES OF THINGS YOU NEVER KNEW HAD NAMES

18 SAYINGS OF OSCAR WILDE

16 WELL-KNOWN SAYINGS ATTRIBUTED TO THE WRONG PEOPLE

13 SAYINGS OF WOODY ALLEN

17 PAIRS OF CONTRADICTORY PROVERBS

SO TO SPEAK – THE TRUTH ABOUT 16 COMMON SAYINGS

29 WORDS RARELY USED IN THEIR POSITIVE FORM

18 UNTRANSLATABLE WORDS

7 WORDS IN WHICH ALL THE VOWELS APPEAR IN ALPHABETICAL ORDER

5 REMARKABLE MESSAGES IN BOTTLES

Words

COLUMELLA NASI – see p.319

23 Obscure and Obsolete Words

The average adult recognises 30,000 to 50,000 words, but only uses 10,000 to 15,000. However, there are actually about 1 million words in the English language, some of which – although obscure, forgotten, or rarely used – are worth reviving.

1. BOANTHROPY – A type of insanity in which a man thinks he is an ox.
2. CHANTEPLEURE – To sing and weep at the same time.
3. DIBBLE – To drink like a duck, lifting up the head after each sip.
4. EOSOPHOBIA – Fear of dawn.
5. EUGERIA – Normal and happy old age.
6. EUNEIROPHRENIA – Peace of mind after a pleasant dream.
7. EYESERVICE – Work done only when the boss is watching.
8. FELLOWFEEL – To crawl into the skin of another person so as to share his feelings, to empathise with.
9. GROAK – To watch people silently while they are eating, hoping they will ask you to join them.
10. GYNOTIKOLOBOMASSOPHILE – One who likes to nibble on a woman's earlobes.
11. HEBEPHRENIC – A condition of adolescent silliness.
12. IATROGENIC – Illness or disease caused by doctors or by prescribed treatment.
13. LAPLING – Someone who enjoys resting in women's laps.
14. LIBBERWORT – Food or drink that makes one idle and stupid, food of no nutritional value, 'junk food'.
15. MEUPAREUNIA – A sexual act gratifying to only one participant.
16. NEANIMORPHIC – Looking younger than one's years.
17. ONIOCHALASIA – Buying as a means of mental relaxation.
18. PARNEL – A priest's mistress.
19. PERISTEROPHOBIA – Fear of pigeons.
20. PILGARLIC – A bald head that looks like a peeled garlic.

21. PREANTEPENULTIMATE – Fourth from last.

22. RESISTENTIALISM – Seemingly spiteful behaviour manifested by inanimate objects.

23. SUPPEDANEUM – A foot support for crucifix victims.

33 Names of Things You Never Knew had Names

1. AGLET
The plain or ornamental covering on the end of a shoelace.

2. ARMSAYE
The armhole in clothing.

3. CHANKING
Spat-out food, such as rinds or pits.

4. COLUMELLA NASI
The bottom part of the nose between the nostrils.

5. DRAGÉES
Small beadlike pieces of candy, usually silver-coloured, used for decorating cookies, cakes and sundaes.

6. FEAT
A dangling curl of hair.

7. FERRULE
The metal band on a pencil that holds the eraser in place.

8. HARP
The small metal hoop that supports a lampshade.

9. HEMIDEMISEMIQUAVER
A 64th note. (A 32nd is a demisemiquaver and a 16th note is a semiquaver.)

10-13. JARNS, NITTLES, GRAWLIX and QUIMP
Various squiggles used to denote cussing in comic books.

14. KEEPER
The loop on a belt that keeps the end in place after it has passed through the buckle.

15. KICK or PUNT
The indentation at the bottom of some wine bottles. It gives added strength to the bottle but lessens its holding capacity.

16. **LIRIPIPE**
The long tail on a graduate's academic hood.

17. **MINIMUS**
The little finger or toe.

18. **NEF**
An ornamental stand in the shape of a ship.

19. **OBDORMITION**
The numbness caused by pressure on a nerve; when a limb is 'asleep'.

20. **OCTOTHORPE**
The symbol '#' on a telephone handset. Bell Labs' engineer Don Macpherson created the word in the 1960s by combining octo-, as in eight, with the name of one of his favourite athletes, 1912 Olympic decathlon champion Jim Thorpe.

21. **OPHRYON**
The space between the eyebrows on a line with the top of the eye sockets.

22. **PEEN**
The end of a hammer head opposite the striking face.

23. **PHOSPHENES**
The lights you see when you close your eyes hard. Technically, the luminous impressions are due to the excitation of the retina caused by pressure on the eyeball.

24. **PURLICUE**
The space between the thumb and extended forefinger.

25. **RASCETA**
Creases on the inside of the wrist.

26. **ROWEL**
The revolving star on the back of a cowboy's spurs.

27. **SADDLE**
The rounded part on the top of a matchbook.

28. **SCROOP**
The rustle of silk.

29. **SNORKEL BOX**
A mailbox with a protruding receiver to allow people to deposit mail without leaving their cars.

30. SPRAINTS
Otter dung.

31. TANG
The projecting prong on a tool or instrument.

32. WAMBLE
Stomach rumbling.

33. ZARF
A holder for a handleless coffee cup.

– S.B. & D.W.

18 Sayings of Oscar Wilde

Born in Dublin and educated at Oxford, Oscar Wilde (1854–1900) wrote one novel, *The Picture of Dorian Gray*, and a number of successful plays, including *Lady Windermere's Fan* and *The Importance of Being Earnest*. Considered the master of social comedy, Wilde was an expert craftsman of witty sayings and paradoxes. Even on his deathbed, as he sipped champagne, he quipped, 'I am dying beyond my means.'

1. Murder is always a mistake. One should never do anything that one cannot talk about after dinner.
2. I don't recognise you – I've changed a lot.
3. Always forgive your enemies – nothing annoys them so much.
4. The idea that is not dangerous is unworthy of being called an idea at all.
5. To love oneself is the beginning of a lifelong romance.
6. Anybody can sympathise with the sufferings of a friend, but it requires a very fine nature to sympathise with a friend's success.
7. When one is in love, one always begins by deceiving oneself; and one always ends by deceiving others. That is what the world calls a romance.
8. To get back my youth I would do anything in the world, except take exercise, get up early, or be respectable.
9. I can resist anything except temptation.

10. What is a cynic? A man who knows the price of everything and the value of nothing.

11. Experience is the name everyone gives to their mistakes.

12. We are all in the gutter, but some of us are looking at the stars.

13. There is a luxury in self-reproach. When we blame ourselves we feel that no one else has a right to blame us.

14. Only dull people are brilliant at breakfast.

15. A cigarette is the perfect type of a perfect pleasure. It is exquisite, and it leaves one unsatisfied. What more can one want?

16. Nothing succeeds like excess.

17. In this world there are only two tragedies. One is not getting what one wants, and the other is getting it.

18. Education is an admirable thing, but it is well to remember from time to time that nothing that is worth knowing can be taught.

16 Well-Known Sayings Attributed to the Wrong People

1. Anybody who hates children and dogs can't be all bad.
   Attributed to: W.C. Fields
   Actually said by: Leo Rosten (at a dinner, introducing Fields): 'Any man who hates dogs and babies can't be all bad.'

2. Go west, young man!
   Attributed to: Horace Greeley
   Actually said by: John Soule (Article, Terre Haute *Express*, 1851)

3. Everybody talks about the weather, but nobody does anything about it!
   Attributed to: Mark Twain
   Actually said by: Charles Dudley Warner (Editorial, Hartford *Courant*, August 24, 1897)

4. Survival of the fittest.
   Attributed to: Charles Darwin
   Actually said by: Herbert Spencer (*Principles of Biology* and earlier works)

5. That government is best which governs least.
Attributed to: Thomas Jefferson
Actually said by: Henry David Thoreau (who put it in quotation marks in 'Civil Disobedience' and called it a motto)

6. Cleanliness is next to godliness.
Attributed to: The Bible
Actually said by: John Wesley (*Sermons*, no. 93, 'On Dress')

7. A journey of a thousand miles must begin with a single step.
Attributed to: Confucius
Actually said by: Lao-Tzu (*Tao Tê Ching*)

8. God helps those who help themselves.
Attributed to: The Bible
Actually said by: Aesop ('The gods help them that help themselves.')

9. God is in the details.
Attributed to: Ludwig Mies van der Rohe
Actually said by: François Rabelais ('The good God is in the details.')

10. If you can't stand the heat, get out of the kitchen.
Attributed to: Harry S Truman
Actually said by: Harry Vaughn (Truman's friend, whom Truman was quoting)

11. Promises are like pie crust, made to be broken.
Attributed to: V.I. Lenin
Actually said by: Jonathan Swift (*Polite Conversation*: 'Promises are like pie crust, leaven to be broken.')

12. Wagner's music is better than it sounds.
Attributed to: Mark Twain
Actually said by: Bill Nye

13. When I hear the word 'culture', I reach for my gun.
Attributed to: Hermann Göring
Actually said by: Hanns Johst (1933 play *Schlageter*: 'Whenever I hear the word "culture", I reach for my Browning.')

14. Winning isn't everything, it's the only thing.
Attributed to: Vince Lombardi
Actually said by: Red Sanders (UCLA football coach; quoted in *Sports Illustrated*, 1955)

15. Spare the rod and spoil the child.
Attributed to: The Bible
Actually said by: Samuel Butler (*Hudibras*, 1664)

16. Float Like a butterfly, Sting like a bee, Your hands can't hit What your eyes can't see.
Attributed to: Muhammad Ali
Actually said by: Drew 'Bundini' Brown (Ali's good friend}

–C.F. & K.A.

13 Sayings of Woody Allen

Born Allan Konigsberg in Brooklyn on December 1, 1935, Allen began writing quips for gossip columnists at the age of 15. After graduating from high school, he landed a job writing for Sid Caesar's classic television comedy series *Your Show of Shows*. In 1961 he branched out from writing to stand-up comedy. He also wrote plays and screenplays before directing his first film, *What's Up, Tiger Lily?*, in 1966. Among his many hits are *Annie Hall* (1977), *Manhattan* (1979) and *Hannah and Her Sisters* (1986).

1. *It seemed the world was divided into good and bad people. The good ones slept better . . . while the bad ones seemed to enjoy the waking hours much more.*
Side Effects, 1981

2. *Don't listen to what your schoolteachers tell you. Don't pay attention to that. Just see what they look like and that's how you know what life is really going to be like.*
Crimes and Misdemeanors, 1990

3. *[Intellectuals] are like the Mafia. They only kill their own.*
Stardust Memories, 1980

4. *Sun is bad for you. Everything our parents told us was good is bad. Sun, milk, red meat, college.*
Annie Hall, 1977

5. *The prettiest [girls] are almost always the most boring, and that is why some people feel there is no God.*
The Early Essays, 1973

6. *Sex alleviates tension and love causes it.*
A Midsummer Night's Sex Comedy, 1982

7. *Nothing sexier than a lapsed Catholic.*
Alice, 1990

8. *Love is deep; sex is only a few inches.*
   Bullets Over Broadway, 1994

9. *I thought of that old joke, you know, this guy goes to a psychiatrist and says, 'Doc, my brother's crazy. He thinks he's a chicken.' And the doctor says, 'Why don't you turn him in?' And the guy says, 'I would but I need the eggs.' Well, I guess that's pretty much how I feel about relationships. You know, they're totally irrational and crazy and absurd . . . but I guess we keep going through it because most of us need the eggs.*
   Annie Hall, 1977

10. *To you, I'm an atheist . . . to God I'm the loyal opposition.*
    Stardust Memories, 1980

11. *I don't want to achieve immortality through my work, I want to achieve it through not dying.*

12. *Someone once asked me if my dream was to live on in the hearts of my people, and I said I would like to live on in my apartment. And that's really what I would prefer.* 1987

13. *There's this old joke. Two elderly women are in a Catskills Mountain resort and one of 'em says: 'Boy, the food at this place is really terrible.' The other one says, 'Yeah, I know, and such small portions.' Well, that's essentially how I feel about life. Full of loneliness and misery and suffering and unhappiness, and it's all over much too quickly.*
    Annie Hall, 1977

17 Pairs of Contradictory Proverbs

1. Look before you leap
   He who hesitates is lost

2. If at first you don't succeed, try, try again
   Don't beat your head against a brick wall

3. Absence makes the heart grow fonder
   Out of sight, out of mind

4. Never put off until tomorrow what you can do today
   Don't cross the bridge until you come to it

5. Two heads are better than one
   Paddle your own canoe

6. More haste, less speed
Time waits for no man

7. You're never too old to learn
You can't teach an old dog new tricks

8. A word to the wise is sufficient
Talk is cheap

9. It's better to be safe than sorry
Nothing ventured, nothing gained

10. Don't look a gift horse in the mouth
Beware of Greeks bearing gifts

11. Do unto others as you would have others do unto you
Nice guys finish last

12. Hitch your wagon to a star
Don't bite off more than you can chew

13. Many hands make light work
Too many cooks spoil the broth

14. Don't judge a book by its cover
Clothes make the man

15. The squeaking wheel gets the grease
Silence is golden

16. Birds of a feather flock together
Opposites attract

17. The pen is mightier than the sword
Actions speak louder than words

– J.Ba.

So To Speak – The Truth About 16 Common Sayings

1. AT A SNAIL'S PACE
The fastest land snail on record is a garden snail named Archie, who won the 1995 World Snail Racing Championship in Longhan, England, by covering 13 inches in 2 minutes. Archie's pace was .0062 mph.

2. JUST A MOMENT
According to an old English time unit, a moment takes 1½

minutes. In medieval times, a moment was either 1/40 or 1/50 of an hour, but by rabbinical reckoning a moment is precisely 1/1,080 of an hour.

3. ALL THE TEA IN CHINA
The United Nations Food and Agricultural Organisation estimates that all the tea in China in 2003 amounted to 800,345 metric tons.

4. BY A HAIR'S BREADTH
Although the breadth of a hair varies from head to head, the dictionary definition of hair's breadth is 1/48 in.

5. ONLY SKIN-DEEP
The depth of human skin ranges from 1/100 in. on the eyelid to 1/5 in. on the back.

6. EATS LIKE A HORSE
A 1,200-lb horse eats about 15 lb of hay and 9 lb of grain each day. This amounts to 1/50 of its own weight each day, or 7 times its own weight each year. The real gluttons in the animal kingdom are birds, who consume more than 90 times their own weight in food each year.

7. A PICTURE IS WORTH A THOUSAND WORDS
The amount paid by magazines for photographs and for written articles varies widely. Both *Travel & Leisure* magazine and *Harper's* magazine pay an average of $350 for a photograph and $1 a word for articles. Based on this scale, a picture is worth 350 words. When *The Book of Lists* first studied this matter in 1978, a picture was worth 2000 words.

8. QUICK AS A WINK
The average wink, or corneal reflex blink, lasts 1/10 sec.

9. QUICKER THAN YOU CAN SAY 'JACK ROBINSON'
When members of *The Book of Lists* staff were asked to say 'Jack Robinson', their speed varied from ½ to 1 sec. It is acknowledged that this may not be a representative sample of the world population.

10. SELLING LIKE HOTCAKES
Sales figures for the International House of Pancakes show that their 1,164 US restaurants sold a total of 700,000,000 pancakes in 2003.

11. **SINCE TIME IMMEMORIAL**
Time immemorial is commonly defined as beyond the memory of any living person, or a time extending so far back as to be indefinite. However, for the purposes of English law, a statute passed in 1275 decreed that time immemorial was any point in time prior to 1189 – the year when Richard I began his reign.

12. **KNEE-HIGH TO A GRASSHOPPER**
According to Charles L. Hogue of the Los Angeles County Museum of Natural History, this figure necessarily depends upon the size of the grasshopper. For the average grasshopper, the knee-high measurement would be about ½ in.

13. **HIGH AS A KITE**
The record for the greatest height attained by a single kite on a single line is 14,509 feet. The kite was flown by a group headed by Richard Synergy at Kincardine, Ontario, Canada, on August 12, 2000.

14. **FASTER THAN A SPEEDING BULLET**
The fastest bullet is a calibre .50 Saboted Light Armor Penetrator-Tracer M962. Used in M2 machine guns, it travels 4,000 feet (.75 mile) per second. The fastest non-military bullet is the .257 Weatherby Spire Point, which travels 3,825 feet (.72 mile) per second.

15. **BLOOD IS THICKER THAN WATER**
In chemistry, water is given a specific gravity, or relative density, of 1.00, because it is used as the standard against which all other densities are measured. By comparison, blood has a specific gravity of 1.06 – only slightly thicker than water.

16. **A KING'S RANSOM**
The largest king's ransom in history was raised by Richard the Lionheart to obtain his release from the Holy Roman Emperor Henry VI in 1194. The English people were forced to contribute almost 150,000 marks to free their sovereign. Nearly as large a ransom was raised by Atahualpa, King of the Incas, when he offered Pizarro a roomful of gold and two roomfuls of silver for his release in 1532. At today's prices, the ransom would be worth more than £4 million (or $7 million). Unfortunately, it was not sufficient to buy Atahualpa his freedom; he was given a mock trial and executed.

29 Words Rarely Used in Their Positive Form

	Negative Form	Positive Form
1.	*Inadvertent*	*Advertent* (giving attention; heedful)
2.	*Analgesia*	*Algesia* (sensitiveness to pain)
3.	*Antibiotic*	*Biotic* (of or relating to life)
4.	*Unconscionable*	*Conscionable* (conscientious)
5.	*Disconsolate*	*Consolate* (consoled, comforted)
6.	*Incorrigible*	*Corrigible* (correctable)
7.	*Uncouth*	*Couth* (marked by finesse, polish, etc; smooth)
8.	*Indelible*	*Delible* (capable of being deleted)
9.	*Nondescript*	*Descript* (described; inscribed)
10.	*Indomitable*	*Domitable* (tamable)
11.	*Ineffable*	*Effable* (capable of being uttered or expressed)
12.	*Inevitable*	*Evitable* (avoidable)
13.	*Feckless*	*Feckful* (effective; sturdy; powerful)
14.	*Unfurl*	*Furl* (to draw in and secure to a staff)
15.	*Disgruntle*	*Gruntle* (to put in good humour)
16.	*Disgust*	*Gust* (inclination; liking)
17.	*Antihistamine*	*Histamine* (a crystalline base that is held to be responsible for the dilation and increased permeability of blood vessels which play a major role in allergic reactions)
18.	*Disinfectant*	*Infectant* (an agent of infection)
19.	*Illicit*	*Licit* (not forbidden by law; allowable)
20.	*Immaculate*	*Maculate* (marked with spots; besmirched)
21.	*Innocuous*	*Nocuous* (likely to cause injury; harmful)
22.	*Deodorant*	*Odorant* (an odorous substance)
23.	*Impeccable*	*Peccable* (liable or prone to sin)
24.	*Impervious*	*Pervious* (being of a substance that can be penetrated or permeated)
25.	*Implacable*	*Placable* (of a tolerant nature; tractable)
26.	*Ruthless*	*Ruthful* (full of compassion or pity)
27.	*Insipid*	*Sipid* (affecting the organs of taste; savoury)
28.	*Unspeakable*	*Speakable* (capable of being spoken of)
29.	*Unwieldy*	*Wieldy* (strong; manageable)

– R.A.

18 Untranslatable Words

Here are 18 words and phrases that have no equivalent in English; edited by the *Book of Lists* authors from Howard Rheingold's *They Have A Word For It*, published by Sarabande.

1. **CAVOLI RISCALDATI (Italian)**
   The attempt to revive a dead love affair. Literally, 'reheated cabbage'. The result of such a culinary effort is usually unworkable, messy and distasteful.

2. **DOHADA (Sanskrit)**
   Unusual appetites and cravings of pregnant women. Dohada is a word older than the English language. There is a scientific basis for dohada: women who want to eat dirt (a condition called pica) or chalk, are attempting to ingest essential minerals.

3. **DRACHENFUTTER (German)**
   A gift brought home from a husband to his wife after he has stayed out late. Literally, 'dragon fodder'. In decades past, men went to bars on Saturday night with the wrapped gifts prepared in advance. This word can also be used for all gifts or acts performed out of guilt for having too much fun, such as gifts from employees to bosses, children to parents, students to teachers, and so on.

4. **ESPRIT DE L'ESCALIER (French)**
   The brilliantly witty response to a public insult that comes into your mind only after you have left the party. Literally, 'the spirit of the staircase'. Observes author Rheingold, 'Sometimes, this feeling about what you ought to have said at a crucial moment can haunt you for the rest of your life.'

5. **KYOIKUMAMA (Japanese)**
   A mother who pushes her children into academic achievement. A derogatory term that literally means 'education mama'. The pressure on Japanese students is severe and intense – but they are hardly the only victims of parental pushing. The American fad for using flashcards and the like, to create infant prodigies, is practised by fathers and mothers.

6. **NAKHES (Yiddish)**
   A mixture of pleasure and pride, particularly the kind that a parent gets from a child. It is something one relishes, as in 'May you only get nakhes from your son!'

7. ONDINNONK (Iroquoian)
This is a noun which describes the soul's innermost desires; the angelic parts of human nature. Listening to one's inner instinct to perform a kindly act is to let our ondinnonk be our guide.

8. RAZBLIUTO (Russian)
The feeling a person has for someone he once loved but now does not. In the original Russian it applies to a man, but has become applicable for both sexes.

9. SCHADENFREUDE (German)
The literal translation is 'joy in damage'. It is the pleasure one feels as a result of someone else's misfortune, like seeing a rival slip on a banana peel. Schadenfreude is not as strong as taking revenge, because it's a thought or a feeling, not an action. But when your noisy neighbour's car breaks down, and you're secretly pleased – that's schadenfreude.

10. TARTLE (Scottish)
To hesitate in recognising a person or thing, as happens when you are introduced to someone whose name you cannot recall. A way out of this social gaffe is to say, 'Pardon my sudden tartle!'

11. PALAYI (Bantu)
A mythical monster that scratches at the door. The very same 'monster' haunts the doors of South Carolina, America and West Africa.

12. KATZENJAMMER (German)
A monumentally severe hangover. The inspiration for the early American comic strip 'The Katzenjammer Kids'. On New Year's Eve, it is common for one German to remark to another, 'You're setting yourself up for a real Katzenjammer.' (The party in question may require some 'Drachenfutter'.)

13. QUALUNQUISMO (Italian)
This describes an attitude of indifference to political and social issues. It is derived from a satirical political journal called *L'uomo qualunque*: the man in the street. For example, a great many people believe that the US president is elected by a majority of qualified voters. In fact, only 29% of all voters led to Ronald Reagan's 'landslide victory' in 1984.

14. BILITA MPASH (Bantu)
This denotes blissful dreams. In English we have nightmares, but no word for waking feeling happy. In Bantu, the word is

further defined as a 'legendary, blissful state where all is forgiven and forgotten'. The African-American equivalent for bilita mpash is a 'beluthathatchee', believed to be traced to African-American slang from its Bantu roots.

15. ZALATWIC (Polish)
Zalatwic means using acquaintances to accomplish things unofficially. It means going around the system to trade, to evade exchanges in cash. Since shortages seem to be a fact of social life, these exchanges can range from the profound (a new apartment) to the menial (a new pair of trainers).

16. HARI KUYO (Japanese)
A hari kuyo is a shrine for broken sewing needles. In Japan's Wakayama Province, every village has a shrine where a periodic service is performed for the broken needles. The belief is that the sewing needles worked hard all their lives and died in the service of those who used them. When they break, they are put to rest on a soft bed of tofu.

17. SALOGOK (Eskimo)
Salogok is young black ice. It is a famous fact that Eskimos have 17 different words for kinds of snow. In *Hunters of the Northern Ice*, a book by Richard K. Nelson, there is an appendix on Eskimo ice-words, titled 'Eskimo Sea-Ice Terminology'. A sample from this work is '*Salogok*: nilas, or black young ice: a thin, flexible sheet of newly formed ice which will not support a man, is weak enough to enable seals to break through it with their heads to breathe, and breaks through with one firm thrust of the unaak.'

18. BIRITULULO (Kiriwana, New Guinea)
Comparing yams to settle disputes. In New Guinean culture nobody discusses what everybody knows concerning sensitive subjects. Breaking this code of polite behaviour results in violent disputes. Yet yams are so important in Kiriwana, that people boast about their own yams, to the point of starting a fight. Settling this fight calms everyone down.

– By permission of the author, Howard Rheingold

7 Words in Which All the Vowels Appear in Alphabetical Order

1. *Abstemious*: adj., practising temperance in living.
2. *Abstentious*: adj., characterised by abstinence.
3. *Annelidous*: adj., of the nature of an annelid.
4. *Arsenious*: adj., of, relating to, or containing arsenic.
5. *Casesious*: adj., having a blue colour.
6. *Facetious*: adj., straining to be funny, flippant, especially at the wrong time.
7. *Fracedinous*: adj., productive of heat through putrefaction.

5 Remarkable Messages In Bottles

1. DELIVER US THIS DAY
   In 1825, one Major MacGregor bottled a message and dropped it into the Bay of Biscay: 'Ship on fire. Elizabeth, Joanna, and myself commit our spirits into the hands of our Redeemer Whose grace enables us to be quite composed in the awful prospect of entering eternity.' The note was found 1½ years later, but the major and his party had already been rescued.

2. DOUBLE JEOPARDY
   In the nineteenth century, a British sailor, perhaps in an attempt to found a lonely hearts club, threw a bottled marriage proposal into Southampton waters as his ship left port for India. At Port Said, on the return journey, he was walking along the quay and saw a bottle bobbing in the water. He retrieved it, opened it and read his own proposal for marriage.

3. THE LAST MESSAGE FROM THE *LUSITANIA*
   In 1916, a British seaman saw a bottle bobbing in the north Atlantic. He fished it from the water, opened it . . . and read the final message sent from the *Lusitania* before it sank, taking with it some 1,198 passengers: 'Still on deck with a few people. The last boats have left. We are sinking fast. The orchestra is still playing bravely. Some men near me are praying with a priest. The end is near. Maybe this note will . . .' And there it ended.

4. BETTER LATE THAN NEVER
   In 1714, Japanese seaman Chunosuke Matsuyama embarked on a treasure hunt in the Pacific. His ship was caught in a gale and sank, but he and 44 shipmates managed to swim to a deserted

coral reef. Matsuyama and his companions eventually died of starvation and exposure, but before they did, Matsuyama attempted to send word home. He wrote the story on chips of wood, sealed them in a bottle, and tossed it into the sea. The bottle washed ashore 150 years later on the beach where Matsuyama grew up.

5. A MESSAGE FROM THE NORTH POLE
In 1948, a Russian fisherman found a bottle in the sand bordering Vilkilski Strait in the Arctic. A message was inside, written in both Norwegian and English. It was incomprehensible even when translated: 'Five ponies and 150 dogs remaining. Desire hay, fish and 30 sledges. Must return early in August. Baldwin.' The bizarre message became clear when it was learned that polar explorer Evelyn Baldwin had sealed the note and sent it in 1902. He managed to survive the Arctic without ever receiving the hay, fish or sledges. Whether or not he made it back in August is unknown.

– J.B.M.

Chapter 13

10 OLYMPIC CONTROVERSIES

6 BIZARRE SPORTS EVENTS

5 FAMOUS PEOPLE WHO INVENTED GAMES

JAMES LANDALE'S 8 REMARKABLE PISTOL DUELS

13 OLYMPIC MEDALLISTS WHO ACTED IN MOVIES

SIR STANLEY MATTHEWS' 11 GREATEST FOOTBALL PLAYERS

RICHARD WILLIAMS' 11 FAVOURITE GOALS

SIR CHRIS BONINGTON'S 9 BEST MOUNTAIN EXPERIENCES

7 NON-BOXERS WHO TOOK ON THE CHAMPIONS

Sports

© Bettman/CORBIS

TOMMY SMITH AND JOHN CARLOS – see p.338

10 Olympic Controversies

1. CRUISING TO THE FINISH LINE (1904 marathon)
The first runner to enter the Olympic stadium at the end of the 1904 marathon was Fred Lorz of New York. He was hailed as the winner, photographed with the daughter of the President of the United States, and was about to be awarded the gold medal when it was discovered that he had stopped running after nine miles and hitched a ride in a car for eleven miles before returning to the course. Lorz was disqualified and the victory was given to Thomas Hicks. Although this was only the third Olympic marathon, Lorz was not the first person to cheat in this way. In the inaugural marathon in 1896, Spiridon Belokas of Greece crossed the finish line in third place, but was disqualified when it was discovered that he had ridden part of the way in a carriage.

2. WITH TOO MUCH HELP FROM HIS FRIENDS (1908 marathon)
Italian Dorando Pietri was the first marathon runner to enter the stadium in London in 1908. However, Pietri was dazed and headed in the wrong direction. Track officials pointed him the right way. But then he collapsed on the track. He rose, but collapsed again . . . and again, and again. Finally the officials, fearful that 'he might die in the very presence of the Queen', carried him across the finish line. This aid led to his disqualification and the gold medal went to John Hayes of the United States.

3. CHAMPION WITH A DARK SECRET (1932 and 1936 women's 100 meters)
Competing for Poland, Stella Walsh won the 100 meters in 1932, equalling the world record three times in the process. Four years later, at the Berlin Olympics, Walsh was beaten into second place by American Helen Stephens. A Polish journalist accused Stephens of being a man in disguise. German officials examined her and issued a statement that Stephens was definitely a woman. Forty-four years later, in 1980, Walsh, by then an American citizen living in Cleveland, was shot to death when she stumbled into the middle of a robbery attempt at a discount store. An autopsy concluded that although Helen Stephens may not have had male sexual organs, Stella Walsh did. All the while that Walsh was winning medals and setting records in women's events, she was, by today's rules, a man.

4. CLOCK VS EYES (1960 100-metre freestyle)
Swimmer Lance Larson of the United States appeared to edge John Devitt of Australia for first place in the 1960 100-metre freestyle. Devitt congratulated Larson and left the pool in disappointment. Larson's official time was 55.1 seconds and Devitt's was 55.2 seconds. Of the three judges assigned the task of determining who finished first, two voted for Larson. However, the three second place judges also voted 2–1 for Larson. In other words, of the six judges, three thought Larson had won and three thought Devitt had won. The chief judge gave the victory to Devitt and four years of protests failed to change the results.

5. THE FOG OF WAR (1968 slalom)
French skier Jean-Claude Killy, competing at home in Grenoble, had already won two gold medals and only needed to win the slalom to complete a sweep of the men's Alpine events. Killy's main challenge was expected to come from Karl Schranz of Austria. But something curious happened as Schranz sped through the fog. According to Schranz, a mysterious figure in black crossed the course in front of him. Schranz skidded to a halt and demanded a rerun. His request was granted and Schranz beat Killy's time and was declared the winner. But two hours later, it was announced that Schranz had been disqualified because he had missed two gates before his encounter with the mysterious interloper. At a four-hour meeting of the Jury of Appeal, the Austrians said that if Schranz missed a gate or two it was because a French soldier or policeman had purposely interfered with him. The French claimed that Schranz had made up the whole story to cover up the fact that he had missed a gate. The Jury voted 3–1 for Killy with one abstention.

6. EXTRA SHOT (1972 basketball)
Since basketball was first included in the Olympic program in 1936, teams from the United Stated had gone undefeated, winning 62 straight games over a 36-year period . . . until the 1972 final against the USSR. In an era before professionals were allowed in the Olympics, and with most of the best American college players taking a pass, the US team was hard-pressed against the seasoned veterans of the Soviet squad. The Americans trailed throughout and did not take their first lead, 50–49, until there were three seconds left in the game. Two seconds later, the head referee, noting a

disturbance at the scorer's table called an administrative time-out. The officials in charge had failed to notice that the Soviet coach, Vladimir Kondrashkin, had called a time-out. With one second on the clock, the USSR was awarded its time-out. When play resumed, they inbounded the ball and time ran out. The US players began a joyous celebration, but then R. William Jones, the British secretary-general of the International Amateur Basketball Federation, ordered the clock set back to three seconds, the amount of time remaining when Kondrashkin originally tried to call time-out. Ivan Edeshko threw a long pass to Sasha Belov, who scored the winning basket. The US filed a protest, which was heard by a five-man Jury of Appeal. Three members of the jury were from Communist countries, and all three voted to give the victory to the USSR. With the final vote 3–2, the United States lost an Olympic basketball game for the first time.

7. WIRED FOR VICTORY (1976 team modern pentathlon)
The favoured team from the USSR was fencing against the team from Great Britain when the British pentathletes noticed something odd about Soviet Army Major Borys Onyshchenko. Twice the automatic light registered a hit for Onyshchenko even though he had not touched his opponent. Onyshchenko's sword was taken away to be examined by the Jury of Appeal. An hour later, Onyshchenko was disqualified. Evidently, he had wired his sword with a well-hidden push-button circuit breaker that enabled him to register a hit whenever he wanted. He was forever after known as Borys Dis-Onyshchenko.

8. THE UNBEATABLE PARK SI-HUN (1988 light middleweight boxing)
The 1988 Summer Olympics were held in Seoul, South Korea, and the Koreans were determined to win gold medals in boxing, one of their strongest sports. This determination turned excessive in the case of light middleweight Park Si-Hun. Park made it to the final with a string of four controversial victories, including one in which he disabled his opponent with a low blow to the kidney. In the final, Park faced a slick, 19-year-old American named Roy Jones, Jr. Jones dominated all three rounds, landing 86 punches to Park's 32. Yet three of the five judges awarded the decision to Park, who won the gold medal. Park himself apologised to Jones. Accusations of bribery lingered for years and it was not until 1997 that an

inquiry by the International Olympic Committee concluded that no bribe had occurred.

9. SCORING SCANDAL SYNCH SWIMMER (1992 solo synchronised swimming)
The two leading synchronised swimmers were Sylvie Fréchette of Canada and Kristen Babb-Sprague of the United States. The competition included a round of figures that counted for 50% of the final score. Fréchette, who was strong in figures, hoped to pick up points to offset the gains that Babb-Sprague was expected to make with her free routine. But one of the five judges, Ana Maria da Silviera of Brazil gave Fréchette's albatross spin up 180° the unusually low score of 8.7. She immediately tried to change the score, claiming she had pushed the wrong button. But before the referee could be notified, the judges' scores were displayed and, according to the rules, that meant they could not be changed. When the free routine was completed the next day, it turned out that da Silviera's low score provided the margin of victory that gave the gold medal to Babb-Sprague. Fourteen months later, the International Swimming Federation awarded Fréchette a belated gold medal, while allowing Babb-Sprague to retain hers.

10. IMPAIRED JUDGMENT (2002 pairs figure skating)
The sport of figure skating has a long history of judging controversies; however the problem reached a head at the Salt Lake City Olympics. Russian skaters had won ten straight Olympic championships in the pairs event. In 2002, Russians Elena Berezhnaya and Anton Sikharulidze were in first place after the short program, with Jamie Sale and David Pelletier of Canada in second. In the free skate, the Russians made a series of technical errors, while the Canadians skated a clean programme. Nonetheless, the judges voted 5–4 to award the gold medals to Berezhnaya and Sikharulidze. The ensuing outrage expressed by the North American media was so great and so prolonged that the International Olympic Committee pressured the International Skating Union into giving a second set of gold medals to Sale and Pelletier. Subsequent investigations revealed behind-the-scenes deals among judges and even possible involvement of organised crime figures. Lost in the uproar was the possibility that the five judges who voted for the Russian pair simply preferred their traditional balletic style, while considering the exuberance of Sale and Pelletier's performance to be glitzy and too 'Hollywood'.

6 Bizarre Sports Events

1. ROCK, PAPER, SCISSORS
   The venerable sport of rock, paper, scissors (rock smashes scissors; scissors cuts paper; paper wraps rock) finally found its place on the world calendar in 2002 with the inauguration of the first international championships. Held in Toronto, Canada the 2003 competition was won by local favourite Rob Krueger. For information see www.rpschamps.com.
2. ROBOT SOCCER
   RoboCup 2004, held in Lisbon, Portugal, brought together dozens of robot soccer teams from nations as far afield as Iran, Latvia, Chile, China, Australia and the United States, although most of the leading entries were from Germany and Japan. Robot teams compete in four senior divisions, including 4-Legged Robot League and Humanoid League, the only category in which the robots are guided by humans with hand-held controllers. For information, see www.robocup2004.pt.
3. ONE-HOLE GOLF TOURNAMENT
   The annual Elfego Baca golf tournament (named after a colourful New Mexico lawyer and politician) consists of only one hole – but it's not your typical hole. The tee is placed on top of Socorro Peak, 7,243 feet above sea level. The hole, which is actually a patch of dirt 60 feet in diameter, is two and a half miles away and 2,550 feet below. The course record, 11, is held by Mike Stanley, who has won the tournament 10 times. The first competition was held in 1969. The 2004 competition was won by Johnny Gonzales with 17 shots. For information, write to Elfego Baca Shoot, John R. Howard and Associates, PO Box 30850, Albuquerque, New Mexico 87108–0850, USA.
4. LAWN-MOWER RACING
   The first national lawn-mower racing championship was held in Grayslake, Illinois, during the Labour Day weekend of 1992. The event was surprisingly controversial. The outdoor Power Equipment Institute, a trade association that represents lawn-mower manufacturers, formally opposed the concept of lawn-mower racing because it does not promote 'the effective and safe use of outdoor power equipment'. Nonetheless, 3,000 spectators had a good time and the proceeds from admissions went to fight Lou Gehrig's disease. Since then, lawnmower racing has spread throughout North America. For information,

write to the US Lawn-Mower Racing Association, 1812 Glenview Rd., Glenview, IL 60025, USA or see www.letsmow.com.

5. STONE THROW
The Unspunnen Festival celebrating Swiss costume and folklore has been held irregularly since 1805. One of the highlights of the festival is the throwing of the 185-pound (83.5 kilograms) Unspunnen Stone. The record throw is 3.61 metres (11 ft 2 in.) set by Josef Küttel of Vitznau at the 1981 festival. The next festival will be held in September 2005. For information, write to the Tourist Office Bernese Oberland, 3800 Interlaken, Switzerland or see www.unspunnenfest.ch.

6. NONVIOLENT HUNTING TOURNAMENT
Archers who don't like to kill animals can enter the National Field Archery Association's 3-D tournaments held throughout the United States. Competitors take aim at life-size dummies of deer, bears, mountain lions, wild pigs and wild turkeys. There are numerous divisions for men and women of all ages, using equipment ranging from *traditional*, with no sights, stabilisers, wheels and cams, to *compound bow*, which allows sight, stabilisers, wheels and cams. For information write to: National Field Archery Association, 31407 Outer I-10, Redlands, CA 92373, USA or see www.fieldarchery.org.

5 Famous People Who Invented Games

1. LEWIS CARROLL (1832–98), British author and mathematician
A wizard at conventional games such as chess and billiards, the creator of *Alice in Wonderland* was a genius at inventing mazes, ciphers, riddles, magic tricks – even a paper pistol that popped when waved through the air. Wherever he travelled, especially to seaside resorts, Carroll always carried a black bag filled with delectable toys and games to enchant prospective female child-friends. His *Game of Logic*, published as a book in 1886, was an attempt to teach a dry, academic subject in a humorous, innovative way. Using 'propositions', 'syllogisms' and 'fallacies', the game, though fairly complicated, was lively and filled with clever statements on everything from dragons and soldiers to pigs, caterpillars and hard-boiled eggs. One of Carroll's syllogisms:

Some new Cakes are unwholesome;
No nice Cakes are unwholesome.
Therefore, some new Cakes are not not-nice.

2. MARK TWAIN (1835–1910), US author
'Mark Twain's Memory-Builder, a Game for Acquiring and Retaining All Sorts of Facts and Dates' was a particularly appropriate game for Twain, who was known for his absentmindedness. Played on a pegboard divided into 100 rectangles (representing the 100 years in a century), the history game tested players' abilities to remember dates of worldwide 'accessions' (to thrones and presidencies), 'battles' and 'minor events' (such as important inventions). A player called out a date and event (such as 1815, Waterloo), then stuck a pin (each player had a set of coloured pins) in the corresponding year and category ('battle'). Penalties were imposed when a player gave an incorrect date and a point system determined the winner. Twain sold the game in 1891 and later revised it, hoping to organise nationwide clubs to compete for prizes. But the overhauled memory-builder proved too complex and was a commercial failure.

3. ROBERT LOUIS STEVENSON (1850–94), Scottish novelist and essayist
The author of *Treasure Island* invented a German-style war game in the winter of 1881–82 while residing in Davos, Switzerland, with his wife, Fanny, and 13-year-old stepson Lloyd. After clearing ample floor space in the lower storey of their chalet, Stevenson, armed with *Operations of War* (a military strategy book), methodically set up a 'theatre of war' and carefully positioned opposing armies of lead soldiers. To shoot down the enemy, players used popguns – ingeniously loaded with 'ems' from Lloyd's small printing press. Face-down cards provided the element of luck in the game, serving up valuable military secrets. The war game never had an official name, nor was it marketed, but Stevenson did write a long magazine article about it which was published in 1898. One reader, H.G. Wells, was so captivated by the game that he created his own – called *Little Wars* (see below).

4. (HELEN) BEATRIX POTTER (1866–1943), British author and illustrator
A shy and repressed little girl, Beatrix Potter turned to animals for companionship. Secreted in her nursery was a menagerie of rabbits, mice, frogs, snails – even bats and a tame hedgehog.

Years later many of her most popular animal characters – Peter Rabbit, Squirrel Nutkin, Jemima Puddle-Duck and Jeremy Fisher – became playing pieces on a board game, 'Peter Rabbit's Race Game', marketed in 1920. To play: choose a character, then roll a die and advance on a path of 122 squares (each player had a separate path) towards the winning goal, 'The Meeting Place in the Wood'. Just one of the obstacles waiting to impede Squirrel Nutkin: 'Nutkin meets his friends and loses a turn while talking'. But there were chances to jump ahead: Square 96 said, 'Old Mr Brown suddenly bites off Nutkin's tail and in terror he bounds off to 98'.

5. H.G. WELLS (1866–1946), British novelist and historian
Wells' book/game *Little Wars* (1913) had simple rules but required an elaborate battleground. Players made houses, churches, castles and sheds by gluing together wallpaper, cardboard and corrugated packing paper; the structures (some over 1 ft high) were handsomely painted to show various details, such as windows and rainwater pipes. H.G. liked to play on an 18-ft battlefield with 200 soldiers and 6 brass cannon (that could fire 1-in. wooden cylinders 9 yards) per side. Playing the game was a serious event for Wells, a boisterous, red-faced commander always ready to rally his troops to anticipated victory. As one friend commented: 'I have seen harmless guests entering for tea, greeted with the injunction, "Sit down and keep your mouth shut" . . . it was a game which began at 10 and only ended at 7:30, in which Wells had illegitimately pressed noncombatants into his army – firemen, cooks, shopkeepers and the like – and in which a magnificent shot from the other end of the floor destroyed a missionary fleeing on a dromedary – the last representation of a nation which had marched so gaily into battle so many hours before.'

– C.O.M.

James Landale's 8 Remarkable Pistol Duels

James Landale is an experienced journalist who currently works as a political correspondent for the BBC. Before joining the corporation in January 2003, he spent ten years working for The Times, *most recently as Assistant Foreign Editor. He also served as the paper's Political Correspondent and Brussels Correspondent. In*

2000/2001 James sailed from the UK to Hawaii in a round-the-world yacht-race sponsored by The Times, his weekly dispatches vividly describing the realities of life at sea. When he is not reporting or writing, he is most likely to be sailing. He lives with his wife, Cath, and daughter, Ellen, in Barnes, southwest London.

James knows all about duels because one of his ancestors took part in one. David Landale shot dead his bank manager in 1826 in Scotland's last fatal pistol duel. James tells the story of this extraordinary encounter in his first book, *Duel – A True Story of Death and Honour*, to be published by Canongate in 2005.

1. A LONG DUEL
   Two officers in Napoleon's army spent 19 years carving each other up in a series of duels that were always bloody but never lethal. Their dispute began in 1794 when Captain Dupont was ordered to stop Captain Fournier attending a party. Fournier took umbrage, challenged Dupont and they fought the first of 17 duels. As the years passed, they drew up a contract. If they came within 100 miles of each other, they would fight, military duty alone excusing a duel. Such was their companionship in honour that on occasion they dined together before fighting. In the end, by 1813, General Dupont tired of fighting General Fournier. He also wished to marry. So he arranged an unusual duel in which they stalked one another in a forest, armed with two pistols. Dupont stuck his coat on a stick and tricked his opponent into firing twice. Dupont spared Fournier's life but told him that if ever they duelled again, he reserved the right to fire two bullets first from a few yards' range. They never fought again. The story formed the basis of Joseph Conrad's story, *The Duel*, and Ridley Scott's 1979 film, *The Duellists*.

2. A PRIME MINISTERIAL DUEL – 1
   In 1798, at a crucial moment in Britain's struggle against Napoleon, the Prime Minister, William Pitt the Younger, chose to risk his life in a seemingly absurd duel. The 39-year-old premier had been criticised in the House of Commons by a hot-headed but insignificant Irish MP. George Tierney had condemned Pitt's plans to beef up the Navy to counter the threat of invasion from France. Pitt was furious, called Tierney a traitor and challenged him to a duel. They fought at three in the afternoon on Putney Heath in southwest London. Pitt's friend, Henry Addington, the Speaker of the British

Parliament, chose to attend as a witness. At 12 paces both men fired twice and, fortunately, missed twice. Some have hinted that the seconds deliberately loaded insufficient gunpowder to avoid a fatal injury. Pitt went on to lead the war effort against Napoleon and introduce income tax to Britain for the first time.

3. A NUDE DUEL
A Member of Parliament once duelled in the nude. Humphrey Howarth, the MP for Evesham, was attending the races at Brighton in 1806 and dined one night at the Castle Inn. There he fell into discussion with the Earl of Barrymore, an Irish peer. Discussion turned into quarrel and they arranged to meet on the race course early next morning. Both men were rogues, and much given to taking the piss. But even Barrymore was astonished as his opponent took his clothes off and presented himself on the duelling ground armed solely with pistol and pants. The seconds and other witnesses burst out laughing, not least because Howarth was by then a fat old man. But Howarth was in earnest. He had spent much of his earlier life as an army surgeon for the East India Company. He knew gunshot wounds were often infected by the dirty clothing that preceded a bullet into flesh. In the end, however, his precaution was redundant. Both he and his opponent missed their targets and resolved their dispute without bloodshed.

4. A PRIME MINISTERIAL DUEL – 2
The Duke of Wellington disapproved of duelling. He believed it fostered indiscipline and wasted good officers. But that did not stop the conqueror of Napoleon indulging in a little combat himself. Nor did the fact that he was 61 years old and Prime Minister put him off either. More than a decade after Waterloo, following several years of political uncertainty, George IV had turned to the aging war hero to re-establish a little order in the Tory party and the country. One of Wellington's first acts was to give Britain's Catholics a greater role in public life in an attempt to avoid unrest in Ireland. The policy divided the Tory party and one peer, the Earl of Winchilsea, a hardline Protestant, questioned Wellington's motives. Letters passed and so, on March 21, 1829, both peers met on Battersea Fields at dawn. Winchilsea, realising by then that he was on a hiding to nothing, refused to point his pistol at Wellington and fired in the air. Wellington fired deliberately wide as well and accepted a written apology. The public were not impressed at their Prime Minister's willingness to risk life and limb for such a

trivial matter and Wellington found himself openly mocked in the press.

5. A SHORT DUEL
Jeffrey Hudson, a dwarf, entered royal service by emerging from a large pie at a party for Charles I. He belonged to the Duke of Buckingham. But Charles's 15-year-old queen, Henrietta Maria, was so enchanted by the little man that she insisted he join the court. She called him Lord Minimus. Charles made him a captain in the Royal Army. But while Hudson was naturally the butt of many jokes, he was also a proud man. One day a young officer called Charles Crofts went too far and teased him for coming off worst in a fight with a turkey cock. For Hudson, this was too much and he challenged Crofts to a duel. The soldier thought he was joking and turned up armed with a water pistol. But Hudson was in earnest and demanded a real duel with real pistols on horseback. This was a shrewd move, for Crofts was fat and slow on a horse. Hudson, however, only 18 inches tall, presented a much tougher moving target. Thus the dwarf escaped injury while his opponent was dead through the heart. This was the last of Hudson's luck. He incurred royal disfavour, was exiled, captured by Barbary pirates and spent the next 25 years in prison in North Africa. In the end, he escaped and retired to his native Rutland, where they still drink a beer named in his honour.

6. A CABINET DUEL
On September 21 1809, at the height of the war against France, two Tory Cabinet ministers fought a duel. One went on to become Prime Minister. The other became the architect of post-Napoleonic Europe. Lord Castlereagh, the Secretary for War, believed – correctly – that George Canning, the Foreign Secretary, was plotting to have him replaced and challenged his colleague to a duel. Both men resigned their posts and met at dawn on Putney Heath in southwest London. Canning, who had never fired a pistol in his life, missed twice. But Castlereagh, with his second shot, lightly wounded his opponent in the left leg. Both men were roundly criticised by both peer and public. George III overlooked Canning and chose a man called Spencer Percival to be Prime Minister instead. Three years later Percival won the dubious honour of becoming the only British PM ever to be assassinated. Canning had to wait until 1827 before securing the premiership, and even then his tenure was

brief; he died unexpectedly three months after entering Downing Street. Castlereagh went on to achieve greatness as a statesman at the Congress of Vienna but was never popular. He committed suicide in 1822 amid allegations of homosexuality and his funeral procession was booed as it entered Westminster Abbey.

7. A VICE-PRESIDENTIAL DUEL
Aaron Burr, the Al Gore of his day, lost the US presidential election in 1800 by a handful of votes. Thomas Jefferson was elected instead and made his defeated opponent Vice President. Burr blamed his defeat on Alexander Hamilton, one of the great figures of the American Revolution. Hamilton – a close friend of Washington, co-framer of the constitution and a former head of the army – had successfully persuaded a tied electoral college to swing behind Jefferson. So when Vice President Burr discovered a few years later that Hamilton had bad-mouthed him in a letter, he issued an instant challenge. Hamilton – by then retired from politics – was opposed to duelling on moral and religious grounds. But the duty of honour was greater and so, on July 11, 1804, both men crossed the River Hudson with their seconds to what is now New Jersey. Burr was determined to shoot his rival dead, which he did. Hamilton, as he was shot, discharged his own pistol into the ground. There was huge public revulsion at the death of such a popular figure and the Vice President found himself on the receiving end of some seriously bad headlines. He was deprived of his New York citizenship and forced into hiding. In later years, he was shunned by society and died destitute on Staten Island in 1836.

8. AN ELEVATED DUEL
Two Frenchmen chose to fight from balloons over Paris because they believed they had 'elevated minds'. Monsieur de Grandpré and Monsieur de Pique quarrelled over a famous opera dancer called Mademoiselle Tirevit, who was mistress of one and lover of the other. So, at 9 a.m. on May 3 1808, watched by a huge crowd, the two Parisians climbed into their aircraft near the Tuileries and rose gently up into the morning air. At about 2,000 ft, when the balloons were about 80 yards apart, de Pique fired his crude blunderbuss and missed. De Grandpré aimed his more effectively. De Pique's balloon collapsed, the basket tipped, and he and his second fell headfirst to their deaths on the rooftops below. De Grandpré and his second, however,

drifted happily away in the light north-westerly breeze before landing safely 20 miles away.

13 Olympic Medallists Who Acted in Movies

1. JOHNNY WEISSMULLER (4 golds; 1924 and 1928 swimming)
While swimming at a club on Sunset Boulevard in Hollywood, Weissmuller was invited to try out for the part of Tarzan. In 1932 he made his film debut in *Tarzan, the Ape Man*. He eventually starred in 11 more Tarzan films.

2. HERMAN BRIX (silver; 1928 shot put)
Brix changed his name to Bruce Bennett, and pursued a successful career that included performances in *Mildred Pierce* (1945) and *The Treasure of Sierra Madre* (1948). He also acted in such clunkers as *The Alligator People* (1959) and *The Fiend of Dope Island* (1961).

3. BUSTER CRABBE (gold; 1932 400-metre freestyle)
Crabbe won his gold medal by one-tenth of a second. He later recalled that that tenth of a second led Hollywood producers to discover 'latent histrionic abilities in me'. In 1933 Crabbe made his film debut as Karpa the Lion Man, in *King of the Jungle*. He eventually appeared in 53 movies, but is best known for his roles as Flash Gordon and Buck Rogers.

4. HELENE MADISON (gold; 1932 100-metre freestyle)
Madison, who once set 16 world records in 16½ months, was invariably described by sportswriters as 'shapely'. After her Olympic triumph, she played an Amazon captain of the guards in the 1933 satire *The Warrior's Husband*. Unfortunately, her performance was undistinguished and she never acted again.

5. SONJA HENIE (3 golds; 1928, 1932 and 1936 figure skating)
Henie's first film, *One in a Million* (1937), was a box-office winner, and nine more followed. Although her acting was never as smooth as her skating, her Hollywood career brought her great financial success.

6.–7. GLENN MORRIS (gold; 1936 decathlon) and ELEANOR HOLM (gold; 1932 100-metre backstroke).
Tarzan's Revenge (1938) starred two Olympic champions as Tarzan and Jane. Unfortunately, Holm was described as

looking 'bored' throughout the film, and reviewers found Morris's performance 'disappointing' and 'listless'. Holm never acted again.

8. HAROLD SAKATA (silver; 1948 light-heavyweight weightlifting)
After the Olympics, Sakata pursued a successful career as a professional wrestler and then moved on to acting. He appeared in eight films, but it was his first role that gained him international stardom – the evil Oddjob in *Goldfinger* (1964).

9. CAROL HEISS (gold; 1960 figure skating)
Heiss, described by *Variety* as 'a fetching lass', made her film debut in the title role in *Snow White and the Three Stooges* (1961). The film was panned, but she received praise for her acting, singing and, of course, her skating. However, she never appeared in another movie.

10. JEAN-CLAUDE KILLY (3 golds; 1968 Alpine skiing)
Killy co-starred as a con-man ski instructor in the mediocre 1972 film *Snow Job*.

11. CORNISHMAN V (2 golds; 1968 and 1972 three-day event)
The only non-human Olympic medallist to pursue a successful film career, Cornishman V helped two different riders to victory in equestrian events. He later appeared in *Dead Cert* (1974), based on a Dick Francis novel, and *International Velvet* (1978).

12. BRUCE JENNER (gold; 1976 decathlon)
Jenner's one and only film appearance was in the loud and awful 1980 film *Can't Stop the Music*. He played a staid lawyer who is drawn into the irresistibly fun New York disco scene.

13. MARK BRELAND (gold; 1984 welterweight boxing)
Breland is one of the few athletes to appear in a movie *before* he appeared in the Olympics. In 1983 he received good reviews for his role in *The Lords of Discipline*. He played the first black cadet in a Southern military academy.

Note: Among the dozens of other Olympic athletes who have appeared in movies are 1924 pole-vault champion Lee Barnes, who served as a stand-in stuntman for Buster Keaton in *College* (1972); 1948 and 1952 decathlon champion Bob Mathias, who appeared in four films, including *It Happened in Athens* (1962) with Jayne Mansfield, and 1952 and 1956 triple jump champion Adhemar

Ferreira da Silva, who appeared in the internationally acclaimed film *Black Orpheus* (1958). Ken Richmond, who won a bronze medal as a wrestler in 1952, was better known as the muscleman who struck the gong at the beginning of J. Arthur Rank films.

Sir Stanley Matthews' 11 Greatest Football Players

Born in 1915, British footballer Sir Stanley Matthews died after a brief illness in February 2000. He is considered perhaps the greatest dribbler in English soccer history. During his unusually long professional career, he played for Stoke City and Blackpool, competing in 752 matches, including 54 international matches. He was the first British player to receive a knighthood. Though he was thin and frail-looking, his skill was such that he was dubbed 'The Wizard of the Dribble'. He first played professionally at 17, and played his last game five days after his 50th birthday, far older than his fellow players. Also known as 'The First Gentleman of Soccer', Matthews was never once booked or sent off by a referee during his 33-year career. After his retirement, he went on to coach a team of Bantu players in South Africa, then coached in Canada and Australia. More than 35,000 fans attended his retirement game, and when he died the flag flew at half-mast in his home football stadiums. A minute's silence was observed before every game for a week after his passing. Sir Stanley donated most of his memorabilia to decorate the walls of a restaurant at the Stoke football club. He contributed this list to *The Book of Lists* in 1995.

1. Johann Cruyff, Netherlands
2. Diego Maradona, Argentina
3. Alfredo Di Stefano, Spain
4. Garrincha, Brazil
5. Ferenc Puskas, Hungary
6. George Best, Northern Ireland
7. Pelé, Brazil
8. Eusébio, Portugal
9. Peter Doherty, Ireland
10. Tom Finney, England
11. Frank Swift, England

Richard Williams' 11 Favourite Goals

Richard Williams is a well-known British journalist who writes about two of the great loves of his life – sport and music. Born in Sheffield and brought up in Nottinghamshire, he worked on *Melody Maker* in the late 1960s and was editor of the paper in the late 1970s. He has written about sport for various national newspapers and is now chief sports writer for the *Guardian*. His published works include books on Phil Spector, Bob Dylan, Miles Davis and Formula 1 racing. His most recent book is *The Last Road Race* (2004).

'A great goal can be the product of patient teamwork or a moment of individual inspiration. To be truly remarkable, however, it needs a suitable context and a meaning that transcends the moment. Puskas' goal at Wembley, for example, taught England a lesson about how far they had fallen in the hierarchy of world football, while Law's strike against his old club was full of tragic resonance. Here are 11 goals that mean something special. Five of them I was there to see (Zidane, Massaro, Storey-Moore, Bergkamp, Owen). Three of them were scored in black and white (Puskas, Di Stefano, Pelé). Storey-Moore's is the only one that was not captured by the cameras, so you will have to take my word for its epic quality. Or you could ask Bob Wilson, who remembers it extremely well.'

1. JAIRZINHO for Brazil v England in the 1970 World Cup at the Jalisco stadium, Guadalajara.
   To decide an enthralling match between two contrasting but well-matched sides, one defending its title and the other on the way to regaining it, a goal fit for a final. After a build-up on the left, involving Rivelino and Paulo Cesar, Tostao retrieves his own blocked shot, fights his way past Alan Ball, Bobby Moore and Tommy Wright, and turns the ball inside to Pelé, who feints like a matador to transfix the remainder of the defence before pushing the ball sideways for the onrushing Jairzinho to smash his shot past Gordon Banks from six yards, continuing the run that will make him the only man in history to score in every round of the World Cup finals.
   Result: Brazil 1, England 0.

2. ZINEDINE ZIDANE for Real Madrid v Bayer Leverkusen in the 2002 European Cup final at Hampden Park, Glasgow.
   At 1–1 in a match that has yet to catch fire, the players are listening for the half-time whistle when Roberto Carlos dinks a pass inside to Zinedine Zidane. For a split-second, as it realises

what the French genius is about to attempt, the stadium holds its breath. And then, from a range of more than 30 yards, Zidane swings his left leg with that balletic grace and brings his boot round to meet the ball with such precision that it flies in a perfect arc, leaving Hans-Jorg Butt helpless as it passes just beneath his crossbar.
Result: Real Madrid 2, Bayer Leverkusen 1.

3. DANIELE MASSARO for AC Milan v Barcelona in the 1994 European Cup final in the Olympic stadium, Athens.
Collecting an aimless ball from Hristo Stoichkov in the second minute of first-half stoppage time, Sebastiano Rossi throws the ball out to Christian Panucci, Milan's young left-back. In the next 47 seconds there will be 13 passes of every variety imaginable, including a perfectly judged back-heel, before Daniele Massaro meets Roberto Donadoni's cut-back with a lethal strike from 15 yards. The others contributing the move are Dejan Savicevic, Zvonimir Boban, Demetrio Albertini, Paolo Maldini, Filippo Galli and Mauro Tassotti.
Result: AC Milan 4, Barcelona 0.

4. FERENC PUSKAS for Hungary v England at Wembley stadium in 1953.
The left-footed drag-back that fooled not only Billy Wright, England's redoubtable captain, but an entire nation preceded one of the Galloping Major's most sublime goals, part of a thrashing that left a permanent scar on the soul of the game's inventors.
Result: Hungary 6, England 3.

5. DIEGO MARADONA for Argentina v Belgium in the 1986 World Cup semi-final in the Azteca stadium, Mexico City.
Like his second goal against England a few days earlier, but even better since he had not first indulged in a bout of cheating. Again he attacked from the right, paralysing an entire defence before delivering the coup de grace.
Result: Argentina 2, Belgium 0.

6. PELÉ for Brazil v Sweden in the 1958 World Cup final in Stockholm.
Sweden took the lead after four minutes, the fools. The goal that finished them off came 10 minutes into the second half, when the 18-year-old Pelé received a ball from the left, flicked it up over his own head, spun round and volleyed the dropping ball past Karl Svensson, the Swedish keeper.
Result: Brazil 5, Sweden 2.

7. **IAN STOREY-MOORE for Nottingham Forest v Arsenal in Division One, December 27, 1971.**
Peter Grummitt rolls the ball to Tommy Gemmell, who plays a short ball to Storey-Moore. From deep in his own half the left-winger sets off, beating the entire Arsenal defence – Bob McNab, Peter Simpson, Frank McLintock and Peter Storey – on a dazzling 75-yard run before clipping the ball past Bob Wilson. Six weeks later the *Daily Express* is calling him 'the gold-plated hyphen' as he moves to Manchester United for £200,000.
Result: Nottingham Forest 1, Arsenal 1.

8. **DENNIS BERGKAMP for Holland v Argentina in the 1998 World Cup quarter-final in the Stade Velodrome, Marseilles.**
Barely half a minute of normal time remains, with the score at 1–1, when Bergkamp controls Frank De Boer's long, high pass with a single delicate touch, turns inside Roberto Ayala and uses the outside of his right boot to drive the ball past Carlos Roa. Minimalist perfection.
Result: Holland 2, Argentina 1.

9. **MICHAEL OWEN for England v Argentina in the 1998 World Cup in the Stade Geoffroy-Guichard, Saint-Etienne.**
After an early goal for each side, the match is boiling when the 18-year-old Owen latches onto the ball in the 15th minute, changes direction twice as he beats three defenders, and finally strikes a wonderful shot past Roa.
Result: Argentina 2, England 2 (Argentina win 4–3 on penalties)

10. **ALFREDO DI STEFANO for Real Madrid v Eintracht Frankfurt in the 1960 European Cup final at Hampden Park, Glasgow.**
The Germans have just scored their second goal, to make it 5–2, when the balding Don Alfredo takes the ball from Francisco Gento on the edge of the centre circle, accelerates on a straight 30-yard run and drives his shot past Loy, the German goalkeeper. From restart to bulging net, exactly 15 seconds.
Result: Real Madrid 7, Eintracht Frankfurt 3.

11. **DENIS LAW for Manchester City v Manchester United at Old Trafford in Division One, 1974.**
No goal was ever freighted with greater poignancy than this. On the last day of the season, United's former hero backheeled the ball past Alex Stepney to send his old club down. Law had not wanted to play in the match, and could not bear to celebrate his goal.
Result: Manchester City 1, Manchester United 0.

Sir Chris Bonington's 9 Best Mountain Experiences

Chris Bonington is Britain's best-known mountaineer. He has been climbing since the 1950s and has led expeditions throughout the world, including two which made the first successful ascents of the South Face of Annapurna and the South West Face of Everest. He was knighted in 1996. Bonington continues to climb and made a first ascent of a peak in the Indian Himalayas in 2003.

'My first choice is my best ever, but after that I've arranged them in chronological order, as it seems invidious to say that any one experience is better than another, they are all so different in what they meant to me.'

1. THE SOUTH WEST RIDGE OF THE WEST SUMMIT OF SHIVLING (1983)
   Biggest isn't necessarily best. It had all the ingredients that made it very special for me. It's a lovely, shapely peak of 6,520 m.; the West summit had never been climbed; the team was small – just Jim Fotheringham and myself; it was spontaneous, since we had come out to climb another mountain, changed our minds and went for Shivling; it was alpine-style, since we packed a sack at the bottom and without any recce or preparation kept going till we got to the top, five days later; the climbing was complex and difficult; the summit was sharp and pointed; we had to find another way down. Altogether the perfect climbing adventure.

2. A CLIMB ON SUILVEN AND A LONG WALK OUT (1952)
   It was my second summer of climbing. My mum gave me £3.00 a week to survive through the summer, climbing around the Scottish Highlands, staying in bothies or Youth Hostels. Tony and I had a few days sleeping in an open vault in the little ruin of Ardvreck Castle on the shore of Loch Assynt when we set out to do a climb on the West Buttress of Suilven. We hitched to Lochinver and then made the long walk in to the foot of Suilven, left our 15-kilo rucksacks with all our stuff for the holiday at the foot, did the climb, of which I can remember little except that the route-finding was challenging. We then did the traverse of the long whaleback of Suilven, with its stunning views of the Northern Highlands, walked back to our rucksacks, picked them up and carried them south over broken pathless ground to the head of Loch Sionascaig and then down its eastern shore

to a bridge over a stream and a path that led over a pass to Linneraineach. It was around 18 miles of rough terrain with very few paths and some of the wildest, loveliest highland country in the British Isles. After all these years I can still remember watching the sun setting over Loch Sionascaig, the numbing tiredness as we completed our walk with the last climb over the col, and the huge relief of finding an empty bothy with a concrete floor that in our exhaustion felt like a feather bed.

3. KING COBRA (1960)
Climbing with Tom Patey was always a delight. After getting back from my first Himalayan expedition to Annapurna II, I joined him for a magical holiday in the northwest Highlands, working our way south from Torridon down to Skye, always climbing new routes (you never did anything else when climbing with Tom, where we did the best climb of all, the first ascent of King Cobra, up the formidable Coireachan Ruadha face of Sgurr Mhiccoinich. Today it's graded HVS (Hard Very Severe) but it is a real adventure climb in a fabulous setting.

4. NORTH FACE OF THE GRANDES JORASSES AND THE TRAVERSE OF THE JORASSES AND ROCHEFORT RIDGE (1962)
There was something very special about these two days. Don Whillans and I had spent the summer first trying the North Wall of the Eiger, and then climbing in the Austrian Alps based in Innsbruck, before starting for home on his motorbike. We called in at the Bernina Alps to climb the North Face of the Badile and then stopped off at Chamonix. The weather was perfect – Don had to get home, but I decided to stay for just one more climb. I met up with Ian Clough and we set out to climb the Walker Spur of the Grandes Jorasses.

It's standard practice to bivouac at the bottom and we did so with about six other parties. Next morning high cloud was blowing in, perhaps sign of a bad weather front. All the others retreated, but I had a hunch that it would clear and so we kept going with the Spur to ourselves. The cloud cleared, the climbing was immaculate and we reached the top in the late afternoon.

We just didn't want it to end, and so instead of descending the easy route to the south, we bivouacked on the summit and the next day traversed the Grandes Jorasses and the Rochefort Ridge to the Torino Hut. It was wonderful classic ridge-climbing.

Ian and I hit that perfect level of teamwork, both of us at the peak of fitness, that makes climbing so special. Three days later we were on the North Wall of the Eiger to make the first British ascent – but our two days on the Jorasses provided an even more memorable experience.

5. COMING DOWN FROM CAMP VI. EVEREST SOUTH WEST FACE (1975)

The South West Face of Everest was a huge challenge – logistics, man management, hard climbing and plenty of uncertainty. There were fun moments, a lot of hard graft and some agonising experiences – in some ways it was the biggest all-round challenge I have ever faced and there was one moment when it all felt worthwhile.

We had just completed the carry from Camp V to our top camp, to put Doug Scott and Dougal Haston in position to make their bid for the summit. They had all they needed, the weather seemed settled and we had done everything we could do – it was now up to them.

On the way down I sat and rested, gazing out over the peaks and tumbled clouds that showed that the monsoon was still with us, but that we were above its effects. Our timing had been spot on. I had a profound sense of peace and a feeling of love for this team of mine that had become so effective and had worked so hard to get us to the position we were now in. All the effort and worry seemed worthwhile – indeed enhanced the sense I had of fulfilment.

6. KONGUR (1981)

In 1979 the Chinese opened eight peaks in China to foreigners. The Mount Everest Foundation decided to organise an expedition to one of these peaks – Kongur, in Sinkiang, at 7,719 m. the second-highest unclimbed peak in the world. We made a recce in 1980 and then in 1981 took part in a large scientific expedition in which us four climbers, Peter Boardman, Joe Tasker, Al Rouse and myself, were both guinea pigs and an alpine-style climbing team.

The climb proved challenging, needing two attempts, and involved crossing a 7,000-m. peak and a knife-edged connecting ridge, four days trapped by a storm in minuscule snow caves and a final push to the summit up steep mixed ground. We bivouacked on top, even trekked over to another top the following morning, just in case it was higher (it wasn't) and then of course had to get all the way down.

7. THE NEEDLE (1992)
The Needle is in the Lemon Mountains of East Greenland. Four of us – Jim Lowther, Rob Ferguson, Graham Little and myself – were flown in by ski plane to land on a covered glacier and then had three weeks of superb climbing on these spectacular granite peaks, making a series of first ascents. The best of the lot was a route up a peak that we called the Needle. It looked a bit like the South West Pillar of the Drus. I climbed it with Graham Little. He led the first pitch off the glacier up a steep wall and led through up an open groove that just went on and on. I think it was one of the best pitches I've ever climbed. It was steep but possible to keep just in balance by bridging, beautiful grey rock with small and subtle holds, reasonable protection, but no sign of a belay ledge and the groove ran out into an overhang at about 40 metres. There were some small holds out on the face. They didn't really seem to go anywhere but there was no choice, I embarked upon them and they took me onto a shallow ramp leading out to the left. Friction climbing, no runners, increasing rope drag and fear. This led into a deep cut groove – Graham from below, yelling no more rope – and I was on a ledge with a crack for an anchor. I let out a whoop of total exhilaration, relief and delight.

The climb went on and on – there were harder pitches that Graham led – and eventually, after 17 hours of climbing, we stood on top of the Needle and gazed around us at a panorama of huge glaciers and rocky peaks, most of them still unclimbed. Other than Jim and Rob, who were on another peak, the nearest human being was some 200 miles away.

8. SEPU KANGRI RECCE (1996)
We flew over an incredible range of mountains in 1982 on our way from Chengdu in southwest China to Lhasa. I guessed correctly that none of them had ever been climbed. In the summer of 1996 my old friend Charlie Clarke, doctor on most of my major expeditions, and I set out to find the highest mountain of the range. All we had was the photograph taken from the air in 1982 and a photograph and very localised map from a book of Tibetan mountains compiled by the China Tibet Mountaineering Association. The only map we could obtain in Lhasa was a roadmap of the whole of Tibet. With that and our interpreter Pasang, we set out in a big pick-up truck for our mountain range, three days' hard driving to the northeast of Lhasa. This took us to the mouth of a valley, at the end of which

we were told was a big snow mountain. It proved to be a peak called Sepu Kangri, which we discovered was a holy mountain rising above a lake. Four families lived in the valley, tending their yak and sheep. They were to become good friends.

Charlie and I walked to good viewpoints in our effort to find a route up our mountain and then drove over 100 miles to make an approach on foot from the other side, hitching a lift on ponies for part of the way with a group of Nomads. The grass was lush and green, rich in wild flowers. Sepu Kangri from the south was even more impressive than it had been from the north.

We felt like the early Himalayan pioneers. It was a wonderful journey of discovery.

9. DANGA II (2000)
The richness of an experience depends so much on the people we share it with. I had always wanted to share with some of my closest family the joy of standing on top of an unclimbed peak and experiencing, for the first time ever, the 360° view from its summit. I did this in the year 2000 with my eldest son Daniel, my brother Gerald and my nephew James. It wasn't a difficult or indeed a very high mountain – I didn't want it to be, for neither Daniel or James were experienced mountaineers and anyway, when you adventure with your nearest and dearest, it pays to be cautious.

Danga II was 6,190 m. high, close to Kangchenjunga, the third-highest peak in the world. The climb was straightforward but the view from the summit was magnificent; most important, however, was sharing that joy with people I love.

7 Non-Boxers Who Took On the Champions

1. LORD BYRON (1788–1824), English poet
Byron sparred with John 'Gentleman' Jackson, the former bareknuckled champion, in the poet's Bond Street rooms. Both men wore 'mufflers' (mittenlike gloves used for sparring in the early days). The poet boxed in a dressing gown, Jackson in knee breeches and a shirt. Byron, with his legendary temper, was reputedly a tough customer in the ring.

2. HESSIE DONAHUE (*fl.* 1890s), US housewife
John L. Sullivan, world heavyweight champion from 1882 to 1892, invited Hessie and her husband, a boxing instructor, to

join his entourage, which was staging boxing exhibitions in theatres around the country. As part of an act they worked out, Hessie, wearing boxing gloves and dressed in a blouse and bloomers, would climb into the ring after Sullivan had disposed of his male challengers, and the two would go at it. During one of their sparring sessions, Sullivan inadvertently hit Hessie in the face, and she countered with a right to the jaw that sent him to the canvas for a full minute. The audience was so delighted that Hessie and Sullivan decided to make a 'knockout' part of their regular routine.

3. PAUL GALLICO (1897–1976), US author
Gallico, author of *The Poseidon Adventure*, was a cub reporter in 1923, assigned to Jack Dempsey's camp at Saratoga Springs prior to the heavyweight champion's title bout with Luis Firpo. Against his better judgement, Gallico asked Dempsey to spar with him for one round. It was, for Gallico, a vivid and somewhat terrifying experience as he was 'stalked and pursued by a relentless, truculent professional destroyer'. He never saw the punch that flattened him; he was aware only of an explosion in his head, and the next instant he was sitting on the canvas grinning stupidly. He struggled to his feet and finished the round propped up in a clinch with Dempsey, absorbing those taps to the neck and ribs that as an observer had seemed so innocuous to him.

4. J. PAUL GETTY (1892–1976), US entrepreneur
The billionaire oil magnate met Jack Dempsey in 1916, when Dempsey was an up-and-coming young fighter, and the two became good friends. Getty, who kept fit in the fully equipped basement gym in his parents' mansion, used to spar with Dempsey. Dempsey once claimed that, in an altercation over a girl, Getty knocked him out with a left uppercut – the only time Dempsey was ever KO'd by anyone.

5. ERNEST HEMINGWAY (1899–1961), US author
During visits to Hemingway's Havana home, former heavyweight champion Gene Tunney would occasionally allow himself to be talked into sparring bare-fisted with the writer, especially if the two had just downed a thermos of frozen daiquiris. Once Hemingway, in a rambunctious mood, tagged Tunney with a hard punch. Incensed, Tunney feinted his friend's guard down and then faked a menacing punch to the face, as he issued a stern warning: 'Don't you ever do that again!'

6. HUGH LOWTHER (1857–1944), British sportsman
Outraged that John L. Sullivan had never fought Jem Smith, the English heavyweight titleholder, the 5th Earl of Lonsdale challenged Sullivan to a bout. According to the earl, he took considerable punishment from the hard-hitting champion – they fought bareknuckle in those days – but dropped Sullivan in the sixth round with a solid blow to the solar plexus. Though at least two people verified Lowther's version, Sullivan's memoirs make no mention of the fight.

7. GEORGE PLIMPTON (1927–2003), US journalist and author
One of Plimpton's early experiments in 'participatory journalism' was taking on Archie Moore, the former light-heavyweight champ, in January 1959. The fight lasted only three rounds, during which Moore cuffed Plimpton around gently, bloodying his nose. The referee called it a draw. Moore was asked how long it would have taken him to polish off his opponent had time been a factor. Moore told Plimpton, "'Bout the time it would take a tree to fall on you, or for you to feel the nip of the guillotine.'

Chapter 14

16 CASES OF PEOPLE KILLED BY GOD

24 STRANGE DEATHS

10 CELEBRATED PEOPLE WHO READ THEIR OWN OBITUARIES

9 PEOPLE WHO DIED LAUGHING

5 PEOPLE WHO DIED PLAYING CARDS

17 HEALTH EXPERTS AND HOW THEY DIED

12 TIMELY DEATHS

PRESERVING OUR HERITAGE – 29 STUFFED OR EMBALMED HUMANS AND ANIMALS

REMAINS TO BE SEEN – 15 PRESERVED BODY PARTS

Death

Courtesy of University College London Library Services

PRESERVING OUR HERITAGE: JEREMY BENTHAM – see p.391

16 Cases of People Killed by God

1. ENTIRE WORLD POPULATION EXCEPT NOAH AND SEVEN RELATIVES (Genesis 6, 7)
   Transgression: Violence, corruption and generalised wickedness.
   Method of execution: Flood.

2. ENTIRE POPULATIONS OF SODOM AND GOMORRAH EXCEPT LOT, HIS WIFE AND THEIR TWO DAUGHTERS (Genesis 19)
   Transgression: Widespread wickedness and lack of respect for the deity.
   Method of execution: Rain of fire and brimstone.

3. LOT'S WIFE (Genesis 19)
   Transgression: Looked back.
   Method of execution: Turned into a pillar of salt.

4. ER (Genesis 38)
   Transgression: Wickedness.
   Method of execution: Unknown.

5. ONAN (Genesis 38)
   Transgression: Refused to make love to his brother Er's widow.
   Method of execution: Unknown.

6. ALL THE FIRSTBORN OF EGYPT (Exodus 12)
   Transgression: Egypt was cruel to the Jews.
   Method of execution: Unknown.

7. PHARAOH AND THE EGYPTIAN ARMY (Exodus 14)
   Transgression: Pursued the Jews.
   Method of execution: Drowned.

8. NADAB AND ABIHU (Leviticus 10)
   Transgression: Offered strange fire.
   Method of execution: Fire.

9. KORAH, DATHAN, ABIRAM AND THEIR FAMILIES (Numbers 16)
   Transgression: Rejected authority of Moses and started own congregation.
   Method of execution: Swallowed by earth.

10. 250 FOLLOWERS OF KORAH (Numbers 16)
    Transgression: Supported Korah.
    Method of execution: Fire.

11. 14,700 ISRAELITES (Numbers 16)
Transgression: Murmured against Moses and his brother Aaron following execution of Korah and his supporters.
Method of execution: Plague.

12. UNKNOWN NUMBER OF RETREATING AMORITE SOLDIERS (Joshua 10)
Transgression: Fought the Israelites.
Method of execution: Hailstones.

13. UZZAH (2 Samuel 6)
Transgression: Touched the ark of God after oxen shook it while pulling it on a cart.
Method of execution: Unknown.

14. 70,000 PEOPLE (2 Samuel 24)
Transgression: King David ordered a census of the population.
Method of execution: Plague.

15. 102 SOLDIERS OF KING AHAZIAH (2 Kings 1)
Transgression: Tried to capture Elijah the Tishbite.
Method of execution: Fire.

16. ANANIAS AND SAPPHIRA (Acts 5)
Transgression: Land fraud.
Method of execution: Unknown.

24 Strange Deaths

1. THE FATEFUL BATH
Pat Burke of St Louis, Missouri, took his first bath in 20 years on August 23, 1903. It killed him. Burke was the second victim of cleanliness in a week at the city hospital, and the third in its history. The first was Billy O'Rourke, who had been bathed on the previous Tuesday. Both men had been scrubbed with a broom.

2. THE FINAL KISS
Li Po (d. 762AD), the great Chinese poet and drunkard, often spouted verses he was too intoxicated to write down. His admirer Emperor Ming Huang served as his secretary and jotted down the poems. Li Po was given a pension that included the right to free drinks whenever he travelled. One well-tanked night he took a boat excursion on a river. Seeing the reflection of the moon on the water, he tried to kiss it, fell overboard and drowned. Some scholars believed he actually died of cirrhosis.

3. THE FATAL SNOOKER SHOT
Mr Raymond Priestley of Melbourne, Australia, was playing snooker in a garage with a friend when he met his doom. He had climbed onto a crossbeam in the ceiling to attempt a trick shot and was hanging upside down by his legs when he slipped. He crashed down on the concrete floor headfirst and later died from brain damage.

4. THE HIRSUTE ACCIDENT
Hans Steininger was known for having the longest beard in the world. One day in September 1567, while he was climbing the staircase leading to the council chamber of Brunn in Austria, Steininger stepped on his beard, lost his balance, fell down the stairs and died.

5. REVENGE OF THE PLANT KINGDOM
On February 4, 1982, 27-year-old David M. Grundman fired two shot-gun blasts at a giant saguaro cactus in the desert outside Phoenix, Arizona. Unfortunately for Grundman, his shots caused a 23-ft section of the cactus to fall on him and he was crushed to death.

6. THE PERFECT LAWYER
Clement L. Vallandigham was a highly controversial Ohio politician who engendered much hostility by supporting the South during the Civil War. Convicted of treason, he was banished to the Confederacy. Back in Ohio after the war, Vallandigham became an extremely successful lawyer, who rarely lost a case. In 1871 he took on the defence of Thomas McGehan, a local troublemaker who was accused of shooting Tom Myers to death during a barroom brawl. Vallandigham contended that Myers had actually shot himself, attempting to draw his pistol from his pocket while trying to rise from a kneeling position.

On the evening of June 16, Vallandigham was conferring in his hotel room with fellow defence lawyers when he decided to show them how he would demonstrate his theory to the jury the next day. Earlier in the day, he had placed two pistols on the bureau, one empty and one loaded. Grabbing the loaded one by mistake, Vallandigham put it in his trouser pocket. Then he slowly pulled the pistol back out and cocked it.

'There, that's the way Myers held it,' he said, and pulled the trigger. A shot rang out and Vallandigham explained, 'My God, I've shot myself!' He died 12 hours later. Vallandigham's client,

Thomas McGehan, was subsequently acquitted and released from custody.

7. THE ELECTRIC GUITARIST
Keith Relf, who had gained fame as the lead singer of The Yardbirds, a 1960s blues-rock group, was found dead at his home in London on May 14, 1976. The cause of death was an electric shock received while playing his guitar. Relf was 33 years old.

8. TOO MUCH OF A GOOD THING
It is almost impossible to die of an overdose of water, but Tina Christopherson managed to do it. The 29-year-old Florida woman, who had an IQ of 189, became obsessed with the idea that she suffered from stomach cancer, a disease which had killed her mother. In an attempt to cleanse her body, Christopherson went on periodic water fasts, during which she ate no food but drank up to four gallons of water a day. By February 17, 1977, she had consumed so much water that her kidneys were overwhelmed and the excess fluid drained into her lungs. She died of internal drowning, otherwise known as 'water intoxication'.

9. THE BURDEN OF MATRIMONY
William Shortis, a rent collector in Liverpool, England, and his wife, Emily Ann, had not been seen for several days. Worried friends and a policeman entered the house on August 13, 1903, and were horrified to discover William, dazed and dying, at the foot of the staircase pinned to the floor underneath the body of his 224-lb wife. A coroner's jury concluded that the elderly couple had been walking up the stairs when Emily Ann fell backwards, carrying her husband with her, but William remained in his unfortunate position for three days, too seriously injured to be able to extricate himself.

10. THE DEADLY DANCE
In August 1981 11-year-old Simon Longhurst of Wigan, England, attended a Sunday afternoon junior disco session where, along with other youngsters, he performed the 'head shake', a New Wave dance in which the head is shaken violently as the music gets faster and faster. The following day, young Simon began suffering headaches and soon a blood clot developed. Three weeks later he died of acute swelling of the brain. The coroner ruled it 'death by misadventure'.

11. **A WISH FULFILLED**
American revolutionary patriot James Otis often mentioned to friends and relatives that, as long as one had to die, he hoped that his death would come from a bolt of lightning. On May 23, 1783, the 58-year-old Otis was leaning against a doorpost in a house in Andover, Massachusetts, when a lightning bolt struck the chimney, ripped through the frame house and hit the doorpost. Otis was killed instantly.

12. **A FATAL TEMPER**
On April 15, 1982, 26-year-old Michael Scaglione was playing golf with friends at the City Park West Municipal Golf Course in New Orleans. After making a bad shot on the thirteenth hole, Scaglione became angry with himself and threw his club against a golf cart. When the club broke, the club head rebounded and stabbed Scaglione in the throat, severing his jugular vein. Scaglione staggered back and pulled the metal piece from his neck. Had he not done so, he might have lived, since the club head could have reduced the rapid flow of blood.

13. **THE WORST NIGHTMARE OF ALL**
In 1924 British newspapers reported the bizarre case of a man who apparently committed suicide while asleep. Thornton Jones, a lawyer, woke up to discover that he had slit his own throat. Motioning to his wife for a paper and pencil, Jones wrote, 'I dreamt that I had done it. I awoke to find it true.' He died 80 minutes later.

14. **A DAREDEVIL'S FINAL FALL**
Bobby Leach was a colourful character who first became famous in 1911, when he went over Niagara Falls in a barrel. He continued to perform dangerous exploits, including parachuting over the falls from an airplane. In April 1926 Leach was walking down a street in Christchurch, New Zealand, when he slipped on a piece of orange peel and broke his leg so badly that it had to be amputated. Complications developed and he died.

15. **KILLED BY JAZZ**
Seventy-nine-year-old cornetist and music professor Nicolas Coviello had had an illustrious career, having performed before Queen Victoria, Edward VII and other dignitaries. Realising that his life was nearing its end, Coviello decided to travel from London to Saskatchewan to pay a final visit to his son. On the way, he stopped in New York City to bid farewell to his

nephews, Peter, Dominic and Daniel Coviello. On June 13, 1926, the young men took their famous uncle to Coney Island to give him a taste of America. The elder Coviello enjoyed himself but seemed irritated by the blare of jazz bands. Finally he could take it no longer. 'That isn't music,' he complained and he fell to the boardwalk. He was pronounced dead a few minutes later. Cause of death was 'a strain on the heart'.

16. DROWNED AT A LIFEGUARDS' PARTY
On August 1, 1985, lifeguards of the New Orleans recreation department threw a party to celebrate their first drowning-free season in memory. Although four lifeguards were on duty at the party and more than half the 200 party-goers were lifeguards, when the party ended, one of the guests, Jerome Moody, 31, was found dead on the bottom of the recreation department pool.

17. STRANGLED BY A GARDEN HOSE
Thirty-five-year-old Richard Fresquez of Austin, Texas, became drunk on the night of May 7, 1983. He tripped on a garden hose, became tangled in it and strangled to death while trying to break free.

18. PERFECT RE-CREATION
On April 23, 1991, Yooket Paen, 57, of Anghton, Thailand, slipped in some mud, grabbed a live wire and was electrocuted. Later that day, her 52-year-old sister, Yooket Pan, was showing some neighbours how the accident happened when she slipped, grabbed the same live wire and was also electrocuted.

19. KILLED BY ART
In 1991 Bulgarian environmental artist Christo erected 1,760 yellow umbrellas along Southern California's Tejon Pass and another 1,340 blue umbrellas in Ibaraki Prefecture north of Tokyo. Each of the umbrellas weighed 48 lb. On October 26, Lori Jean Keevil-Mathews, a 30-year-old insurance agent, drove out to Interstate 5 to view the California umbrellas. Shortly after Keevil-Mathews and her husband got out of their car, a huge gust of wind tore one of the umbrellas loose from its steel screw anchors and blew it straight at Keevil-Mathews, crushing her against a boulder. Christo immediately ordered the dismantling of all the umbrellas in both countries. However, on October 30, another umbrella-related death occurred when 57-year-old crane operator Wasaaki Nakaruma was electrocuted by a power line in Japan as he prepared to take down one of the umbrellas.

20. SELF-INDUCED CAPITAL PUNISHMENT
Michael Anderson Godwin was convicted of murder and sentenced to the electric chair, but in 1983 his sentence was changed to life in prison. On March 5, 1989, Godwin, 28 years old, was trying to fix a pair of earphones connected to the television set in his cell at the Central Correctional Institution in Columbia, South Carolina. While sitting on a steel toilet, he bit into a wire and was electrocuted.

21. THE PERILS OF POLITICS
Nitaro Ito, 41, a pancake-shop operator in Higashiosaka City, Japan, concluded that he needed an extra edge in his 1979 campaign for the House of Representatives. He decided to stage an attack on himself and then draw sympathy by campaigning from a hospital bed. Ito's scheme was to have an employee, Kazuhiko Matsumo, punch him in the face on the night of September 17, after which Ito would stab himself in the leg. After Matsumo had carried out of his part of the plan, Ito stabbed his right thigh. Unfortunately, he cut an artery and bled to death before he could reach his home, 50 m. away.

22. KILLED BY A ROBOT
Ford Motor Company's casting plant in Flat Rock, Michigan, employed a one-ton robot to fetch parts from a storage rack. When the robot malfunctioned on January 25, 1979, 25-year-old Robert Williams was asked to climb up on the rack and get the parts. While he was performing the task, the robot suddenly reactivated and hit Williams in the head with its arms. Williams died instantly. Four years later a jury ordered Unit Handling Systems, the manufacturer of the robot, to pay Williams' family $10 million. Williams is believed to have been the first person killed by a robot.

23. AW CHUTE
Ivan McGuire was an experienced parachutist who spent the afternoon of April 2, 1988, in Louisburg, North Carolina, videotaping parachuting students as they jumped and jumping with them. On his third trip up, McGuire dropped from the airplane and began filming the instructor and student who followed him a second later. McGuire reached back and discovered that he had forgotten to put on his parachute. His videotape, which was shown on the news in nearby Raleigh, recorded McGuire's final words: 'Uh-oh.'

24. SILENCED BY THE LAMBS
Betty Stobbs, 67, put a bale of hay on her bike and went out to feed the sheep at her family farm in Stanhope, England, on January 26, 1999. Forty sheep rushed towards her and began jumping up on the bike to reach the hay, knocking Stobbs into the 100-ft deep Ashes Quarry. Alan Renfry witnessed the incident from his home and was convinced that the sheep were responsible for Stobbs' death.

10 Celebrated People Who Read Their Own Obituaries

1. HANNAH SNELL
Her husband walked out on her and joined the British army. To find him, Hannah Snell also enlisted, posing as a man. During surgery her true sex was discovered. She became a celebrity, and once out of the army she performed in public houses as the Female Warrior. On December 10, 1779, when she was 56, she opened a copy of the *Gentlemen's Magazine* and read her own obituary, which informed her that she had died on a Warwickshire heathland. Perhaps she was superstitious, because reading her death notice snapped something in her mind. Her mental health slowly deteriorated, and in 1789 she was placed in London's Bethlehem Hospital, where she remained insane until she expired in 1792.

2. DANIEL BOONE
The great American frontiersman had retired and settled down in Missouri. In 1818 an American newspaper in the eastern US trumpeted the news that the renowned hunter had been found dead near a deer lick, kneeling behind a tree stump, his rifle resting on the stump, a fallen deer a hundred yards away. The obituary was picked up across the nation. Daniel read it and laughed. Although he could still trap, he was too old and weak to hunt, and could no longer hit a deer even close up. Two years later, aged 86, Boone finally did die. His best-known obituary was seven stanzas devoted to him in Lord Byron's *Don Juan*.

3. LADY JANE ELLENBOROUGH
She was one of the most beautiful and sexual women in all history. Her name was Jane Digby. At 17 she married Lord Ellenborough, Great Britain's lord of the privy seal, then left him to run off with an Austrian prince. During her colourful

career she was the mistress of novelist Honoré de Balzac, King Ludwig of Bavaria and Ludwig's son, King Otto of Greece. Her last marriage of 26 years was to Sheik Medjuel, an erudite Bedouin, head of the Mezrab tribe in the Syrian desert. Returning from a desert trip with Medjuel, the 66-year-old Lady Ellenborough learned that she was dead. Her obituary appeared prominently in *La Revue Britannique*, published in Paris in March 1873. It began: 'A noble lady who had made a great use – or abuse – of marriage has died recently. Lady Ellenborough, some 30 years ago, left her first husband to run off with Count von Schwarzenberg. She retired to Italy, where she married six consecutive times.' The obituary, reprinted throughout Europe, called her last husband 'a camel driver'. The next issue of the publication carried a eulogy of Lady Ellenborough written by her friend Isabel Burton, the pompous and snobbish wife of Burton of Arabia. Mrs Burton claimed she had been authorised to publish the story of Lady Ellenborough's life, based on dictated notes. Appalled, Lady Ellenborough vehemently wrote to the press denying her death – and having dictated an 'authorised' book to Mrs Burton. Lady Ellenborough outlived her obituary by eight full years, dying of dysentery in August 1881.

4. JAMES BUTLER HICKOK

In March 1873 'Wild Bill' Hickok, legendary sheriff and city marshal in the Midwest and a constant reader of Missouri's leading newspaper, the *Democrat*, picked up a copy and learned that he was a corpse. Hickok read: 'The Texan who corralled the untamed William did so because he lost his brother by Bill's quickness on the trigger.' Unsettled by his supposed demise, Wild Bill took pen in hand and wrote a letter to the editor: 'Wishing to correct an error in your paper of the 12th, I will state that no Texan has, nor ever will, "corral William". I wish to correct your statement on account of my people. Yours as ever, J.B. Hickok.' Delighted, the editor of the *Democrat* printed Hickok's letter and added an editorial: 'We take much pleasure in laying Mr Hickok's statement before the readers of the *Democrat*, most of whom will be glad to read from his pen that he is "still on the deck". But in case you should go off suddenly, William, by writing us the particulars we will give you just as fine an obituary notice as we can get up, though we trust that sad pleasure may be deferred for years.' Three years later Hickok was murdered while playing poker.

5. **ALFRED NOBEL**
As the inventor of dynamite, Alfred Nobel, a moody yet idealistic Swede, had become a millionaire. When Nobel's older brother, Ludwig, died of heart trouble on April 12, 1888, a leading French newspaper misread the report and ran an obituary of Alfred Nobel, calling him 'a merchant of death'. Upon seeing the obituary, Nobel was stunned, not by the premature announcement of his passing but by the realisation that in the end he would be considered nothing more than a merchant of death. The printed summary of his life reflected none of his hopes for humanity, his love of his fellow beings, his generosity. The need to repair this false picture was one of several factors that led him to establish, in his will, the Nobel Prize awards to be given to those who did the most in advancing the causes of peace, literature and the sciences.

6. **P.T. BARNUM**
At 80, the great American was ailing and knew that death was near. From his sickbed, he told a friend that he would be happier if he had 'the chance to see what sort of lines' would be written about him after he was dead. The friend relayed this wish to the editor of the *Evening Sun* of New York City. On March 24, 1891, Barnum opened his copy of the *Evening Sun* and read: 'Great and Only Barnum. He Wanted to Read His Obituary; Here It Is.' According to the preface, 'Mr Barnum has had almost everything in this life, including the woolly horse and Jenny Lind, and there is no reason why he should not have the last pleasure which he asks for. So here is the great showman's life, briefly and simply told, as it would have appeared in the *Evening Sun* had fate taken our Great and Only from us.' There followed four columns of Barnum's obituary, illustrated by woodcuts of him at his present age, of him at 41, of his mother, of his deceased first wife Charity, and of the Swedish singer Jenny Lind. Two weeks later, Barnum was dead.

7. **LEOPOLD VON SACHER-MASOCH**
This police commissioner's son, born in Galicia, raised in Austria, was fascinated by cruelty and loved pain and degradation. His first mistress, Anna von Kottowitz, birched him regularly and enjoyed lovers that Sacher-Masoch found for her. His second mistress, Fanny Pistor, signed a contract with him agreeing to wear furs when she beat him daily. She fulfilled the contract and treated him as a servant. He had become a famous writer when he met and married a woman named Wanda. She

thrashed him with a nail-studded whip every day of their 15-year marriage and made him perform as her slave. After she ran off, Sacher-Masoch married a simple German woman named Hulda Meister. By now he was slipping into insanity and he tried to strangle her. In 1895 she had him secretly committed to an asylum in Mannheim and announced to the world that he had died. The press published obituaries praising his talent. Undoubtedly, in lucid moments, he read some of his death notices. He finally did die 10 years later in 1905. Because of Sacher-Masoch's life, psychiatrist Richard von Krafft-Ebing coined the word 'masochism'.

8. MARK TWAIN
In 1897 the noted American author and humorist was in seclusion, grieving over a death in his family, when he learned that he, too, had been declared dead. A sensational American newspaper had headlined his end, stating that he had died impoverished in London. A national syndicate sent a reporter to Mark Twain's home to confirm the news. Twain himself appeared before the bug-eyed reporter and issued an official statement: 'James Ross Clemens, a cousin of mine, was seriously ill two or three weeks ago in London, but is well now. The reports of my illness grew out of his illness. The reports of my death are greatly exaggerated.' Twain finally lived up to his premature obituaries in 1910.

9. BERTRAND RUSSELL
Once in the 1930s, while the English philosopher was visiting Beijing, he became very ill. Japanese reporters in the city constantly tried to see Russell, but were always denied access to him. The journalists decided he must be dead and notified their newspapers of his demise. Word of his death went around the world. Wrote Russell, 'It provided me with the pleasure of reading my obituary notices, which I had always desired without expecting my wishes to be fulfilled. One missionary paper had an obituary notice of one sentence: 'Missionaries may be pardoned for heaving a sigh of relief at the news of Mr Bertrand Russell's death.' All this inspired Russell to compose his own obituary in 1937 for *The Times* of London. He wrote of himself: 'His life, for all its waywardness, had a certain anachronistic consistency, reminiscent of the aristocratic rebels of the early nineteenth century . . . He was the last survivor of a dead epoch.'

He told *The Times* to run it in 1962, the year in which he expected to die. *The Times* did not need it until 1970.

10. EDWARD V. RICKENBACKER
The former auto-racing driver turned fighter pilot emerged from WWI as America's leading ace, with 26 confirmed kills. In peacetime he was an executive in the automobile and aviation industries. With the onset of WWII, Rickenbacker volunteered to carry out missions for the US War Dept. In October 1942, on an inspection tour, Rickenbacker's B-17 went down somewhere in the Pacific Ocean. An intensive air search of the area was made. There was no sign of survivors. Newspapers across the US declared Rickenbacker dead. The following month, on Friday 13 November, there were new headlines. Rickenbacker and seven others were spotted alive in the Pacific. They had survived on a raft for 23 days. Waiting for Rickenbacker when he returned home was a pile of his obituaries. One, in the *New York Daily News*, was a cartoon showing a black wreath floating on water, with the caption 'So Long, Eddie'. Another, in the *New York Journal*, bore the headline 'End of the Roaring Road?' Grinning, Rickenbacker scrawled across it, 'Hell, no!'

Note: Those ten are the editor's favourite cases, but there have been numerous other celebrated persons who read of their deaths while they were alive, among them US President Thomas Jefferson, magician Harry Houdini, dancer Josephine Baker, singer Jeanette MacDonald, novelist Ernest Hemingway and foreign correspondent Edgar Snow. Also, there have been many famous people who, if they did not read about their deaths, heard rumours or announcements that they had gone to the Great Beyond. The modern living dead have included singer Paul McCartney, vague hints of whose demise were supposedly traced to several Beatles records; actress Bette Davis, whose attorney told her that word of her death was spreading throughout New York, to which Miss Davis replied, 'With the newspaper strike on, I wouldn't consider it'; and India's elderly political dissenter J.P. Narayan, who heard Prime Minister Morarji Desai mistakenly deliver a eulogy over his still-warm body in April 1979.

– I.W.

9 People Who Died Laughing

1. CALCHAS (Greek soothsayer, c. 12th century BC)
Calchas, the wisest soothsayer of Greece during the Trojan War, advised the construction of the notorious wooden horse. One day he was planting grapevines when a fellow soothsayer

wandered by and foretold that Calchas would never drink the wine produced from the grapes. After the grapes ripened, wine was made from them and Calchas invited the soothsayer to share it with him. As Calchas held a cup of the wine in his hand, the soothsayer repeated the prophecy. This incited such a fit of laughter in Calchas that he choked and died. Another version of Calchas' death states that he died of grief after losing a soothsaying match in which he failed to predict correctly the number of piglets that a pig was about to give birth to.

2. ZEUXIS (Greek painter, 5th century BC)
It is said that Zeuxis was laughing at a painting of an old woman that he had just completed when his breathing failed and he choked to death.

3. CHRYSIPPUS (Greek philosopher, 3rd century BC)
Chrysippus is said to have died from a fit of laughter on seeing a donkey eat some figs.

4. PHILEMON (Greek poet, c. 236–263)
This writer of comedies became so engulfed in laughter over a jest he had made that he died laughing.

5. PIETRO ARETINO (Italian author, 1492–1556)
Aretino was laughing at a bawdy story being told to him by his sister when he fell backwards in his chair and died of apoplexy.

6. THOMAS URQUHART (Scottish writer and translator, 1611–60)
Best-known for his translation into English of Rabelais' *Gargantua*, the eccentric Sir Thomas Urquhart is said to have died laughing upon hearing of the restoration to the throne of Charles II.

7. MRS FITZHERBERT (English widow, d. 1782)
On a Wednesday evening in April 1782, Mrs Fitzherbert of Northamptonshire went to Drury Lane Theatre with friends to see *The Beggar's Opera*. When the popular actor Mr Bannister made his first appearance, dressed outlandishly in the role of 'Polly', the entire audience was thrown into uproarious laughter. Unfortunately, Mrs Fitzherbert was unable to suppress the laugh that seized her, and she was forced to leave the theatre before the end of the second act. As the *Gentleman's Magazine* reported the following week: 'Not being able to banish the figure from her memory, she was thrown into hysterics, which continued without intermission until she expired on Friday morning.'

8. ALEX MITCHELL (English bricklayer, 1925–75)
Mr and Mrs Mitchell of Brockley Green, Fairstead Estate, King's Lynn, were watching their favourite TV comedy, *The Goodies*. During a scene about a new type of self-defence called 'Ecky Thump', Mr Mitchell was seized by uncontrolled laughter. After half an hour of unrestrained mirth, he suffered a heart attack and died. His wife, Nessie, wrote to *The Goodies* thanking them for making her husband's last moments so happy.

9. OLE BENTZEN (Danish physician, d. 1989)
An audiologist who specialised in developing hearing aids for underdeveloped countries, Bentzen went to see the film *A Fish Called Wanda*. During a scene featuring John Cleese, Bentzen began laughing so hard that his heartbeat accelerated to a rate of between 250 and 500 beats a minute and he was seized by a heart attack and died.

5 People Who Died Playing Cards

1. JOHN G. BENNETT (perfume agent)
Mr Bennett and his wife, Myrtle, lived in a fashionable apartment in Kansas City. One unfortunate Sunday afternoon in the autumn of 1929, the Bennetts sat down with their neighbours, the Hoffmans, to play a friendly game of bridge. Mrs Hoffman later explained, 'As the game went on, the Bennetts' criticisms of each other grew more caustic.' Finally Bennett dealt and bid one spade on a hand that better deserved a pass. Mr Hoffman overcalled with two diamonds, and Mrs Bennett, overeager for a contract, jumped to four spades. In the play of the hand, Bennett was set one. His wife taunted him and they began arguing. John reached across the table and slapped Myrtle, whereupon she told him he was a bum, thus goading him further. John threatened to leave and Myrtle suggested that the Hoffmans depart as well. But before they could go, Myrtle ran into her mother's bedroom, grabbed the family automatic, dashed back and shot her husband twice, killing him. Interestingly, if Bennett had established his club suit before drawing trumps, he might have survived the evening.

2. JAMES BUTLER HICKOK (gunfighter)
When 'Wild Bill' Hickok entered Deadwood, South Dakota, in June of 1876, he had a premonition that he would never leave the gulch alive. On August 2 he was playing poker with three friends in a saloon, laughing and having a good time. Normally

Hickok sat with his back to the wall, but that afternoon Charlie Rich had taken Bill's seat to tease him and had refused to give it up. Jack McCall, whom Hickok had defeated at poker earlier that day, entered the saloon, drew a .45-calibre Colt and shot Wild Bill Hickok through the back of the head, killing him instantly. Wild Bill, who was 39 years old, was holding two pairs, aces and eights, a hand that has since been known as 'the dead man's hand'. He died with a smile on his face.

3. AL JOLSON (entertainer)
   Jolson suffered a heart attack while playing gin rummy with friends in his room in San Francisco's St Francis Hotel on the night of October 23, 1950. He was 64 years old.

4. BUSTER KEATON (comedian)
   Keaton was stricken by a seizure late in the afternoon of January 31, 1966, while playing poker at his home in Hollywood. He expired the following morning at the age of 70.

5. ARNOLD ROTHSTEIN (gambler)
   The man who fixed the 1919 World Series was playing poker in the suite Hump McManus occupied at the Park Central Hotel in New York City when he was shot in the stomach. Rothstein, who owed McManus $320,000 from a previous poker game, stumbled out of the building and was rushed to a hospital, where he refused to name the gunman before he died on November 4, 1928.

17 Health Experts and How They Died

1. STUART M. BERGER (1953–94) Age at death: 40
   The 6 ft 7 in. Berger successfully reduced his weight from 420 to 210 lb. He described his techniques in such bestsellers as *The Southampton Diet* (1984) and *Dr Berger's Immune Power Diet* (1986). Berger claimed that his diet would boost the immune system and promote longevity. He died in his New York City apartment from a heart attack brought on by cocaine abuse and obesity: at the time of his death he weighed 365 lb.

2. SYLVESTER GRAHAM (1794–1851) Age at death: 57
   A clergyman and temperance leader, Graham believed that good health could be achieved through a strict regime which included cold showers, daily exercise and a vegetarian diet. In 1847 he spoke to an audience in Boston and triggered a near riot by

butchers and bakers who were angered by his advocacy of vegetarianism and homemade bread. He was deeply shaken by the attack and his health began to decline. Treatment with stimulants, mineral water and tepid baths proved to be of no lasting help, and he died broken in body and spirit. He is remembered today chiefly for his creation of the Graham cracker, though the present-day commercial product – containing bleached flour, sugar and preservatives – would have horrified him.

3. EUGENE SANDOW (1867–1925) Age at death: 58
Through the application of scientific methods of muscle development, Sandow transformed himself from a weak youth into the 'world's strongest man', as showbusiness promoter Florenz Ziegfeld billed him at the 1893 World's Columbian Exposition in Chicago. In 1911 Sandow was appointed professor of physical culture to King George V. However, Sandow's primary concern was to convince the average man that anyone could achieve strength and vigour by exercising for a little as 20 minutes a day. The strong man pushed himself beyond even his immense capacities when, without any assistance, he lifted a car out of a ditch after an accident. He suffered a severe strain and died soon afterward from a burst blood vessel in the brain. However, some believe that he actually died of syphilis.

4. ÉMILE COUÉ (1857–1926) Age at death: 69
Trained as a pharmacist, Coué became interested in hypnotism and developed a health treatment based on autosuggestion. He told his patients that their health would improve dramatically if, morning and evening, they would repeat faithfully: 'Every day and in every way, I am becoming better and better.' Prior to WWI, an estimated 40,000 patients flocked to his clinic each year and Coué claimed a 97% success rate. Coué kept up a demanding schedule. After one of his lecture tours he returned to his home in Nancy, France, and complained of exhaustion. He died there of heart failure.

5. NATHAN PRITIKIN (1915–85) Age at death: 69
Pritikin was diagnosed with heart disease in his mid-40s. Although he did not have a background in medicine, he spent the next 20 years researching diet and nutrition. He developed a low-fat, low-cholesterol and high-fibre diet that he credited with reversing his heart disease. In 1976 he opened the Pritikin Longevity Center in California to spread the word. He also published eight books on diet and exercise. His programme

gained credibility in 1984 when the National Institutes of Health concluded that lowering cholesterol reduced the risk of heart disease. Unfortunately, at the same time, Pritikin developed leukaemia. The chemotherapy that he underwent to fight the cancer brought about anaemia, kidney failure and severe pain. On February 21, 1985, Pritikin committed suicide in his hospital bed by slashing his wrists with a razor. The leukaemia had probably been caused by a dubious medical technique that Pritikin underwent in 1957. His doctor had prescribed a series of X-ray treatments to destroy a fungal infection causing a skin rash. Afterwards, Pritikin was diagnosed with an elevated white blood cell count, a frequent precursor to leukaemia.

6. ADELLE DAVIS (1904–74) Age at death: 70
'You are what you eat,' claimed Davis, the well-known American nutritionist who advocated a natural diet rich in fresh fruits and vegetables along with large doses of vitamins. When she was diagnosed as having bone cancer at the age of 69, her first reaction was disbelief. 'I thought this was for people who drink soft drinks, who eat white bread, who eat refined sugar, and so on,' she said. Eventually she came to accept her illness as a delayed reaction to the 'junk food' eating habits she had acquired in college and which had lasted until the 1950s. Her hope was that those who had faith in her work would not be disheartened by her fatal illness.

7. MAX BIRCHER-BRENNER (1867–1939) Age at death: 71
One of the first exponents of proper nutrition, Bircher-Brenner advocated the ingestion of raw fruits and vegetables – 'living' food. He also believed that a patient's mind played an important role in the cause of illness and that psychological as well as physical treatment was necessary to cure disease. A premature baby, Bircher-Brenner had been born with a weak heart which doctors said would prevent him from ever living a normal life. Through vigorous physical exercise and careful diet he had attained remarkable health as an adult, but the coronary weakness was not entirely overcome. On January 24, 1939, he died from a ruptured heart vessel.

8. ÉLIE METCHNIKOFF (1845–1916) Age at death: 71
Through extensive longevity research the Nobel Prize-winning bacteriologist concluded that the human body was meant to last 100 to 150 years. He became known particularly for his 'Sour Milk Cure', in which he advocated the consumption of yogurt to

cleanse the large intestine. In addition, he discovered a bacterium (found only in the intestine of dogs) which he believed could further retard the aging process – and he proceeded to inoculate himself with the microbe. Shortly before his death from heart disease, Metchnikoff detailed in his diary the reasons for his untimely demise: 'intense and precocious activities, fretful character, nervous temperament, and tardy start on a sensible regime'.

9. DR ROBERT ATKINS (1930–2003) Age at death: 72
On April 17, 2003, the famous 'low-carb diet doctor', Dr Atkins, died after falling on an icy street and hitting his head. It was in 1972 that Atkins – who had a history of heart disease – published the bestselling *Dr Atkins' Diet Revolution*, which advocated consuming meat, eggs and cheese while shunning all carbohydrates, including wheat bread, all rice and fruits. His books sold more than 15 million copies and became the subject of heated debate: other respected dieticians advise the opposite approach – fruit, fresh vegetables and a largely vegetarian diet. A group of doctors severely critical of Atkins' plan maintain that his programme leads to weight gain and heart disease. Atkins supporters insist that his death was the result of hospitalisation, where, in a coma, he gained 60 lb in fluid retention. Upon entering the hospital, the 6-ft Atkins weighted 195 lb – overweight by the standards of the Center For Heart Disease. He died eight days later at the formidable weight of 265 lb. Defenders of the diet vigorously claim the cause was bloating. His books continue to sell.

10. J.I. RODALE (1898–1971) Age at death: 72
The head of a multimillion-dollar publishing business, Rodale promulgated his belief in 'organic food' (food free from chemicals and artificial additives) supplemented by natural vitamins through his popular magazines *Organic Gardening* and *Prevention*. He was at the height of his fame when he appeared on *The Dick Cavett Show* on June 9, 1971. After describing the dangers of milk, wheat and sugar, Rodale proceeded to say, 'I'm so healthy that I expect to live on and on.' Shortly after the conclusion of the interview, Rodale slumped in his chair, the victim of a fatal heart attack.

11. SEBASTIAN KNEIPP (1821–97) Age at death: 76
As a young seminary student, Kneipp cured himself of an attack of nervous prostration through hydrotherapy. When he became a

priest, he continued his cold-water cures. Eventually he abandoned his priestly duties altogether to give advice to as many as 500 patients a day. The empress of Austria and Pope Leo XIII were among those who consulted him. Kneipp believed that the application of cold water – plus exercise, fresh air, sunshine, and walking barefoot over grass and through snow – could cure virtually any mental or physical disorder. An inflammation of his lungs, which had been weak since childhood, resulted in his death.

12. FRANZ MESMER (1734–1815) Age at death: 80
Mesmer believed that a person became ill when his 'animal magnetism' was out of balance. To correct this condition, the Viennese doctor made use of magnets and held séance-like therapeutic sessions for his patients. Hounded out of Vienna on charges of practising magic, Mesmer moved to Paris, where a royal commission (whose members included Benjamin Franklin and Antoine Lavoisier) concluded that Mesmer's 'cures' were due solely to his patients' imaginations. Mesmer was convinced that he would die in his eighty-first year, as a Gypsy woman had foretold. Her prediction came true two months before his eighty-first birthday, when he succumbed to an extremely painful bladder condition that had troubled him for years.

13. D.C. JARVIS (1881–1966) Age at death: 85
This country doctor became an overnight sensation in 1958 with the publication of *Folk Medicine: A Vermont Doctor's Guide to Good Health*. Part of his appeal derived from the simplicity of his remedies. For example, he suggested that one could stay healthy through a daily dose of two teaspoons each of honey and apple cider vinegar in a glass of water. Jarvis had many supporters, in spite of a Harvard professor's comment that 'This claptrap is strictly for those gullible birds stung by the honey bee.' Jarvis died in a nursing home in Vermont after suffering a cerebral haemorrhage.

14. BERNARD MACFADDEN (1868–1955) Age at death: 87
Billing himself as a kinestherapist, Macfadden ran a chain of health food restaurants and sanitariums that pushed his programme of exercise, fresh air, personal hygiene and wholesome diet. He also published the popular but controversial magazine *Physical Culture*, which featured photos of men and women posing nearly naked – considered obscene by some in the early twentieth century. Throughout his long life Macfadden was almost always in the news for one reason or another – his marriages, his attacks on

the medical establishment, or his founding of a new religion, the Cosmotarian Fellowship. Macfadden celebrated his eighty-third birthday by parachuting 2,500 ft into the Hudson River. The master showman finally succumbed to a urinary tract blockage that he had tried unsuccessfully to combat through fasting.

15. SAMUEL HAHNEMANN (1755–1843) Age at death: 88
A German physician at crosscurrents with the medical beliefs of his day, Hahnemann developed the system of homeopathy. Its basic tenet is that a drug that produces symptoms of illness in a healthy person will cure a sick person who exhibits those symptoms, when that drug is administered in minute doses. Hahnemann died from an inflammation of the bronchial tubes, which had plagued him for 20 years. Although he had come to terms with death ('My earthly shell is worn out,' he stated), his wife was less accepting of the inevitable. She kept his embalmed corpse with her for nine days before giving it up for burial.

16. MARY BAKER EDDY (1821–1910) Age at death: 89
Eddy founded the Christian Science religion after experiencing what she believed to be Christ's method of healing. At the time, she was suffering the effects of a serious fall on the ice. She taught that healing is accomplished not by drugs or medicines but through the affirmation of spiritual truth. Although Eddy enjoyed a remarkably active old age, when her health began to fail she was convinced that it was due to Malicious Animal Magnetism engendered by her enemies. The official verdict was that she died from 'natural causes' after a brief bout of pneumonia. The undertaker who examined the corpse stated: 'I do not remember having found the body of a person of such advanced age in so good a physical condition.'

17. LINUS PAULING (1901–94) Age at death: 93
The only person to win two unshared Nobel Prizes (for Chemistry and Peace, not Medicine), Pauling in 1970 wrote a book arguing that large doses of vitamin C could cure the common cold. Over the years he expanded on his claims, declaring that vitamin C would extend a person's life by decades and ward off cancer and heart disease. Pauling himself took 18,000 mg of vitamin C a day (the recommended daily allowance for adults is 60 mg). Pauling was diagnosed with prostate cancer in December of 1991. He died of complications at his ranch in Big Sur, California, two years later.

– F.B. & C.F.

12 Timely Deaths

We read so often in the newspapers about 'untimely deaths' that it makes one wonder if anyone ever died a 'timely death'. Well, people have, and here are some examples.

1. DOMITIAN (AD51–96), Roman emperor
   Early astrological predictions had warned that he would be murdered on the fifth hour of September 18, AD96. As the date approached, Domitian had many of his closest attendants executed to be on the safe side. Just before midnight marked the beginning of the critical day, he became so terrified that he jumped out of bed. A few hours later he asked the time and was told by his servants (who were conspiring against him) that it was the sixth hour. Convinced that the danger had passed, Domitian went off to take a bath. On the way he was informed that his niece's steward, Stephanus, was waiting for him in the bedroom with important news. When the emperor arrived, Stephanus handed him a list of conspirators and then suddenly stabbed him in the groin. Domitian put up a good fight, but he was overcome when four more conspirators appeared. He died as predicted, on the fifth hour of September 18, AD96.

2. THOMAS JEFFERSON (1743–1826), US president
   The 83-year-old former president was suffering badly from diarrhoea, but he had hopes of lasting until July 4, 1826, the 50th anniversary of the signing of the Declaration of Independence. From his sickbed, he asked, 'This is the fourth?' When he was informed that it was, he died peacefully.

3. JOHN ADAMS (1735–1826), US president
   Adams, like Jefferson, held on until July 4, 1826, before dying at the age of 90. He is reported to have said, 'Thomas Jefferson survives . . . Independence forever,' unaware that his old friend had died a few hours earlier.

4. DR JOSEPH GREEN (1791–1863), English surgeon
   While lying on his deathbed, Dr Green looked up at his own doctor and said, 'Congestion.' Then he took his own pulse, reported the single word, 'Stopped,' and died.

5. HENRIK IBSEN (1828–1906), Norwegian poet and dramatist
   On May 16, 1906, Ibsen was in a coma in his bedroom, surrounded by friends and relatives. A nurse told the others in the room that the famed playwright seemed to be a little better.

Without opening his eyes, Ibsen uttered one word: '*Tvertimod*' ('On the contrary'). He died that afternoon without speaking again.

6. MARK TWAIN (1835–1910), US humorist
Born in 1835, the year of Halley's Comet, Twain often stated that he had come into the world with the comet and would go out of the world with it as well. Halley's Comet next returned in 1910, and on April 21 of that year Twain died.

7. ARNOLD SCHÖNBERG (1874–1951), Austrian composer
Schönberg's lifelong fascination with numerology led to his morbid obsession with the number 13. Born in 1874 on September 13, he believed that 13 would also play a role in his death. Because the numerals seven and six add up to 13, Schönberg was convinced that his 76th year would be the decisive one. Checking the calendar for 1951, he saw to his horror that July 13 fell on a Friday. When that day came, he kept to his bed in an effort to reduce the chance of an accident. Shortly before midnight, his wife entered the bedroom to say goodnight and to reassure him that his fears had been foolish, whereupon Schönberg muttered the word 'harmony' and died. The time of his death was 11:47 p.m., 13 minutes before midnight on Friday July 13, in his 76th year.

8. ELIZABETH RYAN (1892–1979), US tennis player
Elizabeth Ryan won 19 Wimbledon tennis championships between 1914 and 1934 – a record that stood for 45 years. On July 6, 1979, the day before Billie Jean King broke her record by winning a 20th Wimbledon title, the 87-year-old Ryan became ill while in the stands at Wimbledon. She collapsed in the clubhouse and died that night.

9. LEONARD WARREN (1911–60), US opera singer
Warren was performing in Verdi's *La Forza del Destino* on the stage of the Metropolitan Opera in 1960. He had just begun the aria 'O fatal urn of my destiny'. When he reached the word 'fatal', he suddenly pitched forward, dead of a heart attack.

10. CHARLES DAVIES (1927–95), British singer
Davies, age 67, was giving a solo rendition of the old soldiers' song 'Goodbye' at the annual dinner of the Cotswold Male Voice Choir in Echington, England, on January 3, 1995. He finished with the words, 'I wish you all a last goodbye.' As the crowd applauded, Davies collapsed and died.

11. **GEORGE STORY (1936–2000), US journalist**
In 1936 the premier issue of *Life* featured a picture of newborn baby George Story under the headline 'Life Begins'. Over the years, the magazine periodically updated readers about the '*Life* baby', as Story married twice, had children and retired. On April 4, 2000, just days after *Life* had announced that it would cease publication, Story died of heart failure. The final issue of *Life* featured one last article about Story. The headline: 'A Life Ends'.

12. **CHARLES SCHULZ (1922–2000), US cartoonist**
In 1999 Schulz, the creator of the popular comic strip *Peanuts*, announced his decision to retire because of poor health. He died on February 12, 2000, the night before the last original *Peanuts* ran in the Sunday newspapers. The timing was 'prophetic and magical' said close friend and fellow cartoonist Lynn (*For Better or for Worse*) Johnston. 'He made one last deadline. There's romance in that.'

– C.F.

Preserving Our Heritage – 29 Stuffed or Embalmed Humans and Animals

1. **TUTANKHAMEN**
In 1922, while excavating in the Valley of the Kings, English archaeologist Howard Carter discovered the tomb of Tutankhamen, a king of the 18th Dynasty of Egypt, who flourished about 1348BC. The mummy of the pharaoh was encased in a 6-ft coffin containing 2,448 lb of gold. Over the bandages on the king's face was a lifelike gold mask inlaid with precious jewels. A dazzling assortment of rings, necklaces, amulets and other exquisite ornaments were found among the body wrappings. The internal organs of the king had been removed, embalmed and placed in a separate alabaster chest. The mummy, coffin and other valuables from the tomb have toured the world and are currently diplayed at the Egyptian Museum in Cairo.

2. **CHARLEMAGNE**
This ruler of the Holy Roman Empire died in 814. Embalmed, he was dressed in his royal robes, a crown placed on his head, a sceptre placed in his hand, and thus he was propped up in a

sitting position on his marble throne. His preserved body remained on that throne for 400 years. At last, in 1215, Holy Roman Emperor Frederick II removed the corpse, which was found to be in excellent condition. It was buried in a gold and silver casket in the cathedral at Aix-La-Chapelle.

3. EL CID (Rodrigo Díaz de Bivar)
Spanish leader in the war against the Moors, he established the independent kingdom of Valencia. Wounded in battle in 1099 and dying, El Cid's last wish was that his body be embalmed and then seated on his horse, Babieca, during the next battle. When the next battle came – an attack on Valencia by King Bucar of Morocco – and the Spanish were on the verge of defeat, the preserved corpse of El Cid, mounted on his horse, appeared at the head of the troops. Heartened, the Spanish troops rallied and were victorious.

4. INÉS DE CASTRO
When King Pedro of Castile was a young prince, he fell in love with Inés de Castro. His father, fearing political complications, trumped up a charge against Inés and had her beheaded. Pedro waited until he had become king after his father died, then had the assassins' hearts torn out and ordered Inés' body exhumed. Her corpse was dressed, placed on the throne and officially crowned queen. All dignitaries were forced to pay homage by kissing her hand and treating her like a living monarch. Pedro died in 1369.

5. RICHARD II
This English king was deposed in 1399 and probably murdered in 1400. In 1413 Henry V had Richard's body embalmed and put on public display in full royal regalia. Three days later Henry was the chief mourner at Richard's second funeral, during which Richard was interred in Westminster Abbey. At one time there was a hole in the side of the tomb through which visitors could put their hands to touch the king's head. In 1776 an enthusiastic schoolboy thrust his hand in and stole Richard's jawbone. The boy's descendants kept the relic until 1906, when it was finally restored to its rightful resting place.

6. CATHERINE OF VALOIS
Henry V's queen died in 1437. Her grandson, Henry VII, made major alterations to Westminster Abbey, which involved moving her embalmed body. She was placed in a crude coffin constructed of flimsy boards and left above ground. There she

remained a public spectacle for over 200 years. Vergers used to charge a shilling to take off the lid so curious visitors could view her corpse. But seeing wasn't enough for Samuel Pepys, who went to the abbey on his 36th birthday. 'I had the upper part of her body in my hands, and I did kiss her mouth, reflecting upon that I did first kiss a Queene.' The body was finally removed from public view in 1776.

7. DUKE OF MONMOUTH
This English rebel was beheaded in 1685 in one of history's messiest executions (it took 'five chopps'). The body and head were dispatched for burial, but at the last moment it was realised that no portrait existed of the duke. Since he had been the out-of-wedlock son of King Charles II, it was considered important to have one painted. Body and head were returned, sewn back together, dressed – and finally painted. The portrait hangs in the National Portrait Gallery, London.

8. CHARLES BYRNE
This Irish giant lived from 1761 to 1783. He feared that his huge body would be dissected for study, so he paid a group of friends to bury him at sea. But the famous anatomist, John Hunter, who owned a collection of human oddities, was not to be cheated. When Byrne died, Hunter bribed the friends to deliver the body to him. He immediately set about boiling the remains before anyone discovered what had happened. The speed with which he boiled the bones turned them brown. Hunter kept his acquisition secret for more than two years but finally put it on display. Byrne can still be seen in the Hunter Museum at the Royal College of Surgeons in London.

9. 'THE PRESERVED LADY'
Martin van Butchell was an English eccentric who lived from 1735 to 1812. In his marriage contract there was a clause stating he could own certain articles only 'while [his wife] remained above ground'. When she died, he retained title to the property by having her embalmed, dressed in her wedding clothes and placed in a glass-topped case in his drawing room. 'The Preserved Lady' became a great attraction, with Butchell always introducing her as 'My dear departed'. When he remarried, his new wife – irritated by the competition – insisted the corpse be removed. In keeping with the provision that she remain above ground, Butchell presented her to the Royal College of Surgeons,

where she remained on public view until she was cremated by a German bomb during a Luftwaffe raid in May 1941.

10. BARRY
When the fabled Swiss St Bernard who rescued so many travellers trapped in Alpine snowstorms died in 1814, a taxidermist stuffed and mounted him. He may be seen today, remarkably lifelike, standing in the National Museum, Bern, Switzerland.

11. JEREMY BENTHAM
English philosopher and the 'Father of Utilitarianism', Bentham, who died in 1832 at the age of 84, willed his entire estate to the University College Hospital in London – on condition that his body be preserved and placed in attendance at all of the hospital's board meetings. Dr Southward Smith was chosen by Bentham to prepare the philosopher's corpse for viewing. Smith constructed the skeleton and affixed a wax likeness of Bentham's head to it, then attired the body in an appropriate suit and hat. According to Smith, 'The whole was then enclosed in a mahogany case with folding glass doors, seated in his armchair and holding in his hand his favourite walking stick . . . Thus, for the next 92 years, Jeremy Bentham never missed a board meeting.'

12. JULIA PASTRANA
A professional freak, Pastrana (1834–60), a bearded Mexican Indian, was described as the ugliest woman in history and exhibited all over the world. Her manager married her 'for myself alone' and when she became pregnant, made a fortune selling tickets to witness the delivery. The child was stillborn and deformed like his mother. Julia died soon after. Her husband had both mother and child embalmed and placed in a glass case, which he immediately began exhibiting around the world. Her body, still on display, was in Norway at last report.

13. JUMBO
Phineas T. Barnum's famous giant elephant, 10 ft 9 in. at the shoulder, was hit by a freight train and killed in 1885. The showman had Jumbo's carcass stuffed – sending his skeleton to the Smithsonian Institution in Washington, DC – and put the mounted animal on permanent exhibit in Barnum Hall, Tufts University, Medford, Massachusetts. In April 1975 a fire swept Barnum Hall and destroyed Jumbo's remains.

14. **COMANCHE**
When the US Army horse who survived Custer's Last Stand died a national hero, it was decided to preserve and mount him. A University of Kansas naturalist, Professor Lewis Dyche, was paid $450 to do the job. Comanche's insides were given a military funeral. His outsides were preserved, shown at the Columbian Exposition in Chicago in 1893, then permanently placed in the University of Kansas Museum of Natural History in Lawrence. In 1947 General Jonathan Wainwright tried to get Comanche back to be a US Army exhibit in Fort Riley, but failed. In 1950, to save his hide from expanding and contracting, Comanche was placed in an airtight glass case with humidity control and set against an artificial 'sunbaked' setting of soil and grass.

15. **TIM**
Tim was a small mongrel dog who went to Paddington Station in London in 1892 to meet the trains. Attached to his collar was a collection box into which departing passengers dropped coins for a British railways fund for widows and orphans. After a decade's work, Tim died in 1902. He was stuffed and his preserved body – complete with collar and collection box – was placed in a glass case in Paddington Station to continue his good works.

16. **ANDERSON McCREW**
In 1913 a one-legged African-American hobo died after falling off a moving freight train in Marlin, Texas. Anderson (also known as Andrew) McCrew was dead, but he did not rest in peace for 60 years. The morning after his death, he was taken to a funeral parlour and embalmed. When no one appeared to claim the body, a travelling carnival purchased it and displayed McCrew as 'The Amazing Petrified Man – The Eighth Wonder of the World'. When the troupe disbanded 55 years later, McCrew remained in storage until a Dallas widow, Elgie Pace, discovered him. She wanted to give him a decent burial because, as she said to her sister, 'He's a human being. You just can't throw a body in a ditch.' However, she was unable to afford the cost of burial, so she nicknamed him 'Sam' and kept him in the basement. Eventually, a local black undertaker volunteered to give McCrew a funeral. The service was 'beautiful, and very dignified', reported Elgie, and Anderson McCrew was finally laid to rest. Several months later, folksinger Don McLean wrote a song, 'The Legend of Andrew McCrew', which inspired a

radio listener to purchase a gravestone for McCrew. The stone reads: 'Andrew McCrew, "The Mummified Man", Born 1867/Died 1913/Buried 1973'.

17. VLADIMIR ILYICH LENIN
On January 21, 1924, Lenin died, reportedly of a stroke, but possibly of poisoning. The deification process began at once. Lenin's brain was removed, cut into 20,000 sections for study by the Soviet Brain Institute, and then his body was embalmed. It was a poor job and the face became wrinkled and shrunken. By 1926 a Russian doctor, using new embalming fluid which he claimed was based on that used by the ancient Egyptians, re-embalmed the body. A younger, more ascetic look was restored to the face. In 1930 a mausoleum composed of red Ukrainian granite and Karelian porphyry was built in Red Square to contain Lenin's body enclosed in a glass sarcophagus. In a poll taken in April 2004, 56% of Russians wanted Lenin buried, while 35% preferred that he remain above ground.

18. EVA PERÓN
When the wife of Argentine president Juan Perón died in 1952, her husband had her body embalmed. Perón planned to build a mausoleum for his wife, but his government was overthrown in 1955 and he was forced into exile in Spain. Eva Perón's body disappeared and it was assumed that she was buried in an Italian cemetery under a different name. However, by 1971 Perón had retrieved the body and, according to a friend who dined with Perón, the body was present every evening at the dinner table along with Perón and his new wife Isabel. In late 1974, at Isabel's request, Eva Perón was returned to Argentina, where she was placed in an open casket beside the closed casket of her husband. After being briefly displayed, her body was buried in the Duarte family tomb in La Recoleta Cemetary in Buenos Aires.

19. TRIGGER
The world's most famous animal actor, Trigger co-starred with Roy Rogers in 88 films and 100 television shows. An unusually intelligent horse, Trigger was able to untie knots with his teeth and count to 20. Upon his death in 1965 at the age of 33, Trigger was stuffed and mounted. He is on display at the Roy Rogers Museum in Victorville, California, as are Dale Evans' horse, Buttermilk, and their German shepherd dog Bullet.

20. MAO ZEDONG
After Mao, chairman of the Chinese Communist Party, died at 82 on September 9, 1976, he was embalmed. His corpse was placed in a crystal sarcophagus to be displayed permanently to the public in a mausoleum in Tiananmen Square in Beijing. At night, after visitors have gone home, Mao is lowered into an earthquake-proof chamber below the square.

21. ST BERNADETTE
In 1858, at the age of 14, Bernadette Soubirous saw several visions of the Virgin Mary at a spring in Lourdes, France. Bernadette later joined the Sisters of Notre Dame of Nevers, and today the site of the apparitions is one of the most famous Catholic shrines. After her death at the age of 35, Bernadette's body was buried and exhumed three separate times in the next 45 years in attempts to verify the incorruptibility of her corpse (according to Catholic tradition, a sign of sainthood). Although there has been some decomposition, owing in part to numerous examinations, Bernadette's remains are remarkably intact. Her body has been on display in the chapel of the Convent of St Gildard at Nevers since August 3, 1925.

22. ENRICO CARUSO
During the six years that followed his death in 1921, the great Italian tenor surely qualified for the 'best-dressed corpse' list. Each year solicitous friends ordered a new outfit for Caruso's body, which lay on public display in a crystal casket. In 1927 his widow decided enough was enough and had a white granite slab placed over the casket. It now remains sealed and undisturbed with Caruso in old clothes at Del Planto Cemetery near Naples, Italy.

23. BUSHMAN
More than 3 million people viewed the huge, chest-thumping gorilla in Chicago's Lincoln Park Zoo over a period of 20 years. While alive, Bushman often became moody when zoo-goers ignored him. In death, his stuffed and mounted carcass continues to awe visitors at Chicago's Field Museum of Natural History, where he glares from a sealed glass case filled with insecticidal gases.

24. VU KHAC MINH
When Vu, a Buddhist monk, was nearing death in 1639, he asked his followers to leave him alone for 100 days so he could meditate. When his disciples eventually returned, they reportedly

found his perfectly preserved body still in the lotus position. Believing that he had reached nirvana, they preserved his remains with red lacquer. In 2002 monks at his pagoda began restoring the cracked lacquer. X-rays showed that the body was still intact after more than three centuries. Thich Tranh Nhung, the head monk at the pagoda, said that Vu's incorruption 'illustrates the ability of the body to acquire a new level of grace through Buddhist teachings'.

25. 'EL NEGRO'
'El Negro' was the name given to an anonymous Bushman stolen from his grave in 1830 by two French taxidermists, Jules and Edouard Verraux. The body was displayed in a Parisian shop for 50 years before being given to a museum in the town of Banyoles in Spain. The presence of 'El Negro' in Spain led several African nations to threaten a boycott of the 1992 Summer Olympics in Barcelona. In 2000 the embalmed body was returned to Gabarone, Botswana, and given a burial with military honours.

26. BREDO MORSTOEL
Morstoel died of heart failure at the age of 89 in his native Norway in 1989. His grandson, Trygve Brauge, had the body frozen at a cryogenics facility in California, then had it stored in a shed at Brauge's unfinished house in Nederland, Colorado. In 1994 Brauge lost a battle with immigration authorities and was deported to Norway. He arranged to pay $674 per month to locals to deliver dry ice to keep Morstoel from thawing out. Four years later, Morstoel became the subject of a short film, *Grandpa's in the Tuff Shed*, directed by Robin Beeck. Tom Plant, Nederland's representative in the state legislature, tried in 2002 to have March 9 declared 'Frozen Dead Guy Day', pointing out that 'Grandpa Bredo' had been 'a model citizen, never giving the cold shoulder to anyone'. Many representatives were not amused and the motion lost, 35 votes to 27. Despite this setback, Nederland held a festival honouring Morstoel on the weekend of March 9–10. The main events were a showing of *Grandpa's in the Tuff Shed* and a coffin race. A longer sequel, *Grandpa's Still in the Tuff Shed*, was released in 2003.

27. TED WILLIAMS
After the Hall of Fame baseball player died at the age of 83 in 2002, he was taken to the Alcor Life Extension Foundation's cryogenics facility in Scottsdale, Arizona. The decision was

challenged by Williams' eldest daughter, Bobby Jo, since his will stated that he wanted to be cremated and have his ashes scattered off the coast of Florida. Williams' son, John Henry, produced a note in which he, Ted, and Ted's daughter Claudia entered into a pact to freeze themselves after death. The handwritten pact, signed by all three, read, 'JHW, Claudia and Dad all agree to be put in Bio-stasis after we die. This is what we want, to be able to be together in the future, even if it is only a chance.' The suit was settled in December of 2002 and Ted Williams will remain indefinitely in one of Alcor's liquid nitrogen-filled cryogenic tanks.

28. DOLLY
The sheep was famous as the first mammal successfully cloned from an adult. Her birth in 1996 was heralded as a scientific breakthrough but also triggered heated debate about the ethics of cloning. Dolly was put to sleep on February 13, 2003, after developing a fatal lung disease. Her preserved remains were placed on display at the Royal Museum in Edinburgh, Scotland.

29. JOSEPH PAUL JERNIGAN
In 1993 convicted murderer Joseph Paul Jernigan was executed in Texas. Because Jernigan donated his body to science, his body was frozen and shipped to the University of Colorado, where it was 'sliced' into 1,800 cross-sections. Two years later, a 59-year-old Maryland woman was similarly sliced, but into 5,000 segments. These two became the subjects of the Visible Human Project, the first computerised library of human anatomy to be made available to medical researchers around the world.

– I.W., J.Be., C.F. & The Eds

Remains to be Seen – 15 Preserved Body Parts

1. SAARTJE BAARTMAN'S BRAIN AND SEXUAL ORGANS
Baartman was born in the Cape Colony (part of modern-day South Africa) in 1789. Around 1810 she was taken to London by a British navy doctor, who exhibited her in Britain and France as the 'Hottentot Venus'. People paid to gawk at her unusually large buttocks and elongated labia. Baartman was also studied by racial theorists seeking to support notions of

the inherent superiority of European races. After she died in poverty at the age of 27, her brain and sexual organs were preserved and put on display at the Musée de l'Homme (Museum of Man) in Paris. After the ending of apartheid, the government of South Africa began requesting the return of Baartman's remains. In April 2002 the preserved organs, Baartman's skeleton and a plaster cast of Baartman's body that had been on display were handed over at the South African embassy. 'She has recovered her dignity, albeit after many years, with a ceremony that has celebrated her as a true person, and I am very happy about it,' announced Bernard Chevassus-au-Louis, director of the French Museum of Natural History.

2. ST BONAVENTURE'S HEAD

This great Catholic theologian and philosopher is one person who definitely did not rest in peace. Almost 300 years after his death in 1274, his remains were caught in the middle of a French religious war that pitted the Roman Catholic Church against the Protestant Huguenots. In 1562 St Bonaventure's tomb at Lyons was plundered. While his body was publicly burned, the head – said to be perfectly preserved – was saved and hidden by one of the faithful. It disappeared, however, during the French Revolution and has not been seen since.

3. PAUL BROCA'S BRAIN

In one of the less-frequented corners of the Musée de l'Homme (Museum of Man) in Paris are numerous bottles containing human brains. Some belonged to intellectuals, others to criminals. But perhaps the most distinguished of the specimens is that of Paul Broca, a nineteenth-century physician and anthropologist who was the father of modern brain surgery.

4. DEL CLOSE'S SKULL

Close was an improvisational comedian who trained John Belushi, Bill Murray and Mike Myers. Upon his death in 1999, he willed his skull to Chicago's Goodman Theatre to be used as Yorick's skull in productions of *Hamlet*. Close's former improv partner, Charen Halpern, noted, 'It's not the starring role. But Del was always willing to take smaller parts.'

5. GEORGE FREDERICK COOKE'S SKULL

Even though Irish-born actor George Frederick Cooke died in 1812, he continued to get work in bit-parts. Cooke's skull was used in productions of *Hamlet* before being retired to the Thomas Jefferson University Medical School library in Philadelphia.

6. **BARON PIERRE DE COUBERTIN'S HEART**
Lausanne, Switzerland, and Olympia, Greece, are the two most revered sites of the modern Olympic movement. Baron Pierre de Coubertin, the founder of the movement, left a part of himself in each place. His will requested that his body be buried at Lausanne, the site of the International Olympic Committee headquarters. But first his heart was to be removed and placed in a marble column at Olympia, where the ancient games were held.

7. **ALBERT EINSTEIN'S BRAIN**
What might have been the greatest brain of the twentieth century was not buried with the body that housed it. Albert Einstein asked that after his death his brain be removed for study. And when the great physicist died in 1955, this was done. The brain – which was neither larger nor heavier than the norm – was photographed, sectioned into 240 blocks and sent around the country to be studied by specialists. His parietal lobes were discovered to be unusually large.

8. **GALILEO'S FINGER**
The great astronomer died in 1642, but his body was not interred in its final resting place until 1737. During that final transfer to a mausoleum at the Church of Santa Croce in Florence on March 12, an intellectual admirer, Anton Francesco Gori, cut off Galileo's middle finger as a keepsake. After passing through various hands, it was acquired by Florence's Museum of the History of Science, where it is now encased in glass and pointing skyward.

9. **JOSEPH HAYDN'S HEAD**
The Austrian composer died in 1809. Soon after his burial, a prison warden who was an amateur phrenologist – a person who tries to correlate head bumps with character traits – hired grave-robbers to steal the head. The warden examined the skull, then gave it to an acquaintance, and a remarkable 145-year-long odyssey began. The theft of the skull was discovered in 1820, when the family of Haydn's patron had the body disinterred. Eventually they got a skull back, but it wasn't Haydn's. The real item was passed from one owner to

another, some of them individuals, others organisations. Finally, it found a home in a glass case at Vienna's Society of Friends of Music. In 1932 the descendants of Haydn's patrons once again tried to get it back. But WWII and then the cold war intervened – the body was in Austria's Soviet quarter, but the skull in the international zone. It wasn't until 1954 that body and skull were finally reunited.

10. MAJOR JOHN W. POWELL'S BRAIN
Geologist John W. Powell donated his brain to the Smithsonian Institution, of which he was an official, in order to settle a bet with an associate over whose brain was larger. Although Powell's grey matter is still in the museum collection, that of his associate is nowhere to be found, which makes Powell the winner by default.

11. JOSÉ RIZAL'S VERTEBRA
José Rizal, the national hero of the Philippines, was accused of sedition, executed by the Spanish in 1896 and buried without a coffin. He was exhumed in August 1898, after the Americans took Manila. Most of Rizal's remains are interred beneath the Rizal Monument in Luneta – all except one of his cervical vertebrae; the vertebra is enshrined like a holy relic in Fort Santiago.

12. DAN SICKLES' LEG
Sickles was a colourful New York congressman who organised and led a brigade of volunteers at the outbreak of the Civil War. He was involved in some of the bloodiest fighting at Gettysburg, losing his own right leg in the battle. That trauma, however, apparently didn't diminish Sickles' personal flair. He had the leg preserved and sent to Washington, where it was exhibited in a little wooden coffin at the medical Museum of the Library of Congress. Sickles frequently visited it himself.

13. LAZZARO SPALLANZANI'S BLADDER
When Italian biologist Spallanzani died in 1799, his diseased bladder was excised for study by his colleagues. It is currently on display in the Scarpa Room in the University of Pavia in Italy, where it remains a monument to the inquisitive mind.

14.-15. GEORGE WASHINGTON'S HAIR AND TOOTH
In June 1793 George Washington gave a locket containing a

clipping of his hair to his aide-de-camp, Colonel John Trumbull. When Trumbull died, he willed the lock of hair to a first cousin of the president's, Dr James A. Washington, who passed it along to his family as sort of 'hairloom'. George Washington's dentist, John Greenwood, managed to acquire another collectible which the president shed from his person – the last of his natural teeth. Washington sent the tooth to Greenwood to use as a model in making a new set of dentures. The dentist kept the tooth as a souvenir, and it remained in the Greenwood family for generations.

– E.F. & M.J.T.

Chapter 15

DAVE EGGERS' 4 BEST PLACES TO PUT THINGS INTO

12 PRODIGIOUS SAVANTS

15 STRANGE STORIES

11 AMAZING ATTIC EVENTS

27 THINGS THAT FELL FROM THE SKY

PHILIP PULLMAN'S 10 BEST TOOLS, AND ONE MORE

27 THINGS THAT ARE NOT WHAT THEY SEEM

21 BAD PREDICTIONS

10 FUNGUSES THAT CHANGED HISTORY

16 FAMOUS EVENTS THAT HAPPENED IN THE BATHTUB

BRUCE FELTON'S 'WHAT WERE THEY THINKING?: 11 OF THE WORST IDEAS IN RECENT HISTORY'

7 LAST FACTS

Miscellaneous

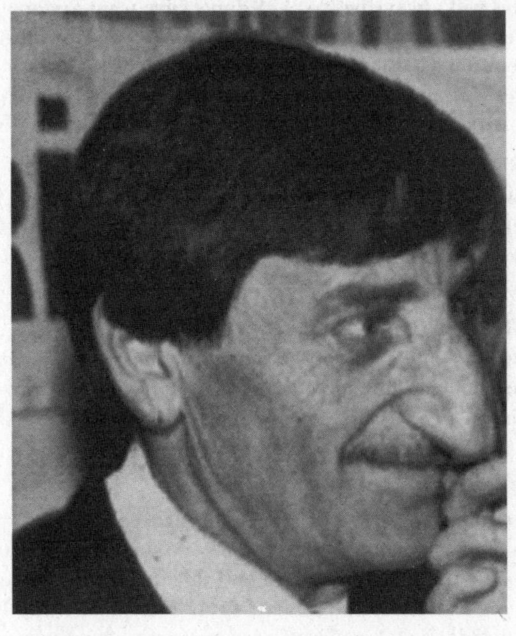

LONG NOSE CHAMPION MEHMET OZYUREK
– see p.9

Dave Eggers' 4 Best Places to Put Things Into

Dave Eggers has written four books and three songs and edits *McSweeney's*.

1. BOXES
   Boxes will always be No. 1. I don't care what anyone else says – boxes are the best. I recommend square ones for most occasions except for occasions involving hats. One of the things I like about boxes is that after you put things into a box, you can close the box with tape. They'll stay closed, all right! Boxes = No. 1.

2. VASES
   Flowers are best, in terms of things to put into vases, but marbles can create a good look, too. The problem with vases is that a lot of things don't fit into them. I guess vases shouldn't be No. 2.

3. CARS
   Cars have one advatange over most things you can put things into: once you put something into a car, you can move it to a different place. Cars can go almost anywhere. Cars should be No. 2.

4. THE GROUND
   This takes more effort than the first three, but it's a good choice in some circumstances, i.e., bones. Make sure the ground you put something into is sturdy and dry. If you put something into wet ground, wrap it in plastic first. That'll save you lots of time and headache later, if you need to get the thing you put into the ground out of the ground. The Ground = No. 4.

12 Prodigious Savants

Savant syndrome is a rare condition in which people suffering from mental retardation, autism or schizophrenia nonetheless possess an unusual ability in a single field, most often relating to music, art or numbers.

1. THOMAS 'BLIND TOM' BETHUNE (1849–1908)
   Although his vocabulary was limited to fewer than 100 words, Blind Tom could play more than 5,000 pieces on the piano, an instrument he had mastered as a four-year-old slave on a Georgia plantation. At the age of 11, he performed at the White

House for President James Buchanan. He learned each piece after hearing it only once; his repertoire included Mozart, Beethoven, Bach and Verdi.

2. ALONZO CLEMONS (1959–)
Clemons, who has an IQ of 40, lives in a home for the developmentally disabled in Boulder, Colorado. An exceptionally talented sculptor, he has sold hundreds of pieces, including one for $45,000. Many buyers have purchased his work unaware that it was created by a mentally handicapped artist.

3.-4. GEORGE and CHARLES FINN (1939–)
Known as the Bronx Calendar Twins, they first attracted national attention when they were featured in a 1966 *Life* magazine article. The brothers can give the day of the week for any date over a period of 80,000 years. They can also recall, in detail, the weather for any day of their lives.

5. THOMAS FULLER (1710–90)
Born in Africa, Fuller was taken to Virginia as a slave in 1724. He was a calculating wonder who could easily multiply nine-digit numbers. At the age of 78, Fuller, who was never able to learn to read or write, was asked, 'How many seconds has a man lived who is 70 years, 17 days and 12 hours old?' Ninety seconds later he gave the answer – 2,210,500,800. Informed that he was wrong, Fuller corrected his interrogator by pointing out that the man had forgotten to include leap years.

6. LESLIE LEMKE (1952–)
Like many prodigious savants, Leslie is blind, was born prematurely and possesses an extraordinary memory. He sings and plays the piano and has appeared on numerous television shows, including *60 Minutes* and *Donahue*. He has also been the subject of two films, *An Island of Genius* and the Emmy-winning *The Woman Who Willed a Miracle*.

7. JONATHAN LERMAN (1987–)
Lerman, who was diagnosed as autistic at the age of 3, has a tested IQ of 53. He began drawing at 10, shortly after the death of his maternal grandfather, Burt Markowitz, who had always insisted that Jonathan had promise. His charcoal drawings, which critics have compared to the works of George Grosz and Francis Bacon, sell for $500 to $1200. A book of his artwork, *Jonathan Lerman: The Drawings of a Boy with Autism*, was published in 2002.

8. KIM PEEK (1951–)
A mathematical savant, Peek, who lives in Salt Lake City, Utah, was the inspiration for the character played by Dustin Hoffman in the 1988 Academy Award-winning film *Rain Man*. His true story is told in the book *The Real Rain Man* (1997).

9. CHRISTOPHER PILLAULT (1982–)
Born in Iran, Pillault is unable to talk, walk or feed himself. He discovered painting in 1993, using his hands, since he can't use his fingers functionally. His paintings, featuring striking, ethereal figures, have been exhibited in France, Italy, Japan and the US. He is also a member of several artists' societies.

10. MATTHEW SAVAGE (1993–)
At the age of three, he was diagnosed with Asperger's disorder, a condition similar to autism. Savage is a professional jazz musician, who leads his own trio, has performed at jazz festivals throughout the US and Canada, and recorded three CDs. He was described as 'amazing' by jazz legend Dave Brubeck. Savage is also prodigious in mathematics – he is learning advanced algebra at the age of 11 – and geography – he represented New Hampshire in the US National Geography Bee in 2004.

11. RICHARD WAWRO (1952–)
Wawro, who is autistic and moderately retarded, started drawing at the age of three. He held his first exhibition in Edinburgh, Scotland, when he was 17. Most of his works are landscapes and seascapes based on images that he has seen just once in books or on television. Wawro can remember where and when he drew each picture. He was the subject of the documentary *With Eyes Wide Open* (1983).

12. STEPHEN WILTSHIRE (1974–)
Although Wiltshire, who lives in London, has the IQ of someone half his age, he is able to glance briefly at a building and then draw it in exquisite detail. Wiltshire has produced three books of drawings, one of which, *Floating Cities*, was a number-one bestseller in Great Britain.

Note: The best book on savant syndrome is *Extraordinary People* by Darold Treffert, MD. It is also worth noting that there exists a school – Hope University, in Anaheim, California – devoted solely to educating gifted, developmentally-challenged adults.

15 Strange Stories

Selected by Paul Sieveking, co-editor of the *Fortean Times*.

The *Fortean Times*, the Journal of Strange Phenomena, is a monthly magazine of news, reviews and research on all types of unusual phenomena and experiences. It was named after philosopher Charles Fort (1874–1932), who thought that data that did not fit the scientific norm should not be excluded or ignored by the scientific community. (To subscribe, write to Fortean Times, PO Box 2409, London NW5 4NP, United Kingdom.)

1. BEES PAY THEIR RESPECTS
   Margaret Bell, who kept bees in Leintwardine, about seven miles from her home in Ludlow, Wales, died in June 1994. Soon after her funeral, mourners were astonished to see hundreds of bees settle on the corner of the street opposite the house where Mrs Bell had lived for 26 years. The bees stayed for about an hour before buzzing off over the rooftops. The local press ran a photograph of the bees, hanging on the wall in a cluster.

2. PHANTOM CAR CRASH
   On December 11, 2002 two motorists called police to report seeing a car veering off the A3 trunk road with headlights blazing at Burpham in Surrey. A thorough search uncovered a car concealed in dense undergrowth and the long-dead driver nearby. It turned out that the crash had happened five months earlier when the driver, Christopher Chandler, had been reported missing by his brother.

3. ENIGMATIC EARTH DIVOT
   An irregular-shaped hole, about 10 ft by 7 ft with 2 ft vertical sides, was found on remote farmland near Grand Coulee, Washington State, in October 1984. It had not been there a month earlier. 'Dribblings' of earth and stones led to a three-ton, grass-covered earth divot 75 ft away. It was almost as if the divot had been removed with a 'gigantic cookie cutter', except that roots dangled intact from the vertical sides of both hole and displaced slab. There were no clues such as vehicle tracks and a seismic cause was thought very unlikely, although there had been a mild quake 20 miles away a week before the hole's discovery.

4. BALLOON BUDDIES
   Laura Buxton released a helium-filled balloon during celebrations for her grandparents' gold wedding anniversary in

Blurton, Staffordshire, in June 2001. Attached to the balloon was her name and address and a note asking the finder to write back. Ten days later she received a reply. The balloon had been found by another Laura Buxton in the garden hedge of her home in Pewsey, Wiltshire, 140 miles away. Both Lauras were aged 10 and both had three-year-old black Labradors, a guinea pig and a rabbit. 'I hope we can become best friends,' said the Staffordshire Laura.

5. **HUM MISTY FOR ME**
A noise a bit like amplifier feedback had been heard for three years coming from the right ear of a Welsh pony called Misty, according to the *Veterinary Record* (April 1995). It varied in intensity, but stayed at a constant pitch of 7 kHz. Hearing a buzzing in one's ears is called subjective tinnitus; very much rarer is when other people can hear the noise, a condition called objective tinnitus, the cause of which is a matter of debate.

6. **WHIRLWIND CHILDREN**
A nine-year-old Chinese girl was playing in Songjiang, near Shanghai, in July 1992 when she was carried off by a whirlwind and deposited unhurt in a treetop almost two miles away. According to a wire report from May 1986, a freak wind lifted up 13 children in the oasis of Hami in western China and deposited them unharmed in sand dunes and scrub 12 miles away.

7. **RIVERSIDE MYSTERY**
Gloria Ramirez, 31, died of kidney failure at Riverside General Hospital, California, in February 1994, after being rushed there with chest pains. Emergency room staff were felled by 'fumes' when a blood sample was taken. A strange oily sheen on the woman's skin and unexplained white crystals in her blood were reported. A doctor suffered liver and lung damage, and bone necrosis; at least 23 other people were affected. One hypothesis was that Ramirez, who had cervical cancer, had taken a cocktail of medicines that combined to make an insecticide (organophosphate) but exhaustive tests yielded no clues. The hospital was later demolished. The episode remains a mystery 10 years later.

8. **BOULDERS IN TREES**
In April 1997 a turkey hunter in Yellowwood State Forest, Indiana, came upon a huge sandstone boulder wedged between three branches of an oak tree about 35 ft from the ground. The

arrow-shaped rock was estimated to weigh 500 lb. Subsequently, four more large boulders were found wedged high up in trees elsewhere in the forest. All were in remote areas. None of the trees was damaged and there were no signs of heavy equipment being used or of tornado damage, and no one recalled any mishaps involving dynamite anywhere nearby.

9. HELPFUL VOICES
While on holiday a woman, referred to by the *British Medical Journal* (December 1997) as AB, heard two voices in her head telling her to return home immediately. Back in London, the voices gave her an address that turned out to be a hospital's brain scan department. The voices told her to ask for a scan as she had a brain tumour and her brain stem was inflamed. Though she had no symptoms, a scan was eventually arranged and she did indeed have a tumour. After an operation, AB heard the voices again. 'We are pleased to have helped you,' they said. 'Goodbye.' AB made a full recovery.

10. LA MANCHA NEGRA
A hazard unique to Venezuelan highways is a slippery goo called La Mancha Negra (the black stain), although it's more of a sludge with the consistency of chewing gum. Although the government has spent millions of dollars in research, no one knows what the goo is, where it comes from, or how to get rid of it. It first appeared in 1987 on the road from Caracas to the airport, covering 50 yards, and spread inexorably every year. By 1992 it was a major road hazard all around the capital and it was claimed 1,800 motorists had died after losing control. The problem remains.

11. POSTCARD FAREWELL
When Jim Wilson's father died in Natal, South Africa, in April 1967, both Jim, living in England, and his sister Muriel, living in Holland, were informed. Muriel contacted her husband, who was on business in Portugal, and he flew to South Africa right away. Changing planes at Las Palmas airport in the Canary Islands, he bought a postcard showing holidaymakers on Margate beach, Natal, and sent it to Muriel. It was she who noticed that the photograph showed her father walking up the beach.

12. NOTECASE FROM THE SKY
In October 1975 Mrs Lynn Connolly was hanging washing in her garden in The Quadrant, Hull, when she felt a sharp tap on the

top of her head. It was caused by a small silver notecase, 63 mm by 36.5 mm, hinged, containing a used notepad with 13 sheets left. It was marked with the initials 'SE', 'C8', 'TB' (or 'JB') and 'Klaipeda', a Lithuanian seaport. No one claimed it at the police station, so it was returned to Mrs Connolly. It seems likely it fell only a short distance but from where? If it had dropped from a plane, it would have given her more than a tap.

13. FIERY PERSECUTION
The village of Canneto di Caronia on Sicily's north coast has been plagued by mysterious fires. The trouble began on January 20, 2004 when a TV caught fire. Then things in neighbouring houses began to burn, including washing machines, mobile phones, mattresses, chairs and even the insulation on water pipes. The electricity company cut off all power, as did the railway company, but the fires continued. Experts of all kinds carried out tests, but no explanation was found. The village was evacuated in February, but when people began returning in March the fires resumed. Police ruled out a pyromaniac after they saw wires bursting into flames. Father Gabriel Amorth, the Vatican's chief exorcist, was quoted as blaming demons.

14. BOVINE ENIGMA
On June 28, 2002, in the middle of a spate of unexplained cattle mutilations in Argentina, something macabre was found in a field near Suco, west of Rio Cuarto in San Luis province. Nineteen cows were stuffed into a sheet metal water tank, closed with a conical cap. Nine were drowned, the rest barely alive, having endured freezing temperatures, not to mention the shock of their lives.

15. BOY TURNS INTO YAM
Three pupils of the Evangelist Primary School in the northern Nigerian town of Maiduguri rushed into the headmistress's office in March 2000 and said that a fellow pupil had been transformed into a yam after accepting a sweet from a stranger. The headmistress found the root tuber and took it to the police station for safe-keeping. Following local radio reports, hundreds of people flocked to see the yam and police were hunting for the sweet-giver. What happened next failed to reach the wire services.

11 Amazing Attic Events

1. THE RESIDENCE OF MADAME DE POMPADOUR (1745–50)
Madame Jeanne-Antoinette d'Etoiles was known throughout Paris as one of the most beautiful and cultured women of her day. In 1745 she met King Louis XV of France. The two immediately fell in love, and Madame d'Etoiles obtained a legal separation from her husband. She was then given the title of the Marquise de Pompadour and installed in the attic apartment of Versailles as the king's mistress. Her apartment became known as the meeting place for some of the most celebrated people of France, and her guests were assisted in the steep 100-stair ascent by an elementary lift dubbed the 'flying chair'. But her private life with the king was less than ideal. After two blissful years together, Pompadour lost her physical passion for the king. She feared losing him and believed that a diet of vanilla, truffles and celery would stimulate her desire for sexual activity. It only worsened her already weak physical condition. After five years in the attic, the king moved her to a flat on the ground floor of the palace. It was clear he had now taken new mistresses. Pompadour, however, retained her powerful position as the king's political and artistic adviser until her death in 1764.

2. THE SUICIDE OF THOMAS CHATTERTON (1770)
As a boy, Thomas Chatterton was a prodigious poet and scholar, and early Romantic who at the age of ten wrote on a par with his adult contemporaries. His family was poor, his mother a widowed seamstress, and privacy was difficult to come by in their small Bristol home. So young Thomas set up a writing room in the attic, which he jealously guarded as his secret domain. In the attic room, among his books and papers, stood Ellinor, a life-size doll made of woven rushes, which his mother used for dress fittings. Thomas loved Ellinor and always took care to powder her face and do her hair. However, when he moved to London to pursue his literary career, he left his beloved Ellinor behind. He rented a garret reminiscent of his attic study at home, and thereafter suffering repeated personal and professional disappointments, including failure to sell a series of forgeries he claimed had been written by a fifteenth-century monk, Chatterton took arsenic and died at the age of 17.

3. THE LITERARY GARRET OF EDMOND DE GONCOURT (1885–96)
Edmond and his brother Jules were French novelists. Both are

best remembered for the detailed journals they kept on literary people of the late nineteenth-century. Jules died in 1870, and in 1885 Edmond turned the two attic rooms of the house into a salon. Each Sunday afternoon, he would entertain such notables as Guy de Maupassant and Émile Zola. The following are some excerpts from Edmond's journal on those afternoons.

February 1, 1885 On the French poet Robert de Montesquieu-Fezenac: 'Somebody described his first love affair with a female ventriloquist who, while [he] was straining to achieve his climax, would imitate the drunken voice of a pimp.'

May 24, 1885 Edmond comments on Zola's reaction to the recent death of Victor Hugo: 'He walked around the room as if relieved by his death and as if convinced he was going to inherit the literary papacy.'

April 19, 1896 A description of the removal of Paul Verlaine's death mask: 'The conversation turned to Verlaine's alcoholism and the softening effect it had had on his flesh . . . [Stéphane] Mallarmé had said he would never forget the wet, soggy sound made by the removal of the death mask from his face, an operation in which his beard and mouth had come away too.'

4. MARCONI INVENTS THE WIRELESS TELEGRAPH (1894–96)

Guglielmo Marconi was 20 years old when he began experimenting in earnest with radio waves. Because his father took a dim view of such 'childish' pursuits as physics and even went so far as to destroy his son's electronic equipment, young Marconi had to set up a secret laboratory in the attic of their villa in Bologna. There, among his mother's trays of silkworms, Marconi determined that radio waves could carry a message in Morse code across the room. In time, he proved that the effectiveness of his invention was not bound by the four attic walls, but that it could transmit messages over great distances.

5. THE CONSTRUCTION AND DEMONSTRATION OF THE FIRST TELEVISION (1922–26)

In 1922, British scientist John Logie Baird rented an attic room above an artificial-flower shop at 8 Queen's Arcade in Hastings to continue research on his primitive television sets. He used a tea chest as the base for his motor, a biscuit tin to house the projection lamp, and he held the whole contraption together with darning needles, scraps of wood, string and sealing wax. In 1924, he took his 'working' apparatus to London. There he rented two attic rooms at 22 Frith Street in Soho. He struggled for another two years before he gave the first demonstration of true television on January 26, 1926, for an audience of 50 scientists. The British Broadcasting Corporation inaugurated Baird's system in 1929 and used it until 1935, when a more sophisticated system was adopted.

6. ADOLF HITLER'S ATTEMPTED SUICIDE (1923)
After the failure of his Beer Hall Putsch in Munich, Germany, Hitler hid in an attic bedroom at Uffing, the country estate of his follower Ernst 'Putzi' Hanfstängl. Hitler tried to commit suicide by shooting himself when the police came to arrest him. A police agent managed to disarm him before he could pull the trigger.

7. ESPIONAGE AT PEARL HARBOR, HAWAII (1939–41)
Ruth Kühn was only 17 years old when she became the mistress of Nazi leader Joseph Goebbels. But like all of his mistresses, Ruth was soon discarded. When the affair ended in 1939, Goebbels decided to send Ruth out of Germany. He arranged for her and her parents, Bernard and Friedel, to move to Hawaii and act as espionage agents for the Japanese. Ruth set up a beauty parlour in Honolulu, which became her chief source of information, since it was frequented by American military men's wives. The next step was to figure out a way of transmitting this information to the Japanese. The Kühns devised a simple code system and sent signals from the attic window of their small house overlooking Pearl Harbor. On December 7, 1941, towards the end of the Japanese surprise attack, their signals were noticed by two American naval officers. The US Navy Shore Patrol arrested the family and all were imprisoned for espionage.

8. ANNE FRANK WRITES HER DIARY (1942–44)
Forced into hiding when the Nazis overran the Netherlands, Anne Frank, her parents and sister, and four other Jews, shared a musty Amsterdam attic above a warehouse and office building. They hid there for two years, obtaining food and other necessities from Gentiles on the floor below. Anne, a precocious girl in her early teens, kept a diary in which she chronicled not only the details of their imprisonment, but also her personal feelings about life, love, the future, and her budding sexual awareness. Finally, in August 1944, the Gestapo, acting on a tip by Dutch informers, raided the hiding place. All the Franks

died in concentration camps (Anne of typhus), except Otto Frank, the father. He returned to the attic after the war and found his daughter's diary, which was first published under the title *The Diary of a Young Girl.*

9. THE DISCOVERY OF FRANZ SCHUBERT'S LOST PIANO SCORE (1969)
The score for a fantasy for piano by Franz Schubert was discovered in an attic in Knittlefield, Austria, in 1969. The piece is believed to have been written by the Viennese composer in 1817.

10. THE DISCOVERY OF FRÉDÉRIC CHOPIN'S LOST WALTZES (1978)
Several waltzes dedicated to Clementine de la Panouse were discovered by Vicomte Paul de la Panouse in the attic of the family château near Paris in 1978. The waltzes were stored in a heavy trunk belonging to the French aristocratic family. The waltzes were hidden – along with many other documents – in various locations prior to the German invasion of France during WWII.

11. THE DISCOVERY OF SCHINDLER'S LIST (1998)
When a German couple found an old grey suitcase in a loft belonging to the husband's late parents in Hildesheim, they didn't think much about it, until they saw the name on the handle: O. Schindler. Inside were hundreds of documents, including a list of the names of Jewish labourers that factory owner Oskar Schindler gave the Nazis during World War II. By giving Jewish workers fake jobs and otherwise manipulating the system, Schindler saved 1,200 Jews from extermination. His story inspired Thomas Keneally's novel *Schindler's Ark* (1982) and the movie *Schindler's List* (1993). The documents had apparently been stored in the loft by friends of Schindler and then forgotten. In 1999 the suitcase and its contents were donated to the Yad Vashem Holocaust Museum in Jerusalem.

– L.O. & M.J.T

27 Things That Fell From the Sky

1. HAY
A great cloud of hay drifted over the town of Devizes in England at teatime on July 3, 1977. As soon as the cloud reached the centre of town, it all fell to earth in handful-size lumps. The sky

was otherwise clear and cloudless, with a slight breeze. The temperature was 26°C.

2. GOLDEN RAIN
When yellow-coloured globules fell over suburban Sydney, Australia, in late 1971, the ministry for health blamed it on the excreta of bees, consisting mostly of undigested pollen. However, there were no reports of vast hordes of bees in the area and no explanation as to why they would choose to excrete en masse over Sydney.

3. BLACK EGGS
On May 5, 1786, after six months of drought, a strong east wind dropped a great quantity of black eggs on the city of Port-au-Prince, Haiti. Some of the eggs were preserved in water and hatched the next day. The beings inside shed several layers of skin and resembled tadpoles.

4. MEAT
The famous Kentucky meat-shower took place in southern Bath County on Friday, March 3, 1876. Mrs Allen Crouch was in her garden making soap when pieces of fresh meat the size of large snowflakes began to fall from the cloudless sky. Two gentlemen who tasted it said that it was either mutton or venison. Scientists who examined the material found the first samples similar to lung tissue from either a human infant or a horse. Other later samples were identified as cartilage and striated muscle fibres. The local explanation was that a flock of buzzards had disgorged as a group while flying overhead.

5. A 3,902-LB STONE
The largest meteorite fall in recorded history occurred on March 8, 1976, near the Chinese city of Kirin. Many of the 100 stones that were found weighed over 200 lb; the largest, which landed in the Haupi Commune, weighed 3,902 lb. It is, by more than 1,000 lb, the largest stony meteorite ever recovered.

6. MONEY
On October 8, 1976, a light plane buzzed the Piazza Venezia in Rome and dropped 500-lire, 1,000-lire and 10,000-lire banknotes on the startled people below. The mad bomber was not found.

7. SOOT
A fine blanket of soot landed on a Cranford park on the edge of London's Heathrow Airport in 1969, greatly annoying the local

park keepers. The official report of the Greater London Council said the 'soot' was composed of spores of a black microfungus, *Pithomyces chartarum,* found only in New Zealand.

8. FIVE HUNDRED BIRDS
About 500 dead and dying blackbirds and pigeons landed in the streets of San Luis Obispo, California, over a period of several hours in late November 1977. No local spraying had occurred, and no explanation was offered.

9. FIRE
On the evening of May 30, 1869, the horrified citizens of Greiffenberg, Germany, and neighbouring villages witnessed a fall of fire, which was followed by a tremendous peal of thunder. People who were outside reported that the fire was different in form and colour from common lightning. They said they felt wrapped in fire and deprived of air for some seconds.

10. WHITE FIBROUS BLOBS
Blobs of white material up to 20 ft in length descended over the San Francisco Bay area in California on October 11, 1977. Pilots in San Jose encountered them as high as 4,000 ft. Migrating spiders were blamed, although no spiders were recovered.

11. LUMINOUS GREEN SNOW
In April 1953 glowing green snow was encountered near Mt Shasta, California. Mr and Mrs Milton Moyer reported that their hands itched after touching it and that 'a blistered, itching rash' formed on their hands, arms and faces. The Atomic Energy Commission denied any connection between the snow and recent A-bomb tests in nearby Nevada.

12. MYSTERIOUS DOCUMENTS
The July 25, 1973, edition of the Albany, New York, *Times Union* reported the unusual case of Bob Hill. Hill, the owner of radio station WHRL of North Greenbush, New York, was taking out the station rubbish at 4:15 p.m. when he noticed 'twirling specks' falling from a distance higher than the station's 300-ft transmitter. He followed two of the white objects until they landed in a hayfield. The objects turned out to be two sets of formulae and accompanying graphs, which apparently explained 'normalised extinction' and the 'incomplete Davis-Greenstein orientation'. No explanation has been made public. The Davis-Greenstein mechanism is used in astrophysics.

13. BEANS
Rancher Salvador Targino of João Pessoa, Brazil, reported a rain of small beans on his property in Paraíba State in early 1971. Local agricultural authorities speculated that a storm had swept up a pile of beans in West Africa and dropped them in northeastern Brazil. Targino boiled some of the beans, but said they were too tough to eat.

14. SILVER COINS
Several thousand rubles' worth of silver coins fell in the Gorky region of the USSR on June 17, 1940. The official explanation was that a landslide had uncovered a hidden treasure, which was picked up by a tornado, which dropped it on Gorky. No explanation was given for the fact that the coins were not accompanied by any debris.

15. MUSHROOM-SHAPED THINGS
Traffic at Mexico City airport was halted temporarily on the morning of July 30, 1963, when thousands of greyish, mushroom-shaped things floated to the ground out of a cloudless sky. Hundreds of witnesses described these objects variously as 'giant cobwebs', 'balls of cotton' and 'foam'. They disintegrated rapidly after landing.

16. HUMAN BODY
Mary C. Fuller was sitting in her parked car with her 8-month-old son on Monday morning, September 25, 1978, in San Diego, California, when a human body crashed through the windshield. The body had been thrown from a Pacific Southwest Airlines jetliner, which had exploded after being hit by a small plane in one of the worst disasters in US history. Mother and son suffered minor lacerations.

17. TOADS
Falls of frogs and toads, though not everyday occurrences, are actually quite common, having been reported in almost every part of the world. One of the most famous toad falls happened in the summer of 1794 in the village of Lalain, France. A very hot afternoon was broken suddenly by such an intense downpour of rain that 150 French soldiers (then fighting the Austrians) were forced to abandon the trench in which they were hiding to avoid being submerged. In the middle of the storm, which lasted for 30 minutes, tiny toads, mostly in the tadpole stage, began to land on the ground and jump about in all directions. When the rain let up, the

soldiers discovered toads in the folds of their three-cornered hats.

18. OAK LEAVES
In late October of 1889 Mr Wright of the parish of Penpont, Dumfries, Scotland, was startled by the appearance of what at first seemed to be a flock of birds, which began falling to the ground. Running towards them, he discovered the objects to be oak leaves, which eventually covered an area 1 mile wide and 2 miles long. The nearest clump of oak trees was 8 miles away, and no other kind of leaf fell.

19. JUDAS TREE SEEDS
Just before sunset in August 1897 an immense number of small, blood-coloured clouds filled the sky in Macerata, Italy. About an hour later, storm clouds burst and small seeds rained from the sky, covering the ground to a depth of half an inch. Many of the seeds had already started to germinate, and all of the seeds were from the Judas tree, which is found predominantly in the Middle East and Asia. There was no accompanying debris – just the Judas tree seeds.

20. FISH
About 150 perch-like silver fish dropped from the sky during a tropical storm near Killarney Station in Australia's Northern Territory in February, 1974. Fishfalls are common enough that an 'official' explanation has been developed to cover most of them. It is theorised that whirlwinds create a waterspout effect, sucking up water and fish, carrying them for great distances and then dropping them somewhere else.

21. ICE CHUNKS
In February of 1965, a 50-lb mass of ice plunged through the roof of the Phillips Petroleum plant in Woods Cross, Utah. In his book, *Strangest of All*, Frank Edwards reported the case of a carpenter working on a roof in Kempten – near Düsseldorf, Germany – who was struck and killed in 1951 by an icicle 6 ft long and 6 in. around, which shot down from the sky.

22 PEACHES
On July 12, 1961, unripe peaches were scattered over a small portion of Shreveport, Louisiana, from a cloudy sky.

23. DEADLY WHITE POWDER
On Saturday, July 10, 1976, the citizens of Seveso, Italy, were startled by a sudden loud whistling sound coming from the

direction of the nearby Icmesa chemical factory. The sound was followed by a thick, grey cloud, which rolled towards the town and dropped a mist of white dust that settled on everything and smelled horrible. It was 10 days before the people of Seveso learned that the white dust contained dioxin, a deadly poison far more dangerous than arsenic or strychnine. By then it was too late. The effects of dioxin poisoning had already begun. The area was evacuated, surrounded by barbed wire and declared a contaminated zone. All exposed animals were killed, ugly black pustules formed on the skin of young children, babies were born deformed, and older people began to die of liver ailments. The full extent of the tragedy has still not been felt.

24. SPACE JUNK
In September, 1962, a metal object about 6 in. in diameter and weighing 21 lb crashed into a street intersection in Manitowoc, Wisconsin, and burrowed several inches into the ground. The object was later identified as part of Sputnik IV, which had been launched by the USSR on May 15, 1960. Since 1959 approximately 9,000 parts of spacecraft have fallen out of orbit, and many of them have reached the surface of the Earth. On July 11, 1979, Skylab, the 77-ton US space station, fell out of orbit over the South Indian Ocean and western Australia. The largest piece of debris to reach land was a one-ton tank.

25. THE LARGEST METEORITE
The largest known iron meteorite, weighing more than 60 tons, crashed to Earth in late 1920, landing on a farm in the Hoba district west of Grootfontein in northern Namibia. It has since been declared a national monument and is visited by more than 20,000 tourists a year. A minor international incident occurred in 1989 when 36 Malaysian soldiers serving in a UN peacekeeping force tried to cut pieces from the boulder for souvenirs.

26. HUMAN WASTE
On Sunday, October 18, 1992, Gerri and Leroy Cinnamon of Woodinville, Washington, were watching a football game on TV in their den with Gerri's parents when something crashed through the roof of their living room. 'I expected to see Superman soar through the hole,' said Leroy. Instead they found several baseball-sized chunks of greenish ice. As it melted, it began to smell bad. Two days later the Federal Aviation Administration confirmed that the Cinnamons' roof had been damaged by frozen human waste from a leaky United

Airlines sewage system. 'It's a good thing none of us was killed,' reflected Leroy. 'What would you put on the tombstone?'

Unfortunately, falls of waste blobs are not uncommon. On April 23, 1978, for example, a 25-lb chunk landed in an unused school building in Ripley, Tennessee. Other attacks have occurred in Denver and Chicago. And then there's the story of the unfortunate Kentucky farmer who took a big lick of a flying Popsicle before he discovered what it was.

27. NON-DAIRY CREAMER
White powder of a more innocuous kind began falling on the small town of Chester, South Carolina, in 1969 – shortly after the Borden company started production of a corn syrup-based non-dairy creamer in its local plant. Whenever the plant's exhaust vents clogged, the creamer spewed into the air and landed on people's homes and cars. Although basically harmless, the powder would mix with dew and rain and cause a sticky mess. Said homeowner Grace Dover, 'It gets on your windows and you can't see out. It looks like you haven't washed your windows for a hundred years.' In 1991 Borden paid a $4,000 fine for releasing Cremora beyond plant boundaries. By that time the company had already taken steps to reduce the low-fat rain.

Philip Pullman's 10 Best Tools, and One More

Philip Pullman is one of the world's great storytellers and his trilogy, His Dark Materials, *the adventures of Lyra Belacqua and her friend Will Parry in a richly imagined alternative universe, has been widely acclaimed.* The Amber Spyglass, *the final book in the trilogy, was the first children's book to win the Whitbread Book of the Year Award. A stage adaptation of the three books was an enormous success at the National Theatre in 2004.*

Born in Norwich in 1946, Philip Pullman grew up to become a teacher. Unable at first to afford the tools he wanted, he turned to writing as the alternative to a life of crime. His greatest unfulfilled ambition is to present woodworking programmes on satellite TV. He is reasonably presentable and articulate, and open to offers.

1. THE TORMEK GRINDER
It's no good trying to use edge tools that are blunt, so you have to keep them sharp. Of all the ways I've tried, this is the best.

An ordinary electric bench grinder spins the stone around at such a speed that the steel you're trying to sharpen gets easily overheated and loses its power to hold an edge. The Tormek grinder overcomes that by having a large wheel revolving fairly slowly in a trough of water and an ingenious system of jigs that slip on to the tool rest and hold the chisel, or the gouge, or the scissors, or the carving knife, at exactly the right angle to the stone. It produces the sharpest, most reliable edge you can get.

2. THE JAPANESE PULL SAW
It's so obvious: a saw that cuts on the pull stroke instead of the push. The advantage is that you can have a much thinner blade, because it doesn't have to be stiff, and that means that you can cut a much narrower kerf much more accurately. It cuts dovetails very well.

3. THE BLOCK PLANE
This is a little plane that you hold with one hand. I have two of them, but the one I use most often is a metal one: a Record. It's satisfyingly heavy for such a small thing and beautifully designed: there's a hollow in the top of the throat-adjustment knob for your forefinger so that you can press on the front end and guide it more firmly, and hollows on the sides for your thumb and middle finger, and the lever cap curls over precisely to fit the palm of your hand. You can adjust the depth of the blade and the width of the throat, and it's ideal for planing end-grain. I found that the thing that made most difference (apart from keeping the blade razor-sharp: see 'The Tormek grinder', above) was grinding the sole until it was as smooth and flat as a mirror. Now it just glides over the wood.

4. THE TRY SQUARE
My favourite is a little metal engineer's try square with a 4-in. blade. If you need a long one, use a long one; but this is adequate for most jobs, and it slips very neatly into the pocket, and it feels good in the hand. I bought it from the Gloucester Green market in Oxford, where there are a couple of stalls that sell second hand tools.

5. THE GOUGE
This is a chisel with a blade that's curved in cross-section. The ones I use for carving have a bevel ground on the outside so you can scoop out a hollow. Sharpening on its own isn't enough for these delicate and high-bred creatures: you have to hone the bevel till it shines. Fortunately, the Tormek (see above) has a

leather wheel especially designed for that. Once it's so sharp that it hurts the eye to look at it, the gouge will slice through the wood with nonchalant accuracy.

6. THE CARVER'S CHOPS
'Chop' has the same origin as 'chap', which means jaw or cheek. It's a heavy wooden vice that holds a big workpiece for carving. I made mine out of beech, following a plan by the excellent and learned Anthony Dew, founder and president of the Guild of Rocking Horse Makers.

7. THE X-ACTO KNIFE
In combination with a steel straightedge and a rubber cutting mat, this is unbeatable. Card, paper, leather, even thin plywood all succumb.

8. THE PENCIL
This is one of those things you don't think of as a tool. But whenever you make something out of wood you're going to need a pencil at some point, whether to mark a line for cutting or to jot down calculations for the measurements or to sketch a complicated joint and fix the shape in your mind. I have never found those wide so-called carpenter's pencils with a flat lead any better than an ordinary HB. A few strokes on a piece of fine sandpaper will restore the sharpest of points.

9. THE BELT SANDER
I had to think hard about which power tool to include. Each one I have is utterly necessary, and so is the next one I'm going to buy, as soon as I decide which it is. How can you cut complex shapes without a bandsaw? How did we manage to do anything at all before they invented the router? But if you're making a large piece of furniture, the only way to achieve a perfectly smooth surface without loathsome and back-breaking toil is to use a belt sander. It removes all the bumps and hollows and rough patches, and with progressively finer belts you can get a result that would have taken our ancestors hours, if not days. They might have turned their noses up at the biscuit jointer or the radial-arm saw, but they would have used one of these like a shot.

10. THE JIG
A hammer always looks like a hammer, a screwdriver always looks like a screwdriver. But a jig can look like anything. It's a frame or a holding device that's often made specifically for one

job and then put away in the corner of the workshop and never used again. But you don't throw it away, just in case. It's used to hold a workpiece in exactly the right place relative to the cutting edge or the drill bit or whatever it might be, to ensure that you cut a perfect semicircle on the bandsaw, or drill thirty holes at exactly the right angle, or cut several mortises to exactly the right depth, or . . . I love jigs.

?? THE ENIGMA
This is a beautiful and slender piece of bronze about a foot long. For half its length, it's been beaten out into a flat blade about as wide as a finger, with an edge that's too blunt to cut anything but paper: it's a perfect letter-opener. The other end has been formed into a similar but shorter blade at right angles to the first; and the shorter blade has been bent half way along its length into a flat foot, at right angles to the main shaft, about as long as the middle joint of my thumb. It's been made by hand, and it's worn smooth with use. I guess it was made to tamp down the sand in a mould, but I really have no idea. I use it for scratching my back.

27 Things That Are Not What They Seem

1. A firefly is not a fly – it's a beetle.
2. A prairie dog is not a dog – it's a rodent.
3. India ink is not from India – it's from China and Egypt.
4. A horned toad is not a toad – it's a lizard.
5. A lead pencil contains no lead – it contains graphite.
6. A Douglas fir tree is not a fir – it's a pine.
7. A silkworm is not a worm – it's a caterpillar.
8. A peanut is not a nut – it's a legume.
9. A panda bear is not a bear – it's a raccoon relative.
10. A *cor anglais*, or English horn, is not English and not a horn – it's an alto oboe from France.
11. A guinea pig is not from Guinea and is not a pig – it's from South America and it's a rodent.

12. Shortbread is not a bread – it's a thick biscuit.
13. Dresden china is not made in Dresden – it's made in Meissen.
14. A shooting star is not a star – it's a meteor.
15. A funny bone is not a bone – it's the spot where the ulnar nerve touches the humerus.
16. Chop suey is not a native Chinese dish – it was invented by Chinese immigrants in California.
17. A bald eagle is not bald – it's got flat white feathers on its head and neck when mature, dark feathers when young.
18. A banana tree is not a tree – it's a herb.
19. A cucumber is not a vegetable – it's a fruit.
20. A jackrabbit is not a rabbit – it's a hare.
21. A piece of catgut is not from a cat – it's usually made from sheep intestines.
22. A Mexican jumping bean is not a bean – it's a seed with a larva inside.
23. A Turkish bath is not Turkish – it's Roman.
24. A koala bear is not a bear – it's a marsupial.
25. A sweetbread is not bread – it's from a calf's or lamb's pancreas or thymus.
26. Bombay duck is not a duck – it's a dried fish.
27. A prairie oyster is not an oyster – it's a calf's testicle.

– I.W. & W.D.

21 Bad Predictions

1. THE SUBMARINE
'I must confess that my imagination, in spite even of spurring, refuses to see any sort of submarine doing anything but suffocating its crew and floundering at sea.'
H.G. Wells, British novelist, in *Anticipations*, 1901

The development of the submarine proceeded rapidly in the early twentieth century, and by World War I submarines were a major factor in naval warfare. They played an even more important role in World War II. By the 1960s and 1970s submarines were considered among the most important of all strategic weapons.

2. AIRCRAFT

'We hope that Professor [Samuel] Langley will not put his substantial greatness as a scientist in further peril by continuing to waste his time, and the money involved, in further airship experiments. Life is short, and he is capable of services to humanity incomparably greater than can be expected to result from trying to fly . . . For students and investigators of the Langley type there are more useful employments.'
The New York Times, December 10, 1903

Exactly one week later, the Wright brothers made the first successful flight at Kitty Hawk, North Carolina.

'I confess that in 1901, I said to my brother Orville that man would not fly for fifty years . . . Ever since, I have distrusted myself and avoided all predictions.'
Wilbur Wright, US aviation pioneer, 1908

'The popular mind often pictures gigantic flying machines speeding across the Atlantic and carrying innumerable passengers in a way analogous to our modern steamship . . . It seems safe to say that such ideas must be wholly visionary, and even if a machine could get across with one or two passengers the expense would be prohibitive to any but the capitalist who could own his own yacht.

Another popular fallacy is to expect enormous speed to be obtained. It must be remembered that the resistance of the air increases as the square of the speed and the work as the cube . . . If with 30 horse-power we can now attain a speed of 40 miles per hour, then in order to reach a speed of 100 miles per hour we must use a motor capable of 470 horse-power . . . It is clear that with our present devices there is no hope of competing for racing speed with either our locomotives or our automobiles.'
William H. Pickering, US astronomer, circa 1910, after the invention of the aeroplane

The first transatlantic commercial scheduled passenger air service was June 17 to 19, 1939, New York to England. The fare one way was $375, round trip $675 – no more than a first-class fare on an ocean liner at the time. On October 14, 1922, at Mount Clemens, Michigan, a plane was flown at 216.1 mph.

3. HIGHWAYS

'The actual building of roads devoted to motor cars is not for the near future, in spite of many rumors to that effect.'
Harper's Weekly, August 2, 1902

Conceived in 1906, the Bronx River Parkway, New York, when completed in 1925, was the first auto express highway system in the United States.

4. RADIO

'[Lee] De Forest has said in many newspapers and over his signature that it would be possible to transmit the human voice across the Atlantic before many years. Based on these absurd and deliberately misleading statements, the misguided public . . . has been persuaded to purchase stock in his company.'
A US district attorney prosecuting inventor Lee De Forest for selling stock fraudulently through the US mails for his Radio Telephone Company, 1913

The first transatlantic broadcast of a human voice occurred on December 31, 1923, from Pittsburgh, Pennsylvania, to Manchester, England.

5. BOLSHEVISM

'What are the Bolsheviki? They are representatives of the most democratic government in Europe . . . Let us recognise the truest democracy in Europe, the truest democracy in the world today.'
William Randolph Hearst, US newspaper publisher, 1918

6. ROCKET RESEARCH

'That Professor Goddard and his "chair" in Clark College and the countenancing of the Smithsonian Institution does not know the relation of action to reaction, and of the need to have something better than a vacuum against which to react – to say that would be absurd. Of course he only seems to lack the knowledge ladled out daily in high schools.'
The New York Times, January 12, 1920

The *New York Times* printed a formal retraction of this comment some forty-nine years later, on July 17, 1969, just prior to the Apollo landing on the moon.

'The proposals as outlined in your letter . . . have been carefully reviewed . . . While the Air Corps is deeply interested in the research work being carried out by your organization . . . it

does not, at this time, feel justified in obligating further funds for basic jet propulsion research and experimentation.'
Brigadier General George H. Brett, US Army Air Corps, in a letter to rocket researcher Robert Goddard, 1941

7. AIR STRIKES ON NAVAL VESSELS
'The day of the battleship has not passed, and it is highly unlikely that an airplane, or fleet of them, could ever successfully sink a fleet of navy vessels under battle conditions.'
Franklin D. Roosevelt, US Assistant Secretary of the Navy, 1922

'As far as sinking a ship with a bomb is concerned, you just can't do it.'
Rear Admiral Clark Woodward, US Navy, 1939

8. JAPAN AND THE UNITED STATES
'Nobody now fears that a Japanese fleet could deal an unexpected blow on our Pacific possessions . . . Radio makes surprise impossible.'
Josephus Daniels, former US Secretary of the Navy, October 16, 1922

'A Japanese attack on Pearl Harbor is a strategic impossibility.'
George Fielding Eliot, 'The Impossible War with Japan', *American Mercury*, September 1938

See newspaper headlines for December 7, 1941.

9. COMMERCIAL TELEVISION
'While theoretically and technically television may be feasible, commercially and financially I consider it an impossibility, a development of which we need waste little time dreaming.'
Lee De Forest, US inventor and 'father of the radio', 1926

'[Television] won't be able to hold onto any market it captures after the first six months. People will soon get tired of staring at a plywood box every night.'
Darryl F. Zanuck

10. REPEAL OF PROHIBITION
'I will never see the day when the Eighteenth Amendment is out of the Constitution of the United States.'
William Borah, US senator, 1929

The Eighteenth Amendment was repealed in 1933. Borah was alive to see the day. He did not die until 1940.

11. HITLER
'In this column for years, I have constantly laboured these points: Hitler's horoscope is not a war-horoscope . . . If and when war comes, not he but others will strike the first blow.'
R.H. Naylor, British astrologer for the *London Sunday Express*, 1939

12. THE ATOMIC BOMB
'That is the biggest fool thing we have ever done . . . The bomb will never go off, and I speak as an expert in explosives.'
Admiral William Leahy, US Navy officer speaking to President Truman, 1945

13. LANDING ON THE MOON
'Landing and moving around the moon offers so many serious problems for human beings that it may take science another 200 years to lick them.'
Science Digest, August 1948. It took 21 years.

14. ATOMIC FUEL
'It can be taken for granted that before 1980 ships, aircraft, locomotives, and even automobiles will be atomically fuelled.'
David Sarnoff, US radio executive and former head of *RCA*, 1955

15. THE VIETNAM WAR
'The war in Vietnam is going well and will succeed.'
Robert McNamara, US Secretary of Defence, January 31, 1963

'We are not about to send American boys 9,000 or 10,000 miles away from home to do what Asian boys ought to be doing for themselves.'
Lyndon B. Johnson, US president, October 21, 1964

'Whatever happens in Vietnam, I can conceive of nothing except military victory.'
Lyndon B. Johnson, in a speech at West Point, 1967

16. FASHION IN THE 1970s
'So women will wear pants and men will wear skirts interchangeably. And since there won't be any squeamishness about nudity, see-through clothes will only be see-through for reasons of comfort. Weather permitting, both sexes will go about bare-chested, though women will wear simple protective panties.'
Rudi Gernreich, US fashion designer, 1970

17. THE FALL OF THE BERLIN WALL
'Liberalisation is a ploy . . . the Wall will remain.'
George Will, columnist for *The Washington Post*, November 9 1989
– the day the Berlin Wall fell.

18. COLLAPSE OF THE SOVIET UNION
'We must expect the Soviet system to survive in its present brutish form for a very long time. There will be Soviet labour camps and Soviet torture chambers well into our great-grand-children's lives.'
Newt Gingrich, US Representative (and future Speaker of the House), 1984

19. INVASION OF IRAQ #1
'There is a minimal risk of conflict.'
Heino Kopietz, senior Middle East analyst, on the possibility of Iraq invading Kuwait, in *The Times* of London, July 26, 1990

Iraq invaded Kuwait five days later.

20. 9/11
'Who cares about a little terrorist in Afghanistan?'
Paul Wolfowitz, US Deputy Secretary of Defense, dismissing concerns about al-Qaeda at an April 2001 meeting on terrorism

21. INVASION OF IRAQ #2
'I have no doubt we're going to find big stores of weapons of mass destruction.'
Kenneth Adelman, Defense Policy Board member, in *The Washington Post*, March 23, 2003

'[The war] could last six days, six weeks. I doubt six months.'
Donald Rumsfeld, US Secretary of Defense, to US troops in Aviano, Italy, February 7, 2003

'[My] belief is we will, in fact, be greeted as liberators . . . I think it will go relatively quickly, weeks rather than months.'
Dick Cheney, US Vice President, March 16, 2003

'We are dealing with a country that can really finance its own reconstruction and relatively soon.'
Paul Wolfowitz, US Deputy Secretary of Defense, to the House Budget Committee, February 27, 2003

– K.H.J. & C.F.

10 Funguses That Changed History

1. THE YELLOW PLAGUE (*Aspergillus flavus*)
   A. flavus is an innocent-looking but deadly yellowish mould also called aflatoxin. Undoubtedly the cause of countless deaths throughout history, it was not suspected of being poisonous until 1960. That year, a mysterious disease killed 100,000 young turkeys in England and medical researchers traced the 'turkey-X disease' to *A. flavus* growing on the birds' peanut meal feed. Hardy, widespread and lethal, aflatoxin is a powerful liver cancer agent. Even so, people have long cultivated *A. flavus* – in small amounts – as part of the manufacturing process of soy sauce and sake. But *A. flavus* can get out of control easily. It thrives on warm, damp conditions and as it breeds – sometimes to lethal proportions within 24 hours – the mould produces its own heat, which spurs even faster growth. Some of *A. flavus*' favourite dishes are stored peanuts, rice, corn, wheat, potatoes, peas, cocoa, cured hams and sausage.

2. THE MOULD THAT TOPPLED AN INDUSTRY (*Aspergillus niger*)
   This common black mould, most often found on rotting vegetation, played a key role in the collapse of a major industry. Until the early 1920s, Italy produced about 90% of the world's citric acid, using low-grade lemons. Exported mainly to the US as calcium citrate, this citric acid was a costly ingredient – about a dollar a pound – used in food, pharmaceutical and industrial processing. When American chemists discovered that *A. niger*, the most ordinary of moulds, secreted citric acid as it grew in a culture medium, they seized the opportunity to perfect citric-acid production using the easily grown mould. Charles Pfizer & Co., of Brooklyn, New York, became known as the 'world's largest lemon grove' – without a lemon in sight. Hardworking acres of *A. niger* were soon squirting out such quantities of citric acid that by 1923 the price was down to 25¢ per pound and the Italians were out of business.

3. ST ANTHONY'S FIRE (*Claviceps purpurea*)
   A purplish-black, spur-shaped mass, *C. purpurea* is a formidable and even frightening fungus that has long plagued mankind. But in addition to its horrible effects, *C. purpurea* also has valuable medical uses if the greatest care is taken to use tiny amounts. The fungus is a powerful muscle contractor and can control bleeding, speed up childbirth and even induce abortion.

It is also the source of the hallucinogenic LSD-25. In doses larger than microscopic, *C. purpurea* – commonly called ergot – produces ergotamine poisoning, a grisly condition known in the Middle Ages as St Anthony's fire. There is still no cure for this hideous, often fatal disease caused by eating fungus-infected rye. The victim suffers convulsions and performs a frenzied 'dance'. This is often accompanied by a burning sensation in the limbs, which turn gangrenously black and fall off. Some victims of medieval ergotism went insane and many died. In AD994 more than 40,000 people in two French provinces died of erogotism, and in 1722 the powerful fungus forced Peter the Great of Russia to abandon his plan to conquer Turkey when, on the eve of the Battle of Astrakhan, his entire cavalry and 20,000 others were stricken with ergotism. The last recorded outbreak of ergot poisoning was in the French village of Pont-Saint-Esprit in 1951.

4. THE NOBEL MOULD *(Neurospora crassa)*
The humble bread mould *N. crassa* provided the means for scientists to explore the most exciting biological discovery of the twentieth century: DNA. As anyone with an old loaf of bread in the bread box knows, *N. crassa* needs only a simple growing medium and it has a short life cycle. With such co-operative qualities, this reddish mould enabled George Beadle and Edward Tatum to win the Nobel Prize in Medicine/Physiology in 1958 for discovering the role that genes play in passing on hereditary traits from one generation to the next. By X-raying *N. crassa*, the researchers produced mutations of the genes, or components of DNA, and then found which genes corresponded with which traits.

5. THE BLUISH-GREEN LIFESAVER
(*Penicillium notatumchrysogenum*)
A few dots of a rather pretty bluish-green mould were Dr Alexander Fleming's first clue to finding one of the most valuable lifesaving drugs ever developed. In 1928 he noticed that his petri dish of staphylococcus bacteria had become contaminated with symmetrically growing, circular colonies of *P. notatum*. Around each speck, all the bacteria were dead. Fleming further found that the mould also killed pneumonia, gonorrhea and diphtheria germs – without harming human cells. The unassuming bluish-green mould was beginning to look more interesting, but Fleming could not isolate the active element. Not until 1939 did Howard Florey and Ernst Chain identify penicillin, a

secretion of the growing mould, as the bacteria-killer. The first important antibiotic, penicillin revolutionised treatment of many diseases. Fleming, Florey and Chain won the Nobel Prize in Physiology/Medicine in 1945 for their pioneering work with the common fruit mould that yielded the first 'miracle drug'.

6. THE GOURMET'S DELIGHT (*Penicillium roquefortii*)
According to an old legend, a French shepherd forgot his lunch in a cave near the town of Roquefort and when he found it weeks later, the cheese had become blue-veined and was richly flavoured. No one knew why this happened until American mycologists discovered the common blue mould *P. roquefortii* in 1918. All blue cheeses – English stilton, Italian gorgonzola, Norwegian gammelost, Greek kopanisti and Swiss paglia – derive their tangy flavour from the energetic blue mould that grows rapidly in the cheese, partially digesting it and eventually turning the entire cheese into mould. Of course, it's more appetising to say that *P. roquefortii* ripens the cheee instead of rotting it, but it's the same process.

7. THE FAMINE-MAKER (*Phytophthona infestans*)
The political history of the world changed as a result of the unsavoury activity of *P. infestans*, a microscopically small fungus which reduced Ireland to desperate famine in 1845. Hot, rainy July weather provided perfect conditions for the white fungus to flourish on the green potato plants – most of Ireland's food crop – and the bushes withered to brown, mouldy, stinking clumps within days. The entire crop was devastated, causing half a million people to starve to death, while nearly two million emigrated, mostly to the United States. *P. infestans* dusted a powdery white death over Ireland for six years. The fungus spread rapidly and just one bad potato could infect and ruin a barrel of sound ones. British Prime Minister Robert Peel tried to get Parliament to repeal tariffs on imported grain and while the MPs debated, Ireland starved. Relief came so slowly and inadequately that Peel's government toppled the next year, in 1846.

8. THE TEMPERANCE FIGHTER (*Plasmopara viticola*)
A soft, downy mildew infecting American-grown grapes was responsible for nearly ruining the French wine industry. In 1872 the French unwittingly imported *P. viticola* on grafting stock of wine grapes grown in the United States. Within 10 years, the mild-mannered mildew had quietly decimated much

of France's finest old vineyards. But in 1882 botanist Pierre-Marie-Alexis Millardet discovered a miraculous cure for the ravages of *P. viticola*. He noticed that Médoc farmers painted their grape leaves with an ugly paste of copper sulphate, lime and water – to prevent theft. Called Bordeaux mixture, this paste was the first modern fungicide. The vineyards of France recovered as the entire world sighed with relief.

9. MERCHANT OF DEATH (*Saccharomyces cerevisiae*)
Ordinary brewers' yeast, *S. cerevisiae*, used to leaven bread and make ale, was once employed as a wartime agent of death. During WWI, the Germans ran short of both nitroglycerin and the fat used in its manufacture. Then they discovered that the usually friendly fungus *S. cerevisiae* could be used to produce glycerin, a necessary ingredient in explosives. Fermenting the fungus together with sucrose, nitrates, phosphates and sodium sulphite, the Germans produced more than 1,000 tons of glycerin per month. According to some military sources, this enabled them to keep their war effort going for an additional year.
10. THE TB KILLER (*Streptomyces griseus*)
A lowly mould found in dirt and manure piles, *S. griseus* nevertheless had its moment of glory in 1943, when Dr Selman Waksman discovered that it yields the antibiotic streptomycin, which can cure tuberculosis. Waksman went to the United States in 1910 as a Russian refugee and by 1918 he had earned his doctorate in soil microbiology. He had worked with *S. griseus* before, but not until a crash programme to develop antibiotics (a word coined by Dr Waksman himself) was launched did he perceive the humble mould's possibilities for greatness. Streptomycin was first used successfully on human beings in 1945, and in 1952 Dr Waksman was awarded the Nobel Prize in Physiology/Medicine.

– K.P.

16 Famous Events That Happened in the Bathtub

1. POISONING OF PELIAS
According to Greek mythology, Medea murdered Jason's uncle (Pelias, King of Thessaly) by showing his daughters that they

could rejuvenate him if they chopped him up and bathed him in her cauldron of herbs. They believed her, and he died.

2. **MURDER OF AGAMEMNON**
Shortly after his return from the Trojan War, the Greek hero Agamemnon was murdered by his wife, Clytemnestra, who struck him twice with an axe while he was relaxing in the tub.

3. **ARCHIMEDES' DISCOVERY**
While soaking in the bathtub, the Greek scientist Archimedes formulated the law of physics – known as the Archimedean principle – that a body immersed in fluid loses weight equal to the weight of the fluid it displaces. He became so excited about his discovery that he rushed out stark naked into the streets of Syracuse, Sicily, shouting 'Eureka!' ('I have found it!')

4. **BURNING OF ALEXANDRIA**
When the Arabs conquered Alexandria, they were alleged to have burned the 700,000 books in the library to keep up the fires in the city's 4,000 public baths.

5. **QUEEN ANNE'S BURNING BATH**
Anne, Queen of Denmark, was the wife of James I of England. In 1615 gases from her mineral bath momentarily ignited, causing Her Majesty great consternation.

6. **FRANKLIN'S PASTIME**
Benjamin Franklin is reputed to have imported the first bathtub into America. He improved its design and contemporary reports indicate that he carried on much of his reading and correspondence while soaking in the tub.

7. **MARAT'S ASSASSINATION**
Jean-Paul Marat played an active part in the French Revolution. As editor of the journal *L'Ami du Peuple*, he became known as an advocate of extreme violence. The moderate Girondists were driven out of Paris and took refuge in Normandy. There, some of them met and influenced a young woman called Charlotte Corday. Convinced that Marat must die, she went to Paris and bought a butcher's knife. When she arrived at Marat's house on July 13, 1793, he was taking a bath. (He spent many hours in the tub because of a painful skin condition.) Overhearing Corday, he asked to see her. They discussed politics for a few minutes, then Corday drew her knife and stabbed Marat to death in the bathtub.

8. **THE BONAPARTES' ARGUMENT**
While Napoleon was taking a bath one morning in 1803, his brothers Joseph and Lucien rushed in, seething with rage because they had just heard of his plan to sell Louisiana to the Americans. They were furious because he refused to consult the legislature about it. Lucien had worked hard to make Spain return the colony to France and now his work would be for naught. Joseph warned Napoleon that he might end up in exile if he carried out his plan. At this, Napoleon fell back angrily in the tub, splashing water all over Joseph. Napoleon's valet, who was standing by with hot towels over his arm, crashed to the floor in a dead faint.

9. **WAGNER'S INSPIRATION**
Composer Richard Wagner soaked in a tub scented with vast quantities of Mild of Iris perfume for several hours every day while working on his final opera, *Parsifal* (1882). He insisted that the water be kept hot and heavily perfumed so that he could smell it as he sat at his desk, clad in outlandish silk and fur dressing gowns and surrounded by vials and sachets of exotic scents.

10. **MORPHY'S DEATH**
Paul Morphy of New Orleans defeated famous chess players when he was still a child. As an adult, he could play eight games simultaneously while blindfolded. Some people consider him the greatest chess player who ever lived, but from the age of 22 until his death on July 10, 1884, at 47, he played no more chess. Believing that people were trying to poison him or burn his clothes, Morphy became a virtual recluse. On one oppressively hot day he returned from a walk and took a cold bath. In the tub he died from what doctors described as 'congestion of the brain or apoplexy, which was evidently brought on by the effects of the cold water on his overheated body'.

11. **ROSTAND'S WRITING**
Edmond Rostand, French poet and playwright, hated to be interrupted while he was working, but he did not like to turn his friends away. Therefore, he took refuge in the bathtub and wrote there all day, creating such successes as *Cyrano de Bergerac* (1898).

12. **SMITH'S MURDERS**
George Joseph Smith of England earned his living by his almost hypnotic power over women. In 1910 he met Bessie Mundy, married her (without mentioning that he already had a wife)

and disappeared with her cash and clothes. Two years later they met by chance and began living together again. After Smith persuaded Bessie to write a will in his favour, he took her to a doctor on the pretence that she suffered from fits. (Both she and the doctor took his word for it.) A few days later she was found dead in the bathtub, a cake of soap clutched in her hand. Everyone assumed she had drowned during an epileptic seizure. Smith married two more women (Alice Burnham and Margaret Lofty), took out insurance policies on their lives and described mysterious ailments to their doctors. They, too, were found dead in their bathtubs. When Alice Burnham's father read of Margaret Lofty's death, he was struck by its similarity to his daughter's untimely end. The police were notified and Smith was tried for murder and sentenced to be executed. His legal wife, Edith, testified at the trial that she could remember only one occasion when Smith himself took a bath.

13. CARROLL'S ORGY

America was shocked by reports of an orgy on February 22, 1926, at the Earl Carroll Theatre, New York, after a performance of his *Vanities*. To bring a midnight party to a climax onstage, a bathtub was filled with champagne and a nude model climbed in, while the men lined up and filled their glasses from the tub. This was during the Prohibition era, so a federal grand jury immediately began an inquiry into whether or not the tub really did contain liquor and, if so, who had supplied it. Earl Carroll, the producer who staged the party, was convicted of perjury for telling the grand jury that no wine had been in the bathtub. He was sentenced to a year and a day in prison, plus a $2,000 fine. After he suffered a nervous breakdown on the way to the penitentiary, his fellow prisoners were ordered never to mention bathtubs in his presence.

14. KING HAAKON'S FALL

On June 29, 1955, the reign of King Haakon VII, who had ruled Norway from the time of its independence in 1905, effectively came to an end when the beloved monarch fell in the royal bathtub at his palace in Oslo. The elderly king lingered on for over two years before succumbing on September 21, 1957, to complications resulting from his fall.

15. GLENN'S CAREER

The momentum of what contemporary experts considered to be an unstoppable political career was interrupted in 1964 when astronaut hero John Glenn fell in the bathtub and had to withdraw from his race for senator from Ohio. He was finally elected to the Senate in 1974.

16. MORRISON'S DEATH
Rock idol Jim Morrison was living in exile in an apartment in Paris. On the morning of July 3, 1971, he was found dead in his bathtub. The cause of death was ruled 'heart failure'. He was 27 years old.

– P.S.H., L.B. & J.Be.

Bruce Felton's What Were They Thinking? 11 of the Worst Ideas in Recent History

Bruce Felton is the co-author of *The Best, Worst & Most Unusual: Noteworthy Achievements, Events, Feats & Blunders of Every Conceivable Kind*, *Felton and Fowler's Famous Americans You Never Knew Existed* and the author of *What Were They Thinking?: Really Bad Ideas Throughout History*.

1. SENATOR SOUP
Victor Biaka-Boda, the Ivory Coast's representative in the French Senate, returned to his home district in January 1950 to campaign for re-election. It wasn't a smart career move. Later that month, his belongings and bones were found near the village of Bouafle. The leftovers were shipped to police labs in Paris for analysis, but it was plainly obvious that Biaka-Boda had ended his days in a tureen. However, until the facts were in, a successor could not be named and his constituents had to forego representation. It took the French Overseas Ministry another two years to acknowledge officially that Biaka-Boda had been eaten. Only then could the vacancy be filled. As *The New York Times* delicately put it, 'You cannot have your senator and eat him too.'

2. THE PLOT TO KILL HITLER'S MOUSTACHE
In a study of Adolf Hitler's health and habits during World War II, the Office of Strategic Services – forerunner of the CIA – found that the Führer was 'close to the male-female line', according to Stanley Lovell, wartime director of research and development for the OSS. 'A push to the female side might make

his moustache fall out and his voice become soprano', turning Hitler into a national laughing stock and driving him from power. To make it happen, the OSS bribed Hitler's personal gardener to inject oestrogen into the Führer's food. Inevitably, this absurd 'destabilization program' failed. Lovell speculates that either Hitler's official tasters noticed something funny about the carrots or, more likely, the gardener was a double-crosser who kept the bribe and discarded the hormones.

3. JUST THE FAX, MA'AM
When residents of Seoul, South Korea, complained that police emergency phone lines were often busy, the Metropolitan Police Administration added two emergency *fax* lines.

4. BADGE OF EXCELLENCE
The US Consumer Product Safety Commission paid $1,700 for 80,000 promotional buttons with the slogan, 'Think Toy Safety' in the 1970s. But the buttons turned out to be more of a menace than any toy ever concocted by the most socially irresponsible toy manufacturer. The metal tags had sharp edges and metal tab fasteners that broke off easily and were a sure bet to be swallowed by small children. Also, the buttons were coated with lead paint. Eventually, the Commission recalled the buttons with an eye to recycling them or just scuttling the lot.

5. THE HILLS ARE ALIVE WITH THE SOUND OF SPLICING
A movie theatre manager in Seoul, South Korea, decided that the running time of *The Sound of Music* was too long. He shortened it by cutting out all the songs.

6. FINANCIAL AID FOR THE DIFFERENTLY HANDED
Juniata College, in Huntingdon, Pennsylvania, offers a scholarship to left-handed students with financial need. The stipend was established by alumni Frederick and Mary Francis Beckley, who were dropped from the college tennis team in 1919 solely because of their left-handedness. Other excessively specialised scholarships include:

– The International Boar Semen Scholarship, a $500 stipend earmarked for the study of swine management at the undergraduate level. IBS is a division of Universal Pig Genes, Inc.

– The $500 NAAFA-NEC Scholarship, awarded to obese college-bound high-school seniors by the New England Chapter of the National Association to Advance Fat Acceptance.

– The Zolp Scholarship, available exclusively to Loyola University (Chicago) students named 'Zolp'.

7. **BALLOON TALK**
In 1917, more than a decade before the first talking films, inventor Charles Pidgin patented a breakthrough way to simulate speech on screen. Before filming, balloons 'made of rubber or any other suitable material' are concealed in each performer's mouth. The balloons are imprinted with dialogue; characters simply blow up their balloons on cue, allowing their lines to be read just as if they were comic strip figures.

8. **HONK IF YOU LOVE RADIATION SICKNESS, BIRTH DEFECTS AND THE END OF CIVILISATION AS WE KNOW IT**
The Nevada state legislature authorised a new licence plate in 2002 depicting a mushroom cloud from an atomic explosion. The design symbolised the 928 nuclear weapons tests conducted in the Nevada desert from 1945 through 1992. Ultimately, however, the Nevada Department of Motor Vehicles rejected the concept, noting that 'any reference on a licence plate to weapons of mass destruction is inappropriate and would likely offend our citizens'.

9. **BIG SPENDER**
In the fourteenth century Mansa Musa held sway over the Mali Empire, among the most powerful and far-reaching Islamic kingdoms of its time. Musa was an enlightened leader who sought peace with his neighbours, fostered the arts and built majestic structures. He also liked to have a good time. In 1324 he led 60,000 followers on a pilgrimage to Mecca; a retinue of 500 slaves bearing solid gold sceptres accompanied them. Along the way, Musa stopped off in Cairo for a few months of revels and relaxation. He spent so much gold in the Egyptian capital that the national economy collapsed. Musa and his followers continued on to Mecca and returned to Mali all but broke; it was years before Egypt recovered from the emperor's excesses.

10. **SCHUMANN'S FINGER-RACK**
As a young man, composer Robert Schumann (1810–56) showed great promise as a concert pianist. Unfortunately, the middle and fourth fingers of his right hand lacked suppleness and agility. To whip some discipline into the wayward digits, he invented a device that held them in place and stretched them while the others played freely. Schumann's homemade finger-rack turned out to be so effective that he wound up crippling his

fingers. On doctor's orders, he marinated his hand regularly in a restorative bath of warm animal guts, but the injury was permanent, and Schumann never played seriously again.

11. THE ANNALS OF ACADEME
At its 1989 commencement ceremonies, Ohio's Central State University awarded boxer Mike Tyson an honorary doctorate in humane letters.

7 Last Facts

1. BABE RUTH'S LAST HOME RUN
Ruth hit his 714th and last major-league home run, a towering out-of-the-park drive off Pittsburgh Pirates' pitcher Guy Bush, on May 25, 1935. However, 11 years later the owner of the Veracruz Blues of the Mexican League hired the famous slugger for $10,000 to come and bat once in a game against the Mexico City Reds. The pitcher, Ramon Brazana, threw three balls and was removed from the game. A reliever was brought in and threw his first pitch straight down the middle. The 51-year-old Ruth hit it deep into the right-field bleachers, much to the delight of 10,000 Mexican fans.

2. THE LAST AMERICAN KILLED IN THE VIETNAM WAR
Kelton Rena Turner, an 18-year-old Marine from Los Angeles, was killed in action on May 15, 1975, two weeks after the evacuation of Saigon, in what became known as the Mayaguez incident. His body was never recovered.

3. THE LAST VICTIM OF SMALLPOX
On October 26, 1977, Ali Maow Maalin, a hospital cook in Somalia, became the last person to contract smallpox through natural transmission when he chose to tend an infected child. The child died but Maalin survived. In September 1978 Janet Parker, an English medical photographer, was exposed to smallpox as the result of a laboratory accident. She subsequently died. The virologist in charge of the lab felt so guilty that he committed suicide. On May 8, 1980, the World Health Organisation declared smallpox eradicated. However, some samples remain in laboratories in Atlanta and Moscow.

4. THE LAST CRANK PHONE IN THE UNITED STATES
On July 12, 1990 American's last hand-cranked, party-line telephone system was replaced by private-line, touch-tone

technology. The system had serviced the 18 year-round residents of Salmon River Canyon, near North Fork, Idaho.

5. THE LAST MISS CANADA
In 1991 women's groups successfully lobbied to have the Miss Canada contest cancelled, claiming that it was degrading to women. The last Miss Canada, Nicole Dunsdon, completed her reign in October 1992.

6. THE LAST VOLKSWAGEN BEETLE
The VW Beetle, little changed since its debut in 1936, became the most popular automobile in history, with 21,529,464 cars rolling off the assembly lines. Production of the car ceased in Germany in 1978, but continued in Mexico where the Beetle was particularly popular as a taxi. After 2000, sales dropped in Mexico, due to free trade agreements that flooded the market with a variety of inexpensive cars with better gas mileage. A decision by Mexico City's local government to grant future licences only to taxis with four doors helped seal the two-door Beetle's fate. The last Beetles were produced at a plant in Pueblo, Mexico, on July 30, 2003. The very last car was sent to a museum at Volkswagen headquarters in Wolfsburg, Germany.

7. THE LAST MESSAGE FROM THE AUTHORS TO THE READERS
We hope you have enjoyed *The Book of Lists*. If you have any comments or suggestions, please write to: viciousgnu@aol.com

Index

A

Abbandando, Frank 'The Dasher', 198
Abbey, Edward, 296
Abbott & Costello, 91
Abbott, Jack Henry, 307
Abdullah, Crown Prince, 233
Accardo, Tony 'Joe Batters', 198
Acker, Jean, 175
Acree Jr, Alfred, 197
actors, 119–20
    becoming politicians, 228–31
    and great roles, 37–41
    Olympic medalists as, 350–2
    see also movies
Adams, Douglas, 2
Adams, John, 386
Adams, Richard, 295
Adamson, Stuart, 81
Addington, Henry, 346–7
Adelman, Kenneth, 429
Adler, David, 291
Adler, William M., 305
Adoula, Cyril, 255
Adren, Sharon, 179
Afghan Mujahedin, 256–7
Agee, James, 46
Agrippina the Younger, 26
Aguilera, Christina, 174
Aguirre, Lope de, 243
aircraft, 425, 427
Aiuppa, Joseph 'Ha Ha', 189, 199
Akkad, Moustapha, 61
Al-Bashir, Omar, 234
al-Fayed, Dodi, 107
Al-Mussallat, Subha Tulfah, 30
Alba, Felipe de, 175
Alba, Thea, 89–90
Albritton, Cynthia, 223
alcohol, 102–7
Alcott, Louisa May, 281
Alderman, Israel 'Icepick Willie', 199
Aldiss, Brian, 304–5
Alexander the Great, 108, 244, 267
Alexander VI, Pope, 28
Alexander, Jason, 175
Alexander, Texas, 79
Ali, Hadji, 86
Ali, Monica, 294
Allen, Paul, 165
Allen, Woody, 45, 177, 324–5
Allende, Salvador, 239
alligators, 131, 142
Allison, Audrey, 77
Allison, Joe, 77
Alvarez, Santiago, 63
Aman, Zeenat, 173
Amberg, Louis 'Pretty', 199
American Academy of Otolaryngology
    Museum, 263
Amin, Idi, 236
Amirah, Che, 212
Amorth, Father Gabriel, 410
Amory, Cleveland, 176
Amos, Tori, 12
Anderson, Lindsay, 64, 80
Anderson, Pamela, 179–80
Andress, Ursula, 44
Andrews, Julie, 180
Angelou, Maya, 46, 285
Angola Mercenary Force, 256
animals, 125–52
    before the law, 202–10
    children and wild, 134–8
    crime, 202–10
    discovery of large, 145–9
    eating humans, 129–31
    extinction, 138–40, 143–4
    lake and sea monsters, 149–51
    lifespan of, 142–3
    penis lengths of, 132
    preservation of, 388–96
    rights, 208–9, 220–1
    strange behaviour of, 140–2
    unusual mating habits, 126–8
Anker, Julian, 175
Anne, Queen, 434
anthems, 68–70
Antique Vibrator Museum, 263
ants, 141, 156
aphrodisiac foods, 180–2
Appel, George, 214
Arago, Jacques, 299
Arbenz, Jacobo, 254
Arbuckle, Fatty, 50

Archimedes, 434
Aretino, Pietro, 378
Aristide, Jean-Bertrand, 257–8
Arkin, Alan, 59
Arlen, Richard, 50
Armen, Jean Claude, 137
arms import/export, 243
Arnaz, Desi, 74
Arnold, Benedict, 26
Arnold, Hannah Waterman, 26
Arnold, Roseanne, 174
Art Ensemble of Chicago, 83
Art and Science of Love, 183
Arthur, Jean, 175
arts, 66–93
  art attack, 116, 371
  barmy quiz questions, 91–3
  blues songs, 79
  Bob Dylan lines, 77–8
  country songs, 76–7
  drummers of note, 84–5
  early names of bands, 68
  found unexpectedly, 74–5
  gigs, 81–3
  jazz musicians, 75–6
  national anthems, 68–70
  theatre productions, 79–81
  variety acts, 89–91
  works painted over, 71–3
  worst song titles, 70–1
  wretched performers, 86–9
Ashe, Arthur, 16
assassination, 250–3
Atkins, Chet, 71
Atkins, Dr Robert, 383
atomic bombs, 428, 439
attic events, 411–14
Attila the Hun, 244
Atwood, Margaret, 302
Atzerodt, George, 104
Auad, Carlos Henrique, 197
Aubrey, John, 161
Austen, Jane, 280, 292
authors *see* literature
Axelrod, Robert, 308

B

Baartman, Saartje, 396–7
Babb-Sprague, Kristen, 341
Babington, R., 274
Bacall, Lauren, 36, 43
Bach, Johann Sebastian, 5, 303, 405
Bach, Richard, 295
Bacon, Francis, 405
Baer, Jo, 173
Bailly, Jean, 205
Baird, John Logie, 412–13
Baker, Josephine, 377
Baldwin, Evelyn, 334
Ball, Lucille, 74
Balliett, Whitey, 297
balloons, 407–8, 439
Balzac, Honoré de, 374
Band, Albert, 59
bands, early names of, 68
Bangles (band), 68
Bankhead, Tallulah, 119–20
Barclay James Harvest, 81–2
Bardot, Brigitte, 213, 220–1
Barents, Willem, 17
Barnes, Lee, 351
Barnett, Doris, 221–2
Barnum, P.T., 375, 391
Barrett, Andy, 191
Barrymore, Drew, 176
Barrymore, Earl of, 347
Barrymore, John, 13
Barton, Roy, 108
basketball, 339–40
Basra Mass Poisoning, 249
bathtub events, 279, 367, 433–7
Battle of the Little Big Horn, 104–5
Baudelaire, Charles, 296
Bauer, Steve, 220
Bauhaus (band), 82
Bay of Pigs Invasion Force, 255
Beach Boys, 68
Beadle, Jeremy, 91–3
bears, 129, 135, 142, 151
Beat movement, 285
Beatles, 68
Beckett, Samuel, 180, 296
Beckham, David, 15, 156
bed, working in, 160–3
Beeck, Robin, 395
Beer, Stafford, 308
Beery, Wallace, 176
Beethoven, Ludwig van, 5, 303, 405

INDEX

Bell, Margaret, 407
Bellin, Howard, 219–20
Bellini, Giovanni, 71
Belokas, Spiridon, 338
Belov, Sasha, 340
Belushi, John, 2, 397
Benchley, Peter, 294
Bennett, John G., 379
Bentham, Jeremy, 365, 391
Bentzen, Ole, 379
Berezhnaya, Elena, 341
Berg, Alban, 62
Berger, Stuart M., 380
Bergerac, Cyrano de, 8
Bergkamp, Dennis, 355
Bergman, Ingrid, 39, 49
Bering, Vitus, 17
Berlin, Irving, 20
Berlin Wall, 429
Bernhardt, Sarah, 11
Bernstein, Leonard, 80
Best, George, 352
bestiality, 204
Bethune, Thomas 'Blind Tom', 404–5
Biaka-Boda, Victor, 437
Bible, 17–19, 184–5, 323–4, 366–7
Bierce, Ambrose, 177
Biggins, Joe, 56
Bill Hayley and His Comets, 68
Bill W., 105
billionaires, 163–7
bin Laden, Osama, 5, 29, 234
Bircher-Brenner, Max, 382
birds, 138–40, 416
Bishop, Jesse Walter, 214
Bissell, Richard, 312
Black Sabbath, 68
Blackfoot, J.D., 71
Blades, James, 84
Blake, Amanda, 221
Blake, William, 282
Bland, Sir Christopher, 309–11
Blatty, William Peter, 62
Bloch, Mark, 288
Block, Mandy, 115–16
Blondie, 68
Bloody Mary, 108
blues songs, 79
Boardman, Peter, 366
body parts, 100–1, 396–400
Bogart, Humphrey, 13, 36, 39, 41, 43, 49
Bok, Christian, 301
Bokassa, Jean-Bedel, 236
Bolan, Marc, 2
Bonaparte, Joseph, 435
Bonaparte, Lucien, 435
Bonaparte, Napoleon, 5, 185, 217, 244–5, 346–7, 435
Bond, Edward, 80
Bond, James (bird expert), 140
Bonham, Jon, 85
Bonington, Sir Chris, 356–60
books *see* literature
booksellers, 295–6
Boone, Daniel, 373
Boone, Richard, 59
Booth, John Wilkes, 27, 104, 262
Booth, Mary Ann Holmes, 27
Borah, William, 427
Borges, Jorge Luis, 160, 308
Borgia, Cardinal Rodrigo, 28
Borgia, Cesare, 28
Boston Molasses Flood, Great, 247–8
Boston Tea Party, 103
Botticelli, Sandro, 72
Boulle, Pierre, 314
Bourdain, Anthony, 58–9
Bowden, Pvt Daniel, 197
Bowles, Jane, 313
Bowles, Paul, 313
Bowman, Ruth, 73
boxes, 404
boxing, 340–1, 360–2
Boyer, Charles, 36, 49
Boyle, Michael 'Umbrella Mike', 199
Bradbury, Ray, 46, 314
Bradford City FC, 156
Bradford, Keith, 192
Brahe, Tycho, 8
Brahms, Johannes, 263
Braine, John, 160
Branagh, Kenneth, 36–7
Brand, Stewart, 308
Brando, Marlon, 37, 41
Brandreth, Gyles, 299–300
Brauge, Trygve, 395
Brazana, Ramon, 440
Brecht, Bertolt, 46, 80

Breland, Mark, 351
Brennan, Walter, 50
Brett, Brig Gen George H., 427
Brigati, Eddie, 223
Briseno, Theodore J., 213
British Lawnmower Museum, 263–4
Brix, Herman, 350
Broca, Paul, 397
Broccoli, Albert, 39
Bronx Calendar Twins, 405
Brook, Peter, 80
Broshears, Minister Raymond, 251
Brown, Cathy, 290
Brown, Charles Wayne, 221
Brown, Drew 'Bundini', 324
Brown, James, 84
Brown, Richard 'Rabbit', 79
Brown, Tina, 13, 180
Browning, Elizabeth Barrett, 10, 298
Bucar, King of Morocco, 389
Buchalter, Louis 'Lepke', 199
Buchanan, President James, 405
Buchinger, Matthew, 90
Buckingham, Duke of, 348
Buffalo Bill, 91
Buffett, Warren, 163–4
Bukowski, Charles, 46
bulls, 190, 209
Bunyan, Clive, 195
Burdon, Eric, 223
Burgess, Anthony, 106
Burke, Martha, 218–19
Burke, Pat, 367
Burmann, Gottlob, 300
Burnham, Alice, 436
Burns, Robert, 282
Burr, Aaron, 349
Burroughs, Edgar Rice, 136
Burroughs, William S., 284, 294, 297, 313–14
Burstyn, Ellen, 50
Burton, Dee, 288
Burton, Isabel, 379
Burton, Mark, 223
Burton, Richard, 35–6
Bush, Barbara, 27
Bush, President George, 11, 238
Bush, President George W., 27, 258
Bush, Guy, 440
Bushman (gorilla), 394
Bussey, Woodrow W., 218
Butchell, Martin van, 390–1
Butler, Samuel, 324
Buxton, Laura, 407–8
Buzzcocks (band), 82
Byrds (band), 68
Byrne, Charles, 390
Byron, Lord, 360

Caan, James, 59
Cabot family, 216
Cage, John, 308
Cage, Nicolas, 15
Cagney, James, 37, 49
Caillaux, Henriette, 210–11
Cain, James M., 293
Calchas (soothsayer), 377–8
Calmette, Gaston, 210–11
calories, 122
Cambodian Coup, 255–6
camels, 142
Cameron, James, 45
Camus, Albert, 281
Canada, Miss, 441
Canning, George, 348–9
Cannon, Dr Walter, 96
Capone, Al, 27, 198–201
Capone, Teresa, 27
Capote, Truman, 46, 297
Capranica, Robert R., 286
Caravaggio, 116
careers *see* work and money
Carlos the Jackal, 234
Carlos, John, 337
Carman, Marie Élénore Maillé de, 28
Caroline of Brunswick, Princess, 103–4
Carpio, Lope de Vega, 300
Carrey, Jim, 56
Carroll, Earl, 436
Carroll, Lewis, 292, 343–4
cars, 404
Carson, Johnny, 178
Carter, Benny, 76
Carter family, 77
Carter, Helena Bonham, 36–7
Carter, Howard, 388
Carter, President Jimmy, 256

INDEX

Caruso, Enrico, 10, 394
Carver, Raymond, 313
Casanova, 159
Cash, Johnny, 71, 76–7
Caspian Sea, 91
Cassady, Neal, 284
Casson, Benny, 225
Castillo, Luis Angel, 251
Castlereagh, Lord, 348
Castro, Fidel, 219, 235, 253
Castro, Inés De, 389
Cather, Willa, 312
Catherine of Valois, 389–90
cats, 133–4, 143, 207–9
Cattanei, Vannozza dei, 28
Ceausescu, Nicolae, 263
celebrities, 15–16
 marriage and, 175–6
 reading own obituary, 373–7
 see also famous people; people
Céline, Louis Ferdinand, 314
censorship, 173
Cervantes, Miguel de, 280
Cézanne, Paul, 72–3
Chain, Ernest, 431–2
Champagne, Jeanne, 218
Chandka Forest Elephant Stampede, 250
Chandler, Christopher, 407
Chandler, Jeff, 60
Chandler, Raymond, 46, 282, 304, 315
Chapin, Dr James P., 146
Chaplin, Charlie, 5, 43–4, 57, 60
Charlemagne, 388–9
Charles I, 348
Charles II, 30, 390
Charlotte, Princess, 104
Chatterton, Thomas, 411
cheeses, mammoth, 98–100
Cheney, Dick, 429
Cherry Sisters, 86–7
Chesselet, Alyn, 217–18
Chevalier Jackson collection, 262
Chevalier, Maurice, 61
Chicago (band), 68
Chicago Seven, 212–13
children, 134–8
Chinese Brigade in Burma, 254
Chopin, Frédéric, 414
Christian VI, King (Denmark), 102
Christo, 371
Christopherson, Tina, 369
Churchill, Winston, 5, 15, 162
CIA, 219, 250–3, 254–8
Cinnamon, Gerri, 419–20
Cinnamon, Leroy, 419–20
circuses, 199, 208
Clapton, Eric, 84
Clark, Guy, 214
Clark, Stanley, 84
Clarke, Charlie, 359
Clarke, Kenny, 76
Claudius I, Emperor, 26
Clement, Jack, 71
Clemons, Alonzo, 405
Cleveland, President Grover, 262
Clift, Montgomery, 38, 41
Clinton, President Bill, 2–3, 11–12
Close, Del, 397
Coates, Ronald, 87
Cobain, Kurt, 2
Cohen, Herb, 223
Colbert, Claudette, 39
Cole, Lloyd, 83
Coll, Vincent 'Mad Dog', 200
Collins, Jackie, 13
Collins, Tom, 109
Colombo, Joseph, 55
Colossus of Rhodes, 267
Columbus, Christopher, 17
Columbus Industrial Association, 122
Comanche (horse), 392
comedies, 65
commanders, 241–3
Confucius, 323
Congo Mercenary Force, 255
Connery, Sean, 38–9, 44
Connolly, Mrs Lynn, 409–10
conquerors, 244–5
Conrad, Joseph, 314, 346
Constant, Emmanuel 'Toto', 258
Constantine the Great, 114
Cooke, George Frederick, 397–8
Cooper, Gary, 41, 49–50
Cooper, Jackie, 54
Cooper, James Fenimore, 297
Cooper, Merian C., 42
Coppola, Francis Ford, 40
Corbett, Jim, 130

Corbin, Myrtle, 6
Corday, Charlotte, 434
Corelli, Marie, 304
Coren, Stanley, 152
Cornishman V (horse), 351
Cortes, Hernando, 245
Corti, Alfonso, 100
Costa, Mario, 51
Cottin, Angelique, 118
Coué, Émile, 381
countries, 243, 245–6, 267–8
country songs, 76–7
Courtenay-Latimer, Ms M., 147
Cousins, Gregory, 106
Coviello, Nicolas, 370–1
Crabbe, Buster, 350
Cranagh, Lucas, 72
Credence Clearwater Revival, 68
Crichton, Michael, 46
crime, 189–225
  animals and insects, 202–10
  films, 58–9
  lawsuits, 215–55
  stolen objects, 190–2
  stupid thieves, 193–8
  underworld nicknames, 198–202
  verdicts and riots, 210–14
  witticisms of condemned, 214–15
Criquielion, Claude, 220
crises, personal, 96–8
crocodiles, 129, 140
Crofts, Charles, 348
Cronin, David, 221
Crosby, John, 52
Crowe, Cameron, 45
Crowhurst, Donald, 305–6
Cruise, Tom, 56
Cruyff, Johann, 352
crying in public, 2–4
Cukor, George, 54
Cummings Jr, Marshall George, 195
Cutler, R.B., 251
Cuvier, Baron Georges, 145
Cyrus the Great, 244

D

Da Vinci, Leonardo, 161
Dahl, Roald, 46, 302–3
Daigle, Beatrice, 218
Dalai Lama, 254
Dali, Salvador, 13
Daltrey, Roger, 13
Dan White Case, 213
Danga II (mountain), 360
Dangerfield, Rodney, 178
Daniels, Josephus, 427
Dante, 10
Darby, Rev John, 92
Darwin, Charles, 5, 322
Dassin, Jules, 58
David, Christian, 250
David, Warrior King, 3
Davies, Charles, 387
Davies, Martin, 290
Davis, Adelle, 382
Davis, Bette, 38, 377
Davis, Gov Gray, 230
Davis, Miles, 76
Dawkins, Richard, 309
De Coubertin, Baron Pierre, 398
De Mille, Nelson, 304
De Palma, Brian, 59
Dean, Carl, 180
Dean, James, 2, 39
death, 96–7, 365–400
  by laughing, 377
  by playing cards, 379–80
  cases killed by God, 366–7
  of health experts, 380–5
  obituaries, 373–7
  and preservation, 388–96
    body parts, 396–400
  of Princess Diana, 107
  strange, 367–73
  timely, 386–8
del Valle, Eladio, 251
Dell Computers, 164–5
Dell, Michael, 164–5
Dellwo, Lt Thomas, 241
Demento, Dr, 70–1
Demetrios I, Patriarch, 173
Demme, Jonathan, 39
Dempsey, Jack, 361
Denghai, Xu, 116
Depeche Mode (band), 68
Desai, Prime Minister Morarji, 377
Deschevaux-Dumesnil, Suzanne, 180
Devitt, John, 339

Dexter, Pete, 313
Di Stefano, Alfredo, 352, 355
Diamond, Jared, 309
Diana, Princess, 2, 107
Diana, temple of, 266
Dias, Bartholomeu, 268
Diaz, Dayami, 224
Dick, Philip K., 305
Dickens, Charles, 5, 280, 292, 303, 314
Dickinson, Emily, 311
dictators, 231–6
Dietrich, Marlene, 64, 119
Digby, Jane, 373–4
Diller, Phyllis, 121
Dillinger, John, 60, 186–7
disasters, unusual, 246–50
Disraeli, Benjamin, 92, 178
documentaries, 63–4
Dodd, Phineas, 215
dogs, 143, 152, 209–10, 223–4, 392
    Dog Collar Museum, 262
Doherty, Peter, 352
Doisneau, Robert, 172
Dolly (sheep), 396
Dom Pérignon, 108
Dombey, Samuel, 21–2
Domitian, Emperor, 386
Donahue, Hessie, 360–1
Donahue, Howard, 252
Donellan, Declan, 81
Donen, Stanley, 62
Doody, Rachelle, 117
Dos Santos, Jean Baptista, 6
Dostoevsky, Fyodor, 304
Doto, Joseph 'Joe Adonis', 200
Douglas, Helen Gahagan, 228
Douglas, Kirk, 38, 44
Douglas, Melvyn, 228
Downes, Jon, 149
Doyle, Sir Arthur Conan, 280, 304
Dreiser, Theodore, 297
Dreyfus Affair, 210
Dreyfus, Alfred, 210
drinks, 108–9
drummers of note, 84–5
Du Maurier, Daphne, 280
Duchamp, Marcel, 159
duels, 345–9
Duff, James, 215–16
Dumas, Alexander, 119
Dumas, Blanche, 6
Dunaway, Faye, 38
Dunlop, John, 298
Dunn, Mark, 301
Dunsdon, Nicole, 441
Dupont, Captain, 346
Durutti Column (band), 83
Durzo, Johnny, 71
Duvalier, François 'Papa Doc', 236–7
Duvalier, Jean-Claude 'Baby Doc', 236–7
Duvalier, Michelle, 237
Dwan, Allan, 51
Dyche, Prof Lewis, 392
Dyer, Geoff, 78–9
Dylan, Bob, 70, 77–8
Dzhugashvili, Ekaterina Gheladze, 28

E

earth surface names, 16–17
Eastern Sea (moon), 92
Eastwood, Clint, 92, 177, 228, 279
eBay sales, 156
Eckler, A. Ross, 300
Eddy, Mary Baker, 385
Edeshko, Ivan, 340
Edison, Thomas, 171
Edward IV, King, 93
Edward VII, King, 370
Edwards, Blake, 180
Edwards, Frank, 418
Edwards, Geoff, 221
Egan, Richard, 51
Eggers, Dave, 404
Eiffel Tower, 91
Eiger, 357–8
Einstein, Albert, 5, 398
Eisenhower, Mamie, 163
Eisenstadt, Alfred, 171
Eisenstein, Sergei, 241
El Cid, 389
'El Negro', 395
Elder, Kate, 9
Eldridge, Roy, 76
Eldridge, Walter, 208
elephants, 142, 208, 250, 391
Elford, F.C., 289
Eliot, George Fielding, 427
Elizabeth I, Queen, 8, 93

Elizabeth II, Queen, 92
Ellenborough, Lady Jane, 373–4
Ellenborough, Lord, 373
Ellis, Albert, 183
Ellis, Brett Easton, 282
Emerald, Connie, 51
Eminem (band), 15
Empire State Building Crash, 248–9, 273
Eno, Brian, 308–9
entertainment, wretched, 86–9
Erben, Dr Herman F., 50
Eric the Red, 268
esoteric studies, 285–91
Estrada, Joseph, 228
Eusébio (footballer), 352
Eustachio, Bartolommeo, 100
Evans, Harold, 180
Evans, Hilary, 117
Everage, Dame Edna, 225
Everest, 358
explosions, 248–9
expulsion from school, 12–15
extinction, 138–40, 143–4
Exxon Valdez Oil Spill, 106–7
Eyre, Richard, 79–81
Eyton, Audrey, 295

F

Fabris, Jean, 73
fact stranger than fiction, 305–7
Fadiman, Clifton, 297
Failed Soviet Coup, 107
Faisal, King (Saudi Arabia), 173
Fallopius, Gabriel, 100–1
famous people
  bands, 68
  expelled from school, 12–15
  insomniacs, 119–20
  inventing games, 343–5
  as librarians, 159–60
  meetings of, 9–12
  mothers of infamous men, 26–30
  and mothers' maiden name, 5
  working in bed, 160–3
  writers, 46–8
  see also celebrities; movies; people
Fantin, Mario, 285
Fantin-Latour, Ignace, 161–2
Faraday, Michael, 116
fashion, 428
Faulkner, William, 20, 46, 293, 297, 312
Faure, Elie, 303
FBI, 250, 253
Felton, Bruce, 437–40
Ferguson, Rob, 359
Ferrell, Mary, 252
Ferrie, David 'Carlos', 251
Ferron, Jacques, 204–5
Feu, Paul de, 176
fiction, fact stranger than, 305–7
Field, Henry, 287
Fields, W.C., 38, 106, 119, 322
Files, James, 253
films *see* movies
Finch, Peter, 172
Fink, Jon-Stephen, 286
Finn, George and Charles, 405
Finn, Mickey, 108–9
Finney, Tom, 352
Finnis, Col John, 241
fires, 248, 410, 416
Firpo, Luis, 361
fish, 141, 147, 418
Fitzgerald, F. Scott, 46, 163, 293, 297, 304, 314
Fitzherbert, Mrs, 103, 378
Flaubert, Gustave, 14, 297
Fleming, Dr Alexander, 431–2
Fleming, Ian, 39
Fleming, Victor, 54
Florey, Howard, 431–2
Floyd, Charles 'Pretty Boy', 200
Flynn, Errol, 38, 50
Foldi family, 6
Foley, Kevin, 223–4
Fonda, Jane, 38
Fondriest, Maurizio, 220
Fong-fond, Josephine Siao, 54
Food and Agriculture Organization of the United Nations (FAO), 132
food and health, 95–122
  alcohol and events, 102–7
  aphrodisiacs, 180–2
  body parts, 100–1
  calorie consumption, 122
  cheeses, mammoth, 98–100
  death of experts, 380–5
  drink names, 108–9

insomnia, 119–22
Italian soups, 109–10
Italian wines, 110–11
medical conditions, 116–19
personal crises, 96–8
recipes, 112–14
sausage events, 114–16
football, 352–5
Ford, Dorothy, 57
Ford, Harrison, 56
Forest, Lee De, 426
Forsyth, Frederick, 295
Fort, Charles, 407
Foster, Jodie, 39
Fournier, Captain, 346
Fowles, John, 12, 294, 315
Fox, Margaret, 218
Fox, Robin, 308
Frambini, Rev Bob, 191
Francis, Dick, 351
Franciscan friars, 207
Frank, Anne, 2, 413–14
Frank, Otto, 414
Franklin, Benjamin, 434
Fréchette, Sylvie, 341
Frederick II, Holy Roman Emperor, 389
French, James Donald, 214
French Revolution, 160
Fresquez, Richard, 371
Freud, Sigmund, 5
Friedkin, William, 62–3
Friel, Anna, 174
Frisch, Karl von, 309
Frost, Robert, 312
Fuentes, Carlos, 46
Fuller, Mary C., 417
Fuller, Thomas, 405
funguses, 430–3

Gable, Clark, 11, 39, 60
Gabor, Zsa Zsa, 175
Gadd, Steve, 84–5
Gaddis, William, 297
Galileo, 398
Gallico, Paul, 361
Galluccio, Frank, 200
Garbo, Greta, 49–50
Garden of Eden, 269–71
Gardner, Ava, 190
Garland, Judy, 57, 119
Garrincha (footballer), 352
Gascoigne, Paul, 3
Gaskill, Bill, 80
Gates, Bill, 165
Gaughan, Dick, 83
Gay Book of Lists, 132
gay rights, 172–4, 213
Genet, Jean, 285, 314
Genghis Khan, 244
Genker, Charles 'Monkey Face', 200
Genovese, Eugene, 309
George III, King, 103, 348
George IV, King, 103–4, 347
George V, King, 381
George VI, King, 93
Gernreich, Rudi, 428
Getty, J. Paul, 361
Ghanem, Alia, 29
Gibson, Don, 77
Gibson, Harry, 70
Gibson, Mel, 56
Gielgud, Sir John, 57
gigs, 81–3
Gillespie, Dizzy, 75–6
Gillingham Fire 'Demonstration', 248
Gingrich, Newt, 429
Ginsberg, Allen, 79, 284–5
Girardelli, Signora, 90
Gish, Lillian, 11
glasnost, 107
Glass, David, 167
Glenn, John, 436–7
Gluck, James Fraser, 75
Goddard, Professor Robert, 426–7
Godwin, Michael Anderson, 372
Goebbels, Joseph, 413
Goethe, Johann Wolfgang von, 5
Goetzinger, Bryan, 191–2
Golikov, Capt Yevgeny, 241
Goncourt, Edmond de, 411–12
Gonzales, Johnny, 342
Gonzales, José, 198
Goodhall, David, 193
Gooding Jr, Cuba, 45
Gorbachev, Mikhail, 4, 107
Gordon, Gen Charles, 270–1
Göring, Reichsmarschall Hermann, 323

Gorki, Arshile, 73
Gorki, Maxim, 80
Graham, Benjamin, 164
Graham, Sylvester, 380–1
Grandes Jorasses, 357–8
Grandpré, Monsieur de, 349–50
Grandy, Fred, 228
Grant, Cary, 39, 49
Grant, Ulysses S., 20
Gray, Rose, 110–11
Great Pyramid of Cheops, 265
Greeley, Horace, 322
Green, Dr Joseph, 386
Greene, Graham, 46–7, 304, 313
Greenwood, John, 400
Greer, Germaine, 176
Grienebner, Hans, 207
Griffith, D.W., 11, 51, 53
Grizzard, Lewis, 177
Grosz, George, 405
ground, 404
Grundman, David N., 368
Guarini, Justin, 89
Guatemalan Rebel Army, 254
Guevara, Ernesto 'Che', 2, 16
Guidarelli, Guidarello, 171
Guillou, Joseph, 115
gunmen, 250–3
Gurney, Gene, 290
Gustavus II, King (Sweden), 241
Guyart, Guillaume, 204
Guzik, Jake 'Greasy Thumb', 200–1
Gypsy Rose Lee, 262
Gysin, Brion, 314

H

Haakon VII, King (Norway), 436
Hackman, Gene, 39, 40
Hagenbeck, Karl, 145
Hahnemann, Samuel, 385
Haile Selassie, 238
Haitian Coups, 257–8
Hakim, Abdel, 175
Hale, Sarah J., 192
Haley, Alex, 92, 294
Haley, Bill, 60
Hall, Loran, 251
Hall, Peter, 80
Hall, Ron, 305–6
Halpern, Charen, 397
Hamer, Rep Thomas L., 20
Hamilton, Alexander, 349
Hammerstein, Oscar, 86
Hammett, Dashiell, 47
Hammond, Joyce, 203
Hanfstängl, Ernst 'Putzi', 413
Hanging Gardens of Babylon, 265
Hanks, Tom, 45, 56
Hansen, Tom, 217
Hardin, Garrett, 308
Hardwood, H.C., 299
Hardy, Oliver, 179
Hargis, David, 24–5
Harlan, Lt Richard, 241
Harness, Charles, 305
Harrelson, Charles V., 250
Harrelson, Woody, 250
Harris, Robert Alton, 214
Harrison, Harry, 305
Harrison, Jim, 313
Hartley, L.P., 281
Hartmann, Sadakichi, 87
Harvey, Tom, 108
Harveywallbangers, 108
Hassan, King (Morocco), 115
Haston, Dougal, 358
Hawking, Stephen, 296
Hawkins, Coleman, 76
Hawthorne, Nathaniel, 311
Hayden, Sterling, 58
Haydn, Joseph, 398–9
Haywood, Ritchie, 85
Hazelwood, Captain Joseph, 106
Head, Murray, 172
health *see* food and health
Hearst, William Randolph, 14, 200, 426
Heart, Busty, 225
Heath, Ted (musician), 85
Heck, Heinz, 144
Heck, Lutz, 144
Hefner, Hugh, 163
Heine, Heinrich, 177
Heiss, Carol, 351
Heller, Joseph, 281, 294, 297
Hemingway, Ernest, 5, 47, 361, 377
  literature, 280, 293, 297–8, 312–14
Hemingway, Mariel, 174
Hendricks, Scott, 71

Hendrix, Jimi, 2, 223
Henie, Sonja, 350
Henrietta Maria, Queen, 348
Henry IV, King, 91
Henry V, King, 389
Henry VII, King, 93, 389
Hepburn, Audrey, 59
Hepburn, Katharine, 35, 54, 178
Herpen, Ruth van, 173
Herrera, Carlos, 109
Hertogh, Adeline, 212
Hertogh, Maria, 212
Heston, Charlton, 39–40
Hickey Jr, George, 252–3
Hickok, James Butler 'Wild Bill', 374, 379–80
Hicks, Kirsten, 133
Hicks, Thomas, 338
Higgins, George V., 313
Hill, Bob, 416
Hilton, James, 304
Hines, Earl 'Fatha', 76
hippopotamuses, 126, 142, 145–6
Hirot, B.C., 262
history
  and esoteric studies, 285–91
  funguses and, 430–3
  movies and, 60–2
  worst ideas in recent, 437–40
Hitchcock, Alfred, 60
Hitler, Adolf, 28–9, 60, 413, 437–8
  world affairs and, 239, 244, 428
Hitler, Klara Pölzl, 28–9
Hobbes, Thomas, 161
Hodges, Mike, 58
Hodgson, Bob, 197
Hoffman, Abbie, 212
Hoffman, Dustin, 41
Hogg, Thomas Jefferson, 14
Hogshire, Jim, 290
Holden, Edith, 295
Holden, William, 38, 43, 54
Holdstock, Robert, 305
Holloway, Stanley, 37
Holly, Buddy, 20
Holm, Eleanor, 350–1
Holmes, T.H., 96
Holt, John T., 219
Honecker, Erich, 237
Hooker, John Lee, 3
Hooper, Tobe, 59
Hoover, J. Edgar, 160
Hopkins, Anthony, 39
Horne, Lena, 63
Horsley, Tom, 217–18
Hoskins, Bob, 59
Houdini, Harry, 377
Howarth, Humphrey, 347
Hu Jintao, 232
Hudson, Jeffrey, 348
Hudson, Rock, 50–1
Hugo, Victor, 412
Hume, David, 14, 159
Humphries, Barry, 225
Humphry, Mrs, 292
Huncke, Herbert, 284
Hung, William, 89
Hunt, 'Golf Bag' Sam, 201
Hunter, John, 390
Hussein, Saddam, 30, 237
Huston, John, 41, 58, 62
Huston, Walter, 49
Huxley, Aldous, 47, 298

I

ibn Mussad Abdel Aziz, Prince Faisal, 173
Ibn-Saud, King (Saudi Arabia), 17
Ibsen, Henrik, 386–7
Icelandic Phallological Museum, 261, 264
ideas, worst, 437–40
Iggy Pop (band), 82
incestuous couples, 184–5
indestructable people, 21–6
infamous men, mothers of, 26–30
insects, 202–10
insomnia, 119–22
Inter-Parliamentary Union, 246
Irving, Amy, 59
Irving, Washington, 9–10
Irwin, May, 171
Isherwood, Christopher, 47
Italians, 100–1, 109–11
Ito, Nitara, 372

J

Jackson, President Andrew, 99
Jackson, Glenda, 229

Jackson, Janet, 15, 89
Jackson, John 'Gentleman', 360
Jackson, Michael, 5
Jackson, Peter, 16
Jackson, Gen Thomas 'Stonewall', 241–2
Jagger, Mick, 5
Jahaleen, Eid Saleb al, 198
Jairzinho (footballer), 353
James I, King, 102, 434
James, Henry, 311
James, Jesse (bandit), 29
James, Jesse S., 290
James, Skip, 79
James, Steve, 64
James, Zerelda Cole, 29
Janek, Miroslav, 64
Jarvis, D.C., 384
Jay, Ricky, 89–91
Jaynes, Julian, 306
jazz, 75–6, 370–1
Jefferson, President Thomas, 5, 99, 217, 323, 349
 death of, 377, 386
Jenkins, Florence Foster, 87–8
Jenner, Bruce, 351
Jennings, Humphrey, 64
Jernigan, Joseph Paul, 396
Jersey, Lady, 103
Jobs, Steve, 166
John II, King (Portugal), 268
Johnson, Allison, 117
Johnson, Vice President Andrew, 104
Johnson, Chris, 290
Johnson, J.J., 76
Johnson, President Lyndon B., 428
Johnson, Robert, 79
Johnson, Samuel, 298
Johnson, Terry, 195
Johnson, Virginia E., 183
Johnston, Lynn, 388
Johnston, Sir Harry, 145
Johst, Hanns, 323
Jolie, Angelina, 37
Jolson, Al, 380
Jones, Ben, 229
Jones, John Paul, 85
Jones Jr, Roy, 340–1
Jones, Penn, 251
Jones, R. William, 340
Jones, Thornton, 370
Jones, Virginia Lucille, 179
Joplin, Janis, 2
Jordan, Michael, 3–4
Joubert, Joseph, 178
Joy Division (band), 82
Joyce, James, 292, 298
Jumbo the elephant, 391

K

Kabila, Laurent, 238
Kabotchnik, Harry, 216
Kafka, Franz, 120, 281
Kama Sutra, 182–3
Kamprad, Ingvar, 165
Kapoor, Shashi, 173
Karloff, Boris, 41
Karpis, Alvin 'Kreepy', 201
Kawthar of Tunisia, 175
Kazan, Elia, 44
Kazin, Alfred, 298
Keating, Ronan, 156
Keaton, Buster, 44, 351, 380
Keats, John, 283
Keevil-Matthews, Lori Jean, 371
Kelly, Gene, 62, 191–2
Kelly, George 'Machine Gun', 201
Keneally, Thomas, 414
Kennedy Onassis, Jacqueline, 61, 251, 253
Kennedy, President John F., 2, 11–12, 61, 250–3
Kennedy Shriver, Eunice, 230
Kennedy, William, 47
Kenyon, John, 10
Kerouac, Jack, 284
Khamba Horsemen, 254
Khomeini, Ayatollah, 263
Khrushchev, Nikita, 61
Kichizo, Ishida, 187
Kidd, Capt William, 103
Kidd, Walter, 289
Killy, Jean-Claude, 14, 339, 351
Kilsey, W.L., 98
Kim IL Sung, 231
Kim IL Sung Gift Museum, 262–3
Kim Jong IL, 227, 231, 235, 263
King, B.B, 285
King Cobra (mountain), 357

King, Henry, 50
King Jr, Martin Luther, 2, 285
King, Marjorie, 109
King, Rodney, 190, 213
King, Stephen, 5, 59–60, 294
Kinks (band), 82
Kinsey, Alfred C., 182–4
kisses, 170–5
Kneipp, Sebastian, 383–4
Knowles, Roderic, 291
Koestler, Arthur, 304
Kolingba, Gen Andre, 236
Komodo dragons, 146
Komodo dragons129
Kondrashkin, Vladimir, 340
Kongur (mountain), 358
Koons, Stacey C., 213
Kopietz, Heino, 429
Kottowitz, Anna von, 375
Krafft-Ebing, Richard von, 376
Krakauer, Jon, 306
Kramer, Stanley, 41
Kravitz, Lenny, 89
Kubrick, Stanley, 44, 58, 63
Kuehl, Sheila, 229
Kugler, Kay, 192
Kühn, Ruth, 413
Kurd Rebels, 256
Küttel, Josef, 343

L

La Brash, George E., 220
La Cava, Gregory, 54
La Manch Negra, 409
La Rue, Al 'Lash', 57
Laattsch, Joe, 196
Ladd, Alan, 39
Lafayette, Marquis de, 190
Laloo, 6
Lamarr, Hedy, 39, 49
Lancaster, Burt, 39
Landale, James, 345–9
Langley, Professor Samuel, 425
Lanzmann, Claude, 64
Lao-Tzu (writer), 303, 323
Larkin, Philip, 160
L'Armée Clandestine, 255
Larson, Lance, 339
Lashkevich, Capt, 242
Lasser, Louise, 45
Laurents, Arthur, 80
LaVigne, Michelle, 291
Law, Denis, 355
Lawrence, D.H., 78, 292
Lawrence, Syd, 85
lawsuits, unusual, 215–25
Laytner, Ron, 252
Le Carré, John, 304
Le, Stephen, 196
Leach, Bobby, 370
Leadbelly, 79
Leahy, Admiral William, 428
Led Zeppelin (band), 68, 85
Lee, Bruce, 2
Lee, Harper, 281
Lee, Tommy, 179–80
Legman, Gershon, 182
Lehrer, Lonnie, 209–10
Leifer, Carol, 178
Leigh, Janet, 51
Leigh, Vivien, 34, 38
Lemke, Leslie, 405
Lemon Mountains, 359
Lenin, V.I., 323, 393
Lennon, John, 2, 178
Lentini, Francesco, 1, 6–7
Leonard, Elmore, 312
Leonard, Eric, 209
leopards, 130, 137
Lepage, Robert, 81
Lerman, Jonathan, 405
Lewis, Sinclair, 293, 298
Li Po (poet), 367
Libbera, Jean, 7
librarians, 159–60
Life of Pi (Yann Martel), 275–6
lifespan of animals, 142–3
Lighthouse of Pharos, 267
Limbaugh, Rush, 3
limbs and digits, extra, 6–7
Lincoln, Abraham, 5, 27, 104, 177
Lind, Jenny, 375
Lindblom, Gerhard, 287
Lineker, Gary, 63
lines
  beginning novels, 280–2
  Bob Dylan's, 78–9
  ending novels, 314–15

erroneously attributed, 49–50
of national anthems, 68–70
lions, 130, 143
lipograms, 299–301
Lipton, Kenneth, 222
Lisciarelli, Arturo, 10
literature, 279–315
American authors, 311–12
authors, favourite, 304
books
fact stranger than fiction, 305–7
mind-changing, 308–9
for a new planet, 302–3
reference, 309–11
unlikely how-to, 291–2
histories and esoteric studies, 285–91
lipograms, 299–301
novels
beginnings to, 280–2
favourite, 312–13
last lines of, 314–15
poets earning a living, 282–5
reviews, 296–9
science fiction, 304–5
strange stories, 407–40
surprise best sellers, 295–6
titles
original, 292–4
scholarly, 78–9
writers, 302–4
Little Feat (band), 85
Little, Graham, 359
Lloyd, Arthur, 90
Locke, John, 14
Loeffelbein, L., 288
Lofty, Margaret, 436
Logan, Joshua, 54
Lollobridgida, Gina, 51
Lomax, Alan, 309
Lombard, Carole, 51
Lombardi, Vince, 323
Lombardo, Tullio, 170
Lon Nol, 256
Longfellow, Henry Wadsworth, 161
Longhurst, Simon, 369
Lonsdale, 5th Earl of, 362
Loren, Sophia, 229
Lorre, Peter, 36
Lorz, Fred, 338
lost property, 264
Louis XI, King (France), 160
Louis XV, King (France), 160, 411
Louis XVIII, (France), 74
Louise L., 7
love *see* sex, love and marriage
Lovell, Stanley, 437
Loveridge, Marguerite, 51
Lowell, Amy, 119
Lowther, Hugh, 362
Lowther, Jim, 359
Loy, Myrna, 39
Luciano, Charles 'Lucky', 201
Ludendorff, Gen Erich, 105
Ludwig, King (Bavaria), 374
Luetgert, Adolph, 115
Lumet, Sidney, 63
Lumley, Joanna, 156
Lund, David, 85
Lupino, Ida, 51
Luria, A.R., 306
Lutz, Tom, 3
Lydekker, Richard, 145
Lyne, Adrian, 63
Lynryd Skynyrd (band), 68
lynx spiders, 128

M

Maalin, Ali Maow, 440
McAlea, Edward, 194
McCall, Jack, 380
McCartney, Paul, 377
McCrew, Anderson, 392–3
McDonald, Hugh, 252
MacDonald, Jeanette, 377
Macdonald, Kevin, 63–4
Macfadden, Bernard, 384–5
McGehan, Thomas, 368–9
MacGraw, Ali, 40
McGregor, Ewan, 40
MacGregor, Major, 333
Macgregor, Robert 'Rob Roy', 109
McGuire, Ivan, 372
McIntyre, James, 99
McKellan, Sir Ian, 38
Mackenzie, John, 59
MacKinnon, John, 148
Mackowski, Carmen, 219
MacLaine, Shirley, 61

McLaughlin, Terence, 287
MacLaurin, Dr C., 185
MacLean, Charles, 306–7
McLean, Don, 392
MacLeish, Archibald, 159
McLeod, Duncan, 215
McManus, Hump, 380
McMurtry, Larry, 47
McNamara, Robert, 428
McQueen, Steve, 40
Madison, Helene, 350
Madonna, 174, 191
Madsen, Michael, 40
Madsen, Wayne, 258
Mafia, 198–202, 250–1, 253
Magellan, Ferdinand, 268
Magherini, Dr Graziella, 116
Mahmud of Ghazni, 245
maiden names, 5
Mailer, Norman, 47, 307
Malcolm X, 2, 92
Mallarmé, Stéphane, 412
Malloy, Michael, 22–3
Mamas and the Papas, 68
Mamet, David, 57
Manilow, Barry, 224
Manivet, Jean-Pierre, 221
Mankiewicz, Joseph, 35–6, 62
Mann, Michael, 59
Mansfield, Jayne, 351
Mansi, Sandra, 150
Mao Tse Tung, 16, 159, 394
Maradona, Diego, 352
Marat, Jean-Paul, 434
Marciano, Rocky, 2
Marconi, Guglielmo, 412
Marcos, Ferdinand, 264
Marcos, Imelda, 264
Marcus, Col David, 242
Margarita (cocktail), 109
Maria Hertogh Custody Case, 212
Marikina City Footwear Museum, 264
Markowitz, Burt, 405
Marley, Bob, 2
Marquez, Gabriel García, 280
marriage *see* sex, love and marriage
Marsh, Mae, 51
Marshall, Chief Justice John, 262
Martel, Yann, 275–6
Martial (poet), 178, 183
Martin, Jean, 205
Martin, Martin, 306
Martin, Ricky, 89
Marvin, Lee, 38
Marx, Groucho, 55, 120, 178
Marx, Karl, 5, 307
Mary I, Queen, 108
Mary Queen of Scots, 108
Masiello, Joe, 191
Mason, Bobbie Ann, 313
Massaro, Daniele, 354
Massie, Robert K., 309
Masters, William H., 183
Mather, Cotton, 204
Mathias, Bob, 351
mating habits, 126–8
Matsumo, Kazuhiko, 372
Matsuyama, Chunosuke, 333–4
Matthau, Walter, 65
Matthews, Sir Stanley, 352
Maud, Queen, 16–17
Maugham, W. Somerset, 177, 304, 314
Maupassant, Guy de, 10, 412
Mausolus, King (Caria), 266
Max Planck Institute, 143
Mayle, Peter, 296
Mayo, Gerald, 217
Maysles, Albert, 64
Maysles, David, 64
Meacham, John, 196
medical conditions, 116–19
Medical Museum of the Armed Forces Institute of Pathology, 186
Medjuel, Sheik, 374
Meister, Hulda, 376
Meliton of Chalcedon, Metropolitan, 173
Mellencamp, John, 16
Melville, Herman, 280, 311, 315
Melville, Jean-Pierre, 58
Mencken, H.L., 177
Mengistu Haile Mariam, 238
Menninger, Bonar, 252
Mercouri, Melina, 229
Meriweather, Charles A., 193
Mesmer, Franz, 384
messages in bottles, 333–4
Metchnikoff, Élie, 382–3

meteorites, 415, 419
Meyer, Dr Alfred, 96
Meyer, Kathleen, 291
Michelangelo, 8, 72, 116
Mickey Finn (cocktail), 108–9
Microsoft Corporation, 155, 165
Milding, William, 14th Earl of Streatham, 135
Miles, Carl, 208–9
Milk, Harvey, 213
Millardet, Pierre-Marie-Alexis, 433
Miller, Arthur, 47
Miller, B.J., 192
Miller, Elva, 88–9
Miller, Henry, 303–4
Ming Huang, Emperor, 367
Minnelli, Vincent, 62
Minnock, Tommy, 89
Mirren, Helen, 59
Mitchell, Alex, 379
Mitchell, Attorney Gen John, 213
Mitchell, Margaret, 293, 314
Mitchell, Nelly, 222–3
Mitchum, Robert, 58
Mittermeier, Dr Russell, 147
Mobuto, Sese Seko (Joseph), 238, 255
Modrow, John, 291
Mogwai (band), 83
monkeys, 138, 203, 205–6
Monmouth, Duke of, 390
Monroe, Marilyn, 2, 44, 262
monsters, lake and sea, 149–51
Montague, J.F., 286
Montaigne, Michel de, 177
Montesquieu-Fezenac, Robert de, 412
Moody, Jerome, 371
Moon, Keith, 85
moon landings, 428
Moon, Mary, 150
Moore, Archie, 362
Moore, Demi, 56
Moorman, Mary, 250
Mootageri, Shivshankari Yamanappa, 7
Moran, Thomas 'Butterfingers', 201–2
Morgan, Frank, 38
Morgan, George, 77
Morphy, Paul, 435
Morris, Errol, 63
Morris, Glenn, 350
Morris, W.B., 251
Morrison, Jim, 2, 437
Morstoel, Bredo, 395
Morton, Nails, 203
Moscone, George, 213
mothers
  of infamous men, 26–30
  maiden names of, 5
Motion, Andrew, 77–8
mountain climbing, 356–60
movies, 32–65
  comedies, 65
  crime films, 58–9
  discovery of stars, 50–2
  documentaries, 63–4
  favourite, 62–3
  film scenes cut, 41–5
  lines erroneously attributed, 49–50
  love on set, 34–7
  Olympic medalists and, 350–2
  as part of history, 60–2
  roles turned down, 37–41
  scariest scenes, 59–60
  tales of, 52–7
  writers working for, 46–8
Moyer, Milton, 416
Mozart, Wolfgang Amadeus, 5, 405
Mswati III, King (Swaziland), 235–6
MTV Celebrity Kissfest, 174
Mugabe, Robert, 232–3
Muhammad Ali, 324
Mundy, Bessie, 435–6
Murdoch, Iris, 12
Murphy, A.C., 288
Murray, Bill, 397
Musa, Mansa, 439
Museum of Bad Art, 262
museums, 262–4
Museveni, President Yoweri, 236
music *see* arts
Mussolini, Alessandria, 229
Mussolini, Benito, 14, 29
Mussolini, Rosa Maltoni, 29
mutilations, 410
Mütter Museum, 262
Myers, Mike, 397
Myers, Tom, 368
Myslivecek, Josef, 8

N

Nabokov, Vladimir, 280, 298
Nakaruma, Wasaaki, 371
names
  of body parts, 100–1
  changed by accident, 20
  drink, 108–9
  earth surface, 16–17
  of famous bands, 68
  maiden, 5
  underworld nicknames, 198–202
  unfortunate product, 158
  unlikely place, 268
  unnamed women, 17–19
  of unusual things, 319–21
Narayan, J.P., 377
Nashe, Thomas, 314
Nat Turner Rebellion, 104
Nath, N., 71
national anthems, 68–70
Naylor, R.H., 428
Neale, Dianne, 118
Nebuchadnezzar, 265
Needle (mountain), 359
Nelson, Lester 'Baby Face', 202
Nero, 26
Neruda, Pablo, 284
Nevins, Allan, 9
Newley, Anthony, 223
Newman, Paul, 40
Newton, Caroline, 170
Newton, Dennis, 196
Newton, Isaac, 5
Newton, Krandel Lee, 223
Nguema, Teodoro Obiang, 233–4
Nicaraguan Contras, 257
Nichols, Nichelle, 172
Nicoletti, Charles, 253
Nietzsche, Friedrich, 178, 303, 307
Nightingale, Florence, 262
Nile, River, 91
Nixon, Richard, 4, 228
Niyazov, Saparmurat, 234–5
Nobel, Alfred, 375
Nobel, Ludwig, 375
Noble, Herbert 'The Cat', 24
Noebel, David A., 286
Noriega, Felicidad, 191
Noriega, Manuel, 191, 238–9
noses, famous, 8–9
Novak, Kim, 54
novels *see* literature
nuclear weapons test, 439
Nung Mercenaries, 255
Nye, Bill, 323
Nyman, Lena, 61

O

Oates, Joyce Carol, 311–12
O'Banion gang, Dion, 203
Obasanjo, President Olusegun, 240
O'Connor, Flannery, 312
O'Hare, Virginia, 219–20
Oliver, Jamie, 156
Olivier, Laurence, 34
Olympics, 91, 338–41, 350–2
O'Neal, Ryan, 51
Ono, Yoko, 178
Onyshchenko, Major Boris, 340
Ophuls, Marcel, 64
Orlovsky, Peter, 284–5
Orwell, George, 281, 314
Osborne, John, 47
Osbourne, Ozzy, 179
O'Sullivan, Maureen, 42, 49, 54
Oswald, Lee Harvey, 61, 250–3
Otis, James, 370
Otto, King (Greece), 374
Outkast (band), 89
Ouwens, Major P.A., 146
Owen, Michael, 355
Ozyurek, Mehmet, 9, 403

P

Pace, Elgie, 392
painting *see* arts
Palmer, William, 214
Paluck, Jason, 190
Panouse, Clementine de la, 414
Park, Si-Hun, 340
Parker, Charlie, 76
Parker, Dorothy, 47
Parker, Janet, 440
Parker, Matthew, 8
Parker, Robert M., 311
Parton, Dolly, 180
Pasternak, Boris, 159
Pastrana, Julia, 391

INDEX

Patey, Tom, 357
Patton, Charles, 79
Paul VI, Pope, 173
Paul, Henri, 107
Paule, Barbara, 134
Pauling, Linus, 385
Pausanias, 266
Pavlov, Valentin, 107
peaches, 418
Peaks, Tawny, 224–5
Pearl Harbor, 413
Pearson, Karl, 286
Peck, Gregory, 41
Pedro, King of Castile, 389
Peek, Kim, 406
Peel, John, 81
Peel, Robert, 432
Pelé (footballer), 352, 354
Pelias, King (Thessaly), 433–4
Pelletier, David, 341
Pellito, Penny, 220
penguins, 126
penicillin, 431–2
penises, 132, 185–7, 264
Pennsylvania Society of the Order of Founders and Patriots of America, 216
people, 1–30
- almost indestructable, 21–6
- drinks named after, 108–9
- earth's surface and, 16–17
- electric, 118
- extra limbs and digits, 6–7
- with famous noses, 8–9, 170
- had they lived to 2005, 2
- with namechanges, 20
- who cried in public, 2–4
- women of the Bible, 17–19

Pepys, John 'Stumpey', 85
Pepys, Samuel, 298, 390
Percival, Spencer, 348
Percy, Walker, 298, 313
Pere Ubu (band), 82
Perec, Georges, 301
Perelman, S.J., 47
Perez, Joanne, 74
performers, wretched, 86–9
Perkins, Elizabeth, 45
Perón, Eva, 393
Perón, Juan, 160, 393
Perot, Ross, 166–7
Perrault, Charles, 170
Peruvian Regiment, 255
Petiot, Ferdinand L., 108
Petrides, Gilbert, 73
Pettiford, Oscar, 76
Petty, Tom, 11
Pfeiffer, Michelle, 39
Philips, Shaun, 133
Philon, 265–6
Phoenix, River, 2
Picasso, Pablo, 5
Pickens, Tyrone, 195
Pickering, William H., 425
Pietri, Dorando, 338
pigs, 132, 205
Pillault, Christopher, 406
Pimm's (cocktail), 108
Pinochet, Augusto, 239
Pinter, Harold, 47
Pique, Monsieur de, 349
Pistor, Fanny, 375
Pitt the Younger, William, 346–7
Pittsburg Gasometer Explosion, 248
Pittsburgh Pirates, 440
Pius XI, Pope, 159
Pizarro, Francisco, 245
Pizzo, Cecilia M., 217
Plainsong (band), 83
Plant, Tom, 395
Plante, Joseph, 196
Plaster Caster, Cynthia, 223
Plath, Sylvia, 2, 280
Pleasant, Wally, 71
Plimpton, George, 362
Pliny the Elder, 265
Plymouth Brethren, 92
Poe, Edgar Allan, 14, 311
poets, 282–5
poison, 249, 418–19
Pol Pot, 239
Polanski, Roman, 55
politicians, 228–31
politics *see* war, politics and world affairs
Pomeroy, Sarah C., 288
Pompadour, Madame de, 411
population, 267–8

porcupines, 127, 143
Potter, (Helen) Beatrix, 344–5
Powell, Lawrence M., 213
Powell, Major John W., 399
Powell, William, 60
Power, Tyrone, 36
predictions, bad, 424–9
Preminger, Otto, 54
Prescott, Peter, 298
'Preserved Lady', 390–1
Presley, Elvis, 2, 4, 11, 291
Prevette, Johnathan, 174
Priestley, Raymond, 368
Pritikin, Nathan, 381–2
Proclaimers (band), 82–3
Proulx, Annie, 313
Proust, Marcel, 162, 280, 303
proverbs, 325–6
Pryor, Richard, 14
Puccini, Giacomo, 10
Pujol, Joseph, 90
Pullman, Philip, 420–3
Puskas, Ferenc, 354
Putnam, George, 9
Puzo, Mario, 55, 281, 314

quiz questions, 91–3

R

Rabelais, François, 303, 323
radios, 425
Raft, George, 41
Rahe, T.H., 96
rain, 215, 273–5, 415
Rainey, Ma, 79
Raleigh, Sir Walter, 214
Rama Rao, N.T., 229–30
Ramachandran, M.G., 173
Ramirez, Gloria, 408
Ramones (band), 82
Rank, J. Arthur, 84, 352
Rankin, Ian, 81–3
Rasputin, Grigori, 21, 186
Reader, John, 309
Reagan, Nancy, 11
Reagan, President Ronald, 34, 213, 230, 256–7
recipes, 112–14
Redd, G.C., 71
Redding, Otis, 2
Redford, Robert, 40–1
Reeves, Keanu, 40
Relf, Keith, 369
REM (band), 83
Remarque, Erich Maria, 312
Renfry, Alan, 373
Renoir, Jean, 60
Residents (band), 83
Ressler, Robert K., 307
Reuben, Dr David, 45
Rhine, J.B., 133
Rice, John C., 171
Rich, Buddie, 85
Rich, Charlie, 380
Richard II, King, 389
Richardson, Janet, 118
Richelieu, Cardinal de, 161
Richmond, Clifford A., 289
Richmond, Ken, 352
Rickenbacker, Edward V., 377–9
Riga, Peter de, 300
Righteous Brothers, 68
Rimbaud, Arthur, 283
Ringling Brothers Circus, 199
riots, 210–14
Rizal, José, 399
Rizzo, Dr Peter, 70
Rob Roy (cocktail), 109
Robbins, Jerome, 80
Roberts, Julia, 56
Roberts, Tiffany, 118
Robertson, Patrick (writer), 52–7
Robida, Albert, 305
Robinson, Tom, 82
Rochefort Ridge, 357–8
rocket research, 426–7
Rodale, J.I., 383
Rodgers, James W., 215
Rodin, François Auguste, 171
Rodney King Beating Trial, 213–14
Rogers, Ginger, 54
Rogers, Roy, 393
Rogers, Ruth, 109–10
Rohan-Csermak, Géza de, 286
Rohl, David, 269
Rolling Stones, 64, 83
Romero, George, 59

Rooney, Mickey, 57
Roosevelt, President Franklin D., 427
Roosevelt, President Theodore, 120
Rorty, Richard, 309
Rostand, Edmond, 435
Rosten, Leo, 322
Roth, Philip, 280, 294
Rothstein, Arnold, 380
Rouse, Al, 358
Rowling, J.K., 294
Royer, Jean, 90
Ruby, Jack, 252
Ruddy, Albert S., 55
Rudolf I, King (Hapsburg), 8
Ruiz, Maria del Carmen y, 219
Rumsfield, Donald, 429
Runyon, Damon, 199
Russell, Bertrand, 376
Russell, Jane, 60
Russell, Lillian, 215–16
Russell, Tony, 61
Ruth, Babe, 11, 440
Rutledge, Leigh, 132
Ryan, Elizabeth, 387
Ryzhkov, Nikolai, 4

Sacco, Nicola, 211
Sacher-Masoch, Leopold, 375–6
Sada, Abe, 187
Sade, Marquis de, 28
Sagal, Katey, 190–1
St Anthony, 191
St Bernadette, 394
St Bonaventure, 397
St Paul, 266
St Pierre Snake Invasion, 246–7
Saint, Eva Marie, 41
Sakata, Harold, 351
Sale, Jamie, 341
Salinger, J.D., 281
Salle, David, 73
Saltzman, Harry, 39
Salvadoran Death Squads, 257
Samples, Gordon, 288
Samuelson, Bill, 221
Sanders, Red, 323
Sandow, Eugene, 381
Sarnoff, David, 428
Sarti, Lucien, 250
sausage events, 114–16
Savage, Matthew, 406
Savalas, Telly, 52
savants, 404–6
Saverland, Thomas, 170
Sawyer, Mary, 192
sayings, 321–2, 324–5, 326–8
Scaglione, Michael, 370
Scagnetti, Jack, 279, 290
Schachtman, Tom, 307
Schell, Maximilen, 64
Schindler, Oskar, 414
Schlesinger, John, 172
Schnabel, Julian, 73
Schomburgk, Hans, 145–6
Schönberg, Arnold, 387
Schopenhauer, Artur, 307
Schott, Ben, 85
Schranz, Karl, 339
Schubert, Franz, 414
Schulz, Charles, 388
Schumann, Robert, 439–40
Schwabe, Calvin W., 112
Schwartz, Sheldon, 71
Schwarz, Marco, 148
Schwarzenberg, Count von, 374
Schwarzenegger, Arnold, 5, 230–1
Schwarzkopf, Norman, 4
Sclater, P.L., 270
Scorsese, Martin, 59
Scott, Bernadette, 25
Scott, Doug, 358
Scott, Ridley, 346
Scottsboro Boys, 211
Screen Actors Guild, 57
Seale, Bobby, 212
Seiler, Lewis, 171
Self, Will, 305–7
Sennett, Mack, 50
September 11th, 428
Sepu Kangri, 359–60
Sertoli, Enrico, 101
sex, love and marriage, 169–87
    aphrodisiacs, 180–2
    celebrity marriages, 175–6
    incestuous couples, 184–5
    meeting mates, 178–80
    memorable kisses, 170–5

- movie stars and, 34–7
- perfect woman, 176
- preserved sex organs, 185–7
- sexual intercourse, 182–4
- thoughts on, 177–8

Shah, Nadir, 242
Shakespeare, William, 5, 80, 100, 298
Sharpe, Mrs Hollis, 193–4
Shatner, William, 172
Shaw, Clay, 251
Shaw, George Bernard, 5, 48
Shcherbakov, Deputy Prime Minister, 107
Shea, Mary, 206
Shearer, Norma, 51
Sheen, Charlie, 16
Sheen, Martin, 40
sheep, 131–2, 135, 143
Shelley, Mary, 305
Shelley, Percy Bysshe, 14
Shepard, Sam, 48
Shiloh Baptist Church Panic, 247
Shimkonis, Paul, 224–5
shipwreck survival tips, 275–6
Shivling (mountain), 356
Shortis, Emily Ann, 369
Shortis, William, 369
Shortman, Dr Kenneth, 144
Shriver, Maria, 230
Siamese twins, 262
Sickles, Dan, 399
Siegel, Benjamin 'Bugsy', 202
Sieveking, Paul, 407
Sihanouk, Prince Norodom, 255
Sikharulidze, Anton, 341
Silva, Adhemar Ferreira da, 351–2
Silviera, Ana Mari da, 341
Simmons, Jean, 44
Simon and Garfunkel, 68
Simon, Neil, 48
Simon, Randall, 115–16
Simpson, Joe, 63
Simpson, Wallis, 179
Sinatra, Frank, 5, 37, 61
Sinclair, Upton, 115
Singer, Isaac Bashevis, 304
Singh, Rev J.A.L., 136
Skids (band), 81
Skutch, Alexander F., 287
sky, objects falling from, 414–20
Slyke, Rev D.O. Van, 271
smallpox, 440
Smith, Bessie, 79
Smith, Dr Southward, 391
Smith, George Joseph, 435–6
Smith, James, 147
Smith, Jem, 362
Smith, Joseph, 271
Smith, Martin Cruz, 282
Smith, Penny, 156
Smith, Pvt Billy Dean, 241
Smith, Tommy, 337
Smith, Will, 40
Smithsonian Institution, 186
snakes, 128, 130, 246–7
Snell, Hannah, 373
snow, 272–5, 416
Snow, Edgar, 377
Snow, Hank, 77
Socrates, 177
Sondheim, Stephen, 80
songs, 70–1, 76–9
Sonny and Cher, 68
Soto, Hernando de, 308
Soule, John, 322
soups, Italian, 109–10
Soutre, Jean Rene, 252
Sozio, Ciro, 285
Spacek, Sissy, 59
Spallanzani, Lazzaro, 399
Sparks Circus, 208
Spears, Britney, 174–5
Spencer, Herbert, 322
spiders, 128, 416
Spinal Tap (band), 85
sports, 337–62
- bizarre events, 342–3
- boxing champions, 360–2
- football, 352–5
- inventing games, 343–5
- mountain experiences, 356–60
- Olympics, 338–41, 350–2
- pistol duels, 345–50

squid, 126, 129
Stalin, Joseph, 28
Staller, Ilona, 230
Stallone, Sylvester, 5, 56, 58, 231
Stamm, Orville, 90
Stanley, Mike, 342

Stanley, Robert H., 273
Stapledon, Olaf, 305
Starks, Jabo, 84
Starr, Ray, 71
Starr, Ringo, 84
Stein, Peter, 80
Steinbeck, John, 48, 293, 312
Steininger, Hans, 368
Stephens, Helen, 338
Stephenson, Nicola, 174
Steppenwolf (band), 68
Stevens, Wallace, 283
Stevenson, Robert Louis, 162, 292, 344
Stewart, Jimmy, 230
Stobbs, Betty, 373
Stockholm International Peace Research (SIPRI), 243
Stoker, Bram, 281
stolen objects, 190–2
Stoppard, Tom, 48
Storey, David, 80
Storey-Moore, Ian, 355
Story, George, 388
Strauss, Erwin S., 292
Strick, Joseph, 50
Strindberg, August, 159
Striptease Museum, 262
Stroessner, Alfredo, 239
Stuart, Gloria, 45
Stubblefield, Clyde, 84
Sturgis, Frank, 253
submarines, 424–5
Suharto, 240
Suilven, 356–7
Sukarno, President, 254
Sulabh International Museum Of Toilets, 263
Sullivan, John L., 360–1
Sumatran Rebels, 254
Supremes (singers), 68
Suskind, Patrick, 281
Suu Kyi, Aung San, 232
Swanson, Gloria, 38, 43, 176
Swift, Frank, 352
Swift, Jonathan, 298, 323
swimming, 339, 341
Swinburne, Algernon Charles, 10
Sykes, Gloria, 216

T

Tagore, Rabindranath, 303
Tait, Charles, 53
Talking Heads (band), 68
Tamerlane (chieftain), 244
Tarantino, Quentin, 40
Targino, Salvador, 417
Tasker, Joe, 358
Tasman, Abel Janzoon, 17
tattoos, 15–16
Tatum, Art, 76
Taylor, A.G., 289
Taylor, Charles, 193, 240
Taylor, Elizabeth, 35–6, 177
tears in public, 2–4
temperature, 272–4
Templeton, Richard G., 289
Temptations (band), 68
Tennyson, Alfred, Lord, 150
Testa, Barbara, 75
Texas City Chain Reaction Explosions, 249
Than Shwe, General, 232
Thatcher, Lady Margaret, 156
theatre productions, 79–81
Theron, Charlize, 52
Thich Tranh Nhung, 395
thieves, 193–8
Third Battle Of The Aisne River, 105
Thomas, Dylan, 2
Thomas, Jeffrey, 176
Thompson, Emma, 36
Thompson, Fred, 230–1
Thompson, Jim, 48
Thoreau, Henry David, 311, 323
Thornley, Kerry, 251–2
Thornton, Billy Bob, 37
tigers, 131, 143
Tillman, Cpl Pat, 242
Tirevit, Mademoiselle, 349
Titian, 71
Tocqueville, Alexis de, 309
Todd, Brent, 134
Tolkien, J.R.R., 38
Tolstoy, Leo, 281, 292, 298
Tom Collins (cocktail), 109
Tomalin, Nicholas, 305–6
tomb of King Mausolus, 266
tools, best, 420–3

Toomey, Regis, 171
Torrigiano, Pietro, 8
Tourog, Norman, 54
Tracy, Spencer, 35
travel, 261–76
  ancient world wonders, 265–7
  bizarre weather, 272–5
  Garden of Eden sites, 269–71
  least populous nations, 267–8
  lost property, 264
  museums, 262–4
  shipwreck survival, 275–6
  unlikely placenames, 268
Travolta, John, 40
Treffert, Darold, 406
Trench, Brinsley Le Poer, 271
Trevino, Chris, 134
Trevino, Jennifer, 134
trials and riots, 210–14
Trigger (horse), 393
Trimmer, Capt John W., 292
Trotsky, Leon, 15
Truman, President Harry S., 228, 323
Trumbull, Col John, 400
Truss, Lynne, 296
Tse Tsan Tai, 270
Tubb, Ernest, 77
Tulp, Dr Nicholas, 135
Tune, Mehmet, 133
Tunney, Gene, 361
Turnbull, Colin, 306
Turner, Dr Monica, 16
Turner, Kelton Rena, 440
Turner, Lana, 52
Turner, Nat, 104
Tutankhamun, King, 220, 388
Twain, Mark, 75, 120, 322–3, 344
  death and, 376, 387
  literature, 281, 312
  work, money and, 161
Tyson, Mike, 16, 440

U

U2 (band), 82
Uganda kob, 126
Ukrainian Partisans, 254
Upton, Albert, 4
Urbain, Professor Achille, 147
Urquhart, Sir Thomas, 378
Urwin, Alan, 25–6
Urzua, Capt Pedro De, 242–3
Utrillo, Maurice, 73

V

Vader, John, 222
Valens, Ritchie, 2
Valentino, Rudolph, 175–6
Vallandigham, Clement L., 368–9
van der Rohe, Ludwig Miles, 323
van Gogh, Vincent, 74–5
Vanzetti, Bartolomeo, 211
variety acts, 89–91
vases, 404
Vaughn, Harry, 323
Vega, Lope de, 81
Velez, Edward, 198
Velvet Underground (band), 68
Venezuelan Coup, 258
Ventura, Jesse, 231
Verdi, Guiseppe F.F., 405
Vergez, Jacques, 237
Verlaine, Paul, 283, 412
Verrell, Ronnie, 85
Vespucci, Amerigo, 16
Victoria, Queen, 16, 99, 304, 370
Vidal, Gore, 48
Vidor, King Wallis, 177
Vietnam War, 428, 440
Volk, Jules, 71
Volkswagen Beetle, 441
Voltaire, François, 298
Von Stroheim, Erich, 60
Vonnegut, Kurt, 299, 305
Voss, Sergeant Carl, 56
Vries, Peter de, 178
Vu Khac Minh, 394–5

W

Wagner, Richard, 62, 435
Waite, Dr Arthur Warren, 23
Waksman, Dr Selman, 433
Wallace, Amy, 10
Wallace, Edgar, 48
Wallace, Irving, 10, 304
Walsh, Raoul, 52
Walsh, Stella, 338
Walter Reed Army Medical Centre, 187
Walton, Sam, 167

war, politics and world affairs, 227–58
actors and politics, 228–31
armies of the CIA, 254–8
arms import/export, 243
commanders and own troops, 241–3
dictators, 231–6
disasters, unusual, 246–50
gunmen and Kennedy, 250–3
men conquering miles, 244–5
women in legislatures, 245–6
Warner, Charles Dudley, 322
Warner, Jack, 230
Warren, Leonard, 387
Warwick, Dionne, 20
Warwick, John, 50
Washington, Booker T., 247
Washington, President George, 5, 9–10, 190, 272, 349, 399–400
Washington, Dr James A., 400
Watts, Charlie, 84
Wawro, Richard, 406
Wayne, John, 52
weather, bizarre, 272–5
Weaver, Larry, 70
Webster, Stephen, 195
Weddell, James, 17
Wedders, Thomas, 8
Weising, George P., 287
Weissmuller, Johnny, 42, 49, 350
Welch, Denton, 314
Welles, Orson, 62
Wellington, Duke of, 9, 347–8
Wells, Bombardier Billy, 84
Wells, H.G., 292, 305, 345, 424
Wesley, John, 323
West, Mae, 49, 106, 163
West, Nathaniel, 48
Westheimer, Manfred 'Fred', 179
Westheimer, Ruth, 179
Wharton, Edith, 162
Wheeler, Billy Edd, 71
White, Dan, 213
White, Geneva, 252
White, Ricky, 252
White, Rev Robert L., 190
White, Roscoe, 252
Whitman, Gov Christine Todd, 210
Whitman, Walt, 283, 299, 303, 311
Wilde, Oscar, 177, 263, 314, 321–2
Wilder, Billy, 44, 62
Wilder, Thornton, 48
Wildman, Daniel, 90
Wilkerson, Billy, 52
Wilkes, Charles, 17
Will, George, 429
Willard, Clarence, 90–1
Williams, Betty Lou, 7
Williams, Hank, 77, 79
Williams, Richard, 353–5
Williams, Robert, 372
Williams, Ted, 395–6
Williams, Tennessee, 48
Williams, William Carlos, 284, 312
Willis, Bruce, 56
Willson, Henry, 51
Wilson, Calvin, 195
Wilson, Jim, 409
Wilson, Owen, 15
Wiltshire, Stephen, 406
Winchilsea, Earl of, 347
Wind, Timothy E., 213
Windsor, Duke of, 179
wine, Italian, 110–11
Winfrey, Oprah, 20
Wingate, David, 144
Winokur, Jon, 178
Wolfe, Fred, 71
Wolfe, Tom, 48
Wolfowitz, Paul, 429
Wolfram, Stephen, 308
wolves, 131, 134–8
Womack, Tommy, 71
woman, perfect, 176
wonders, ancient world, 265–7
Wood, Frederick Charles, 215
Wood Jr, John H., 250
Wood, J.T., 266
Wood, Natalie, 44
Woods, Tiger, 5
Woodward, Joanne, 41
Woodward, Rear Admiral Clark, 427
Woolf, Virginia, 299
words, 326–45
with alphabetical vowels, 333
contradictory proverbs, 325–6
messages in bottles, 333–4
names of things, 319–21
obscure and obsolete, 318–19

sayings, 321–2, 324–5, 326–8
untranslatable, 330–2
used in negative form, 329
Wordsworth, William, 10
work and money, 155–67
billionaires' careers, 163–7
eBay unusual sales, 156
librarians, 159–60
poets earning a living, 282–5
product names, 156
very odd jobs, 156–8
working in bed, 160–3
world affairs *see* war, politics and world affairs
Worthington, A.M., 289
Wozniak, Stephen, 166
Wray, Fay, 42
Wright brothers, 15, 424
Wright, Ernest Vincent, 300
writers, 46–8, 119–20, 302
see also literature
Wyman, Jane, 34, 171

Y

Yanayev, Gennady, 107
Yardbirds (band), 369
Yates, Peter, 58
Yates, Simon, 63
Yeltsin, Boris, 107
Yitzhaki, Major Ishmael, 191
Yooket Paen, 371
Yooket Pan, 371
Young, Lester, 76
Young, Terence, 59
Yussupov, Prince Felix, 21, 186

Z

Zannuck, Darryl F., 427
Zappa, Frank, 223
Zeus (statue), 265–6
Zidane, Zinedine, 353–4
Zola, Émile, 210, 412
Zwerin, Charlotte, 64

Franz Liszt